HUMAN PERSPECTIVES:

Introductory Readings for Sociology

HUMAN PERSPECTIVES:

Introductory Readings for Sociology

edited by

HOWARD M. SHAPIRO

and

ROBERT GLINER

THE FREE PRESS *New York*

COLLIER–MACMILLAN LIMITED *London*

The Free Press
A Division of The Macmillan Company
866 Third Avenue, New York, New York 10022

Collier-Macmillan Canada Ltd., Toronto, Ontario

Library of Congress Catalog Card Number: 78–143501

printing number
1   2   3   4   5   6   7   8   9   10

To Lynne, Beth, Kevin, and Meegan

Contents

Preface

These selections introduce the discipline of sociology through the study of human perspectives. Our intent is to show how variations in an individual's life in society affect his beliefs, attitudes, and values—what we, and others, have called his perspective. Sociologists Peter Berger and Thomas Luckmann have called this process "the social construction of reality." Thus we reject the premise that directly observable behaviors are the only allowable subject matter for social science. The individual's perceptions—how he sees his world—are a social reality that demand our attention. Descriptions of this reality and the social processes that construct it constitute the first part of this book.

Social reality is not an ultimate truth; it exists in and is constructed through human experience. Sociologists are increasingly aware that each man partly creates the meaning of his own existence. Existential analyses of social life are therefore presented in Part II.

The following sections describe a variety of different meanings that individuals construct out of their lives. Such differences in meaning occur because each individual's existence is distinct from that of his fellows. So that the reader may easily see the relationship between the studies presented here and those in other sociological sources, we follow the practice of dividing social life into major sociological categories. Differences in social life have been examined in terms of variations in, for example: language, class, family, and ethnicity. While such a division of man's existence does injustice to the notion of the "wholeness" of one's perspective, it allows a closer look at the differing aspects of social life that enter into the individual's construction of meaning for his own life and the world around him.

We present a variety of selections. Some are primarily theoretical; some report empirical research. Many of the most important statements regarding the issues involved in this volume have been made by classical sociologists such as Mannheim, Weber, and Simmel. Thus, the theme of this book has roots in a long tradition in sociology.

To summarize, each of us constructs our existence and its meaning on the basis of experience. An integral part of this experience is social life. Variations in social life, then, must necessarily result in varying perspectives. It is impossible for each of us to have the same perspective. A platitudinous remark, perhaps, but people continue to destroy one another in the attempt to

have their perspective accepted as the ultimate reality. If this book helps illustrate that each person, each group must construct its own meanings, and
that we should learn to understand and accept one another's different perspectives, then we shall have accomplished a great deal beyond introducing
sociology through the study of human perspectives.

H.M.S. Durham, New Hampshire
R.G. San Jose, California

Notes on Contributors

Peter L. Berger is Professor of Sociology at Rutgers University. He has written extensively in the fields of sociology of religion and sociology of knowledge as well as in other areas. Among his major works is *The Social Construction of Reality*, written with Thomas Luckmann. He is the author of *Invitation to Sociology*.

Tamotsu Shibutani is Professor of Sociology at the University of California, Santa Barbara. His main area of interest is social psychology. He has written a number of articles and books among which is *Society and Personality*.

Karl Mannheim was Professorial Lecturer in Sociology at the London School of Economics and Political Science at the time of his death in 1947. His writings are among the most important in the sociology of knowledge. Among his works in this area is *Ideology and Utopia*.

Charles Hampden-Turner is a Fellow of the Cambridge Institute, Cambridge, Massachusetts. His major interest is in radicalization in the social sciences.

Stanford M. Lyman is Associate Professor of Sociology at the University of California, San Diego. His primary area of interest has been social deviance. He has written a number of articles in this area as well as *Accounts in Deviance and Respectability*.

Marvin B. Scott is Associate Professor of Sociology at Sonoma State College. His main area of interest is also social deviance.

Jack D. Douglas is Associate Professor of Sociology at the University of California, San Diego. He has written a number of works in social deviance and on the creation of sociological knowledge. Among his books are *The Social Meaning of Suicide* and *American Social Order*.

Alfred R. Lindesmith is Professor of Sociology at Indiana University. His major area of investigation is drug use. He has written *Opiate Addiction* and *The Addict and the Law* in this area.

Anselm L. Strauss is Professor of Sociology at the University of California Medical School, San Francisco. His primary interest is social psychology. Among his major works are *Mirrors and Masks* and *The Discovery of Grounded Theory*, written with Barney Glazer.

Gary J. Miller is Assistant Professor of Sociology at Indiana University. His main area of investigation has been in sociolinguistics and family sociology.

Leonard Schatzman is Associate Professor of Sociology at the University of California School of Nursing, San Francisco. His major area of interest is social psychology. He has contributed a number of articles to social science journals.

Lee Rainwater is Professor of Sociology at Harvard University. His principal area of investigation is the family life of disadvantaged people. He is the author of a number of articles and books including *Family Design.*

Gerald Handel is Associate Professor of Sociology and Director of the Social Research Laboratory at City College, CUNY. His primary research interest is in the social psychology of the family. Among his publications is *Family Worlds,* written with Robert D. Hess.

William H. Form is Professor of Sociology at Michigan State University. He has investigated, among other issues, the relationship between socioeconomic structure and ideology. His publications include *Industrial Sociology,* written with Delbert Miller.

Joan Huber Rytina is Assistant Professor of Sociology at the University of Notre Dame. Her major interest is in stratification and ideology. She has written a number of articles in this area.

Robert K. Merton is Professor of Sociology and Associate Director of the Bureau of Applied Research at Columbia University. He has contributed significantly to the development of sociological theory in general and to a number of substantive areas. Among his major works is *Social Theory and Social Structure.*

Robert Dubin is Professor of Sociology at the University of California, Irvine. His major areas of interest are industrial sociology and sociological theory construction. He has written a number of works in both of these areas, among which is *Theory Building.*

John Holt is a Consultant with the Fayerweather Street School in Cambridge, Massachusetts. He is an outspoken critic of the educational system. His most recent book is *The Underachieving School.*

Robert Dreeben is Associate Professor of Education at the University of Chicago. He received his Ph.D. in Sociology from Harvard University. His major concern is the social psychology of education. He has contributed articles on this subject to leading educational journals.

Paul L. Dressel is Assistant Provost and Director of the Office of Institutional Research at Michigan State University. His research interests are in higher education and evaluation of general education. He is a frequent contributor to education journals.

Irving J. Lehmann is Professor of Evaluation Services at Michigan State University. His major research interest is in student attitudes and values. He has contributed articles in this area to leading educational journals.

William W. Lambert is Professor of Psychology, Sociology, and Anthropology at Cornell University. Among his primary research interests are child development and culture and personality. He has published widely in these and other areas. Among his books is *Social Psychology,* written with Wallace Lambert.

David Reiss is Chief of the Section on Experimental Group and Family Studies of the Adult Psychiatry Branch of the National Institute of Mental Health. His research focuses on family dynamics and cognition. He has written a series of articles on this subject.

Sandra L. Bem is Assistant Professor of Psychology at Carnegie-Mellon University. Her major area of interest is social psychology.

Daryl J. Bem is Associate Professor of Psychology and Industrial Administration at Carnegie-Mellon University. He also specializes in social psychology, particularly attitude and self-perception studies. He has contributed articles to major psychology journals on a variety of issues.

Max Weber was Professor of Sociology at the University of Munich at the time of his death in 1920. His work on sociological theory and method as well as his contributions to a number of substantive areas are of major importance in contemporary sociology. Among his major works are *The Theory of Social and Economic Organization* and *Economy and Society.*

Michael Parenti is Associate Professor of Political Science at the University of Vermont. His research interests are in ethnic politics and political power. Among his publications is *The Anti-Communist Impulse.*

Elliot Liebow is an anthropologist with the Public Health Service of the United States Department of Health, Education and Welfare. His research interests are urban anthropology and minority groups.

Fred L. Strodtbeck is Professor of Sociology and Psychology at the University of Chicago. His major research interests are small groups, social psychology, and family sociology. Among his publications is *Variations in Value Orientations,* written with Florence Kluckhohn.

John H. Burma is Professor of Sociology at Grinnell College. His major interests are minority groups and social deviance. Among his publications is *Spanish-Speaking Groups in the United States.*

Arthur J. Vidich is Professor of Sociology and Anthropology at the New School for Social Research. His areas of interest are community analysis and political sociology. He has written a number of articles and books among which is *Reflections on Community Studies,* written together with Joseph Bensman and Maurice Stein.

Joseph Bensman is Professor of Sociology at the City University of New York. His primary interests are in community analysis and social stratification. Among his publications is *Mass, Class, and Bureaucracy,* written with Bernard Rosenberg.

Thomas J. Scheff is Professor of Sociology at the University of California, Santa Barbara. His major interests are deviant behavior and social psychology. He has written a number of articles and books, among them *Being Mentally Ill.*

Georg Simmel was Professor at the University of Strasbourg when he died in 1918. His work on conflict, small groups, and social psychology is of major significance to contemporary sociology. Many of his articles and essays are available in English translation.

Kingsley Davis is Professor of Sociology and Director of the Institute of Population and Urban Research at the University of California, Berkeley. He has contributed to a number of areas of sociology—among them social stratification and the sociology of youth. Among his major works is *Human Society.*

Theodore Roszak is Professor of History at California State College, Hayward. He is primarily interested in contemporary American society and in the youth movement. He has written a number of articles in these areas.

Maurice Zeitlin is Associate Professor of Sociology at the University of Wisconsin. His major interest is political sociology, particularly Latin-American politics. Among his many publications is *Revolutionary Politics and the Cuban Working Class*.

PART I

SOCIAL REALITY

Sociologists study patterns of interactions as they exist in interpersonal relationships, in small groups, in large-scale organizations, and in societies at
large. They also study the behavior patterns in the major institutions of society
such as government, economy, religion, education, and family. Another aspect
of sociological study is analysis of variations in behavior in terms of class,
ethnic, and racial status. By such means sociologists attempt to describe and
explain social life. The concepts and approaches used indicate what is sociologically "real" or what exists to be described and explained about man's collective existence. Here we will rely on such concepts and approaches, not to
elaborate or elucidate them, but rather to introduce another basic approach to
sociological investigation. This approach, the theme of the book, is the description and explanation of the reality which people construct as participants
in the social process. We are thus concerned with describing perspectives and
investigating what social life has to do with them. As sociologists, our concern
is with the effect of living within and in terms of groups, organizations, and
institutions, rather than the effect of an individual's unique experience on his
perspective. There are articles in this section which lay the foundation for
our investigation. These articles provide the theoretical base for an analysis of the relationship between individuals' perspectives and their collective experience. Social reality in this context is the varying realities which
groups of individuals construct and maintain; we will explore the social determination of these realities.

Sociology as a Form
of Consciousness

PETER L. BERGER

This selection from Peter Berger's *Invitation to Sociology* introduces the sociological perspective, the discipline of sociology, and sets forth the themes that underlie many of the selections that appear in this reader. These themes—the "debunking" motif, the "unrespectability" motif, and the "relativizing" motif—characterize the perspective which the sociologist brings to the study of social reality.

By the debunking motif, Berger means that the sociologist is oriented to "see through" or "look behind" the official version of reality. For instance, the political organization of a community as set forth in its civic regulations or the explanations for marriage set forth as cultural ideals do not suffice for the person with a sociological perspective. This debunking motif is apparent, for example, in Max Weber's study on Protestantism and capitalism, in Emile Durkheim's analysis of the social factors leading to suicide, and in Vilfredo Pareto's work on social class and ideology. The unrespectability motif has been an important theme particularly in American sociology. The sociologist is conscious not only of reality as it exists in the chamber of commerce, in the church, and in the school, but also of the reality of the unrespectable world of gambling, nonmarital sex, and other areas of "deviance." Berger cites the work of Thorstein Veblen and the "Chicago" sociologists such as Robert Park and Everett Hughes in this regard. The study of the unrespectable world demands a recognition of various ways of constructing reality and of differing value systems. This brings up the third motif—relativization. The sociological perspective leads one to see "a world in which values have been radically relativized."

All footnotes will be found at the end of their respective selections.

LET us examine the proposition that sociological perspective involves a process of "seeing through" the façades of social structures. We could think of this in terms of a common experience of people living in large cities. One

From *Invitation to Sociology*, pp. 31–46, 48–49, by Peter L. Berger, copyright © 1963 by Peter L. Berger. Reprinted by permission of Doubleday & Company, Inc., and Penguin Books Ltd.

of the fascinations of a large city is the immense variety of human activities taking place behind the seemingly anonymous and endlessly undifferentiated rows of houses. A person who lives in such a city will time and again experience surprise or even shock as he discovers the strange pursuits that some men engage in quite unobtrusively in houses that, from the outside, look like all the others on a certain street. Having had this experience once or twice, one will repeatedly find oneself walking down a street, perhaps late in the evening, and wondering what may be going on under the bright lights showing through a line of drawn curtains. An ordinary family engaged in pleasant talk with guests? A scene of desperation amid illness or death? Or a scene of debauched pleasures? Perhaps a strange cult or a dangerous conspiracy? The facades of the houses cannot tell us, proclaiming nothing but an architectural conformity to the tastes of some group or class that may not even inhabit the street any longer. The social mysteries lie behind the facades. The wish to penetrate to these mysteries is an analogon to sociological curiosity. In some cities that are suddenly struck by calamity this wish may be abruptly realized. Those who have experienced wartime bombings know of the sudden encounters with unsuspected (and sometimes unimaginable) fellow tenants in the air-raid shelter of one's apartment building. Or they can recollect the startling morning sight of a house hit by a bomb during the night, neatly sliced in half, the facade torn away and the previously hidden interior mercilessly revealed in the daylight. But in most cities that one may normally live in, the facades must be penetrated by one's own inquisitive intrusions. Similarly, there are historical situations in which the facades of society are violently torn apart and all but the most incurious are forced to see that there was a reality behind the facades all along. Usually this does not happen and the facades continue to confront us with seemingly rocklike permanence. The perception of the reality behind the facades then demands a considerable intellectual effort.

A few examples of the way in which sociology "looks behind" the facades of social structures might serve to make our argument clearer. Take, for instance, the political organization of a community. If one wants to find out how a modern American city is governed, it is very easy to get the official information about this subject. The city will have a charter, operating under the laws of the state. With some advice from informed individuals, one may look up various statutes that define the constitution of the city. Thus one may find out that this particular community has a city-manager form of administration, or that party affiliations do not appear on the ballot in municipal elections, or that the city government participates in a regional water district. In similar fashion, with the help of some newspaper reading, one may find out the officially recognized political problems of the community. One may read that the city plans to annex a certain suburban area, or that there has been a change in the zoning ordinances to facilitate industrial development in another area, or even that one of the members of the city council has been accused of using his office for personal gain. All such matters still occur on the, as it were, visible, official or public level of political life. However, it would be an exceedingly naive person who would believe that this kind of information gives him a rounded picture of the political reality of that community. The sociologist will want to know above all the constituency of the "informal power structure" (as it has been called by Floyd Hunter, an American sociologist interested in such studies), which is a configuration of men and their power that cannot be found in any statutes, and probably cannot be read about in the newspapers. The political scientist or the legal expert might find it very interesting to compare the city charter with the constitutions of other similar communities. The sociologist will be far more concerned with discovering the way in which powerful vested interests influence or even control the actions of officials elected under the charter. These vested interests will not be found in city hall, but rather in the executive suites of corporations that may not even be located in that community, in the private mansions of a handful of powerful men, perhaps in the offices of certain labor unions or even, in some instances, in the headquarters of criminal organizations. When the sociologist concerns himself with power, he will "look behind" the official mechanisms that are supposed to regulate power in the community. This does not necessarily mean that he will regard the official mechanisms as totally ineffective or their legal definition as totally illusionary. But at the very least he will insist that there is another level of reality to be investigated in the particular system of power. In some cases he might conclude that to look for real power in the publicly recognized places is quite delusional.

Take another example. Protestant denominations in this country differ widely in their so-called "polity," that is, the officially defined way in which the denomination is run. One may speak of an episcopal, a presbyterian or a congregational "polity" (meaning by this not the denominations called by these names, but the forms of ecclesiastical government that various denominations share—for instance, the episcopal form shared by Episcopalians and Methodists, the congregational by Congregationalists and Baptists). In nearly all cases, the "polity" of a denomination is the result of a long historical development and is based on a theological rationale over which the doctrinal experts continue to quarrel. Yet a sociologist interested in studying the government of American denominations would do well not to arrest himself too long at these official definitions. He will soon find that the real questions of power and organization have little to do with "polity" in the theological sense. He will discover that the basic form of organization in all denominations of any size is bureaucratic. The logic of administrative behavior is determined by bureaucratic processes, only very rarely by the workings of an episcopal or a congregational point of view. The sociological investigator will then quickly "see through" the mass of confusing terminology denoting officeholders in the ecclesiastical bureaucracy and correctly identify those who hold executive power, no matter whether they be called "bishops," or "stated clerks" or "synod presidents." Understanding denominational organization as belonging to the much larger species of bureaucracy, the sociologist will then be able to grasp the processes that occur in the organization, to observe the internal and external pressures brought to bear on those who are theoretically in charge. In other words, behind the facade of an "episcopal polity" the sociologist will perceive the workings of a bureaucratic apparatus that is not terribly different in the Methodist Church, an agency of the Federal government, General Motors or the United Automobile Workers.

Or take an example from economic life. The personnel manager of an industrial plant will take delight in preparing brightly colored charts that show the table of organization that is supposed to administer the production process. Every man has his place, every person in the organization knows from whom he receives his orders and to whom he must transmit them, every work team has its assigned role in the great drama of production. In reality things rarely work this way—and every good personnel manager knows this. Superimposed on the official blueprint of the organization is a much subtler, much less visible network of human groups, with their loyalties, prejudices, antipathies and (most important) codes of behavior. Industrial sociology is full of data on the operations of this informal network, which always exists in varying degrees of accommodation and conflict with the official system. Very much the same coexistence of formal and informal organization are to be found wherever large numbers of men work together or live together under a system of discipline—military organizations, prisons, hospitals, schools, going back to the mysterious leagues that children form among themselves and that their parents only rarely discern. Once more, the sociologist will seek to penetrate the smoke screen of the official versions of reality (those of the foreman, the officer, the teacher) and try to grasp the signals that come from the "underworld" (those of the worker, the enlisted man, the schoolboy).

Let us take one further example. In Western countries, and especially in America, it is assumed that men and women marry because they are in love. There is a broadly based popular mythology about the character of love as a violent, irresistible emotion that strikes where it will, a mystery that is the goal of most young people and often of the not-so-young as well. As soon as one investigates, however, which people actually marry each other, one finds that the lightning-shaft of Cupid seems to be guided rather strongly within very definite channels of class, income, education, racial and religious background. If one then investigates a little further into the behavior that is engaged in prior to marriage under the rather misleading euphemism of "courtship," one finds channels of interaction that are often rigid to the point of ritual. The suspicion begins to dawn on one that, most of the time, it is not so much the emotion of love that creates a certain kind of relationship, but that carefully predefined and often planned relationships eventually generate the desired emotion. In other words, when certain conditions are met or have been constructed, one allows oneself "to fall in love." The sociologist investigating our patterns of "courtship" and marriage soon discovers a complex web of motives related in many ways to the entire institutional structure within which an individual lives his life—class, career, economic ambition, aspirations of power and prestige. The miracle of love now begins to look somewhat synthetic. Again, this need not mean in any given instance that the sociologist will declare the romantic interpretation to be an illusion. But, once more, he will look beyond the immediately given and publicly approved interpretations. Contemplating a couple that in its turn is contemplating the moon, the sociologist need not feel constrained to deny the emotional impact of the scene thus illuminated. But he will observe the machinery that went into the construction of the scene in its nonlunar aspects—the status index of the automobile from which the contemplation occurs, the canons of taste and tactics that determine the costume of the contemplators, the many ways in which language and demeanor place them socially, thus the social location and intentionality of the entire enterprise.

It may have become clear at this point that the problems that will interest the sociologist are not necessarily what other people may call "problems." The way in which public officials and newspapers (and, alas, some college textbooks in sociology) speak about "social problems" serves to obscure this fact. People commonly speak of a "social problem" when something in society does not work the way it is supposed to according to the official interpretations. They then expect the sociologist to study the "problem" as they have defined it and perhaps even to come up with a "solution" that will take care of the matter to their own satisfaction. It is important, against this sort of expectation, to understand that a sociological problem is something quite different from a "social problem" in this sense. For example, it is naive to concentrate on crime as a "problem" because law-enforcement agencies so define it, or on divorce because that is a "problem" to the moralists of marriage. Even more clearly, the "problem" of the foreman to get his men to work more efficiently or of the line officer to get his troops to charge the enemy more enthusiastically need not be problematic at all to the sociologist (leaving out of consideration for the moment the probable fact that the sociologist asked to study such "problems" is employed by the corporation or the army). The sociological problem is always the understanding of what goes on here in terms of social interaction. Thus the sociological problem is not so much why some things "go wrong" from the viewpoint of the authorities and the management of the social scene, but how the whole system works in the first place, what are its presuppositions and by what means it is held together. The fundamental sociological problem is not crime but the law, not divorce but marriage, not racial discrimination but racially defined stratification, not revolution but government.

This point can be explicated further by an example. Take a settlement house in a lower-class slum district trying to wean away teen-agers from the publicly disapproved activities of a juvenile gang. The frame of reference within which social workers and police officers define the "problems" of this situation is constituted by the world of middle-class, respectable, publicly approved values. It is a "problem" if teen-agers drive around in stolen automobiles, and it is a "solution" if instead they will play group games in the settlement house. But if one changes the frame of reference and looks at the situation from the viewpoint of the leaders of the juvenile gang, the "problems" are defined in reverse order. It is a "problem" for the solidarity of the gang if its members are seduced away from those activities that lend prestige to the gang within its own social world, and it would be a "solution" if the social workers went way the hell back uptown where they came from. What is a "problem" to one social system is the normal routine of things to the other system, and vice versa. Loyalty and disloyalty, solidarity and deviance, are defined in contradictory terms by the representatives of the two systems. Now, the sociologist may, in terms of his own values, regard the world of middle-class respectability as more desirable and therefore want to come to the assist-ance of the settlement house, which is its missionary outpost *in partibus infi-delium*. This, however, does not justify the identification of the director's headaches with what are "problems" sociologically. The "problems" that the sociologist will want to solve concern an understanding of the entire social situation, the values and modes of action in *both* systems, and the way in which the two systems coexist in space and time. Indeed, this very ability to look at a situation from the vantage points of competing systems of interpreta-tion is, as we shall see more clearly later on, one of the hallmarks of sociologi-cal consciousness.

We would contend, then, that there is a debunking motif inherent in socio-logical consciousness. The sociologist will be driven time and again, by the very logic of his discipline, to debunk the social systems he is studying. This unmasking tendency need not necessarily be due to the sociologist's tempera-ment or inclinations. Indeed, it may happen that the sociologist, who as an individual may be of a conciliatory disposition and quite disinclined to disturb the comfortable assumptions on which he rests his own social existence, is nevertheless compelled by what he is doing to fly in the face of what those around him take for granted. In other words, we would contend that the roots of the debunking motif in sociology are not psychological but methodological. The sociological frame of reference, with its built-in procedure of looking for levels of reality other than those given in the official interpretations of society, carries with it a logical imperative to unmask the pretensions and the propa-ganda by which men cloak their actions with each other. This unmasking im-perative is one of the characteristics of sociology particularly at home in the temper of the modern era.

The debunking tendency in sociological thought can be illustrated by a variety of developments within the field. For example, one of the major themes in Weber's sociology is that of the unintended, unforeseen consequences of human actions in society. Weber's most famous work, *The Protestant Ethic and the Spirit of Capitalism,* in which he demonstrated the relationship between certain consequences of Protestant values and the development of the capitalist ethos, has often been misunderstood by critics precisely because they missed this theme. Such critics have pointed out that the Protestant thinkers quoted by Weber never intended their teachings to be applied so as to produce the specific economic results in question. Specifically, Weber argued that the Calvinist doctrine of predestination led people to behave in what he called an "inner-worldly ascetic" way, that is, in a manner that concerns itself intensively, systematically and selflessly with the affairs of this world, especially with economic affairs. Weber's critics have then pointed out that nothing was further from the mind of Calvin and the other leaders of the Calvinist Reformation. But Weber never maintained that Calvinist thought *intended* to produce these economic action patterns. On the contrary, he knew very well that the intentions were drastically different. The consequences took place regardless of intentions. In other words, Weber's work (and not only the famous part of it just mentioned) gives us a vivid picture of the *irony* of human actions. Weber's sociology thus provides us with a radical antithesis to any views that understand history as the realization of ideas or as the fruit of the deliberate efforts of individuals or collectivities. This does not mean at all that ideas are not important. It does mean that the outcome of ideas is commonly very different from what those who had the ideas in the first place planned or hoped. Such a consciousness of the ironic aspect of history is sobering, a strong antidote to all kinds of revolutionary utopianism.

The debunking tendency of sociology is implicit in all sociological theories that emphasize the autonomous character of social processes. For instance, Emile Durkheim, the founder of the most important school in French sociology, emphasized that society was a reality *sui generis,* that is, a reality that could not be reduced to psychological or other factors on different levels of analysis. The effect of this insistence has been a sovereign disregard for individually intended motives and meanings in Durkheim's study of various phenomena. This is perhaps most sharply revealed in his well-known study of suicide, in the work of that title, where individual intentions of those who commit or try to commit suicide are completely left out of the analysis in favor of statistics concerning various social characteristics of these individuals. In the Durkheimian perspective, to live in society means to exist under the domination of society's logic. Very often men act by this logic without knowing it. To discover this inner dynamic of society, therefore, the sociologist must frequently disregard the answers that the social actors themselves would give to his questions and look for explanations that are hidden from their own awareness. This essentially Durkheimian approach has been carried over into the theoretical approach now called functionalism. In functional analysis society is analyzed in terms of its own workings as a system, workings that are often obscure or opaque to those acting within the system. The contemporary American sociologist Robert Merton has expressed this approach well in his concepts of "manifest" and "latent" functions. The former are the conscious and deliberate functions of social processes, the latter the unconscious and unintended ones. Thus the "manifest" function of antigambling legislation may be to suppress gambling, its "latent" function to create an illegal empire for the gambling syndicates. Or Christian missions in parts of Africa "manifestly" tried to convert Africans to Christianity, "latently" helped to destroy the indigenous tribal cultures and thus provided an important impetus toward rapid social transformation. Or the control of the Communist Party over all sectors of social life in Russia "manifestly" was to assure the continued dominance of

the revolutionary ethos, "latently" created a new class of comfortable bureaucrats uncannily bourgeois in its aspirations and increasingly disinclined toward
the self-denial of Bolshevik dedication. Or the "manifest" function of many
voluntary associations in America is sociability and public service, the
"latent" function to attach status indices to those permitted to belong to such
associations.

The concept of "ideology," a central one in some sociological theories,
could serve as another illustration of the debunking tendency discussed. Sociologists speak of "ideology" in discussing views that serve to rationalize the
vested interests of some group. Very frequently such views systematically dis-
tort social reality in much the same way that an individual may neurotically
deny, deform or reinterpret aspects of his life that are inconvenient to him.
The important approach of the Italian sociologist Vilfredo Pareto has a central
place for this perspective and . . . the concept of "ideology" is essential for
the approach called the "sociology of knowledge." In such analyses the ideas
by which men explain their actions are unmasked as self-deception, sales talk,
the kind of "sincerity" that David Riesman has aptly described as the state of
mind of a man who habitually believes his own propaganda. In this way, we
can speak of "ideology" when we analyze the belief of many American physicians that standards of health will decline if the fee-for-service method of payment is abolished, or the conviction of many undertakers that inexpensive
funerals show lack of affection for the departed, or the definition of their
activity by quizmasters on television as "education." The self-image of the
insurance salesman as a fatherly adviser to young families, of the burlesque
stripper as an artist, of the propagandist as a communications expert, of the
hangman as a public servant—all these notions are not only individual assuage-
ments of guilt or status anxiety, but constitute the official self-interpretations of
entire social groups, obligatory for their members on pain of excommunication.
In uncovering the social functionality of ideological pretensions the sociologist
will try not to resemble those historians of whom Marx said that every corner
grocer is superior to them in knowing the difference between what a man is and
what he claims to be. The debunking motif of sociology lies in this penetration
of verbal smoke screens to the unadmitted and often unpleasant mainsprings
of action.

It has been suggested above that sociological consciousness is likely to
arise when the commonly accepted or authoritatively stated interpretations of
society become shaky. As we have already said, there is a good case for thinking of the origins of sociology in France (the mother country of the discipline)
in terms of an effort to cope intellectually with the consequences of the French
Revolution, not only of the one great cataclysm of 1789 but of what De
Tocqueville called the continuing Revolution of the nineteenth century. In the
French case it is not difficult to perceive sociology against the background of
the rapid transformations of modern society, the collapse of facades, the defla-
tion of old creeds and the upsurge of frightening new forces on the social scene.
In Germany, the other European country in which an important sociological

movement arose in the nineteenth century, the matter has a rather different appearance. If one may quote Marx once more, the Germans had a tendency to carry on in professors' studies the revolutions that the French performed on the barricades. At least one of these academic roots of revolution, perhaps the most important one, may be sought in the broadly based movement of thought that came to be called "historicism." This is not the place to go into the full story of this movement. Suffice it to say that it represents an attempt to deal philosophically with the overwhelming sense of the relativity of all values in history. This awareness of relativity was an almost necessary outcome of the immense accumulation of German historical scholarship in every conceivable field. Sociological thought was at least partly grounded in the need to bring order and intelligibility to the impression of chaos that this array of historical knowledge made on some observers. Needless to stress, however, the society of the German sociologist was changing all around him just as was that of his French colleague, as Germany rushed towards industrial power and nationhood in the second half of the nineteenth century. We shall not pursue these questions, though. If we turn to America, the country in which sociology came to receive its most widespread acceptance, we find once more a different set of circumstances, though again against a background of rapid and profound social change. In looking at this American development we can detect another motif of sociology, closely related to that of debunking but not identical with it—its fascination with the unrespectable view of society.

In at least every Western society it is possible to distinguish between respectable and unrespectable sectors. In that respect American society is not in a unique position. But American respectability has a particularly pervasive quality about it. This may be ascribed in part, perhaps, to the lingering aftereffects of the Puritan way of life. More probably it has to do with the predominant role played by the bourgeoisie in shaping American culture. Be this as it may in terms of historical causation, it is not difficult to look at social phenomena in America and place them readily in one of these two sectors. We can perceive the official, respectable America represented symbolically by the Chamber of Commerce, the churches, the schools and other centers of civic ritual. But facing this world of respectability is an "other America," present in every town of any size, an America that has other symbols and that speaks another language. This language is probably its safest identification tag. It is the language of the poolroom and the poker game, of bars, brothels and army barracks. But it is also the language that breaks out with a sigh of relief between two salesmen having a drink in the parlor car as their train races past clean little Midwestern villages on a Sunday morning, with clean little villagers trooping into the whitewashed sanctuaries. It is the language that is suppressed in the company of ladies and clergymen, owing its life mainly to oral transmission from one generation of Huckleberry Finns to another (though in recent years the language has found literary deposition in some books designed to thrill ladies and clergymen). The "other America" that speaks this language can be found wherever people are excluded, or exclude themselves, from the world of middle-class propriety. We find it in those sections of the working class that have not yet proceeded too far on the road of *embourgeoisement,* in slums, shantytowns and those parts of cities that urban sociologists have called "areas of transition." We find it expressed powerfully in the world of the American Negro. We also come on it in the subworlds of those who have, for one reason or another, withdrawn voluntarily from Main Street and Madison Avenue—in the worlds of hipsters, homosexuals, hoboes and other "marginal men," those worlds that are kept safely out of sight on the streets where the nice people live, work and amuse themselves *en famille* (though these worlds may on some occasions be rather convenient for the male of the species "nice people"—precisely on occasions when he happily finds himself *sans famille*).

American sociology, accepted early both in academic circles and by those concerned with welfare activities, was from the beginning associated with the "official America," with the world of policy makers in community and nation. Sociology today retains this respectable affiliation in university, business and government. The appellation hardly induces eyebrows to be raised, except the eyebrows of such Southern racists sufficiently literate to have read the footnotes of the desegregation decision of 1954. However, we would contend that there has been an important undercurrent in American sociology, relating it to that "other America" of dirty language and disenchanted attitudes, that state of mind that refuses to be impressed, moved or befuddled by the official ideologies.

This unrespectable perspective on the American scene can be seen most clearly in the figure of Thorstein Veblen, one of the early important sociologists in America. His biography itself constitutes an exercise in marginality: a difficult, querulous character; born on a Norwegian farm on the Wisconsin frontier; acquiring English as a foreign language; involved all his life with morally and politically suspect individuals; an academic migrant; an inveterate seducer of other people's women. The perspective on America gained from this angle of vision can be found in the unmasking satire that runs like a purple thread through Veblen's work, most famously in his *Theory of the Leisure Class,* that merciless look from the underside at the pretensions of the American *haute bourgeoisie.* Veblen's view of society can be understood most easily as a series of non-Rotarian insights—his understanding of "conspicuous consumption" as against the middle-class enthusiasm for the "finer things," his analysis of economic processes in terms of manipulation and waste as against the American productivity ethos, his understanding of the machinations of real estate speculation as against the American community ideology, most bitterly his description of academic life (in *The Higher Learning in America*) in terms of fraud and flatulence as against the American cult of education. We are not associating ourselves here with a certain neo-Veblenism that has become fashionable with some younger American sociologists, nor arguing that Veblen was a giant in the development of the field. We are only pointing to his irreverent curiosity and clear-sightedness as marks of a perspective coming from those places in the culture in which one gets up to shave about noon on Sundays. Nor are we arguing that clear-sightedness is a general trait of unrespectability. Stupidity and sluggishness of thought are probably distributed quite fairly throughout the social spectrum. But where there is intelligence and where it manages to free itself from the goggles of respectability, we can expect a clearer view of society than in those cases where the oratorical imagery is taken for real life.

A number of developments in empirical studies in American sociology furnish evidence of this same fascination with the unrespectable view of society. For example, looking back at the powerful development of urban studies undertaken at the University of Chicago in the 1920s we are struck by the apparently irresistible attraction to the seamier sides of city life upon these researchers. The advice to his students of Robert Park, the most important figure in this development, to the effect that they should get their hands dirty with research often enough meant quite literally an intense interest in all the things that North Shore residents would call "dirty." We sense in many of these studies the excitement of discovering the picaresque undersides of the metropolis—studies of slum life, of the melancholy world of rooming houses, of Skid Row, of the worlds of crime and prostitution. One of the offshoots of this so-called "Chicago school" has been the sociological study of occupations, due very largely to the pioneering work of Everett Hughes and his students. Here also we find a fascination with every possible world in which human beings live and make a living, not only with the worlds of the respectable occupations, but with those of the taxi dancer, the apartment-house janitor, the professional boxer or the jazz musician. The same tendency can be discovered in the course of American community studies following in the wake of the famous *Middletown* studies of Robert and Helen Lynd. Inevitably these studies had to bypass the official versions of community life, to look at the social reality of the community not only from the perspective of city hall but also from that of the city jail. Such sociological procedure is *ipso facto* a refutation of the respectable presupposition that only certain views of the world are to be taken seriously. . . .

We would now say explicitly that sociology is so much in tune with the temper of the modern era precisely because it represents the consciousness of a world in which values have been radically relativized. This relativization has become so much part of our everyday imagination that it is difficult for us to grasp fully how closed and absolutely binding the world views of other cultures have been and in some places still are. The American sociologist Daniel Lerner, in his study of the contemporary Middle East (*The Passing of Traditional Society*), has given us a vivid portrait of what "modernity" means as an altogether new kind of consciousness in those countries. For the traditional mind one is what one is, where one is, and cannot even imagine how one could be anything different. The modern mind, by contrast, is mobile, participates vicariously in the lives of others differently located from oneself, easily imagines itself changing occupation or residence. Thus Lerner found that some of the illiterate respondents to his questionnaires could only respond with laughter to the question as to what they would do if they were in the position of their rulers and would not even consider the question as to the circumstances under which they would be willing to leave their native village. Another way of putting this would be to say that traditional societies assign definite and permanent identities to their members. In modern society identity itself is uncertain and in flux. One does not really know what is expected of one as a ruler, as a parent, as a cultivated person, or as one who is sexually normal. Typically, one then requires various experts to tell one. The book club editor tells us what culture is, the interior designer what taste we ought to have, and the psychoanalyst who we are. To live in modern society means to live at the center of a kaleidoscope of ever-changing roles.

Reference Groups as Perspectives

TAMOTSU SHIBUTANI

The focus on human perspectives as an approach to social life demands an adequate social psychology. Shibutani makes an important contribution to this end with his discussion of the concept of "reference groups." He points to three distinct uses of the concept: "(1) groups which serve as comparison points; (2) groups to which men aspire; and (3) groups whose perspectives are assumed by the actor."

Shibutani states that, because people have perspectives, they conceive of order in the world and, therefore, can act in terms of such order. Shibutani goes on to show how perspectives are the products of social interaction. The relationship between interaction and perspective is explored in his discussion of communication channels.

In mass societies consisting of many possible reference groups and communication channels, perspectives are constantly subject to change. The study of perspectives and their social determinants, that is, reference group processes, is, Shibutani believes, fundamental to the analysis of social order and social change.

ALTHOUGH [Herbert] Hyman coined the term scarcely more than a decade ago, the concept of reference groups has become one of the central analytic tools in social psychology, being used in the construction of hypotheses concerning a variety of social phenomena. The inconsistency in behavior as a person moves from one social context to another is accounted for in terms of a change in reference groups; the exploits of juvenile delinquents, especially in interstitial areas, are being explained by the expectations of peer-group gangs; modifications in social attitudes are found to be related to changes in associations. The concept has been particularly useful in accounting for the choices made among apparent alternatives, particularly where the selections seem to be contrary to the "best interests" of the actor. Status problems—aspirations of social climbers, conflicts in group loyalty, the dilemmas of marginal men—have also been analyzed in terms of reference groups, as have the differential sensitivity and reaction of various segments of an audience to mass communication. It is recognized that the same generic processes are involved in these phenomenally diverse events, and the increasing popularity of the concept attests to its utility in analysis.

As might be expected during the exploratory phases in any field of inquiry,

Reprinted from *The American Journal of Sociology*, Vol. LX, May, 1955, pp. 562–569, by permission of the author and the publisher, The University of Chicago Press.

however, there is some confusion involved in the use of this concept, arising largely from vagueness of signification. The available formal definitions are inconsistent, and sometimes formal definitions are contradicted in usage. The fact that social psychologists can understand one another in spite of these ambiguities, however, implies an intuitive recognition of some central meaning, and an explicit statement of this will enhance the utility of the concept as an analytic tool. The literature reveals that all discussions of reference groups involve some identifiable grouping to which an actor is related in some manner and the norms and values shared in that group. However, the relationship between these three terms is not always clear. Our initial task, then, is to examine the conceptions of reference group implicit in actual usage, irrespective of formal definitions.

One common usage of the concept is in the designation of that group which serves as the point of reference in making comparisons or contrasts, especially in forming judgments about one's self. In the original use of the concept Hyman spoke of reference groups as points of comparison in evaluating one's own status, and he found that the estimates varied according to the group with which the respondent compared himself. Merton and Kitt, in their reformulation of Stouffer's theory of relative deprivation, also use the concept in this manner; the judgments of rear-echelon soldiers overseas concerning their fate varied, depending upon whether they compared themselves to soldiers who were still at home or men in combat. They also propose concrete research operations in which respondents are to be asked to compare themselves with various groups. The study of aspiration levels by Chapman and Volkmann, frequently cited in discussions of reference-group theory, also involves variations in judgment arising from a comparison of one's own group with others.[1] In this mode of application, then, a reference group is a standard or check point which an actor uses in forming his estimate of the situation, particularly his own position within it. Logically, then, *any* group with which an actor is familiar may become a reference group.

A second referent of the concept is that group in which the actor aspires to gain or maintain acceptance: hence, a group whose claims are paramount in situations requiring choice. The reference group of the socially ambitious is said to consist of people of higher strata whose status symbols are imitated. Merton and Kitt interpret the expressions of willingness and felt readiness for combat on the part of inexperienced troops, as opposed to the humility of battle-hardened veterans, as the efforts of newcomers to identify themselves with veterans to whom they had mistakenly imputed certain values.[2] Thus, the concept is used to point to an association of human beings among whom one seeks to gain, maintain, or enhance his status; a reference group is that group in which one desires to participate.

In a third usage the concept signifies that group whose perspective constitutes the frame of reference of the actor. Thus, Sherif speaks of reference groups as groups whose norms are used as anchoring points in structuring the perceptual field,[3] and Merton and Kitt speak of a "social frame of reference" for interpretations.[4] Through direct or vicarious participation in a group one comes to perceive the world from its standpoint. Yet this group need not be one in which he aspires for acceptance; a member of some minority group may despise it but still see the world largely through its eyes. When used in this manner, the concept of reference group points more to a psychological phenomenon than to an objectively existing group of men; it refers to an organization of the actor's experience. That is to say, it is a structuring of his perceptual field. In this usage a reference group becomes any collectivity, real or imagined, envied or despised, whose perspective is assumed by the actor.

Thus, an examination of current usage discloses three distinct referents for a single concept: (1) groups which serve as comparison points; (2) groups to which men aspire; and (3) groups whose perspectives are assumed by the actor. Although these terms may be related, treating together what should be clearly delineated as generically different can lead only to further confusion. It is the contention of this paper that the restriction of the concept of reference group to the third alternative—that group whose perspective constitutes the frame of reference of the actor—will increase its usefulness in research. Any group or object may be used for comparisons, and one need not assume the role of those with whom he compares his fate; hence, the first usage serves a quite different purpose and may be eliminated from further consideration. Under some circumstances, however, group loyalties and aspirations are related to perspectives assumed, and the character of this relationship calls for further exploration. Such a discussion necessitates a restatement of the familiar, but, in view of the difficulties in some of the work on reference groups, repetition may not be entirely out of order. In spite of the enthusiasm of some proponents there is actually nothing new in reference-group theory.

Culture and Personal Controls

Thomas pointed out many years ago that what a man does depends largely upon his definition of the situation. One may add that the manner in which one consistently defines a succession of situations depends upon his organized perspective. A perspective is an ordered view of one's world—what is taken for granted about the attributes of various objects, events, and human nature. It is an order of things remembered and expected as well as things actually perceived, an organized conception of what is plausible and what is possible; it constitutes the matrix through which one perceives his environment. The fact that men have such ordered perspectives enables them to conceive of their ever changing world as relatively stable, orderly, and predictable. As Riezler puts it, one's perspective is an outline scheme which, running ahead of experience, defines and guides it.

There is abundant experimental evidence to show that perception is selective; that the organization of perceptual experience depends in part upon what is anticipated and what is taken for granted. Judgments rest upon perspectives, and people with different outlooks define identical situations differently, responding selectively to the environment. Thus, a prostitute and a social worker walking through a slum area notice different things; a sociologist should perceive relationships that others fail to observe. Any change of perspectives —becoming a parent for the first time, learning that one will die in a few months, or suffering the failure of well-laid plans—leads one to notice things previously overlooked and to see the familiar world in a different light. As Goethe contended, history is continually rewritten, not so much because of the discovery of new documentary evidence, but because the changing perspectives of historians lead to new selections from the data.

Culture, as the concept is used by Redfield, refers to a perspective that is shared by those in a particular group; it consists of those "conventional understandings, manifest in act and artifact, that characterize societies." [5] Since these conventional understandings are the premises of action, those who share a common culture engage in common modes of action. Culture is not a static entity but a continuing process; norms are creatively reaffirmed from day to day in social interaction. Those taking part in collective transactions approach one another with set expectations, and the realization of what is anticipated successively confirms and reinforces their perspectives. In this way, people in each cultural group are continuously supporting one another's perspectives, each by responding to the others in expected ways. In this sense culture is a product of communication.

In his discussion of endopsychic social control Mead spoke of men "taking the role of the generalized other," meaning by that that each person approaches his world from the standpoint of the culture of his group. Each perceives, thinks, forms judgments, and controls himself according to the frame of reference of the group in which he is participating. Since he defines objects, other people, the world, and himself from the perspective that he shares with others, he can visualize his proposed line of action from this generalized standpoint, anticipate the reactions of others, inhibit undesirable impulses, and thus guide his conduct. The socialized person is a society in miniature; he sets the same standards of conduct for himself as he sets for others, and he judges himself in the same terms. He can define situations properly and meet his obligations, even in the absence of other people, because, as already noted, his perspective always takes into account the expectations of others. Thus, it is the ability to define situations from the same standpoint as others that makes personal controls possible. [6] When Mead spoke of assuming the role of the generalized other, he was not referring to people but to perspectives shared with others in a transaction.

The consistency in the behavior of a man in a wide variety of social contexts is to be accounted for, then, in terms of his organized perspective. Once one has incorporated a particular outlook from his group, it becomes his orientation toward the world, and he brings this frame of reference to bear on all new situations. Thus, immigrants and tourists often misinterpret the strange things they see, and a disciplined Communist would define each situation differently from the non-Communist. Although reference-group behavior is generally studied in situations where choices seem possible, the actor himself is often unaware that there are alternatives.

The proposition that men think, feel, and see things from a standpoint peculiar to the group in which they participate is an old one, repeatedly emphasized by students of anthropology and of the sociology of knowledge. Why, then, the sudden concern with reference-group theory during the past decade? The concept of reference group actually introduces a minor refinement in the long familiar theory, made necessary by the special characteristics of modern mass societies. First of all, in modern societies special problems arise from the fact that men sometimes use the standards of groups in which they are *not* recognized members, sometimes of groups in which they have never participated directly, and sometimes of groups that do not exist at all. Second, in our mass society, characterized as it is by cultural pluralism, each person internalizes several perspectives, and this occasionally gives rise to embarrassing dilemmas which call for systematic study. Finally, the development of reference-group theory has been facilitated by the increasing interest in social psychology and the subjective aspects of group life, a shift from a predominant concern with objective social structures to an interest in the experiences of the participants whose regularized activities make such structures discernible.

A reference group, then, is that group whose outlook is used by the actor as the frame of reference in the organization of his perceptual field. All kinds of groupings, with great variations in size, composition, and structure, may become reference groups. Of greatest importance for most people are those groups in which they participate directly—what have been called membership groups—especially those containing a number of persons with whom one stands in a primary relationship. But in some transactions one may assume the perspective attributed to some social category—a social class, an ethnic group, those in a given community, or those concerned with some special interest. On the other hand, reference groups may be imaginary, as in the case of artists who are "born ahead of their times," scientists who work for "humanity," or philanthropists who give for "posterity." Such persons estimate their endeavors from a postulated perspective imputed to people who have not yet been born. There are others who live for a distant past, idealizing some period in history and longing for "the good old days," criticizing current events from a standpoint imputed to people long since dead. Reference groups, then, arise through the internalization of norms; they constitute the structure of expectations imputed to some audience for whom one organizes his conduct.

The Construction of Social Worlds

As Dewey emphasized, society exists in and through communication; common perspectives—common cultures—emerge through participation in common communication channels. It is through social participation that perspectives shared in a group are internalized. Despite the frequent recitation of this proposition, its full implications, especially for the analysis of mass societies, are not often appreciated. Variations in outlook arise through differential contact and association; the maintenance of social distance—through segregation, conflict, or simply the reading of different literature—leads to the formation of distinct cultures. Thus, people in different social classes develop different modes of life and outlook, not because of anything inherent in economic position, but because similarity of occupation and limitations set by income level dispose them to certain restricted communication channels. Those in different ethnic groups form their own distinctive cultures because their identifications incline them to interact intimately with each other and to maintain reserve before outsiders. Different intellectual traditions within social psychology—psychoanalysis, scale analysis, *Gestalt,* pragmatism—will remain separated as long as those in each tradition restrict their sympathetic attention to works of their own school and view others with contempt or hostility. Some social scientists are out of touch with the masses of the American people because they eschew the mass media, especially television, or expose themselves only condescendingly .Even the outlook that the *avant-garde* regards as "cosmopolitan" is culture-bound, for it also is a product of participation in restricted communication channels—books, magazines, meetings, exhibits, and taverns which are out of bounds for most people in the middle classes. Social participation may even be vicarious, as it is in the case of a medievalist who acquires his perspective solely through books.

Even casual observation reveals the amazing variety of standards by which Americans live. The inconsistencies and contradictions which characterize modern mass societies are products of the multitude of communication channels and the ease of participation in them. Studying relatively isolated societies, anthropologists can speak meaningfully of "culture areas" in geographical terms; in such societies common cultures have a territorial base, for only those who live together can interact. In modern industrial societies, however, because of the development of rapid transportation and the media of mass communication, people who are geographically dispersed can communicate effectively. Culture areas are coterminous with communication channels; since communication networks are no longer coterminous with territorial boundaries, culture areas overlap and have lost their territorial bases. Thus, next-door neighbors may be complete strangers; even in common parlance there is an intuitive recognition of the diversity of perspectives, and we speak meaningfully of people living in different social worlds—the academic world, the world of children, the world of fashion.

Modern mass societies, indeed, are made up of a bewildering variety of social worlds. Each is an organized outlook, built up by people in their interaction with one another; hence, each communication channel gives rise to a separate world. Probably the greatest sense of identification and solidarity is to be found in the various communal structures—the underworld, ethnic minorities, the social elite. Such communities are frequently spatially segregated, which isolates them further from the outer world, while the "grapevine" and foreign-language presses provide internal contacts. Another common type of social world consists of the associational structures—the world of medicine, of organized labor, of the theater, of café society. These are held together not only by various voluntary associations within each locality but also by periodicals like *Variety,* specialized journals, and feature sections in newspapers. Finally, there are the loosely connected universes of special interest—the world of sports, of the stamp collector, of the daytime serial—serviced by mass media programs and magazines like *Field and Stream.* Each of these worlds is a unity of order, a universe of regularized mutual response. Each is an area in which there is some structure which permits reasonable anticipation of the behavior of others, hence, an area in which one may act with a sense of security and confidence.[7] Each social world, then, is a culture area, the boundaries of which are set neither by territory nor by formal group membership but by the limits of effective communication.

Since there is a variety of communication channels, differing in stability and extent, social worlds differ in composition, size, and the territorial distribution of the participants. Some, like local cults, are small and concentrated; others, like the intellectual world, are vast and the participants dispersed. Worlds differ in the extent and clarity of their boundaries; each is confined by some kind of horizon, but this may be wide or narrow, clear or vague. The fact that social worlds are not coterminous with the universe of men is recognized; those in the underworld are well aware of the fact that outsiders do not share their values. Worlds differ in exclusiveness and in the extent to which they demand the loyalty of their participants. Most important of all, social worlds are not static entities; shared perspectives are continually being reconstituted. Worlds come into existence with the establishment of communication channels; when life conditions change, social relationships may also change, and these worlds may disappear.

Every social world has some kind of communication system—often nothing more than differential association—in which there develops a special universe of discourse, sometimes an argot. Special meanings and symbols further accentuate differences and increase social distance from outsiders. In each world there are special norms of conduct, a set of values, a special prestige ladder, characteristic career lines, and a common outlook toward life—a Weltanschauung. In the case of elites there may even arise a code of honor which holds only for those who belong, while others are dismissed as beings somewhat less than human from whom bad manners may be expected. A social world, then, is an order conceived which serves as the stage on which each participant seeks to carve out his career and to maintain and enhance his status.

One of the characteristics of life in modern mass societies is simultaneous participation in a variety of social worlds. Because of the ease with which the individual may expose himself to a number of communication channels, he may lead a segmentalized life, participating successively in a number of unrelated activities. Furthermore, the particular combination of social worlds differs from person to person; this is what led Simmel to declare that each stands at that point at which a unique combination of social circles intersects. The geometric analogy is a happy one, for it enables us to conceive the numerous possibilities of combinations and the different degrees of participation in each circle. To understand what a man does, we must get at his unique perspective—what he takes for granted and how he defines the situation—but in mass societies we must learn in addition the social world in which he is participating in a given act.

Loyalty and Selective Responsiveness

In a mass society where each person internalizes numerous perspectives there are bound to be some incongruities and conflicts. The overlapping of group affiliation and participation, however, need not lead to difficulties and is usually unnoticed. The reference groups of most persons are mutually sustaining. Thus, the soldier who volunteers for hazardous duty on the battlefield may provoke anxiety in his family but is not acting contrary to their values; both his family and his comrades admire courage and disdain cowardice. Behavior may be inconsistent, as in the case of the proverbial office tyrant who is meek before his wife, but it is not noticed if the transactions occur in dissociated contexts. Most people live more or less compartmentalized lives, shifting from one social world to another as they participate in a succession of transactions. In each world their roles are different, their relations to other participants are different, and they reveal a different facet of their personalities. Men have become so accustomed to this mode of life that they manage to conceive of themselves as reasonably consistent human beings in spite of this segmentalization and are generally not aware of the fact that their acts do not fit into a coherent pattern.

People become acutely aware of the existence of different outlooks only when they are successively caught in situations in which conflicting demands are made upon them, all of which cannot possibly be satisfied. While men generally avoid making difficult decisions, these dilemmas and contradictions of status may force a choice between two social worlds. These conflicts are essentially alternative ways of defining the same situation, arising from several possible perspectives. In the words of William James, "As a man I pity you, but as an official I must show you no mercy; as a politician I regard him as an ally, but as a moralist I loathe him." In playing roles in different social worlds, one imputes different expectations to others whose differences cannot always be compromised. The problem is that of selecting the perspective for defining the situation. In Mead's terminology, which generalized other's role is to be taken? It is only in situations where alternative definitions are possible that problems of loyalty arise.

Generally such conflicts are ephemeral; in critical situations contradictions otherwise unnoticed are brought into the open, and painful choices are forced. In poorly integrated societies, however, some people find themselves continually beset with such conflicts. The Negro intellectual, children of mixed marriages or of immigrants, the foreman in a factory, the professional woman, the military chaplain—all live in the interstices of well-organized structures and are marginal men.[8] In most instances they manage to make their way through their compartmentalized lives, although personal maladjustments are apparently frequent. In extreme cases amnesia and dissociation of personality can occur.

Much of the interest in reference groups arises out of concern with situations in which a person is confronted with the necessity of choosing between two or more organized perspectives. The hypothesis has been advanced that the choice of reference groups—conformity to the norms of the group whose perspective is assumed—is a function of one's interpersonal relations; to what extent the culture of a group serves as the matrix for the organization of perceptual experience depends upon one's relationship and personal loyalty to others who share that outlook. Thus, when personal relations to others in the group deteriorate, as sometimes happens in a military unit after continued defeat, the norms become less binding, and the unit may disintegrate in panic. Similarly, with the transformation of personal relationships between parent and child in late adolescence, the desires and standards of the parents often become less obligatory.

It has been suggested further that choice of reference groups rests upon personal loyalty to significant others of that social world. "Significant others," for Sullivan, are those persons directly responsible for the internalization of norms. Socialization is a product of a gradual accumulation of experiences with certain people, particularly those with whom we stand in primary relations, and significant others are those who are actually involved in the cultivation of abilities, values, and outlook.[9] Crucial, apparently, is the character of one's emotional ties with them. Those who think the significant others have treated them with affection and consideration have a sense of personal obligation that is binding under all circumstances, and they will be loyal even at great personal sacrifice. Since primary relations are not necessarily satisfactory, however, the reactions may be negative. A person who is well aware of the expectations of significant others may go out of his way to reject them. This may account for the bifurcation of orientation in minority groups, where some remain loyal to the parental culture while others seek desperately to become assimilated in the larger world. Some who withdraw from the uncertainties of real life may establish loyalties to perspectives acquired through vicarious relationships with characters encountered in books.[10]

Perspectives are continually subjected to the test of reality. All perception is hypothetical. Because of what is taken for granted from each standpoint, each situation is approached with a set of expectations; if transactions actually take place as anticipated, the perspective itself is reinforced. It is thus the confirming responses of other people that provide support for perspectives.[11] But in mass societies the responses of others vary, and in the study of reference groups the problem is that of ascertaining *whose* confirming responses will sustain a given point of view.

The Study of Mass Societies

Because of the differentiated character of modern mass societies, the concept of reference group, or some suitable substitute, will always have a central place in any realistic conceptual scheme for its analysis. As is pointed out above, it will be most useful if it is used to designate that group whose perspective is assumed by the actor as the frame of reference for the organization of his perceptual experience. Organized perspectives arise in and become shared through participation in common communication channels, and the diversity of mass societies arises from the multiplicity of channels and the ease with which one may participate in them.

Mass societies are not only diversified and pluralistic but also continually changing. The successive modification of life-conditions compels changes in social relationships, and any adequate analysis requires a study of these transformational processes themselves. Here the concept of reference group can be of crucial importance. For example, all forms of social mobility, from sudden conversions to gradual assimilation, may be regarded essentially as displacements of reference groups, for they involve a loss of responsiveness to the demands of one social world and the adoption of the perspective of another. It may be hypothesized that the disaffection occurs first on the level of personal relations, followed by a weakening sense of obligation, a rejection of old claims, and the establishment of new loyalties and incorporation of a new perspective. The conflicts that characterize all persons in marginal roles are of special interest in that they provide opportunities for cross-sectional analyses of the processes of social change.

In the analysis of the behavior of men in mass societies the crucial problem is that of ascertaining how a person defines the situation, which perspective he uses in arriving at such a definition, and who constitutes the audience whose responses provide the necessary confirmation and support for his position. This calls for focusing attention upon the expectations the actor imputes to others, the communication channels in which he participates, and his relations with those with whom he identifies himself. In the study of conflict, imagery provides a fertile source of data. At moments of indecision, when in doubt and confusion, who appears in imagery? In this manner the significant other can be identified.

An adequate analysis of modern mass societies requires the development of concepts and operations for the description of the manner in which each actor's orientation toward his world is successively reconstituted. Since perception is selective and perspectives differ, different items are noticed and a progressively diverse set of images arises, even among those exposed to the same media of mass communication. The concept of reference group summarizes differential associations and loyalties and thus facilitates the study of selective perception. It becomes, therefore, an indispensable tool for comprehending the diversity and dynamic character of the kind of society in which we live.

Notes

[1] H. H. Hyman, "The Psychology of Status," *Archives of Psychology*, XXXVIII (1942), 15; R. K. Merton and A. Kitt, "Contributions to the Theory of Reference Group Behavior," in R. K. Merton and P. F. Lazarsfeld (eds.), *Studies in the Scope and Method of "The American Soldier"* (Glencoe, Ill.: Free Press, 1950), pp. 42–53, 69; D. W. Chapman and J. Volkmann, "A Social Determinant of the Level of Aspiration," *Journal of Abnormal and Social Psychology*, XXXIV (1939), 225–38.

[2] *Op. cit.*, pp. 75–76.

[3] M. Sherif, "The Concept of Reference Groups in Human Relations," in M. Sherif and M. O. Wilson (eds.), *Group Relations at the Crossroads* (New York: Harper & Bros., 1953), pp. 203–31.

[4] *Op. cit.*, pp. 49–50.

[5] R. Redfield, *The Folk Culture of Yucatan* (Chicago: University of Chicago Press, 1941), p. 132. For a more explicit presentation of a behavioristic theory of culture see *The Selected Writings of Edward Sapir in Language, Culture and Personality*, ed. D. G. Mandelbaum (Berkeley: University of California Press, 1949), pp. 104–9, 308–31, 544–59.

[6] G. H. Mead, "The Genesis of the Self and Social Control," *International Journal of Ethics*, XXXV (1925), 251–77, and *Mind, Self and Society* (Chicago: University of Chicago Press, 1934), pp. 152–64. Cf. T. Parsons, "The Superego and the Theory of Social Systems," *Psychiatry*, XV (1952), 15–25.

[7] Cf. K. Riezler, *Man: Mutable and Immutable* (Chicago: Henry Regnery Co., 1950), pp. 62–72; L. Landgrebe, "The World as a Phenomenological Problem," *Philosophy and Phenomenological Research*, I (1940), 38–58; and A. Schuetz, "The Stranger: An Essay in Social Psychology," *American Journal of Sociology*, XLIX (1944), 499–507.

[8] Cf. E. C. Hughes, "Dilemmas and Contradictions of Status," *American Journal of Sociology*, L (1945), 353–59, and E. V. Stonequist, *The Marginal Man* (New York: Charles Scribner's Sons, 1937).

[9] H. S. Sullivan, *Conceptions of Modern Psychiatry* (Washington, D.C.: W. H. White Psychiatric Foundation, 1947), pp. 18–22.

[10] Cf. R. R. Grinker and J. P. Spiegel, *Men under Stress* (Philadelphia: Blakiston Co., 1945), pp. 122–26; and E. A. Shils and M. Janowitz, "Cohesion and Disintegration in the Wehrmacht in World War II," *Public Opinion Quarterly*, XII (1948), 280–315.

[11] Cf. G. H. Mead, *The Philosophy of the Act* (Chicago: University of Chicago Press, 1938), pp. 107–73; and L. Postman, "Toward a General Theory of Cognition," in J. H. Rohrer and M. Sherif (eds.), *Social Psychology at the Crossroads* (New York: Harper & Bros., 1951), pp. 242–72.

The Social Determination
of Knowledge

KARL MANNHEIM

Karl Mannheim was perhaps the single most influential figure in the sociology of knowledge. The following selection is an excerpt from an essay entitled "The Sociology of Knowledge," which constitutes the last chapter of his *Ideology and Utopia*.

Mannheim is concerned with verifying the social or existential (for him these concepts are synonymous) determination of thinking. He proposed that this can be done if we can show that: (a) knowing is not based entirely on "theoretical factors" such as immanent laws, nature, logic, or an inner force, but also on existential factors that exist in social experience; and (b) existential factors penetrate the forms, content, scope, and intensity of our perspectives. A major portion of this selection is devoted to these two points. To understand the concept of knowledge as given in point (a), Mannheim contends that we must study ideas in the context of the experience of the individuals who possess them, not as entities unto themselves. All think-ing (which he refers to as the formulation and treatment of problems) is based on such experiences, which are largely social rather than individual. Thoughts "arise out of the collective purposes of a group which underlie the thought of the individual. . . ."

Mannheim, then, sees various groups, each with its own collective historical experiences, as the existential bases of perspectives. Social processes such as competition among conflicting groups or the rela-tions between generations give rise to varying perspectives.

The second point concerns the extent to which such existential factors affect our perspective. Social processes are found to be crucial in the determination of thought. For instance, although the exact (physical) sciences may be cumulative, Mannheim contends that this is not so easily demonstrated with regard to the cultural (social) sci-ences. Ultimately, every period has its own approach and point of view. When assessing art or knowledge in general (Mannheim appears to be referring to social science knowledge) we can specify the social-

Pp. 267–286 from *Ideology and Utopia* by Karl Mannheim. Reprinted by permission of Harcourt Brace Jovanovich, Inc., and Routledge & Kegan Paul Ltd.

historical setting in which a work occurred since it exemplifies a particular perspective.

Mannheim gives a definition of perspective—"the manner in which one views an object, what one perceives in it, and how one construes it in his thinking." He also provides some examples of what to look for in an analysis of perspective and applies these to an analysis of nineteenth-century German political perspectives. Not only are particular concepts dependent on group experience, but so are the basic categories of thought. Mannheim discusses how German political groups on the left used different categories of thought from those on the right in regard to the same issues. Another aspect of perspective is that it includes a "thought-model" which predisposes a person to consider an object (object being broadly defined as anything which one thinks about) in a certain way. For example Marxism contains a thought-model which predisposes its adherents to consider problems in a certain perspective.

Varied groups constitute modern social life and an individual's perspective is largely shaped by his group experience. Men no longer find their perspective shared by all persons with whom they communicate. A result of this situation is "talking past one another." Mannheim contends that we can avoid doing this by considering thought in terms of "relationism" and "particularization." In relationism we recognize that thoughts are related "to a certain mode of interpreting the world which, in turn, is ultimately related to a certain social structure. . . ." With particularization we delimit the view to be analyzed. We specify the scope and the extent of validity of the view in question.

Although some of Mannheim's conceptualizations are difficult, his work is a fundamental contribution to sociology and we should keep in mind the main outlines of his discussion.

WE will present the sociology of knowledge as a theory of the social or existential determination of actual thinking. It would be well to begin by explaining what is meant by the wider term "existential determination of knowledge" ("*Seinsverbundenheit* [1] *des Wissens*"). As a concrete fact, it may be best approached by means of an illustration. The existential determination of thought may be regarded as a demonstrated fact in those realms of thought in which we can show (*a*) that the process of knowing does not actually develop historically in accordance with immanent laws, that it does not follow only from the "nature of things" or from "pure logical possibilities," and that it is not driven by an "inner dialectic." On the contrary, the emergence and the crystallization of actual thought is influenced in many decisive points by extra-theoretical factors of the most diverse sort. These may be called, in contradistinction to purely theoretical factors, existential factors. This existential determination of thought will also have to be regarded as a fact (*b*) if the influence of these existential factors on the concrete content of knowledge is of more than mere peripheral importance, if they are relevant not only to the genesis of ideas, but penetrate into their forms and content and if, furthermore, they decisively determine the scope and the intensity of our experience and observation, i.e. that which we formerly referred to as the "perspective" of the subject.

Social Processes Influencing the Process of Knowledge

Considering now the first set of criteria for determining the existential connections of knowledge, i.e. the role actually played by extra-theoretical factors in the history of thought, we find that the more recent investigations undertaken in the spirit of the sociologically oriented history of thought supply an increasing amount of corroborative evidence. For even to-day the fact seems to be perfectly clear that the older method of intellectual history, which was oriented towards the *a priori* conception that changes in ideas were to be understood on the level of ideas (immanent intellectual history), blocked recognition of the penetration of the social process into the intellectual sphere. With the growing evidence of the flaws in this *a priori* assumption, an increasing number of concrete cases makes it evident that (*a*) every formulation of a problem is made possible only by a previous actual human experience which involves such a problem; (*b*) in selection from the multiplicity of data there is involved an act of will on the part of the knower; and (*c*) forces arising out of living experience are significant in the direction which the treatment of the problem follows.

In connection with these investigations, it will become more and more clear that the living forces and actual attitudes which underlie the theoretical ones are by no means merely of an individual nature, i.e. they do not have their origin in the first place in the individual's becoming aware of his interests in the course of his thinking. Rather, they arise out of the collective purposes of a group which underlie the thought of the individual, and in the prescribed outlook of which he merely participates. In this connection, it becomes more clear that a large part of thinking and knowing cannot be correctly understood, as long as its connection with existence or with the social implications of human life are not taken into account.

It would be impossible to list all the manifold social processes which, in the above sense, condition and shape our theories, and we shall, therefore, confine ourselves to a few examples (and even in these cases, we shall have to leave the detailed proof to the instances cited in the index and bibliography).

We may regard competition as such a representative case in which extra-theoretical processes affect the emergence and the direction of the development of knowledge. Competition [2] controls not merely economic activity through the mechanism of the market, not merely the course of political and social events, but furnishes also the motor impulse behind diverse interpretations of the world which, when their social background is uncovered, reveal themselves as the intellectual expressions of conflicting groups struggling for power.

As we see these social backgrounds emerge and become recognizable as the invisible forces underlying knowledge, we realize that thoughts and ideas are not the result of the isolated inspiration of great geniuses. Underlying even the profound insight of the genius are the collective historical experiences of a group which the individual takes for granted, but which should under no conditions be hypostatized as "group mind." On closer inspection it is to be seen that there is not merely one complex of collective experience with one exclusive tendency, as the theory of the folk-spirit maintained. The world is known through many different orientations because there are many simultaneous and mutually contradictory trends of thought (by no means of equal value) struggling against one another with their different interpretations of "common" experience. The clue to this conflict, therefore, is not to be found in the "object in itself" (if it were, it would be impossible to understand why the object should appear in so many different refractions), but in the very different expectations, purposes, and impulses arising out of experience. If, then, for our explanation we are thrown back upon the play and counterplay of different impulses within the social sphere, a more exact analysis will show that the cause of this conflict between concrete impulses is not to be looked for in theory itself, but in these varied opposing impulses, which in turn are rooted in the whole matrix of collective interests. These seemingly "pure theoretical" cleavages may, in the light of a sociological analysis (which uncovers the hidden intermediate steps between the original impulses to observe and the purely theoretical conclusion), be reduced, for the most part, to more fundamental philosophical differences. But the latter, in turn, are invisibly guided by the antagonism and competition between concrete, conflicting groups.

To mention only one of the many other possible bases of collective existence, out of which different interpretations of the world and different forms of knowledge may arise, we may point to the role played by the relationship between differently situated generations. This factor influences in very many cases the principles of selection, organization, and polarization of theories and points of view prevailing in a given society at a given moment. (This is given more detailed attention in the author's essay entitled "Das Problem der Generationen." [3]) From the knowledge derived from our studies on competition and generations, we have concluded that what, from the point of view of immanent intellectual history, appears to be the "inner dialectic" in the development of ideas, becomes, from the standpoint of the sociology of knowledge, the rhythmic movement in the history of ideas as affected by competition and the succession of generations.

In considering the relationship between forms of thought and forms of society, we shall recall Max Weber's [4] observation that the interest in systematization is in large part attributable to a scholastic background, that the interest in "systematic" thought is the correlate of juristic and scientific schools of thought, and that the origin of this organizing form of thought lies in the continuity of pedagogical institutions. We should also mention at this point

Max Scheler's [5] significant attempt to establish the relationship between various forms of thought and certain types of groups in which alone they can arise and be elaborated.

This must suffice to indicate what is meant by the correlation between types of knowledge and of ideas, on the one hand, and the social groups and processes of which they are characteristic.

The Essential Penetration of the Social Process into the "Perspective" of Thought

Are the existential factors in the social process merely of peripheral significance, are they to be regarded merely as conditioning the origin or factual development of ideas (i.e. are they of merely genetic relevance), or do they penetrate into the "perspective" of concrete particular assertions? This is the next question we shall try to answer. The historical and social genesis of an idea would only be irrelevant to its ultimate validity if the temporal and social conditions of its emergence had no effect on its content and form. If this were the case, any two periods in the history of human knowledge would only be distinguished from one another by the fact that in the earlier period certain things were still unknown and certain errors still existed which, through later knowledge were completely corrected. This simple relationship between an earlier incomplete and a later complete period of knowledge may to a large extent be appropriate for the exact sciences (although indeed to-day the notion of the stability of the categorical structure of the exact sciences is, compared with the logic of classical physics, considerably shaken). For the history of the cultural sciences, however, the earlier stages are not quite so simply superseded by the later stages, and it is not so easily demonstrable that early errors have subsequently been corrected. Every epoch has its fundamentally new approach and its characteristic point of view, and consequently sees the "same" object from a new perspective.

Hence the thesis that the historico-social process is of essential significance for most of the domains of knowledge receives support from the fact that we can see from most of the concrete assertions of human beings when and where they arose, when and where they were formulated. The history of art has fairly conclusively shown that art forms may be definitely dated according to their style, since each form is possible only under given historical conditions and reveals the characteristics of that epoch. What is true of art also holds *mutatis mutandis* good for knowledge. Just as in art we can date particular forms on the ground of their definite association with a particular period of history so in the case of knowledge we can detect with increasing exactness the perspective due to a particular historical setting. Further, by the use of pure analysis of thought-structure, we can determine when and where the world presented itself in such, and only in such a light to the subject that made the assertion, and the analysis may frequently be carried to the point where the more inclusive question may be answered, *why* the world presented itself in precisely such a manner.

Whereas the assertion (to cite the simplest case) that twice two equals four gives no clue as to when, where, and by whom it was formulated, it is always possible in the case of a work in the social sciences to say whether it was inspired by the "historical school," or "positivism," or "Marxism," and from what stage in the development of each of these it dates. In assertions of this sort, we may speak of an "infiltration of the social position" of the investigator into the results of his study and of the "situational-relativity" (*"Situationsgebundenheit"*), or the relationship of these assertions to the underlying reality.

"Perspective" in this sense signifies the manner in which one views an object, what one perceives in it, and how one construes it in his thinking. Perspective, therefore, is something more than a merely formal determination of thinking. It refers also to qualitative elements in the structure of thought, elements which must necessarily be overlooked by a purely formal logic. It is precisely these factors which are responsible for the fact that two persons, even if they apply the same formal-logical rules, e.g. the law of contradiction or the formula of the syllogism, in an identical manner, may judge the same object very differently.

Of the traits by which the perspective of an assertion may be characterized, and of the criteria which aid us to attribute it to a given epoch or situation, we will adduce only a few examples: analysis of the meaning of the concepts being used; the phenomenon of the counter-concept; the absence of certain concepts; the structure of the catgorical apparatus; dominant models of thought; level of abstraction; and the ontology that is presupposed. In what follows, we intend to show, by means of a few examples, the applicability of these identifying traits and criteria in the analysis of perspective. At the same time, it will be shown how far the social position of the observer affects his outlook.

We will begin with the fact that the same word, or the same concept in most cases, means very different things when used by differently situated persons.

When, in the early years of the nineteenth century, an old-style German conservative spoke of "freedom" he meant thereby the right of each estate to live according to its privileges (liberties). If he belonged to the romantic-conservative and Protestant movement he understood by it "inner freedom," i.e. the right of each individual to live according to his own individual personality. Both of these groups thought in terms of the *"qualitative conception of freedom"* because they understood freedom to mean the right to maintain either their historical or their inner, individual distinctiveness.

When a liberal of the same period used the term "freedom," he was thinking of freedom *from* precisely those privileges which to the old-style conservative appeared to be the very basis of all freedom. The liberal conception was, then, an *"equalitarian conception of freedom,"* in the case of which "being free" meant that all men have the same fundamental rights at their disposal. The liberal conception of freedom was that of a group which sought to overthrow the external, legal, non-equalitarian social order. The conservative idea of freedom, on the other hand, was that of a stratum which did not wish to see any changes in the external order of things, hoping that events would continue in their traditional uniqueness; in order to support things as they were, they also had to divert the issues concerning freedom from the external political realm to the inner non-political realm. That the liberal saw only one, and the conservative only another, side of the concept and of the problem was clearly and demonstrably connected with their respective positions in the social and political structure.[6] In brief, even in the formulation of concepts, the angle of vision is guided by the observer's interests. Thought, namely, is directed in accordance with what a particular social group expects. Thus, out of the possible data of experience, every concept combines within itself only that which, in the light of the investigators' interests, it is essential to grasp and to incorporate. Hence, for example, the conservative concept of *Volksgeist* was most probably formulated as a counter-concept in opposition to the progressive concept of "the spirit of the age" (*Zeitgeist*). The analysis of the concepts in a given conceptual scheme itself provides the most direct approach to the perspective of distinctively situated strata.

The absence of certain concepts indicates very often not only the absence of certain points of view, but also the absence of a definite drive to come to grips with certain life-problems. Thus, for example, the relatively late appearance in history of the concept "social" is evidence for the fact that the questions implied in the concept "social" had never been posited before, and likewise that a definite mode of experience signified by the concept "social" did not exist before.

But not only do the concepts in their concrete contents diverge from one another in accordance with differing social positions, but the basic categories of thought may likewise differ.

So, for example, early nineteenth century German conservatism (we draw most of our illustrations from this epoch because it has been studied more thoroughly from a sociological point of view than any other), and contemporary conservatism too, for that matter, tend to use morphological categories which do not break up the concrete totality of the data of experience, but seek rather to preserve it in all its uniqueness. As opposed to the morphological approach, the analytical approach characteristic of the parties of the left, broke down every concrete totality in order to arrive at smaller, more general, units which might then be recombined through the category of causality or functional integration. Here it becomes our task not only to indicate the fact that people in different social positions think differently, but to make intelligible the causes for their different ordering of the material of experiences by different categories. The groups oriented to the left intend to make something new out of the world as it is given, and therefore they divert their glance from things as they are, they become abstract and atomize the given situation into its component elements in order to recombine them anew. Only that appears configuratively or morphologically which we are prepared to accept without further ado, and which, fundamentally, we do not wish to change. Still further, by means of the configurative conception, it is intended to stabilize precisely those elements which are still in flux, and at the same time to invoke sanction for what exists because it is as it is. All this makes it quite clear to what extent even abstract categories and principles of organization, which are seemingly far removed from the political struggle, have their origin in the meta-theoretical pragmatic nature of the human mind, and in the more profound depths of the psyche and of consciousness. Hence to speak here of conscious deception in the sense of creating ideologies is out of the question.

The next factor which may serve to characterize the perspective of thought is the so-called thought-model; i.e. the model that is implicitly in the mind of a person when he proceeds to reflect about an object.

It is well known, for instance, that once the typology of objects in the natural sciences was formulated, and the categories and methods of thought derived from these types became models, it was thenceforth hoped to solve all the problems in the other realms of existence, including the social, by that method. (This tendency is represented by the mechanistic-atomistic conception of social phenomena.)

It is significant to observe that when this happened, as in all similar cases, not all the strata of society oriented themselves primarily to this single model of thought. The landed nobility, the displaced classes, and the peasantry were not heard from during this historical period. The new character of cultural development and the ascendant forms of orientation towards the world belonged to a mode of life other than their own. The forms of the ascendant world-perspective, modeled on the principles of natural science, came upon these classes as if from the outside. As the interplay of social forces brought other groups, representing the above-mentioned classes and expressing their life-situation, into the forefront of history, the opposing models of thought, as, for instance, the *"organismic"* and the *"personalistic"* were played off against the "functional-mechanistic" type of thought. Thus Stahl, for instance, who stood at the apex of this development, was already able to establish connections between thought-models and political currents.[7]

Behind every definite question and answer is implicitly or explicitly to be found a model of how fruitful thinking can be carried on. If one were to trace in detail, in each individual case, the origin and the radius of diffusion of a certain thought-model, one would discover the peculiar affinity it has to the social position of given groups and their manner of interpreting the world. By these groups we mean not merely classes, as a dogmatic type of Marxism would have it, but also generations, status groups, sects, occupational groups, schools, etc. Unless careful attention is paid to highly differentiated social groupings of this sort and to the corresponding differentiations in concepts, categories, and thought-models, i.e. unless the problem of the relation between super- and sub-structure is refined, it would be impossible to demonstrate that corresponding to the wealth of types of knowledge and perspectives which have appeared in the course of history there are similar differentiations in the sub-structure of society. Of course we do not intend to deny that of all the above-mentioned social groupings and units class stratification is the most significant, since in the final analysis all the other social groups arise from and are trans-formed as parts of the more basic conditions of production and domination. None the less the investigator who, in the face of the variety of types of thought, attempts to place them correctly can no longer be content with the undifferentiated class concept, but must reckon with the existing social units and factors that condition social position, aside from those of class.

Another characteristic of the perspective is to be found by investigating the level of abstraction, beyond which a given theory does not progress, or the degree to which it resists theoretical, systematic formulation.

It is never an accident when a certain theory, wholly or in part, fails to develop beyond a given stage of relative abstractness and offers resistance to further tendencies towards becoming more concrete, either by frowning upon this tendency towards concreteness or declaring it to be irrelevant. Here, too, the social position of the thinker is significant.

Precisely in the case of Marxism and the relation it bears to the findings of the sociology of knowledge can it be shown how an interrelationship can often be formulated only in that form of concreteness which is peculiar to that particular standpoint. It can be shown in the case of Marxism that an observer whose view is bound up with a given social position will by himself never succeed in singling out the more general and theoretical aspects which are implicit in the concrete observations that he makes. It might have been expected, for instance, that long ago Marxism would have formulated in a more theoretical way the fundamental findings of the sociology of knowledge concerning the relationship between human thought and the conditions of existence *in general,* especially since its discovery of the theory of ideology also implied at least the beginnings of the sociology of knowledge. That this impli-cation could never be brought out and theoretically elaborated, and at best only came partially into view, was due, however, to the fact that, in the con-crete instance, this relationship was perceived only in the thought of the opponent. It was probably due, furthermore, to a subconscious reluctance to think out the implications of a concretely formulated insight to a point where the theoretical formulations latent in it would be clear enough to have a dis-quieting effect on one's own position. Thus we see how the narrowed focus which a given position imposes and the driving impulses which govern its insights tend to obstruct the general and theoretical formulation of these views and to restrict the capacity for abstraction. There is a tendency to abide by the particular view that is immediately obtainable, and to prevent the question from being raised as to whether the fact that knowledge is bound up with existence is not inherent in the human thought-structure as such. In addition to this, the tendency in Marxism to shy away from a general, sociological formulation may frequently be traced to a similar limitation which a given point of view imposes on a method of thinking. For instance, one is not even allowed to raise the question whether "impersonalization" (*Verdinglichung*), as elaborated by Marx and Lukács, is a more or less general phenomenon of consciousness, or whether capitalistic impersonalization is merely one particular form of it. Whereas this overemphasis on concreteness and historicism arises out of a particular social location, the opposite tendency, namely the immediate flight into the highest realms of abstraction and formalization, may, as Marxism has rightly emphasized, lead to an obscuring of the concrete situation and its unique character. This could be demonstrated once more in the case of "formal sociology."

We do not wish in any way to call into question the legitimacy of formal sociology as one possible type of sociology. When, however, in the face of the tendency to introduce further concreteness into the formulation of sociological problems, it sets itself up as the only sociology, it is unconsciously guided by motives similar to those which prevented its historical forerunner, the bourgeois-liberal mode of thought, from ever getting beyond an abstract and generalizing mode of observation in its theory. It shies away from dealing historically, concretely, and individually with the problems of society for fear that its own inner antagonisms, for instance the antagonisms of capitalism itself, might become visible. In this it resembles the crucial bourgeois discussion of the problem of freedom, in which the problem usually was and is posited only theoretically and abstractly. And even when it is so posited, the question of freedom is always one of political, rather than of social, rights, since, if the latter sphere were considered, the factors of property and class position in their relation to freedom and equality would inevitably come to light.

To summarize: the approach to a problem, the level on which the problem happens to be formulated, the stage of abstraction and the stage of concreteness that one hopes to attain, are all and in the same way bound up with social existence.

It would be appropriate finally to deal with the underlying substratum in all modes of thought, with their presupposed ontologies and their social differentiations. It is precisely because the ontological substratum is fundamentally significant for thinking and perceiving that we cannot deal adequately in limited space with the problems raised thereby, and we refer therefore, to more elaborate treatments to be found elsewhere.[8] At this point, let it suffice to say that, however justified the desire of modern philosophy may be to work out a "basic ontology," it is dangerous to approach these problems naïvely, without first taking into account the results suggested by the sociology of knowledge. For if we approached this problem naïvely, the almost inevitable result would be that, instead of obtaining a genuine basic ontology, we would become the victims of an arbitrary accidental ontology which the historical process happens to make available to us.

These reflections must suffice in this connection to clarify the notion that the conditions of existence affect not merely the historical genesis of ideas, but constitute an essential part of the products of thought and make themselves felt in their content and form. The examples we have just cited should serve to clarify the peculiar structure and the functions of the sociology of knowledge.

The Special Approach Characteristic of the Sociology of Knowledge

Two persons, carrying on a discussion in the same universe of discourse— corresponding to the same historical-social conditions—can and must do so quite differently from two persons identified with different social positions. These two types of discussion, i.e. between socially and intellectually homogeneous participants and between socially and intellectually heterogeneous participants, are to be clearly distinguished. It is no accident that the distinction between these two types of discussion is explicitly recognized as a problem in an age like ours. Max Scheler called our contemporary period the "epoch of equalization" (*Zeitalter des Ausgleichs*), which, if applied to our problems, means that ours is a world in which social groupings, which had hitherto lived more or less isolated from one another, each making itself and its own world of thought absolute, are now, in one form or another, merging into one another. Not only Orient and Occident, not only the various nations of the west, but also the various social strata of these nations, which previously had been more or less self-contained, and, finally, the different occupational groups within these strata and the intellectual groups in this most highly differentiated world —all these are now thrown out of the self-sufficient, complacent state of taking themselves for granted, and are forced to maintain themselves and their ideas in the face of the onslaught of these heterogeneous groups.

But how do they carry on this struggle? As far as intellectual antagonisms are concerned, they usually do so with but few exceptions by "talking past one another"; i.e. although they are more or less aware that the person with whom they are discussing the matter represents another group, and that it is likely that his mental structure as a whole is often quite different when a concrete thing is being discussed, they speak as if their differences were confined to the specific question at issue around which their present disagreement crystallized. They overlook the fact that their antagonist differs from them in his whole outlook, and not merely in his opinion about the point under discussion.

This indicates that there are also types of intellectual intercourse between heterogeneous persons. In the first, the differences in the total mental structure remain obscurely in the background in so far as the contact between the participants is concerned. Consciousness for both is crystallized about the concrete issue. For each of the participants the "object" has a more or less different meaning because it grows out of the whole of their respective frames of reference, as a result of which the meaning of the object in the perspective of the other person remains, at least in part, obscure. Hence "talking past one another" is an inevitable phenomenon of the "age of equalization."

On the other hand, the divergent participants may also be approached with the intention of using each theoretical point of contact as an occasion for removing misunderstandings by ascertaining the source of the differences. This will bring out the varying presuppositions which are implied in the two respective perspectives as consequences of the two different social situations. In such cases, the sociologist of knowledge does not face his antagonist in the usual manner, according to which the other's arguments are dealt with directly. He seeks rather to understand him by defining the total perspective and seeing it as a function of a certain social position.

The sociologist of knowledge has been accused, because of this procedure, of avoiding the real argument, of not concerning himself with the actual subject-matter under discussion, but, instead, of going behind the immediate subject of debate to the total basis of thought of the assertor in order to reveal it as merely one basis of thought among many and as no more than a partial perspective. Going behind the assertions of the opponents and disregarding the actual arguments is legitimate in certain cases, namely, wherever, because of the absence of a common basis of thought, there is no common problem. The sociology of knowledge seeks to overcome the "talking past one another" of the various antagonists by taking as its explicit theme of investigation the uncovering of the sources of the partial disagreements which would never come to the attention of the disputants because of their preoccupation with the subject-matter that is the immediate issue of the debate. It is superfluous to remark that the sociologist of knowledge is justified in tracing the arguments to the very basis of thought and the position of disputants only if and in so far as an actual disparity exists between the perspectives of the discussion resulting in a fundamental misunderstanding. As long as discussion proceeds from the same basis of thought, and within the same universe of discourse, it is unnecessary. Needlessly applied, it may become a means for side-stepping the discussion.

The Acquisition of Perspective as a Pre-condition for the Sociology of Knowledge

For the son of a peasant who has grown up within the narrow confines of his village and spends his whole life in the place of his birth, the mode of thinking and speaking characteristic of that village is something that he takes entirely for granted. But for the country lad who goes to the city and adapts himself gradually to city life, the rural mode of living and thinking ceases to be something to be taken for granted. He has won a certain detachment from it, and he distinguishes now, perhaps quite consciously, between "rural" and "urban" modes of thought and ideas. In this distinction lie the first beginnings of that approach which the sociology of knowledge seeks to develop in full detail. That which within a given group is accepted as absolute appears to the outsider conditioned by the group situation and recognized as partial (in this case, as "rural"). This type of knowledge presupposes a more detached perspective.

This detached perspective can be gained in the following ways: (*a*) a member of a group leaves his social position (by ascending to a higher class, emigration, etc.); (*b*) the basis of existence of a whole group shifts in relation to its traditional norms and institutions,[9] (*c*) within the same society two or more socially determined modes of interpretation come into conflict and, in criticizing one another, render one another transparent and establish perspectives with reference to each other. As a result, a detached perspective, through which the outlines of the contrasting modes of thought are discovered, comes within the range of possibility for all the different positions, and later gets to be the recognized mode of thinking. We have already indicated that the social genesis of the sociology of knowledge rests primarily upon the last mentioned possibility.

Relationism

What has already been said should hardly leave any doubt as to what is meant when the procedure of the sociology of knowledge is designated as "relational." When the urbanized peasant boy characterizes certain political, philosophical, or social opinions to be found among his relatives as "rustic," he no longer discusses these opinions as a homogeneous participant, that is, by dealing directly with the specific content of what is said. Rather he relates them to a certain mode of interpreting the world which, in turn, is ultimately related to a certain social structure which constitutes its situation. This is an instance of the "relational" procedure. We shall deal later with the fact that when assertions are treated in this way it is not implied that they are false. The sociology of knowledge goes beyond what, in some such crude way as this, people frequently do to-day, only in so far as it consciously and systematically subjects all intellectual phenomena without exception, to the question: In connection with what social structure did they arise and are they valid? Relating individual ideas to the total structure of a given historico-social subject should not be confused with a philosophical relativism which denies the validity of any standards and of the existence of order in the world. Just as the fact that every measurement in space hinges upon the nature of light does not mean that our measurements are arbitrary, but merely that they are only valid in relation to the nature of light, so in the same way not relativism in the sense of arbitrariness but *relationism* applies to our discussions. Relationism does not signify that there are no criteria of rightness and wrongness in a discussion. It does insist, however, that it lies in the nature of certain assertions that they cannot be formulated absolutely, but only in terms of the perspective of a given situation.

Particularization

Having described the relational process, as conceived by the sociology of knowledge, the question will inevitably be raised: what can it tell us about the validity of an assertion that we would not know if we had not been able to relate it to the standpoint of the assertor? Have we said anything about the truth or falsity of a statement when we have shown that it is to be imputed to liberalism or to Marxism?

Three answers may be made to this question:—

(a) It may be said that the absolute validity of an assertion is denied when its structural relationship to a given social situation has been shown. In this sense there is indeed a current in the sociology of knowledge and in the theory of ideology which accepts the demonstration of this sort of relationship as a refutation of the opponents' assertion, and which would use this method as a device for annihilating the validity of all assertions.

(b) In opposition to this, there may be another answer, namely that the imputations that the sociology of knowledge establishes between a statement and its assertor tells us nothing concerning the truth-value of the assertion, since the manner in which a statement originates does not affect its validity. Whether an assertion is liberal or conservative in and of itself gives no indication of its correctness.

(c) There is a third possible way of judging the value of the assertions that the sociologist of knowledge makes, which represents our own point of view. It differs from the first view in that it shows that the mere factual demonstration and identification of the social position of the assertor as yet tells us nothing about the truth-value of his assertion. It implies only the suspicion that this assertion might represent merely a partial view. As over against the second alternative, it maintains that it would be incorrect to regard the sociology of knowledge as giving no more than a description of the actual conditions under which an assertion arises (factual-genesis). Every complete and thorough sociological analysis of knowledge delimits, in content as well as structure, the view to be analyzed. In other words, it attempts not merely to establish the existence of the relationship, but at the same time to particularize its scope and the extent of its validity. The implications of this will be set forth in greater detail.

What the sociology of knowledge intends to do by its analysis was fairly clearly brought out in the example we cited of the peasant boy. The discovery and identification of his earlier mode of thought as "rural," as contrasted with "urban," already involves the insight that the different perspectives are not merely particular in that they presuppose different ranges of vision and different sectors of the total reality, but also in that the interests and the powers of perception of the different perspectives are conditioned by the social situations in which they arose and to which they are relevant.

Already upon this level the relational process tends to become a particularizing process, for one does not merely relate the assertion to a standpoint but, in doing so, restricts its claim to validity which at first was absolute to a narrower scope.

A fully developed sociology of knowledge follows the same approach which we have illustrated above in the case of the peasant boy, except that it follows a deliberate method. With the aid of a consistently elaborated analysis of the perspective, particularization acquires a guiding instrument and a set of criteria for treating problems of imputation. The range and degree of comprehension of each of these several points of view becomes measurable and delimitable through their categorical apparatus and the variety of meanings which each presents. The orientation towards certain meanings and values which inheres in a given social position (the outlook and attitude conditioned by the collective purposes of a group), and the concrete reasons for the different perspectives which the same situation presents to the different positions in it thus become even more determinable, intelligible, and subject to methodical study through the perfection of the sociology of knowledge.[10]

With the growing methodological refinements in the sociology of knowledge, the determination of the particularity of a perspective becomes a cultural and intellectual index of the position of the group in question. By particularizing, the sociology of knowledge goes a step farther than the original determination of the facts to which mere relationism limits itself. Every analytical step undertaken in the spirit of the sociology of knowledge arrives at a point where the sociology of knowledge becomes more than a sociological description of the facts which tell us how certain views have been derived from a certain *milieu*. Rather it reaches a point where it also becomes a critique by redefining the scope and the limits of the perspective implicit in given assertions. The analyses characteristic of the sociology of knowledge are, in this sense, by no means irrelevant for the determination of the truth of a statement; but these analyses, on the other hand, do not by themselves fully reveal the truth because the mere delimitation of the perspectives is by no means a substitute for the immediate and direct discussion between the divergent points of view or for the direct examination of the facts. The function of the findings of the sociology of knowledge lies somewhere in a fashion hitherto not clearly understood, between irrelevance to the establishment of truth on the one hand, and entire adequacy for determining truth on the other. This can be shown by a careful analysis of the original intention of the single statements of sociology of knowledge and by the nature of its findings. An analysis based on the sociology of knowledge is a first preparatory step leading to direct discussion, in an age which is aware of the heterogeneity of its interests and the disunity of its basis of thought, and which seeks to attain this unity on a higher level.

Notes

[1] Here we do not mean by "determination" a mechanical cause-effect sequence: we leave the meaning of "determination" open, and only empirical investigation will show us how strict is the correlation between life-situation and thought-process, or what scope exists for variations in the correlation. [The German expression *"Seinsverbundenes Wissen"* conveys a meaning which leaves the exact nature of the determinism open.]

[2] For concrete examples cf. the author's paper "Die Bedeutung der Konkurrenz im Gebiete des Geistigen," *op. cit.*

[3] *Kölner Vierteljahrshefte für Soziologie* (1928), vol. viii.

[4] Cf. Max Weber, *Wirtschaft und Gesellschaft, op. cit.*, particularly the section on the sociology of law.

[5] Cf. especially his works, *Die Wissenformen und die Gesellschaft*, Leipzig, 1926, and *Die Formen des Wissens und der Bildung*, i, Bonn, 1925.

[6] Cf. the author's "Das konservative Denken," *Archiv für Sozialwissenschaft und Sozialpolitik*, vol. 57, pp. 90 ff.

[7] The history of theories of the state, especially as viewed by F. Oppenheimer in his *System der Soziologie* (vol. ii, "Der Staat") is a treasure of illustrative material.

[8] Cf. the author's "Das konservative Denken" (*loc. cit.*, pp. 489 ff., and especially p. 494), and pp. 88 ff., 98 ff., 193 ff. of this volume.

[9] A good example is furnished by Karl Renner, in *Die Rechtsinstitute des Privatrechts* (J. C. B. Mohr, Tübingen, 1929).

[10] For further details, cf. the treatment of the relationship of theory and practice, *supra*, Part III, where we have endeavored to carry out such a sociological analysis of the perspective.

PART II

SOCIOLOGY AND EXISTENTIALISM

Although we are examining the social determination of reality, this does not bind us to an absolutist social determinism concerning how people construct meaning in their lives. Man can still be seen as capable of creating, choosing, and of changing in order to provide himself with meaning. The fact that he lives within certain constraints, in terms of rules which large numbers of people agree to follow, does not alter his individuality. His individuality, his personal reality, exists in terms of collective existence. Without routinized social processes, the social order, all that exists is chaos. Men make rules, that is, share values, as a way of constructing meaning in the face of the nothingness of an a priori existence. The existential perspective requires us to see man's social life as man-made. As such, the patterns of behavior and shared beliefs are constantly being re-created and changed. No particular behavior or belief is ultimate essence or truth. As sociologists we study the processes of social life in order to grasp the existential bases from which individuals construct their particular meaning and behavior—their social reality.

Recently this perspective, as represented in the articles in this section, has appeared with renewed vigor in sociology. Existentialism is, however, not new to sociology. Many of the ideas which are being employed today are found in the works of such early sociologists as Max Weber and Georg Simmel.

The Existential Perspective

CHARLES HAMPDEN-TURNER

In the following excerpt from Hampden-Turner's book *Radical Man*, the existential view is presented particularly as it relates to the assumptions of social science. This perspective holds that each individual must be the final arbiter of his values and rules for behavior and that each individual is to some extent free to choose among alternative values and behaviors.

Man, according to this perspective, is a synthesizer of experience, but the interpretation he will make of that experience is not simply determined by natural laws or by the society in which he finds himself. It is from his interactions with other people, often but not always within the institutional framework of the larger community, that he determines the rules and values of his existence. On the basis of such rules and values man invests his life with meaning.

Hampden-Turner presents eight statements on the existential perspective and explains and discusses them in turn. He provides a clear and powerful statement of this point of view and shows how each of his statements contributes to the theoretical base of an existential sociology.

I HAVE argued that we need a fresh perspective in the social sciences in order to appreciate the radical, creative and integrative side of human personality. . . . I shall explore the full ramifications of the words "man exists freely. . . ."

Existence comes from the Latin ex-istere meaning to *stand out*. I shall later be referring to the process of *investment* or man investing personal meanings, since what I wish to convey is the transitive nature of the process. The human personality is invested beyond the mind into the social environment, so that man is conceived as a radiating center of meaning.

In the diagram below, the box in the center represents the human mind with inputs on the left and outputs on the right. The top half of the diagram is expressed in existential terms. The lower half with dotted lines is expressed in the terms of behavioral learning theory.

From *Radical Man*, pp. 19–29, by Charles Hampden-Turner, Schenkman Publishing Company, Inc., Cambridge, Mass., copyright © 1970.

INPUTS	MIND	OUTPUTS
Confirmations of experience and novel perceptions	Synthesizing Symbolizing and Exploring Capacities	Investments of personal meanings and experience
Various reinforcements under certain stimulus conditions	Basic Drives and Intervening Variables	Responses in the form of physical and verbal behavior

Under the following heads I shall explore the evidence for man's existence and the ramifications thereof.

1. The synthesizing capacity
2. The symbolizing capacity
3. The exploring capacity
   (which require:)—
4. A field theory—not a monadic one
5. The concept of freedom within the law—not strict determinism
6. Relational facts not objective facts
7. Alternate involvement with self and others—not detachment
8. Value full investigation—not value free.

In the bottom half of the diagram above we see that behaviorists work with the concepts of "stimuli," "reinforcements," the "basic drives" of the person such as hunger and sex, and the characteristics of his "responses," such as strength, frequency and direction. Lately neo-behaviorists have been more and more concerned with "intervening variables"—e.g., age, intelligence, personality type, I.Q., and diagnostic categories. They believe that "reinforcement" under certain "stimulus conditions" will "shape the drives" of specified types of people so that their "responses" can be predicted. The more sophisticated of these experiments have multiple intervening variables.[1]

The advantage of this technique is that it permits the application of most of the traditional scientific principles . . . including the hypothetico-deductive method, fairly strict empiricism (depending on the nature of the "intervening variables"), replication, precision, mathematics and analysis. Its disadvantages . . . are that it ignores, minimizes, or distorts the radical human capacities for synthesizing, symbolizing, and exploring. I hope to show that these capacities are so salient that they justify a reversal of the behavioral perspective itself.

1. The Synthesizing Capacity

There has been a series of experiments by José Delgado thought by many to usher in a new millenium for behaviorism. By implanting electrodes in certain parts of the brain, angry bulls have been halted in mid-charge to become as docile as Ferdinand, monkeys have eaten ravenously at the press of a button and then rejected the food when other parts of their brains were stimulated. But after detailed study of neural pathways and the synapses which permit new connections between circuits Delgado wrote:—

> . . . it should be emphasized that the source of mental information is totally *extracerebral*. The brain can accept, reject or react against received information, or establish associations between past and present sensory inputs. Originality and invention are merely a novel combination of old data, and original thought could not be produced by the naive brain of a newborn baby. Shakespeare did not invent English, nor Einstein, mathematics. . . . The elements which form our personality are borrowed from the environment and from the past. Only their combination and the feelings they create within us are unique.[2]

Here, then, from the pinnacle of S-R achievement we have an admission (hedged around with "merely's" and "only's") of man's capacity to select information, synthesize and resynthesize it. We know that even apes can do this. Wolfgang Kohler describes how an ape which he had observed from birth and which had never used a stick as a tool and never seen one used (although he had played with one), suddenly broke a branch from a bush growing within his cage and, stripping it of leaves and twigs, pushed it through the bars of the cage to retrieve a banana. He accomplished this not by trial and error, but by one fluent series of actions following a period of seeming reflection.[3] Cats have been faced with the problem of obtaining a piece of meat which is suspended in the middle of a closed cage by a piece of string which passes through the top of the cage and is attached to the ceiling. They survey the situation, pause a moment, then leap upon the top of the cage and draw up the string with the meat at the end.[4]

Arthur Koestler has described these elementary acts of creation as "bisociation" of two or more "thought matrices."[5] The wanting-to-reach-and-eat-the-banana matrix is suddenly visualized as capable of combination with the playing-with-sticks matrix and in the absence of a stick "the bush-consisting-of-sticks" is seen as relevant too. The animals can *select* only a stick from out of the "bush matrix" and only the raking in motion from the "playing matrix." Coded information from one neural circuit travels across the synapse into another circuit, and two images are combined.[6]

From apes let us move to Gutenberg and his invention of the printing press. He recollected seeing the carved wooden blocks which were used to stamp playing cards. Later he watched molten coins poured into moulds, and he recalled that seals could be used to stamp paper. But none of these could solve his problem of how to mass produce bibles for a pilgrimage—until months later when he watched a wine press in action. In a flash he saw the solution. "A simple substitution which is a ray of light . . . God hath revealed to me the secret . . ." he wrote. He visualized moulds for every letter of the alphabet in which type could be cast like coins, the type face like a giant seal could be attached to a press, and the press could stamp vellum "like your foot when it multiplies its print. There is the Bible!" [7]

Let us return to the diagram for a moment. Behaviorists would argue that every part of Gutenberg's "response," the printing press, can be traced to prior "reinforcements" and "contiguous stimuli," or to quote Delgado, we have "merely a novel combination of old data." But this combination is no less than revolutionary *so that the input has been totally transformed by this human brain into a novel output.*

What do I mean by "totally transformed"? In the first place there is a transformation in human significance. Print technology was perhaps our greatest leap into modernity and rang up the curtain on the Renaissance. We cannot say this of playing cards or winepresses—a fact that illustrates how incredibly more significant can be the combination of parts than the parts themselves. Combination can produce totally new entities—neither a bush, a plaything, nor the need for a banana is a tool—but the selective syntheses of these matrices can produce the idea of a tool, with its endless ramifications leading up to space technology.

A synthesis can increase energy output a thousandfold or more. How long would it have taken to carve every word of the Bible on wooden blocks? This synthesis transformed the capacity to communicate, helped to fashion the notion of information storage and retrieval, disseminated the Bible so widely that a moral Reformation soon swept Europe. Finally it led to vast increases in the human capacity to symbolize and transmit symbols.

2. The Symbolizing Capacity

If man stands out from his past "reinforcements" by weaving remembered experiences into a personal synthesis, then he stands out also when he chooses symbols to *stand for* those experiences.

Suppose that one were thrown by Nazis into a death camp, as was Viktor Frankl,[8] or that like Albert Camus and Jean Paul Sartre one were forced to live under the Occupation. It would be hard to conceive of more "negative reinforcements" designed to obtain predictable "responses" from victims. And to some extent the predictions were correct, for thousands collaborated, perished, and gave up hope: but a sizable minority found the courage to rebel and this they did by finding fresh meanings, by relabelling the same reality that was overwhelming their compatriots.[9]

For existentialists like Sartre and Camus the absurdity and horror of their environment instead of forcing them to be products of absurdity convinced them of their freedom and that human beings themselves were the sole source of value. "We were never more free than under the Nazis," wrote Sartre. Here he is using "free" in the special existential sense as *the discrepancy between the tyrannical pressures upon him and his capacity to generate meanings which contradicted this environment.*

Similarly Frankl had to experience the degradation of a concentration camp to discover how powerful was his human capacity to emit meaning in the face of chaos. His light shone all the more brightly because the darkness was so total. When aid and comfort were finally extinguished in his surroundings he discovered a personal power which not only sustained him and his companions but laid the ground work for his Third Psychiatric Revolution.[10]

Existential philosophies have a way of strengthening themselves in the face of adversity, for the more evil and inchoate is the environment, the more is the existentialist convinced that only his own affirmation of value and his rebellion in the face of death itself (the final absurdity) can project meaning into the world. He only needs a few memory traces whose combination is meaningful to combat a contemporary assault of "negative reinforcements." Man is free to choose between symbols, and to label pressures upon him as legitimate or illegitimate, free to resymbolize, and free to synthesize and re-synthesize those symbols into structured fields of meaning by which he exists.

3. The Exploring Capacity

Man stands out in yet another way. Instead of passively waiting to be bombarded with "stimuli" he actively explores his environment, using his incomplete knowledge in search for the missing elements in his mental "map."

Behaviorists have never been comfortable with the "exploratory drive." While "hunger drives" in animals can be "shaped" almost completely in controlled conditions, the drive for exploration which *seeks the unknown* cannot be "shaped" by events *known* to be "reinforcing." Even were I to admit that "novelty is reinforcing," this would not enable me to predict that a certain "reinforcement" would produce a certain "response" since that "response" might still be seeking the unknown—that is something different from what was previously "reinforced." Whichever way you stretch the elastic concept of "reinforcement," the exploratory capacity introduces an unpredictable element, and where exploration is combined with man's synthesizing and symbolizing capacities this produces an intentional and a focused capacity to search.

Even in caged animal experiments—and these conditions minimize the freedom to explore—it has long been known that rats will learn a maze merely by being placed in it without reward.[11] They will run the gauntlet of an electrified grill for the sake of exploring strange objects [12] and leave food unfinished when their curiosity is aroused.[13] Rhesus monkeys solve manual puzzles more easily when *no* food or "reinforcers" are inside.[14] Indeed appetite makes them clumsy and impatient. Similarly hungry babies and unmothered monkeys are notoriously unexplorative. The need to know emerges when physiological and emotional needs reach some level of satisfaction.

When man searches he may be looking for a piece to link two or more information matrices and so create a systematic body of thought. He may have a symbol and be seeking the experience for which it stands. Successful exploration can expand his symbolizing, synthesizing, and experiential capacities, and this expanded consciousness can in turn guide his further exploration. In view of the total transformation of incoming messages wrought by the human mind, its capacity to seek out certain messages in preference to others, and its astonishing freedom to synthesize and code its store of memories, I submit that "man exists freely."

In light of this existence let me pause to restate the opening question in this book. If with Bacon we seek a knowledge which is power, then what would most contribute to the knowledge and power of man—a psychology that traced *backwards* from a radio telescope to dim memories of jungle drums and smoked glass, or a psychology that reveals the synthesizing, developing, and expanding process of the human mind in dialogue with other minds? Even were I convinced (and I am not) that man was nine-tenths "caused to behave" and one-tenth seeking, synthesizing and symbolizing, I would still explore the latter realm and thereby make my existential choice of being as responsible as the human condition allows. As Arthur Miller once put it,

> What is needed are people who, quite simply, know how to think, who know how to synthesize knowledge and find connections between distantly related phenomena, who seek constantly to relate rather than isolate experience.[15]

Given this existential perspective a number of ramifications follow that profoundly affect the usual assumptions of psychosocial investigation.

4. A Field Theory—Not a Monadic One

Once we accept that man is a synthesizer of fragmentary experience and a synthesizer of his own earlier syntheses, then analysis, the breaking down of the life field into fragments, must be recognized as a potentially regressive process [16] and one that can blind an investigator to the struggle of living organisms to achieve higher levels of developmental organization.

For the basic property that differentiates living matter from dead matter is not found in a physical or chemical description of the constituents. A heap of dead ingredients can have the same chemical properties as a live organism. Life is a peculiar *state of organization*—a vital synthesis of parts.[17]

Most attempts at theory building in the social sciences assume a *monadic* theory—one in which the relationships *between* unit entities are explained by some property of the *units themselves.*[18] In other words first you analyze social reality into separate units—making sure they are "mutually exclusive and collectively exhaustive"—and *then* you discover how these units interact and relate. What is overlooked in this almost standard procedure is the possibility that the overall organization of the pieces is what imparts to them the very property of life and that their meanings are not intrinsic but depend on how they are synthesized.

Suppose we meet a man who proclaims loudly and often that his home is his castle. Depending on how he organized this attitude into an overall *gestalt* he might for all we know:

> be a radical protesting illegal seizure of his pamphlets by the police,
> be a racist objecting to open housing ordinances,
> be a psychotic convinced that he is William the Conqueror,
> or be an English peer of the realm attempting to attract tourists to his ancestral seat.

To treat such statements as "basic data" and "building blocks" for a science could be extremely hazardous.

What a psychology of existence needs is a *field* theory rather than a monadic one. Our symbolic language is comprehended through its overall structure which carries the meaning, so that we retain the meaning while often forgetting the verbal units in which it was expressed, and we substitute our own units when we relay the meaning to others. Hence an existential perspective is holistic in the sense that *the whole must be grasped in order to comprehend the function of the parts.*[19]

Much of social science is getting laboriously nowhere by trying to correlate artificially separated units of attitude and behavior whose intrinsic meaning is at best ambiguous and inconstant. And the attempt to invent a private language where words have only one precise meaning leads to some very simple ideas being expressed in turgid prose at extraordinary length.[20] In fact the multi-faceted symbol with several contiguous meanings plays a vital part in creating a synthesis between matrices. When social science purges itself of ambiguity it may reduce the capacity of its researchers to think creatively, which might explain why so many of its writings hardly keep the mind alive.

5. The Concept of Freedom within the Law
—Not Strict Determinism

"The freedom of living things is a freedom not *without* the law but *within* the law," writes Floyd Matson.[21] In contrast to this view the polarity of freedom *versus* determinism is commonly expressed along with conviction that science rests squarely upon determinism.

The existential perspective regards this and many other polarities as reconcilable. The capacity to synthesize, symbolize and explore, though leading to unique results, is still a lawful process containing measurable uniformities. In existential philosophy man is free yet bound by his human condition, recognition of the certainties of this condition is regarded as the springboard of freedom, and all free men may still be required to regard certain truths as inalterable.[22]

In biology the concept of equipotentiality recognizes that while an organism will unfold and seems directed by a genetic code to seek an end state of maturation—there are still many degrees of freedom in the paths taken to this end.[23] If parts of an organism are removed other parts will take over their function. Minced and scrambled tissues reorganize themselves while certain organs regenerate. Where normal paths are blocked ingenious and circuitous paths will be substituted. In some organisms, for instance the mushroom, the tangle of fibres is quite unpredictable but not the final smooth curvature to which these fibres aim. In man codes of thought and morals seem to have supplemented the genetic code and while we can seldom predict on the basis of his ideological or his genetic code the exact behaviors a man will emit, we can predict *the direction* and understand to what ends the partial processes are being subordinated.

This subordination of man's motor skills, verbal units, and fixed sub-assemblies to the overall style and purpose of his existence is completely missed by those who regard freedom as some unreliable link in an otherwise flawless chain of cause and effect.[24] Existentially man lives in a "world of freedom." Everything in that world is directed and triggered into action by the structures of his existence. Even if Delgado were to intrude upon my brain and stimulate it so that I poured out an endless succession of cups of tea, I might still combine this with my own value matrix and pour it over him and his contraptions. My body and my world though hedged on many sides by compulsion are freed by my capacities for existence to serve overall ends.[25]

6. Relational Facts Not Objective Facts

The old habits of mind also contrast objectivity with subjectivity—usually to the detriment of the latter. This originates in the habit of detachment and analysis, but specifically in the Cartesian dichotomy between the mind and external reality. So thoroughly has this view permeated our discourse that we are seldom aware of how narrowly it channels our thought. The eye is regarded as a retinal mirror, reflecting what is out there in the "real world" of physical objects located in public space.

After summarizing many research studies that demonstrate the impact of human thought and knowledge upon perception, Arthur Koestler bids us trace with soap the outline of our faces reflected in the mirror.[26] The image is actually much smaller than our heads. That we do not exclaim, "My God, my head has shrunk!," testifies to the fact that we *know* our heads remain of constant size and this knowledge adjusts our vision. In many other ways our knowledge and expectancy, our symbols and syntheses, control the way we see.

Instead of facts being "out there" separate from me and passively reflected in my brain, the existential perspective regards all perceived facts as organized by my style of existence—an integrated structure of *relational facts,* which thus transcend another false dichotomy—that between subjective and objective. As Rollo May has put it:

> Existentialism, in short, is the endeavor to understand man by cutting below the cleavage between subject and object which has bedeviled Western thought and science since shortly after the Renaissance. This cleavage Binswanger calls "the cancer of all psychology up to now. . . ." [27]

So while all behaviorists regard "reinforcements," "stimuli," and "responses," etc. as separate objective facts, the existentialists see the creation, investment and confirmation of meanings as a total process radiating from the individual. Labelling the parts of this process is purely for convenience, as we might draw attention to different aspects of a total organism without ever assuming its separateness.

It is often assumed that existentialism is wholly subjective—an error which springs from a Cartesian cast of mind unable to suspend its structures. From here the conclusion is drawn that only objectivity can be validated. But most existentialists regard objectivity as nothing more than a consensus among investigators as to how a phenomenon is to be regarded and measured. Hence calls for objectivity are like calls for consensus politics—they affirm the most obvious and the least controversial. In fact, creative styles of existence tend to be self-validating. A creative man will have distinctive kinds of thought processes that we can measure, will report his experience in certain ways, communicate that experience to others, and leave impacts on his environment. Every stage of this process is validated by earlier or later stages so that they are *congruent.* Lack of congruence alerts the investigator to pseudo existence, misreports, or unreliable instruments. The particular fault can often be identified by which of the measures are out of line.

7. *Alternative Involvement With Self and Others —Non Detachment*

The existential knower cannot by definition practice the traditional scientific detachment. He is studying relational facts, and the attempt to detach himself could destroy these. Even where he is observing the mutuality of others, the source of his insight will run dry with the source of his concern, since his own feelings and powers of identification are important clues to the shared human condition. If man exists he inevitably influences what he studies, and his only choice is to become aware of what he contributes to the relationship and to ensure that it facilitates the developmental process in which he himself is involved.

Yet there is one kind of "detachment" which is necessary. In order to understand others one must achieve at least a momentary suspension of self-concern in order to comprehend *their* perspectives—to switch from self-involvement to other-involvement. A man with the disciplined capacity to understand why his most cherished idea is a dead duck from the perspectives of his listeners is still attached to human concerns.

8. Value Full Investigation—Not Value Free

Were men caused to behave only by previous "reinforcements" and "stimuli" and were these enough or almost enough to predict the human "responses," then the professed values of such men would be only verbalized noises for what had actually "reinforced" them. The investigators would then be wise to discard such values as explanations for behavior since description carries no prescription and you cannot get an "Ought" from an "Is." If, on the other hand, men are synthesizers of symbols and these totally transform "reinforcements" into novel existence then *personal values are the partial blueprints for these transformations*. Where men choose between aspects of their past experience to create their preferred combinations then moral choice is at the very heart of existence and cannot be exorcised from the investigator or his subjects. To detach oneself and treat others like so many objects is not to be value-free but to choose to devalue others.

The moment we conceive of creativity and communication as mediated by codes of values, then we must ask which values facilitate successful and creative communication and which impede this process. The thousands of values which we urge one another to adopt can only be fashioned and exchanged if those *core* values supportive of creativity and communication themselves are constantly affirmed. In this existential view, radical man daily invests prescriptions in his environment which can become descriptive realities. In every "Ought" lies an embryonic "Is." . . .

Notes

[1] The most convincing summary and exposition of current neo-behaviorism is contained in *Social Learning and Personality Development* by Albert Bandura and Richard H. Walters, New York: Holt, Rinehart and Winston, 1965.

[2] "Manipulation of Behavior by Direct Stimulation of The Brain." Paper presented at the Columbia University Seminars on Technology and Social Change, Nov. 1966, Mimeo., p. 19.

[3] See *The Mentality of Apes,* Harmondsworth: Pelican Books, 1957.

[4] See E. R. Hilgard, *Theories of Learning*, London: Methuen, 1958, p. 65.

[5] *The Act of Creation*, New York: Macmillan, 1964, p. 35 f.

[6] "Manipulation of Behavior by Direct Stimulation of The Brain," *op. cit.*, p. 10.

[7] Quoted by Arthur Koestler in *The Act of Creation, op. cit.*, p. 123.

[8] A description of his conversion to existentialism is in *Man's Search for Meaning* (formerly entitled *From Death Camp to Existentialism*) New York: Washington Square Press, 1963.

[9] This process is well described by Camus in *Resistance, Rebellion, and Death*, New York: Modern Library, 1960, see especially pp. 1–25, "Letters to a German Friend."

[10] *Man's Search for Meaning, op. cit.*

[11] Harlow, H. F., *Psychol. Review*, 60, 1953, pp. 23–32.

[12] See H. W. Nissen's contribution in *Current Theory and Research in Motivation*, Jones, M. R. (ed.), University of Nebraska Press, 1954.

[13] See D. E. Berlyne, *Conflict, Arousal and Curiosity*, New York: McGraw-Hill, 1960, p. 119.

[14] Harlow, H. F., *op. cit.*

[15] Quoted by Penelope Gilliat in the London *Observer*, 1965. Exact reference mislaid.

[16] For a persuasive and scholarly account of man fragmented by scientific premises, see *The Broken Image* by Floyd W. Matson, New York: Braziller, 1964.

[17] Ludwig von Bertalanffy was making this and related points as early as 1927. His views are at last gaining a respectful hearing and are well summarized in *Problems of Life*, New York: Harper Torchbooks, 1960.

[18] The distinction between monadic and field theories is well made by Abraham Kaplan in the *Conduct of Inquiry*, San Francisco: Chandler, 1964.

[19] This idea is developed by Arthur Koestler in his distinction between the Chain of Words and The Tree of Language, see *The Ghost in The Machine, op. cit.*, pp. 19–45.

[20] C. Wright Mills has teased grand theorists, especially Talcott Parsons. He recites whole pages from Parsons and then summarizes them in one short paragraph each. See *The Sociological Imagination*, New York: Grove Press, 1961, pp. 25–49.

[21] *The Broken Image, op. cit.*, p. 76.

[22] This and similar points are made in John Wild's excellent exposition on *Existence and The World of Freedom*, Englewood Cliffs: Prentice-Hall, 1963.

[23] See *Problems of Life, op. cit.*

[24] *The Ghost in The Machine, op. cit.*, p. 19 *et. seq.*

[25] *Ibid.*, pp. 45–58.

[26] *The Act of Creation, op. cit.*, p. 120.

[27] See "Origins of the Existential Movement" by Rollo May, in *Existence: A New Dimension in Psychiatry and Psychology*, Rollo May (ed.), New York: Clarion Books, 1967, p. 11. For an excellent summary of the arguments for and against behaviorism and phenomenology, see *Behaviorism and Phenomenology*, V. W. Wann (ed.), University of Chicago Press, 1964.

Toward a Sociology of the Absurd

STANFORD M. LYMAN AND MARVIN B. SCOTT

"The world is essentially without meaning." From this fundamental assumption, Lyman and Scott proceed to explain how a new sociology,
founded on existentialism and phenomenology, studies how man creates meaning in his life. The authors contend that human action is
fundamentally based on interpersonal conflict. Therefore in order to
study the social construction of reality they employ a *game model* of
interaction while assuming a model of man in conflict.

Lyman and Scott contend that their approach to sociology is in
opposition to functionalism on a number of major points, each of
which can be interpreted to revolve around the freedom, awareness,
and personal values of the individual member of society. They also see
the Sociology of the Absurd as being in opposition to a policy-oriented
or melioristic sociology.

This excerpt concludes with the authors indicating their debt to
drama (Theatre of the Absurd), philosophy (Camus), and sociology
(Simmel) for the foundations of a sociology of existential man.

A NEW wave of thought is beginning to sweep over sociology. Aspects
of the wave have been given an assortment of names—"labeling theory,"
"ethnomethodology," and "neo-symbolic interactionism"—but these do not
cover its entire range of critique and perspective. A new name must be found
to cover a concept which presents not only a unique perspective on conventional sociology but is also a radical departure from the conventional.

We feel an appropriate name is *the Sociology of the Absurd.*

The term "absurd" captures the fundamental assumption of this new wave:
The world is essentially without meaning. In contrast to that sociology which
seeks to discover the *real* meaning of action—a sociological reality, such as
the *functional* meaning of social behavior—this new sociology asserts that all
systems of belief, including that of the conventional sociologists, are arbitrary.
The problems previously supposed to be those of the sociologist are in fact
the everyday problems of the ordinary man. It is he who must carve out

meanings in a world that is meaningless. Alienation and insecurity are fundamental conditions of life—though they are experienced differently by individuals and groups—and the regular rehumanization of man is everyman's task.

The Sociology of the Absurd draws its philosophical inspiration from existentialism and phenomenology. The works of Edmund Husserl are particularly crucial to its originating ideas.[1] Moreover, the interpreters of Husserl—especially Alfred Schutz [2] and Maurice Merleau-Ponty [3]—are major sources of intellectual perspectives, fundamental concepts, and promising insights. On the basis of its debt to phenomenology and existentialism the Sociology of the Absurd might be called an existential phenomenology for sociology.

From existentialism the Sociology of the Absurd derives its emphases on human freedom and the life-long process of "becoming"; on the nexus between the reality which is "out there" and the man who is thinking, feeling, apprehending "inside" himself; and on the broader view of man as an integral being, composed not only of *cogito,* but also of feeling, sensing, and apprehending. Finally, on the basis of existentialist thought the Sociology of the Absurd restores the individual to his rightful place as the principal agent of action, the central subject of sociology. Together with Kierkegaard, Sartre, and Jaspers, the sociologists of the new wave seek to place man at the center of study—as he already is in fact at the center of thought and action.[4]

From phenomenology, the Sociology of the Absurd derives its emphasis on certain aspects of human activity, such as intentionality, consciousness, and subjective meaning. Human intentions, contrary to the position of the Watsonian behaviorists, are definable to both social actors and their observers, not by some special technique possessed solely by experts or mystics, but rather by means of the most ordinary—but as yet not fully understood—mechanisms of perception carried on in everyday life.[5] Human consciousness should be the principal object of study in sociology, and this has been suggested in the work of Max Weber [6] and in the early formulations of Parsons' theory of action.[7] But methodological problems restricted research, and it has not yet excited the intellectual interest it deserves.

Phenomenology, and especially existential phenomenology, appears to have laid the basis for a solution to the methodological problem of subjective knowledge and objective existence, and in this the new sociology finds a grounding for new research. As Tiryakian has observed, existential phenomenology "seeks to elucidate the existential nature of social structures by uncovering the surface institutional phenomena of the everyday, accepted world; by probing the subterranean, noninstitutional social depths concealed from public gaze, by interpreting the dialectic between the institutional and the non-institutional. . . ."[8]

Now what specifically is the nature of human action from the viewpoint of the Sociology of the Absurd? Action consists of the pursuit of ends by social actors capable of deliberating about the line of activity they undertake and of choosing among alternatives to the same end. This does not mean that men always precede action by deliberation. This is manifestly not the case. What it does mean is that men are capable of giving an account of their actions either as preactivity mental images of the action, its consequences and meanings, or as post hoc retrospective readings of completed acts. As images either before or after completion, these constructions emerge as statements made by the actor which give meaning to his actions.[9] These constructions are not unintelligible to others. Most important, these statements constitute the actual meaning, though not necessarily the cause, of these actions, and thus are the basic data of the new sociology. Instead of adopting an undisguised skepticism of what humans say—a skepticism deeply rooted in the positivist and behaviorist traditions—the Sociology of the Absurd rejects the question of the truth value in face of the significance of the meaning value of these statements. In this respect the new sociology draws on yet another new intellectual strand, that introduced by the ordinary language philosophers who now contribute so much to linguistics and psychology.[10]

It follows from the emphasis on freedom and becoming in existentialist thought that human action should be considered, as Parsons once put it, "voluntaristic." [11] Without this idea of voluntarism, human activity would be "mere behavior." [12] Instead, in concert with Parsons' early view of the theory of action,[13] the sociologist of the Absurd sees activity in discernible units of action—episodes, encounters, situations—to which the actor gives meaning; meaning beyond merely the sense of a set of physical objects. Thus humans are not necessarily the creatures of social or psychological forces—class, caste, race, or deep-lying unconscious states—which *determine* their behavior in the situation. The age-old problem of freedom versus determinism is not a problem of objective philosophy but rather of the actor's construction of reality, his image of freedom and constraint. The Sociology of the Absurd conceives of man as being constructed—and of constructing—social reality in every situation. From this point of view mental illness, for instance, is a social construction, not an absolute, unambiguous disease.[14]

If life consists of encounters, episodes and engagements among persons pursuing goals of which they are consciously aware, or about which they can be made aware, then it appears that the fundamental structure of human action is *conflict*. This is true even if individuals are pursuing the same ends, since each is out to maximize his own interests. Thus, even two lovers in an erotic embrace, as Simmel once noted,[15] may be regarded in conflict since each may be seeking to outdo the other in demonstrating affection or providing the other with feeling. If one begins with the conception of human action as interpersonal conflict, two important implications (for theory) follow. The first concerns the kind of model of *interaction* most useful for the analysis of the social world; the second is the heuristic model of *man* most fruitful for the analysis of interaction.

Concerning the first, it seems that a *game model* is most suited for the analysis of interaction as our conception of the game model derives from the conception of man as a goal-seeking, voluntaristic, intentional actor. It follows from these characteristics that in any engagement he will employ, more or less consciously, stratagems and tactics to attain the end intended. It also follows that others participating in the engagement may be viewed as allies, opponents, or neutrals according to the goal sought and the means employed. The game model, we hold, is fruitful for the analysis of all social interactions, but it is especially so for the study of problematic statuses, such as homosexuals, paranoids, minorities, and the stigmatized in general. . . . We have emphasized the game model, including a discussion of the nature and types of games, the role of game-strategy behavior in understanding the sick and stigmatized, the relation of spatial considerations to game strategies and personal identities, and the type of character and self-presentation associated with strategies and tactics.

With regard to the second, the Sociology of the Absurd assumes a model of man in conflict—with others, with society, with nature, and even with himself. Even though much of sociology has refused to adopt this conception of man,[16] it recommends itself as the most powerful *heuristic* device for the study of man-in-society.[17] In passing it may be noted that the recent findings in animal ethology—especially the works of Konrad Lorenz [18]—lend a curious kind of support to our conception. More significant, however, are the fruitful settings for intellectual problems provided by the adoption of this model of man. By beginning with the assumption that social life is one of conflict, it follows that every social situation is problematic for those involved. With this model the sociologist must continually search for mechanisms that permit the production—and reproduction in a continuous series of engagements—of stable, uniform and persistent interaction.[19] Thus the sociologist is induced by this model to persistently try and solve the riddle that originally set the discipline in motion: how is society possible? The sociologist must view man as the maker and remaker of social existence, as the producer and reproducer of stable engagements, as the craftsman of society and the ever-renewed social order.

The Sociology of the Absurd does not aim at building a "social system." Indeed system building would go against the grain. This new sociology is perhaps best characterized as a conceptual style of theoretical ideas and sensitizing concepts tied together not by logic or system, but rather by the underlying existential-phenomenological assumptions stated above. In this respect it is worth contrasting the Sociology of the Absurd with functionalism.[20]

The Sociology of the Absurd stands in opposition to functionalism on five major contentions. First, functionalism is interested in understanding human action in terms of forces unperceived by the actor. Functionalism assumes a determined world inhabited by creatures who are for the most part unaware of the forces that shape their destinies and who live by the illusion and self-deception of their own imagined freedom. The Absurd, on the contrary, holds that there is an existential continuum between freedom and determinism constructed and reconstructed by the social actors individually or in concert. Thus some men are more free than others; some are more constrained than they know. The Absurd is concerned with man's intentions and consciousness, with his "felt" state of freedom or fatalism, and with the consequences that flow therefrom.

Second, functionalism holds that the various parts of society are non-arbitrary since they contribute to the integration of the whole. The Absurd, on the other hand, holds that all elements of society are arbitrary. These elements have no fixed, stable, and irreducible meaning. They certainly are not part of an organic system with a built-in end purpose—homeostasis. This imagery of society which functionalism inherited from Aristotle and his followers lends itself to the radical separation of events from processes, and in many cases to a peculiar sociological emphasis on processes detached from events or particular episodes.[21] The Absurd emphasizes the individual and the and the episodic—the event—and perceives this as the factor emerging from the participants' social construction of reality.

Third, functionalism regards the social order as rooted in a basic interdependence and cooperation. As the functionalists see it, men, through the socialization process, internalize norms, and fit into roles. These roles, in turn, are meshed together to form interlocking role-sets, or institutions. Aside from our disagreement with the empirical validity of this interpretation (we believe, for example, that society in the modern complex world is better described as a collection of conflicting subcultures,[22] which in their relations manage to maintain some pattern of stability by the employment of social mechanisms as yet imperfectly understood by sociologists), we hold that the functionalist perspective is heuristically weak because it begs the basic question for which sociology was founded. By assuming cooperation and interdependence *a priori,* by pressing society on to a teleological Procrustean bed, by conceiving of society as an organism or a mechanism, functional theory cannot make the social order problematic; it can assume that society is possible but not *discover* how it is possible.

Fourth, because functionalism sees man as a determined creature played upon by forces largely seen "as through a glass, darkly," it opts to study man from the point of view of the observer. Functionalism pays little attention to the perceptions made by men about their own activities. Rather it regards these as founded on ignorance of the real forces that shape human action.[23] The Absurd on the other hand rejects the *a priori* existence of a determined world discoverable by sociologists. It regards man as an actor who builds up his actions on the basis of his goals and of his continuing attempts to define and redefine the situation. Thus, the social world is studied from the point of view of the actors who construct it.

Finally, functionalism postulates a common value system in society. We hold, on the other hand, that in modern complex societies there are few if any common, binding values. Values and norms are pluralistically applicable on the basis of situations, persons, and times.[24] Thus what is crucial is the definition of the situation. And this definition is not simply "given." Rather, it is a bargain struck for the time being by the participants in the episode. For values to be employed, for norms to be operational, there must be "negotiation" of situations and identities, and obviously the participants have significant stakes in this negotiation. Only when these interactants are agreed upon who they are and what they are do they give and receive accounts—excuses and justifications—the linguistic devices that shore up fractured social situations.

Because we cannot assume value consensus, we have a second reason for supposing the social world to be problematic. Every investigation carried out under the aegis of the Sociology of the Absurd is approached with a sense of astonishment that a social order exists. *The puzzle, the mystery of how social order somehow emerges from the chaos and conflict predicated by the inherently meaningless is the motive for the study of social phenomena.*

Much sociology has been motivated by social meliorism.[25] Although we might laud the endeavors to improve the world, and certainly recognize the multi-faceted problems in modern societies, for several reasons we cannot subscribe to the thesis that social engineering or social change is the primary objective of the Sociology of the Absurd. First, no sociological enterprise directed at healing the social ills, improving the body politic, or salvaging cultural remnants can approach the subject from the standpoint of the Sociology of the Absurd. A consciously naïve but intellectual inquiry into how social order is possible supersedes questions of policy and priority in such a manner as to make the latter not only irrelevant but also a hindrance.

Second, once sociologists consciously adopt meliorism as their principal objective, they seek to influence policy-makers. Influence requires a rhetoric calculated to convince those in power that one has both the appropriate ideas and the techniques with which to make the studies that are convincing to policy-makers. Thus, the policy-oriented sociologist is more likely to be inclined to low-level theorizing, quantification, axiomatic system building, and whatever other rhetorical stratagems are likely to be persuasive.[26]

Finally, sociological meliorism is a contradiction of the nature of man and society as assumed by the Sociology of the Absurd. Meliorism, were it to be the aim of sociology, assumes that sociologists are philosopher-kings, or to put it more accurately, philosophers *of* the people and advisers *to* the kings. The sociologist of the Absurd is simply an observer of the social scene and thus does not suffer from the conceit and arrogance of the social engineer who would reshape the world according to what he lays down as "objective" ethics.

It follows from this, however, that the sociologist of the Absurd can maximize his observations and reflections in the freest of societies. Such a society is not one in which the practicing social scientist is restricted in his opportunities for observation. This does not mean a society devoid of privacy, but one in which the sociologist takes his chances to see what he can see, observing the nooks and crannies, crevices and interstices as well as the broad range of open spaces and public situations. A society marked by police regulation and extensive sumptuary legislation is unlikely to produce much good sociology, just as it is unlikely to produce much excellent art or literature.

It would be untrue, however, to say that restricted societies are unamenable to sociological inquiry. The sociologist of the Absurd must be a careful observer in any situation, and his awarness and exact description of the political, legal, social, and moral restraints on the individual is part of his task. He must, insofar as possible, apprehend the exact definition the individual has of his own freedom and of the constraints upon it in every encounter, so that he can, as part of his description, locate the person precisely in the continuum between humanism and fatalism. He must uncover ideology and utopia in each man, wish and transfiguration in each situation. The sociologist of the Absurd, by his very description of society, by his everlasting unfolding and illumination of the modes and styles of social order, can summon men to build the world of their dreams, but he cannot build it for them.

Although the Sociology of the Absurd is a new wave, it grows out of contemporary issues and new ideas in other arenas of progressive thought and action. Undoubtedly one of the most important of these is the Theatre of the Absurd, a school of dramatic thought limned by such names as Beckett, Ionesco, and Genet. Indeed our definition of the Absurd derives from Ionesco's in his essay on Kafka: "Absurd is that which is devoid of purpose. . . . Cut off from his religious, metaphysical, and transcendental roots, man is lost; all his actions become senseless, absurd, useless." [27]

If the Theatre of the Absurd illustrates the meaninglessness of the world, the Sociology of the Absurd *describes* man's constant *striving for meaning* in the face of the faceless Monolith. The Sociology of the Absurd emphasizes the episodic in man's life; it deemphasizes, though it does not discount, the predecessors and successors of contemporary man. It sees man as Simmel saw some men and Camus saw all men—as strangers. Thus Simmel wrote:

> If wandering is the liberation from every given point in space, and thus the conceptional opposite to fixation at such a point, the sociological form of the "stranger" presents the unity, as it were, of these two characteristics. . . . The stranger is thus being discussed here, not . . . as the wanderer who comes today and goes tomorrow. . . . He is fixed within a particular spatial group, or within a group whose boundaries are similar to spatial boundaries. But his position in this group is determined, essentially, by the fact that he has not belonged to it from the beginning, that he imports qualities into it, which do not and cannot stem from the group itself.[28]

And Camus:

> A world that can be explained by reasoning, however faulty, is a familiar world. But in a universe that is suddenly deprived of illusions and of light, man feels a stranger. His is an irremediable exile, because he is deprived of memo-

ries of a lost homeland as much as he lacks the hope of a promised land to come. This divorce between man and his life, the actor and his setting, truly constitutes the feeling of Absurdity.[29]

Simmel characterizes the stranger as an awe-inspiring, fearsome contributor; Camus as a victim of the irrelevant past and unpromising future. The sociologist, seeing man as the stranger, emphasizes the problematic nature of his existence. Essentially a contemporary, the stranger must struggle to establish the meaning of each new moment, even if only to get through it and be confronted by the next moment, and the next. Further he must sort out his relationships, appropriately sharing his affections between strangers and brothers, acquaintances and lovers. He is annoyed by the importunity of unwarranted fellowship; estranged by the coldness of unrequited affection; threatened by the powers of the mighty; frightened by the terror of the unknown; and doomed by the inevitability of death. And always he is confronted with life—things, events, people—which demand responses, require interpretation, cry out for meaning. Thus the Sociology of the Absurd studies existential man, the creature who strives aften sense in a senseless world.

Notes

[1] Edmund Husserl, *Phenomenology and the Crisis of Philosophy*, N.Y.: Harper Torchbooks, 1965. See also *The Phenomenology of Internal Time-Consciousness*, Bloomington and London: Indiana University Press, 1964. These two works will introduce the reader to Husserl's style and general orientation. For an explication, interpretation and extension of Husserl's philosophy, see *Phenomenology: The Philosophy of Edmund Husserl and Its Interpretation*, edited by Joseph J. Kockelmans, Garden City, N.Y.: Doubleday Anchor, 1967.

[2] Alfred Schutz, *Collected Papers*, The Hague: Martinus Nijhoff, 1962, 1964, 1966. Three volumes. Edited by Maurice Natanson, Arvid Brodersen, and I. Schutz, respectively. See also Schutz's *The Phenomenology of the Social World*, translated by George Walsh and Frederick Lehnert, Evanston, Ill.: Northwestern University Press, 1967.

[3] Maurice Merleau-Ponty, *The Structure of Behavior*, Boston: Beacon, 1963; *In Praise of Philosophy*, Evanston, Ill.; Northwestern University Press, 1963; *Sense and Non-Sense*, Evanston, Ill.: Northwestern University Press, 1964; *The Primacy of Perception and Other Essays*, Evanston, Ill.: Northwestern University Press, 1964; and *Signs*, Evanston, Ill.: Northwestern University Press, 1964.

[4] See Edward A. Tiryakian, *Sociologism and Existentialism*, Englewood-Cliffs, N.J.: Prentice-Hall, 1962, 71–76.

[5] Edmund Husserl, "The Thesis of the Natural Standpoint and Its Suspension," in Kockelmans, *op. cit.*, 68–79.

[6] Max Weber, *The Theory of Social and Economic Organization*, N.Y.: Oxford University Press, 1947, 88.

[7] Talcott Parsons, *The Structure of Social Action*. Glencoe: The Free Press, 1949, 79–81, 732–33, 750–51.

[8] Edward A. Tiryakian, "Existential Phenomenology and the Sociological Tradition," *American Sociological Review*, 30 (October, 1965), 687.

[9] See G. E. M. Anscombe, *Intention*, Ithaca: Cornell University Press, 1966, 1–61.

[10] For an introduction to ordinary language philosophy, see Antony Flew, editor, *Logic and Language, First Series*, Oxford: Basil Blackwell, 1960. Our own thinking on language and meaning has been strongly influenced by the following Ludwig Wittgenstein, *Philosophical Investigations*, Oxford: Basil Blackwell, 1959; J. L. Austin, *Philosophical Papers*, Oxford: Clarendon Press, 1961; Gilbert Ryle, *The Concept of Mind*, N.Y.: Barnes and Noble, 1949; and D.S. Shwayder, *The Stratification of Behavior*, N.Y.: Humanities Press, 1965. Anthropologists are far ahead of sociologists in their recognition of the fundamental importance of the study of language. See John J. Gumperz and Dell Hymes, editors, *The Ethnography of Communications*,

a special publication of the *American Anthropologist*, 66 (December, 1964). Whatever recognition sociologists have given the study of language falls under the rubric of "sociolinguistics." For a sampling, see William Bright, editor, *Sociolinguistics*, Hague: Mouton, 1966.

[11] Parsons, *op. cit.*, 10–12, *et passim*.

[12] For a general discussion, see Edward C. Devereux, Jr., "Parsons' Sociological Theory," *Social Theories of Talcott Parsons*, edited by Max Black, Englewood Cliffs, N.J.: Prentice-Hall, 1961.

[13] For an analysis of the early and more recent changes in Parsons' frame of reference, see John Finley Scott, "The Changing Foundations of the Parsonian Action Scheme," *American Sociological Review*, 28 (October, 1963), 716–35.

[14] See Thomas Szasz, *The Myth of Mental Illness*, N.Y.: Delta, 1967. See also Michel Foucalt, *Madness and Civilization*, N.Y.: Pantheon, 1965.

[15] Georg Simmel, "The Adventure," *Georg Simmel, 1858–1918*, edited by Kurt H. Wolff, Columbus: Ohio State University Press, 1959, 249–252.

[16] Tiryakian has argued that existentialism might benefit from the sociological conception of man as interdependent. "Sociologism, to reiterate an earlier point, does not view the relation between the individual and society as one marked by conflict, for it stresses ultimately the needs and contributions of each to the other." See *Sociologism and Existentialism, op. cit.*, 167. Our conception is that the conflict between individual and society, or individual and individual may not be "marked," although sometimes it is, but it is always present, though sometimes repressed or hidden from view. Further, though men may "ultimately" contribute to one another's needs, they act out relations which are full of conflict in the actual episodes of their lives.

[17] A conflict model was employed by early sociologists derived from their awareness of the conflicts between classes, races, and states. See for example Ludwig Gumplowicz, *Outlines of Sociology*, edited by Irving L. Horowitz, N.Y.: Paine-Whitman, 1963. A modern sociology of conflict has been urged by Lewis Coser. See his *The Functions of Social Conflict*, Glencoe: The Free Press, 1956, and *Continuities in the Study of Social Conflict*, N.Y.: The Free Press, 1967.

[18] Konrad Lorenz, *On Aggression*, N.Y.: Harcourt, Brace and World, 1966.

[19] Thus the value of Sigmund Freud's *Civilization and Its Discontents* is not to be found in its empirical validity, but rather in its conception of man in opposition to society and thus in a position to regard all social situations as problematic.

[20] For a clear and systematic statement on functionalism, see Robert K. Merton, "Manifest and Latent Functions," in *Social Theory and Social Structure*, N.Y.: The Free Press, 1968, 73–138.

[21] See Kenneth E. Bock, *The Acceptance of Histories*, Berkeley: University of California Press, 1956, 49–56; and Marvin B. Scott, "Functional Foibles and the Analysis of Social Change," *Inquiry*, 9 (1966), 205–14.

[22] See Milton M. Gordon, *Assimilation in American Life*, N.Y.: Oxford University Press, 1964, 132–232.

[23] The point is nicely made by Floyd Matson, *The Broken Image*, N.Y.: Braziller, 1964, 54–101.

[24] See Joseph Fletcher, *Situation Ethics*, Philadelphia: The Westminster Press, 1966.

[25] See C. Wright Mills, *The Sociological Imagination*, N.Y.: Oxford University Press, 1959, 84–90.

[26] We are indebted for this point to Jack Douglas.

[27] Quoted in Martin Esslin, *The Theatre of the Absurd*, Garden City: Doubleday Anchor, 1961, xxi.

[28] Georg Simmel, "The Stranger," *The Sociology of Georg Simmel*, Glencoe: The Free Press, 1950, 402.

[29] Quoted in Esslin, *op. cit.*, xix.

Freedom and Constraint
in Constructing Meanings

JACK D. DOUGLAS

For Douglas the proper role of sociology is to study how men construct meaning in the course of the situations they encounter in everyday life. The existential question is how much freedom and constraint is involved in this meaning-making. Douglas believes that both are present and that they exist in varying degrees among individuals and societies.

Human social life functions through culture (shared symbols) and this constrains the meanings that members of a particular culture can construct. Within any culture, however, there are a variety of abstract meanings that can be used in constructing meaning in any particular situation. Such abstract meanings allow men to be free within their cultural context. At the same time these abstract rules and beliefs provide the basis for communication in particular situations, and since their meanings are partially independent of the situation they also act as a constraining force.

Most individuals, however, do not usually look upon such routinized meanings primarily as constraints. This is because people recognize that the human quality exists only by interaction with other humans. Douglas' answer to the existential question is that we are both free and constrained by social life. The task of sociology is to study how meaning is created under these conditions—not to attempt to prove the case for social determinism.

Man is free to construct his social world and constrained by that social world: Man is both the creator of society and created by society. . . .

MUCH of the disagreement regarding the issue of individual freedom and social determinism has resulted from a confusion over the meanings of "freedom." Freedom is one of those terms in the Western societies that are essentially problematic; that is, the term has many different meanings, even in the abstract. This is apparent in the works of philosophers, scholars, and other writers. There are fundamental arguments over the meaning of freedom, so much so that even the scholars are forced to make use of terms such as "freedom from" and "freedom to" as distinctions between the basically different "types" of freedom. This centuries-old confusion has been the source of many arguments in the Western world, resulting in a vast metaphysical and philosophical polemic.

The proponents of free will theory and of human freedom have certainly never believed that the human beings they observed were in any way *completely* free, unconstrained or unpredictable. On the contrary, metaphysicians themselves have been aware of the patterning that exists in human behavior. For example, in *Enchirdion* Saint Augustine made a basic distinction between *libertas* and *libertad* in order to distinguish between the "absolute freedom" of man before the fall and the kind of "relative free choice" that man had after the fall. This relatively free choice after the fall was constrained by the evil passions of human beings resulting from that notable event. Philosophers, historians, and most other men of the Western world have long been aware of the existence of social customs, or the "cake of customs" as Bagehot called it. They have noted since Herodotus that there are patterned differences in human beliefs and actions between different societies; they have certainly recognized that there are some similarities in basic needs and feelings. It is equally apparent that there is some general social order among most groups of human beings and in the everyday lives of most people. It is perfectly apparent that the world is not a random event, so that anyone who ever thought that a theory of freedom or free will meant that the world would be disordered, or completely random, was simply missing the point.

The issue concerning human freedom is twofold. First, there is the question of whether human beings choose what they do *because* something previously existing and *external* to them has made them what they are in such a way that they will choose to respond to the order they find in the world in the way in which they do. Second, there is the issue of whether human beings are able to alter the nature of their world (and possibly themselves) in order to fulfill their own desires and beliefs, regardless of where those desires and beliefs originally came from.

Clearly no one has been able to demonstrate that human actions are entirely or even predominantly the result of what has been put into them. No one has yet been able to predict in detail what human beings will do in specific situations. In its extreme form, this belief must remain nothing more than an article of faith until such demonstrations through prediction are provided. It is also clear, however, that the number of things that go into any individual human being and into any specific situation facing him are so exceedingly complex that it would be almost impossible to expect to get highly specific predictability. It is likely that human consciousness is a special factor in any given human being which acts to some degree independently of external phenomena to bring order and to structure decisions from the mass of complex factors interacting within himself and between him and the situation he faces. To the degree both that he does not control the inputs from the situation, and to which he himself has been socialized to have certain feelings and beliefs, without being able to change those feelings and beliefs, he is not free. But to the degree that he acts as an independent factor in ordering those internal and external phenomena, he is free. To this degree one would expect to find some irreducible element of unpredictability in human events. But it is the second issue, that of whether individuals *can* alter situations, that is the most relevant for our purposes.

. . . there are some very simple societies in which individuals normally take the social rules, social beliefs, and so on, to be absolute. There are also true believers or fundamentalists in our own society, though very few, who are, apparently, innocent of any doubts concerning their own social rules and beliefs. In our pluralistic society individuals have been subject to all kinds of conflicts and changes in social rules and beliefs, so it is very difficult for them not to come to see social rules and beliefs as at least partially relativistic, and not be "cynical," "skeptical," "hypocritical," or "sophisticated." This is especially true of individuals living in a highly technological society as our own, in which so many share a generalized rational orientation toward things. It is even more difficult for those living in a rapidly changing and democratic society, in which they are frequently remaking the rules, to view the rules and beliefs as absolute. Anyone involved in remaking rules and introducing new rules is aware that the rules are not a necessary part of the structure of reality. If he can make the rules, then anyone else could do so too. Living in an age of mass education and mass communication, he knows that others have arrived at very different rules and beliefs.

In a complex and rapidly changing society, then, we would have to expect on *prima facie* grounds that individuals would not take an absolutist view of social rules and social beliefs. But we must not conclude that this relativistic attitude is universal in our society or that, even if we were to grant that it is a dominant attitude, that there would be no social constraint on the individual's construction of social rules and beliefs.

We have already argued that the complex nature of the physical and social world, combined with the nature of man and the nature of social meanings themselves, makes it clear that the individual *must* rely upon his own constructions of unique interpretations to fit the inevitably unique situations that he encounters in everyday life. In this sense, then, man is necessarily free. But we have not yet investigated the question of whether he is free in the sense of being able to affect the inputs into his constructions: Do individuals have any control over what goes into their own constructions or are these inputs (i.e., beliefs, rules, immediate situations, biographical details, social position, and so on) quite beyond his control, provided for him, whether he realizes it or not, by the society in which he lives? These are the crucial *con-*

ditions under which choices are made and these determine how significant and effective any freedom in decision-making can be.

All men are probably free to some degree to affect the conditions of their choices and, thence, their acts and the consequences of their acts. All men with reasonably normal physical capacities can rearrange the immediate physical situation as they find it, and in this sense they are free (unless, as rarely happens, there is someone acting to constrain their immediate physical actions). But there is far more question concerning the ability of men to affect the other conditions of their choices and actions. There are two issues in this problem: (1) are individuals free to determine the inputs of symbolic resources into their constructions of the meanings of situations at hand? and (2) are individuals free to determine the social nature of the situations for which they are constructing such meanings? In both cases I believe that the answer is clearly that men are both free and constrained, but that the degrees of each vary greatly across societies and for individuals within any one society. The most obvious aspect of freedom is the first, which is essentially the ability of individuals to control the meanings of things for themselves. . . .

Unless we assume the programming of man by the gods or the fates, it is clear that man has created culture over the eons, that man is the *culture (shared symbol) creator*. Symbol creation and transmission is what distinguishes man from all other animals. Unless we are to deny all of the evidence of the transmission of culture and of cultural relativity, we must recognize as well that men are constrained by culture, that they are not free to construct just anything, that they are themselves creatures of culture. As Berger and Luckmann have put it so well, man and society are necessarily involved in a dialectical process, each one creating the other and each being created by the other, each one cause and effect of the other.[1]

The evidence of great individual freedom in our pluralistic society in constructing situational meanings is everywhere at hand. The great majority of individuals have available to them a wide variety of abstract meanings, which they can make use of in constructing the meanings they choose for the situation they face. For example, taking a traditional, Puritanical view of sex one might expect that a member of American society faced with a non-marital sexual possibility would apply the general rule "no sex outside of marriage," meaning that he would have to do all of his activity within such a constraining rule—and would no doubt find that he couldn't get much done with it. (This has, in fact, been the assumption of all too many of the early sociological works on "deviance.") But this is certainly not so today. Any reasonably sophisticated young American would come to such a situation well-equipped with a barrage of resources from which he would hope to construct a fine legitimization for whatever he intends to do: Freudian theory, Kinsey data, glorifications of love, hip lingo, Eastern glorifications of communication with the inner being—and birth control manuals. The fact that he might, depending on his social group and his particular date, have to make use of such rhetorical devices would indicate that the old rule may still have some constraining effect; but the acceptance of this would not deny that the other meanings have force as well (nor would it deny that the old rule has no effect until an individual makes use of it to construct the meanings for the situation-at-hand).

On the whole, individuals in our society today have great freedom in constructing legitimate and plausible meanings from the meaningful resources available to them. In addition, because most people have come to accept and value change, openness, and creativity for their own sake, even to the point in some of the arts of disowning all standards, it is sometimes possible for individuals to create or impart very new ideas and seek to build their lives around them. Artists are able—and encouraged by many—to develop "bizarre" art forms from the sounds of automobile engines, from wires, from tin-cans, and so on almost endlessly. Millions become involved in seeking their own forms of mysticism, nirvana, mystical transcendence, mind-freeing (and clothes-freeing) group relations ("T-group sensitivity training"), and so on. This insistence on the "totally new" and the "totally individual" has grown steadily in Western societies for at least a century and has become a generalized attack on all shared abstractions, on all "forms," as Simmel argued almost fifty years ago.[2]

However, even in a pluralistic society in which so many people come to see the rules and beliefs as relativistic and to recognize their problematic nature, this understanding is by no means consistent or universal. The same individuals who explicitly recognize that "there is no arguing about tastes" or that "there are always exceptions to any rule" may well forget all about this in other situations, both because such constructions of the general meanings of rules and beliefs are themselves situational, and because he may consciously use the presumption of the absolutism of rules and beliefs as a strategy for controlling others. The same man who feels no guilt about theft might well feel guilt about sexual matters because he has very different feelings about the rules governing each realm.

More important than the constraint exercised by individuals' situational views of rules as absolute is the constraint resulting from the shared abstract meanings. As we have already seen, the fact that individuals must construct concrete meanings for the situation-at-hand does not at all mean that "anything goes." On the contrary, the particulars have meanings themselves, which are simply (partially) indeterminate for the actors until they are provided concrete meanings. It is very possible through the constructions of situated meanings, and the cutting off (or compartmentalization) of the situation from other situations, to construct meanings that might well be seen as very much in conflict with the more abstract rules if they were to be compared; but this in no way denies the independent importance of the particular, which in this instance is the abstract meanings or rules.

It is, in fact, only because individuals do share particular abstract meanings that are partially independent of the situations-at-hand that they are able to communicate at all. If they came to situations without trans-situational shared meanings, then they would have to begin by developing some shared meanings for things before they could communicate.

The abstract meanings serve as the basic resources from which concrete meanings must be constructed for the situation-at-hand.

Although there is a great deal of freedom involved in the construction of such situated meanings, the abstract meanings that must be used as common resources by those who want to communicate in the situation-at-hand act as a definite constraint. Abstract rules and beliefs act as a constraint on concrete, situational constructions simply because they have meanings that are partially independent of the situational interpretations that might be provided them; but their primary constraining influence comes from the fact that situational constructions of meanings for the concrete situations become routinized for any group with reasonably stable patterns of interaction.

There are many interpretations of both the relevance and the relatively concrete meanings of the abstract rules and beliefs for the situations individuals *typically* face in everyday life. For example, in our society the shared abstract value on equality ("All men are created equal . . .") is associated with specific and different interpretations for the realms of "justice" and "economics." These interpretations are, in fact, normally expressed in slogans: "Equal justice before the law" and "Equality of opportunity." These slogans are then further associated with various more specific interpretations widely shared in the society (equal justice meaning that status will not be considered in weighing guilt). In line with our previous arguments it should be clear that the more specific we get, the more problematic the meanings will be. But these widely shared situational constructions constrain individual constructions of meanings for the situation-at-hand more than the shared abstract rules and beliefs.

It would be mistaken to conclude that individuals look at such *routinized meanings,* or *typifications,* as Schutz has called them,[3] primarily as constraints. This is true partially because, as should be apparent from our discussion, their constraining effect, while greater than that of abstract meaning, is still not very great. But it is equally true because most people do not look at their social lives primarily in terms of their constraining effects. It is taken-for-granted by most people that their lives are necessarily social and that social interaction itself is of fundamental value. *They can only fulfill their human selves through society.* In addition, because meaningful differences and problems are taken-for-granted by the vast majority of people, individuals come to assume that compromises are necessary in their everyday lives. Although the necessity of compromise constrains the individual, it also allows him to fulfill himself by acting *with* other human beings toward some common goals. But, whether cooperating with others or fighting with them, an individual's constructions of meanings are normally interdependent with the constructive work of others.

Notes

[1] See Peter Berger and Thomas Luckmann, *Social Construction of Reality,* Garden City, New York: Doubleday, 1966, pp. 57–58.

[2] See Georg Simmel, "The Conflict in Modern Culture," in *Georg Simmel: The Conflict in Modern Culture and Other Essays,* tr. and ed., by K. Peter Etzkorn, New York: Teachers College Press, 1968, pp. 11–26.

[3] Certainly one of the best uses of Schutz's idea of "typifications" is the essay by David Sudnow, on "Normal Crimes," in *Social Problems,* 12(1965), pp. 225–276.

PART III

LANGUAGE AND CULTURE

Sociological inquiry is premised on the existence of culture. Culture has been variously defined by such terms as social heritage, design for living, or shared meanings and values. For our purposes, culture is best conceived as symbols shared by a collectivity (usually a society) of people. It is both existential and normative. It is existential in that it typifies what a people "know" to exist. It is normative because it specifies what is right and wrong and what is good and bad. Furthermore, culture provides the set of expectations that guide individuals' relations to the physical universe and, most important to the sociologist, guide their relations with one another. This set of expectations is referred to as the normative structure of society, and is manifested in all of a society's institutions. Since culture is learned and is in the minds of men (while represented by their technology, literature, and material production), the sociologist must be concerned with what a people know and how they come to know it. Human knowing, so far as it is cultural, is based on a set of symbols which constitute a people's language. Some social scientists have gone so far as to equate the study of language with the study of culture. Although we do not accept this position, we do accept the necessity of studying a people's symbol system in order to understand their social life. To study what a people know, we must study the symbols which they use.

Language and the Structure
of Thought

ALFRED R. LINDESMITH AND ANSELM L. STRAUSS

A culture may be seen as a system of shared symbols and their referents—a definition which emphasizes the importance of symbols in
man's social world. Lindesmith and Strauss employ the "symbolic
interaction" approach in their book from which this selection is taken.

The symbol system of a particular culture—its language—is used
to construct the reality perceived by the symbol users. Language is an
important determinant of perspective. Each language contains symbols
which label phenomena in a way particular to that culture. Furthermore, the way the symbol system is organized, the structure of a
language (its grammar, tenses, and other categories), is of basic importance for the way in which the language user thinks. The authors'
discussions of Chinese and Navaho language are examples of these
points.

Lindesmith and Strauss use the concept of "audience" as an
integral part of the thinking process. Thinking proceeds with symbols.
When one thinks, he is communicating to himself the same symbols
that he communicates to others. However, only certain "others", a certain social grouping, are taken into account in his thinking. This
"audience" exists even for the formally constructed systems of logicians, constrained by the language of their culture, and certainly for
the thinking of scientists who discourse within "the scientific community." There is a similarity and complementarity between this concept of audience and Shibutani's discussion of reference groups as
perspectives.

RATHER obviously, the content of a person's thought is affected by
his social environment. The form or manner of his thinking is similarly influenced. E. Sapir . . . suggests the very great importance that particular languages have for the construction of thought and environments. He says:

Human beings do not live in an objective world alone . . . but are very much at the mercy of the particular language which has become a medium of expression for their society. It is quite an illusion to imagine that one adjusts to reality essentially without the use of language and that language is merely an incidental means of solving specific problems of communication or reflection . . . the "real world" is to a large extent unconsciously built up on the language habits of the group. No two languages are ever sufficiently similar to be considered as representing the same social reality. The worlds in which different societies live are distinct worlds, not merely the same worlds with different labels attached.[1]

The very structure of a language tends to influence modes of perception and reasoning. This is perhaps less so in the concrete practical realm than on more abstract planes. One of the best illustrations of this point is the manner in which mathematical reasoning is influenced by the nature of the counting system. Think of the great advantages of Arabic numerals over Roman numerals even for simple problems in arithmetic, not to mention complicated problems in algebra, geometry, and physics. Many branches of modern mathematics probably could not have been developed by using the Roman system, or without the invention of concepts such as negative numbers, zero, decimal, position, fraction, and the like.

The influences of language structure upon the structure of thought are further illustrated by the difficulties of translators. The translation of other languages into English involves more than merely finding equivalent words; the translator is faced with the problem of conveying meanings and nuances of meaning that may be practically impossible to express in English. The Spanish language, for example, has two verbs for "to be"; they are *ser* and *estar*. Their different uses—extremely difficult for a foreigner to master— reflect a mode of thinking resulting from and unique to Spanish culture. The translation of non-European languages into English is even more difficult because the modes of thought are likely to be still more divergent from ours than are those of peoples living within the general European tradition. Differences between Chinese and American thinking are suggested by the following quotation: [2]

Chinese poets seldom talk about one thing in terms of another. . . . If a metaphor is used, it is metaphor directly relating to the theme, not something borrowed from the ends of the earth. . . . For our Western taste, used as we are to the operatic in poetry, that is, the spectacular or shocking effect produced by some unusual analogy or metaphor, the substance of Chinese poems seems often mild or trivial.

The following newspaper account suggests some of the difficulties of the conscientious translator when he attempts to interpret English expressions for the Chinese: [3]

Some of the great difficulties among the diplomats sitting around the international table here [at the United Nations] arise from the differences in languages, alphabets, and, consequently, ways of thinking; and in no tongue is more ingenuity required for accurate, precise translation than Chinese.

The Chinese ideograph script is one of the world's oldest written media, but the talk at Lake Success is so brimful of new ideas, new concepts and new words that, to translate even the basic Charter itself into Chinese, it was necessary to devise almost 2000 new combinations of characters.

A perfect example of the troubles faced here by Chinese translators is the word "uranium," which has a persistent way of cropping up in diplomatic reports. The translators went into a huddle and came out with a decision to call the atomic base "U-metal." That, however, only started their headaches.

The symbol for "U" was found in the Chinese word for grapefruit, which in literal translation is the "U-tree." What was just as disturbing, from a purist point of view, was the discovery that the symbol for metal was contained in the first part of the word for "bell," which literally translated meant "metal boy."

After some cudgeling of brains, however, the calligraphers came up with the proposal to shave off the "tree" part of the "U-tree" character, discard the "boy" part of the "bell" character, and then in the best manner of diplomatic compromise, join the severed remains to form a new symbol: "U-metal" or, as we would say, uranium.

The naïve person tends to regard his native tongue as the "natural language of man," the "best" or "most flexible" one, and in a religious era, as the language of God and His angels. The English-speaking person notes and is tolerant of the peculiarities of French, German, Spanish, and other Indo-European tongues belonging to the same language family as his own. But when he encounters entirely unrelated language structures, such as those of preliterate tongues, he is likely to be nonplussed at first by what appear to him as fundamental deficiencies in intelligibility or as outright departures from common sense, good logic, and good taste.

Although new words may be added to a language with relative ease, the basic structure of a language is highly stable and resists change. Most people who speak a given language are unaware of its structure as something that differs from the structures of other language systems. Consequently, the uniform modes of thought imposed upon them by their native tongue are not recognized or taken into consideration as such, but are accepted as part of the "real nature of the world" or as among the elements of "common sense."

Since most Americans are acquainted only with the general family of Indo-European languages, they are likely to view skeptically the contention that thinking is not essentially the same the world over. They know that the content of thought varies from group to group; that Russians are concerned with other problems than those that vex Americans; that the impoverished rural tenant farmer thinks about other matters than those engaging the attention of the urban financier; and that the day-by-day preoccupations of the natives of the Pacific Islands are vastly different from those of the average American. Nevertheless, one is likely to believe that although the content of thought varies from group to group the form of all "correct" thinking is always and everywhere the same. The divergent modes of thought of other peoples—which actually do exist—are thus often regarded merely as varieties of error.

It would be very interesting and revaling to know what effect the English language may have on our thinking processes. It is probably impossible for anyone operating within the framework of our language to become aware of the influences it exerts upon him without first being acquainted with other languages, preferably non-European ones. For this reason, we shall illustrate our point with materials from the ancient Chinese and Navaho Indian languages, both quite different from our own.[4]

The vocabulary of the ancient Chinese was concrete, specific, picturesque, and descriptive. Thus almost all words were used to evoke complex and specific images. Where English or French people use the word "mountain" in addition to adjectives or descriptive phrases, the Chinese used the following words: *K'i,* bare mountain; *Hou,* mountain covered with vegetation; *Ngan,* high mountain near a river; *Tsou,* high mountain; *Ts'ouei,* a high and vast mountain; and so forth. Seventeen different words could refer to various kinds of mountains.

Words were never used in a general sense (such as "I climb the mountain"), but with concrete reference, as "I climb *that* mountain." The need for this sort of descriptive precision limited the use of general terms. Thus, instead of "husband," the Chinese word *Kia* evoked a definite, specific, concrete image, that of the household of which he is the master.

A great many redoubled words such as *Ye-ye* were used. These have been termed "descriptive auxiliaries." They had a remarkable power of evoking concrete images; they were veritable vocal paintings of noises, movements, feelings, and so forth. Thus *Houci-houci* meant the sound of thunder, *Kui-kui* meant solitude, and *Kouo-kouo* meant a rapid current. One redoubled word might refer to and evoke three or four or more images. For instance, *Yong-yong* referred to the cry of wild birds, indicating at the same time the response of the female to the call of the male and their characteristic manner of flying in pairs, the female flying a bit behind the male. When used in a different context, such a descriptive auxiliary might refer to an entirely different set of images.

Where the Occidental thinker can express his thoughts exactly and quickly, the Chinese had to do so by a kind of symbolization akin to poetic activity. The writer or speaker used various symbols which together conveyed his ideas by evoking specific concrete aspects of things.

The world thus appeared to the Chinese as a complex of specific aspects and images. Chinese thought as reflected by the language was oriented toward particulars, not toward generalizations or abstractions. As R. K. Merton has said, "The ancient Chinese language is not equipped to note concepts, to analyze ideas, or to present doctrines discursively." [5]

The Navaho language likewise offers an instructive contrast to European languages: [6]

[Navaho language] delights in sharply defined categories. It likes, so to speak, to file things away in neat little packages. It favors always the concrete and particular, with little scope for abstractions. It directs attention to some features of every situation, such as the minute distinctions as to direction and type of activity. It ignores others to which English gives a place. Navaho focuses interest upon doing—upon verbs as opposed to noun or adjectives. . . . The important point is that striking divergences in manner of thinking are crystallized in and perpetuated by the forms of Navaho grammar. Take an example of a commonplace physical event: rain. Whites can and do report their perception of this event in a variety of ways: "It has started to rain"; "It is raining"; "It has stopped raining." The Navaho people can, of course, convey these same ideas—but they cannot convey them without finer specifications. To give only a few instances of the sorts of discrimination the Navaho must make before he reports his experiences; he uses one verb form if he himself is aware of the actual inception of the rain storm, another if he has reason to believe that the rain has been falling for some time in his locality before the occurrence struck his attention. One form must be employed if rain is general round about within the range of vision; another if, though it is raining round about, the storm is plainly on the move. Similarly, the Navaho must invariably distinguish between the ceasing of rainfall (generally) and the stopping of rain in a particular vicinity because the rain clouds have been driven off by the wind. The [Navaho] people take the consistent noticing and reporting of such differences . . . as much for granted as the rising of the sun.

Navaho is an excessively literal language, little given to abstractions and to the fluidity of meaning that is so characteristic of English. The inner classification gives a concreteness, a specificity, to all expression. Most things can be expressed in Navaho with great exactness by manipulating the wide choice of stems in accord with the multitudinous alternatives offered by fusing prefixes and other separable elements in an almost unlimited number of ways. . . . The general nature of the difference between Navaho thought and English thought—both as manifested in the language and also as forced by the very nature of the linguistic forms into such patterns—is that Navaho thought is prevailingly so much more specific, so much more concrete. The ideas expressed by the English verb "to go" provide a nice example. To Germans, the English language seems a little sloppy because the same word is used regardless of whether the one who goes, walks or is transported by a train or other agency, whereas in German these two types of motion are always sharply distinguished in the two verbs *gehen* and *fahren*. But Navaho does much more —for example, when one is talking about travel by horse, the speed of the animal may be expressed by the verb form chosen. The following all mean "I went by horseback":

lii shil niya	(at a walk or at unspecified speed)
lii shil yidloozh	(at a trot)
lii shil neeltaa	(at a gallop)
lii shil yilghod	(at a run)

When a Navaho says that he went somewhere he never fails to specify whether it was afoot, astride, by wagon, auto, train, or airplane. This is done partly by using different verb stems which indicate whether the traveler moved under his own steam or was transported, partly by by naming the actual means. Thus, "he went to town," would become:

kintahgoo iiya	He went to town afoot or in a non-specific way.
kintahgoo bil 'i'ii eel	He went to town by boat.
kintahgoo bil o'oor'a	He went to town by wagon.

Moreover, the Navaho language insists upon another type of splitting up of the generic idea of "going," to which German is as indifferent as English. The Navaho always differentiates between starting to go, going alone, arriving at, returning from a point, and so forth. . . . It is not, of course, that these distinctions *cannot* be made in English but that they *are not* made consistently. They seem of importance to English-speakers only under special circumstances, whereas constant precision is a regular feature of Navaho thought and expression about movement.

The study of non-European languages makes it evident that there are different modes of reasoning. Every human being is introduced, as a child, to a system or systems of language embodying certain peculiar and nonuniversal conceptual distinctions. Thus, the child is inducted into traditions of thinking, traditions consisting not only of certain kinds of ideas but of certain ways of thinking.

The point is made particularly clear by a consideration of time divisions. If certain temporal distinctions are not made by one's language, one cannot think in terms of them. Behavior can scarcely be organized, systematized, arranged, defined, regulated, or coordinated in terms of temporal categories of which the person is unaware. While our own language [7]

. . . always expresses tense with perfect definiteness there are languages . . . which are incapable of doing so . . . in Samoyedic [Siberian] only two temporal forms of the verb are recognized . . . one of these . . . signifying present and future . . . the other indicating the past. . . . The minute temporal distinctions which we recognize as "present," "present perfect," "past," "past perfect," "past future," "future," "future perfect," and "past perfect" are impossible in these languages.

A number of languages clearly reveal the efforts which have been made to render intelligible the elusive and abstract nature of time by interpreting it in terms of space. . . . [In Sudan language for example] the locations in space are crudely expressed by means of body-part words, and these spatial expressions then serve as indicators of time . . . here the fundamental intuition of time is quite different from that to which we are accustomed. . . .

[For] some people future and past fuse linguistically into what might be called a "not-now" . . . in Schambala [African] the same word designates the distant past as well as the distant future. For them there exists only a "today" and a "not today."

Other critical categories (such as those of number, action, and quality) also differ in various languages.

Since the language which people use is largely an inheritance from previous generations, the modes of thought of the present are derived from the past. This has its disadvantages as well as its advantages, for the experiences of past generations are not comparable to those of later ones. The errors of the past are tenacious because they become embedded in the language and popular thought, so much so that they become unquestioned assumptions. Scientific progress often depends upon freeing oneself from the implications of popular speech. Note, for example, the sayings that the sun rises in the east, and that members of a race are related to each other by blood. Symbolic logicians make analyses of speech through its logical forms so that the contradictory and ambiguous qualities of sentence forms can be avoided. Recognizing all this, Sapir reminds us that "language is at one and the same time helping and retarding us in our exploration of experience." [8]

In setting forth the general hypothesis that language profoundly influences the forms of thought, we are not saying that a given language rigidly determines the form of thought of the society in which it is spoken. But language so thoroughly interpenetrates the modes of experiencing that at the very least it limits the possibilities of perception and of thinking. It may be argued that language merely reflects the experiences of a people as its vocabulary reflects the interests and concerns of a people; but to say this is either to confine language to the transfer of ideas or to separate it sharply from culture.

Internalized Canons of Thought

Thinking goes on in the form of a symbolic process, an inner conversation; hence thought, like speech, is formulated in terms of the requirements of communicability. More specifically, this means that the thinker, like the speaker, has in mind an audience to which he adapts the formulations of his thought. This audience may at times assume the form of particular persons whose imagined responses are taken into account, or it may assume the form of a conception of "people in general." At other times, the imagined audience may be represented merely by abstract rules, principles, or standards. These may be considered the equivalent of an audience because they derive their authority from social consensus.

All reasoning involves processes of self-criticisms, judgment, appreciation, and control. Socially transmitted traditions of thought determine, among other things, which problems are important and which are unimportant, which questions are crucial and which are trivial, which solutions are to be rejected out of hand and which ones are to be judged acceptable, and so on.

The fact that thinking is a symbolic process means that a thinker can view and criticize his thought processes only from the standpoint (that is, according to the norms) of particular social groups because symbols are group products. To reason "correctly" means to conform to the canons of thought and to the conceptions of right thinking that prevail within a given circle. To be "right" always means "right" from some point of view. The principles of logic are not absolutes. They are not innate, nor are they immutable rules determined by the nature of the world. They do not exist in a realm of "being" independent of the concrete actions of human beings; they belong to people, to groups, and to societies. Their authority is always relative to particular places, particular times, particular groups, and particular types of discourse. Like other conventionalized norms of behavior, the norms of proof, correct reasoning, verification, and scientific method change with the times. They are subject to dispute, criticism, and revision.

Logical classifications and canons are conditioned by the linguistic structures of the society that formulates them. Masson-Oursel [9] for example, reached the conclusion that ancient Greek, Indian, and Chinese logical formulations were not identical, that problems of logic and their solutions reflected the peculiar emphasis and perspectives of each society and the structure of its language. Dewey [10] has suggested that the logical theory formulated by the ancient Greeks reflected their conceptions of the world; and Werkmeister explicitly notes the influences of Greek grammatical structure upon Greek logic:

> The formation of a sentence and its analysis into word units and word classes, as required in Greek language . . . seem to have had their influence upon the development of Aristotle's system of categories . . . the last four categories in particular . . . seem to become fully intelligible only when we relate them to certain basic distinctions which the Greek language recognizes in connection with the verb and verbal action.[11]

The existence of competing logical systems among modern logicians—for example, neo-Thomism (J. Maritain), instrumentalism (J. Dewey), and logical positivism (R. Carnap)—is evidence that even now logical formulations are in a process of change.

C. W. Mills has ably expressed the linkages among thought, audience, and logic which we have suggested above: [12]

> Societal processes enter as determinants into reflection. [There is an] internalized audience with which the thinker converses: a focalized and abstracted organization of attitudes of those implicated in the social field of behavior and experience. . . . The other conditions the thinker and the outcome of their interaction is a function of both interactants. . . . The social and intellectual habits of the audience, as elements in this interaction, condition the statements of the thinker and the fixation of beliefs evolving from that interplay. . . . It is in conversing with this internalized organization of collective attitudes that ideas are logically, that is, implicitly, "tested." Here they meet with recalcitrance and rejection, reformulation and acceptance. The thinker operates logically (applies standardized critiques) upon propositions and arguments (his own included) from the standpoint of the generalized other. . . . It is from this socially constituted viewpoint that one approves or disapproves of given arguments as logical or illogical, valid or invalid.

It is worth noting that no complex society has only one way of reasoning: various types of discourse representing different modes of thinking and of viewing the world exist simultaneously. Among the types of discourse that exist within our own society we may mention the poetic, philosophical, scientific, and religious. Each type implies a unique approach to human experience, and each has its own criteria of validity and relevance. The scientist, for example, cultivates systematic doubt and believes only what empirical evidence forces him to believe. By contrast, the poetic approach requires what Coleridge called a "suspension of disbelief." The scientifically-minded person who is troubled because the poet does not define his terms as he goes along seeks to apply the standards of one type of discourse to another type to which they bear no relation.

These different types of discourse, corresponding to different frames of reference, imply the utilization of different internalized audiences. For example, the modes of reasoning acceptable in poetic circles are significantly different from those of the scientists, and those of the latter are not deemed appropriate in the area of religious and moral beliefs. As individuals move from one activity to another (for example, from the laboratory to the home or the church) they change their frames of reference and their standards of proof, validity, and relevance. For an individual the importance of any given audience varies according to how relevant he considers its opinion to be; thus, the opinions of the scientist's wife concerning his theories, if she is not a scientist herself, are likely to have less influence upon him than her opinions of his table manners.

Notes

[1] E. Sapir, "The Status of Linguistics as a Science," in D. G. Mandelbaum, ed., *Selected Writings in Language, Culture, and Personality*. Berkeley, Calif.: University of California Press, 1949.

[2] W. Bynner, *The Jade Mountain*. New York: Alfred A. Knopf, 1929, p. 27.

[3] *The New York Times*, February 9, 1948, pp. 1, 3.

[4] M. Granet, "Quelques Particularités du Langage et de la Pensée Chinoise," *Revue Philosophique* (1920), pp. 98–128, 161–195.

[5] R. K. Merton, "Sociology of Knowledge," in G. D. Gurvitch and W. E. Moore, *Twentieth-Century Sociology*. New York: Philosophical Library, Inc., 1945, p. 387.

[6] C. Kluckhohn and D. Leighton, *The Navaho*. Cambridge, Mass.: Harvard University Press 1946, pp. 194, 197–201.

[7] W. H. Werkmeister, *A Philosophy of Science*. New York: Harper & Row, Publishers, 1940 pp. 126–129.

[8] E. Sapir, "Time Perspective in Aboriginal American Culture: A Study in Method," in D. G. Mandelbaum. *Selected Writings*, p. 11.

[9] P. Masson-Oursel, *Comparative Philosophy*. New York: Harcourt, Brace & World, Inc., 1926, pp. 114–148.

[10] J. Dewey, *Logic: The Theory of Inquiry*. New York: Holt, Rinehart and Winston, Inc., 1931, p. 81–98.

[11] Werkmeister, *A Philosophy of Science*, pp. 109–110.

[12] C. W. Mills, "Language, Logic, and Culture," *American Sociological Review*, vol. 4 (1939), pp. 672–673.

Linguistic Constructions of Reality

GARY J. MILLER

As we saw in the previous selection, language is an intrinsic part of every culture; through language experiences are organized and given meaning. As Miller shows in this selection, man is born into an ongoing culture which provides him with a symbol system by which he can interact and conceptualize his world. Language, however, also limits his perspective. The Whorfian hypothesis which Miller discusses views language as *the* source of human perspective. This approach has been called linguistic determinism since it asserts that a people's language determines what they see and what they know. The issue of linguistic determinism is not confined to cross-cultural research. Especially in large, complex cultures, intrasocietal linguistic differences are substantial, for example, in terms of social class.

Obviously this [human] world forms no exception to those biological rules which govern the life of all the other organisms. Yet in the human world we find a new characteristic which appears to be the distinctive mark of human life. The functional circle of man is not only quantitatively enlarged; it has also undergone a qualitative change. Man has, as it were, discovered a new method of adapting himself to his environment. Between the receptor system and the effector system, which are to be found in all animal species, we find in man a third link which we may describe as the *symbolic system*. This new acquisition transforms the whole of human life. As compared with the other animals man lives not merely in a broader reality; he lives, so to speak, in a new dimension of reality.

—Ernst Cassirer [1]

IT is difficult to overstate the importance of language and speech in human behavior. In mediating between a stimulus and a response, language plays an important role in determining the stimuli to which we respond. Since the writings of Mead and Dewey have become widely accepted, sociologists no longer conceive of an individual as passively responding to environmental stimuli but realize that selective perception is quite pervasive. This selectivity, which orients the individual to certain aspects of the social world while ignoring other aspects, is partially determined by the language and speech we utilize. For example, the labels we assign to objects can influence the per-

---

This chapter was written especially for this book.

ception of them. Certainly perceptions of people change depending whether they are labelled as a "businessman," "hippie," "homosexual," or "Communist." The extensive work done on stereotyping provides further examples. With somewhat surprising consistency, people "see" the Negro standing on the street corner as loafing or waiting for the welfare office to open rather than waiting for a bus. In the same way we often overlook several neat Negro householders, but triumphantly exclaim, when we encounter the slovenly tenth, "they do depreciate property." In this sense, language is a filter through which we interpret the world. As C. Wright Mills stated:

> It is only by utilizing the symbols common to his group that a thinker can think and communicate. . . . By acquiring the categories of language, we acquire the structured "ways" of a group, and along with the language, the value-implicatives of these "ways." Our behavior and perception, our logic and thought, come within the control of a system of language.[2]

Recently, experimental evidence has demonstrated that the world we perceive (the phenomenal world) is partly determined by language, that is, people see what they have words for. Brown and Lenneberg found that colors for which subjects had one-word names could be identified more often than colors for which they had only phrase-names. In this case, a particular linguistic fact, ease of naming or "codability," had an effect upon recognition, a cognitive process.[3]

Language performance is similar to conditioning—the speaker utilizes an institutionalized medium, one that has conditioned not only his manner of speaking but also his intellectual behavior. He cannot speak without using established words and language structures. This process may have a restricting effect upon the speaker, since the language he uses incorporates into somewhat fixed forms the agreed-upon representations of things, events, and relations. Since people must reach some consensus of word-reactions in order to communicate, they also tend to reach a consensus of individual perceptions. According to Alfred Schutz, man finds himself in surroundings already mapped out for him by others. Only a small fraction of his knowledge originates from his own individual experience; most of it is socially derived. All of our knowledge of the world involves "constructs," that is, a set of abstractions, generalizations, and idealizations which form the basis of our thought organization. There are no such things as facts, pure and simple; we merely grasp certain aspects of reality, namely, those which are relevant to us. In such a system of relevant constructs, language functions to sensitize the speaker to those features of the world that are most relevant.[4]

The Relationship between Language and Thought

The relationship between language and thought still involves considerable controversy. According to one school of thought, a language contains a practically exhaustive listing and classification of the concerns of a group. That is, the categories of a language *reflect* the interests, predilections, and emphases of a given group, community, or culture. For example, the Arabs have approximately 6000 words referring to the camel but until recently had very few that referred to automobiles. As the automobile grew more prominent in their lives, additional words referring to mechanized transportation were added. Likewise, in English we have only one word for snow, while the Eskimos have many, each reflecting a different characteristic of snow. This interpretation views language as adapting to culture. Since it develops in the context of a particular culture, language necessarily reflects the basic features of that culture.

An alternative school of thought suggests that language determines or molds a people's culture, perceptions, and cognitions. This view attributes a much stronger and more controversial role to language, although it does not necessarily contradict the first position. According to this view, the language structure operates as a ready-made metaphysical framework through which the speakers perceive and conceptualize. A person's language is his means of interpreting reality; it shapes his comprehension of the environment and supplies him with his definitions, categories, concepts, and perspectives.

The major expositor of the linguistic determinism hypothesis was Benjamin Lee Whorf.[5] The Whorfian hypothesis, as this position is termed, was developed from Whorf's comparisons of European languages with North and South American Indian languages. According to Whorf, language is, to its own speakers, largely of a background character and outside their control. When linguists examined a large number of languages of widely different patterns:

> It was found that the background linguistic system (in other words, the grammar) of each language is not merely a reproducing instrument for voicing ideas but rather is itself the shaper of ideas, the program and guide for the individual's mental activity, for his analysis of impressions, for his synthesis of his mental stock in trade. . . . We dissect nature along lines laid down by our native languages. . . . We cut nature up, organize it into concepts, and ascribe significances as we do, largely because we are parties to an agreement to organize it this way—an agreement that holds throughout our speech community and is codified in the patterns of our language.[6]

This observation was significant to Whorf; it meant that no person is free to describe nature with absolute impartiality but is confined to certain modes of interpretation. This new principle of relativity held that:

> . . . all observers are not led by the same physical evidence to the same picture of the universe, unless their linguistic backgrounds are similar, or can in some way be calibrated.[7]

The Whorfian hypothesis has sparked a tremendous controversy in linguistics. A number of anthropologists (Kluckhohn, Lee, Hall) have supported the hypothesis, based upon their ethnographic studies of non-Western languages. These investigations have revealed a relationship between linguistic differences and different verbal descriptions of reality. But we must emphasize that the mere convergence of linguistic structures and descriptions of reality does not prove which factor determines the other. In addition, these ethnological descriptions have utilized "language data" about cultural themes rather than providing the necessary nonlinguistic evidence of these cultural themes.

Others have not accepted the hypothesis so readily. Although linguists and social scientists acknowledge the importance of language in the study of culture and social organization, many are hesitant to accept the rigid linguistic determinism of Whorf. There is a question as to whether the connection between language and thought is as direct as Whorf thought it was. For many, a culture cannot be so easily reduced to its language, since culture consists of many unverbalized elements that nevertheless affect perception and behavior. In addition, the mere presence of language differences does not necessarily mean there are also psychological differences, as some investigators have assumed.

Roger Brown has reexamined much of the anthropological evidence supporting the determinist position. He questions whether the absence of a word for an object or event in a language can be asssumed to indicate that the object or event cannot be named. According to Brown, a phenomenon can usually be "named" even though the language contains no particular word for it; it can be named through the use of adjectives. For example, even though English contains only one word for snow, it does not follow that speakers of English cannot distinguish between slushy snow and dry snow. The very fact that we talk about such a difference indicates that we can make the distinction. And mostly certainly small children can tell at a glance whether or not the snow is suitable for making snowballs. Thus, the presence or absence of particular words in a language does not provide much insight into the speaker's perceptions. Ethnological data provide only weak evidence for the determinist position.[8]

Experimental Research

As the above discussion indicates, the collection of instances of linguistic differences and the consequent inference that a cognitive difference also exists is an unsatisfactory approach to the verification of the Whorfian hypothesis. Verification of the hypothesis ultimately depends upon whether it can be shown that a relation does exist between a measure of language structure and an *independent* measure of some nonlinguistic cognitive process. Experimental attempts at verification provide an ideal way of assessing the validity of the hypothesis. We shall now briefly review some of the experimental evidence pertaining to the issue of linguistic determinism.

As Joshua Fishman has indicated, there are two aspects to researching the hypothesis: (1) the measurement of language either as vocabulary or grammar, and (2) the measurement of cognition using either verbal reports of the subjects or some nonlinguistic measurement of cognition (e.g., subjects are asked to point or to indicate perceptions in some nonverbal way, problem solving that is performed motorically and not verbally).[9] Since it has already been indicated that a proper test of the hypothesis should employ a nonverbal measure of cognition and since the Whorfian hypothesis is mainly concerned with grammatical structure, the ideal test will employ measurement of grammatical differences and their effect upon thought or perception as measured nonlinguistically. This, however, is the most difficult avenue for research. Hence there has been little of this type of verification. Most of the research has dealt with the effects of vocabulary differences upon perception and cognition. We shall first deal with this latter type of research.

Experimental research on the effects of vocabulary differences upon thought and perception have usually involved comparing speakers of different languages on some cognitive or perceptual task related to the speech difference. As indicated earlier, Brown and Lenneberg discovered a relationship between possessing a specific name for a color and the ability to distinguish between the color and slightly different colors. In a follow-up study, the same task was administered to Zuni Indian subjects (the Zuni color vocabulary has only one name for orange and yellow). In comparing the English-speaking subjects with the Zuni subjects, it was noted that the Zuni subjects frequently confused orange and yellow colors, whereas the English-speaking subjects did not. Here again we see that a vocabulary difference has an effect upon perception, in this case, recognition of colors.[10] Others have replicated this study, not always with the same results. A major problem in these investigations has been to determine a proper measure of codability or ease of naming —the vocabulary difference of interest. A recent study by Lantz and Stefflre developed a different measure of codability and found that vocabulary differences again resulted in perceptual differences.[11] This latter study was an improvement over earlier studies in that the findings could be more easily generalized and not confined to the particular color array used in the test. Yet we still do not know whether linguistic codability affects perceptual recognition or vice versa. It could be easily argued that perceptual differences across cultures determine the kinds of words people use to describe and name colors rather than that the names we use determine the colors that we recognize. What is needed is a demonstration that language differences cause perceptual differences. One study is relevant to this latter point. Lantz, in a doctoral dissertation, manipulated this relationship experimentally. She taught subjects new names for colored chips which were previously difficult to name and in this way increased the accuracy with which these chips were recognized.[12] This is only one demonstration of a possible causal connection between language and cognition but a valuable one. Of course, further confirmation is needed before much faith can be placed in the hypothesis. The above studies are by no means the only ones relevant to this position, but they do provide a sampling of the kind of empirical work that needs to be done.

The ʳabove types of studies investigated vocabulary differences among languages and, as such, are only low-level tests of the Whorfian hypothesis. They test the effects of concept formation more than they test the effects of language usage. They are not irrelevant to the hypothesis, but better tests utilize grammatical language data rather than vocabulary data.

There are two studies that do examine the effects of grammar on thought and perception. In comparing English and Navaho languages, Carroll and Casagrande noticed that verb-form differences sensitize the speakers to different attributes of physical objects. In an experimental study they found that these verb-form differences were reflected in differences between subjects from the two cultures in pairing pictures of objects on the basis of either shape, size, or color. In another study, Brown found that children were able to match nonsense words as they were used in a sentence with pictures that corresponded to the nonsense word. In the latter case, grammatical usage of a nonsense word structured perception.[13] These two studies are just a first step in the demonstration that grammar can influence perception and thought. Not all studies have provided this amount of support for the Whorfian hypothesis. Further replication of these studies is needed in order to conclude that grammatical differences create different phenomenal worlds for the speakers.

These studies indicate that there might be a principle of relativity operating through the languages that people use. On the basis of existing evidence, however, it is only possible to state that linguistic relativity is only moderately powerful in structuring thought and perception. And, at the same time, not all linguistic differences result in cognitive differences. Osgood, in studies using the semantic differential, has shown that there is universality in some aspects of language and thought, especially in the connotative realm of language.[14] This is a serious counter position to that of Whorf. Obviously, greater specification of the Whorfian hypothesis is needed. Attempts must be made to delimit more sharply the types of language structures and the types of nonlinguistic behavior that do or do not show the Whorfian effect. It is entirely possible that there are areas of language in which the Whorfian hypothesis not relevant. At the same time, in those areas where the hypothesis is relevant, it needs to be determined whether the effect of language can be modified or is resistant to change.

The above studies do provide some support for the hypothesis, but its status is still unclear. In reviewing much of the evidence for linguistic determinism, Brown concludes that:

> The proposed relationships between these variables language and thought have some empirical support but nothing like adequate proof. I don't know of any attempts as yet to show that an independently defined linguistic pattern has

either historical or biographical priority over the thought pattern it is supposed to determine.[15]

The proper role of language in the human thought process still is indeterminate. It appears that we can go beyond the previously expressed position that language is merely a reflection of thought and culture. Whether we can go so far as to say that language determines thought must await further empirical evidence. At present, it appears that the language of a speaker does influence and direct thought processes into prescribed channels. As Hockett concludes, languages differ not so much in terms of what is *possible* to say and think, but rather they differ in terms of what is *relatively easy* to say and think.[16] The above investigations all underscore the fundamental importance of language and speech in *sensitizing* cognition.

Intrasocietal Comparisons

Cross-cultural research has provided insights into the importance of language in human cognition. However, the comparisons of languages from different cultures should not blind us to the many language and speech differences within a culture. Space does not allow a consideration of societies with more than one spoken language and its consequences or with differences in accent.

Just as in intersocietal comparisons, two approaches to the role of language can be taken. First, language can be conceived as a reflection of the social structure with its many subcultural differences. The history and interests of a group of people is often reflected in their language. The idioms and vernacular of sociologists, physicians, soldiers, college students, football players, jazz musicians, and hippies all reflect their respective dominant interests and concerns.

Language is a principal weapon in maintaining the cohesiveness and solidarity of groups. Social solidarity is almost synonymous with linguistic solidarity. Language functions as the badge or symbol of the group; it is a major indicator of the group identity and of its unity. By means of language, the outgroups are marked off from the ingroup. Thus, it is not surprising to find subcultures with their own argot. For example, jazz musicians have their own private language, delinquent groups have their own lingo, the Negro community has historically had its own language, confidence men have special terms for their trade, Marxists repeatedly utilize key phrases and terms indicating their identity and solidarity, and the drug cult of the sixties speaks of trips, acid, and freaking out. Language and speech also can provide insights into the stratification system; speech has historically differentiated the upper-class individual from the working- or lower-class person. One of the first things the upwardly mobile person must learn in order to be accepted into a higher status is its speech style.

A second approach to the role of language is to relate speech differences to cognitive and behavioral differences. Schatzman and Strauss examined social class differences in speech from interviews and found: lower-class descriptions were given as seen through the respondent's own eyes, while middle-class descriptions were given as seen by others; lower-class persons showed a relative insensitivity to differences between their perspective and that of the interviewer, while middle-class persons recognized much more fully the difference; and lower-class descriptions were segmental or limited in scope, while middle-class respondents used overall frames to organize their accounts. From these descriptions of language differences in the two social classes it might be concluded that members of different social classes perceive and think differently, but the investigators stop short of this conclusion (although they lean toward it).[17]

This line of research has been pursued furthest by the British sociologist Basil Bernstein.[18] Bernstein has continued Whorf's interest in the relation between speech and thought by investigating social class differences in speech. He has, however, modified Whorf's interpretation of this relationship. According to Bernstein, the social structure generates distinct speech codes and these codes essentially constrain thought and behavior. The major difference from Whorf is Bernstein's emphasis upon the social structure as the major influence upon culture *through* its effects upon speech style. For Whorf, language and speech had a rather independent existence; he never bothered to examine outside influences upon language and speech. For our purposes in this discussion, however, the implications are nearly identical. Both men have emphasized the causal influence of language and speech upon thought and perception.

Based upon comparisons of speech samples of lower- and middle-class children, Bernstein concludes that lower- and middle-class children utilize different speech codes. Although the connection between social class and type of speech code used is not invariant, it does reflect preponderant usage. In the lower class speech is characterized by a rigidity of syntax and limited use of structural possibilities for sentence organization. Speech is condensed and the statements are highly predictable for any speaker. Middle-class speech, on the other hand, utilizes more sophisticated grammatical structure and can elaborate and differentiate the cognitive elements relevant to a given situation. This ability enables the elaborated code speaker to respond in an organized, rational manner to differing situations.

Since language is one of the most important means of initiating, synthesizing, and reinforcing perceptions, thought, and behavior, Bernstein posits that speech differences create different orders of relevance and different interpretations of experience. Like many of the ethnological studies of language differences across cultures, Bernstein has not yet demonstrated empirically that these speech differences result in cognitive differences. This last link in the chain of reasoning awaits empirical support, some of which has already been provided by Hess and Shipman and by Robinson and Creed. Hess and Shipman found a relationship between type of speech code used and problem-solving ability, while Robinson and Creed established a relationship between speech code and perceptual responses to pictures.[19]

More of this type of evidence is needed before the Bernstein thesis can be unequivocally accepted. A few further comments on the above thesis are in order at this time. Although the relationship between social class and type of speech code used is fairly strong, it is by no means perfect. Not all middle-class speakers use an elaborated code or are all lower-class speakers limited to the restricted code. When Bernstein speaks of lower-class speech and middle-class speech, he is referring to prevailing usages which are by no means universal within each class. Speech codes are also modifiable. If these qualifications are kept in mind, we should not be tempted to stereotype all lower-class speakers as inferior. This tendency would, in all likelihood, produce a stereotypic depiction of lower-class persons that is as debilitating as the recently disproven stereotype of inferior genetic potential.

Secondly, social class differences are not the only differences that can affect speech. Situational differences, group membership, reference groups, and region of the country can also influence the type of speech code used. The emphasis on social class and its relations to speech form stem from its pervasive influence and its theoretical significance. Further work is now needed in specifying the social psychological significance of social class differences. We also need to know exactly what aspects of social class subcultures have an effect upon speech.

Summary

The debate about the centrality of language and speech in the determination of thought and perception has not yet ended. Because they lack solid empirical support, the linguistic determinists have not been able to argue their position convincingly. Yet the evidence is strong enough to point to a relativistic interpretation, at least regarding some aspects of language. By sensitizing the speaker to certain perceptions and thoughts, language plays a central role in delimiting a person's social reality. It is, however, still premature to argue that certain language forms *prevent* the speaker from perceiving and thinking in unconventional ways. At this point in the inquiry, it is only safe to conclude that language and speech condition *habitual* modes of perceiving and thinking. With this in mind, it is not surprising to notice that speakers from different speech communities dissect nature and reality along somewhat different lines. More than likely the African aborigine transported to a busy intersection in a metropolitan area would not come up with the same interpretation of the activity as the native urban dweller would, and not all of this difference in the interpretation would be due to knowledge differences.

Some of the differences in perception and interpretation could undoubtedly be accounted for by the language differences.

The same type of relativity of perception and thought that has been observed across societies may also operate within societies, as the recent work by Basil Bernstein indicates. Different groups within the larger society may dissect social reality differently and create different phenomenal worlds. It may be that some of the difficulty in interaction across social class lines in our society resides in speech differences. No conclusive empirical demonstration has been presented to verify this latter assertion, but it is a most promising avenue for further research.

*

Notes

[1] Ernst Cassirer, *An Essay on Man* (New Haven: Yale University Press, 1944), p. 24.

[2] C. Wright Mills, "Language, Logic, and Culture," *American Sociological Review*, 4 (1939), 677.

[3] Roger Brown and Eric Lenneberg, "A Study in Language and Cognition," *Journal of Abnormal and Social Psychology*, 49 (1954), 454–462.

[4] Alfred Schutz, "Symbol, Reality, and Society," in *Symbols and Society* (New York: Harper, 1955), pp. 193–194, and "Common-Sense and Scientific Interpretation," in *Philosophy of the Social Sciences*, Maurice Natanson, ed. (New York: Random House, 1963), pp. 302–346.

[5] Benjamin Lee Whorf, "Science and Linguistics," *Readings in Social Psychology*, Eleanor Maccoby, et. al., ed. (New York: Holt, Rinehart, & Winston, 1958), pp. 1–9.

[6] Ibid., p. 5.

[7] Ibid., p. 5.

[8] Roger Brown, *Words and Things* (Glencoe: Free Press, 1958), pp. 233–237.

[9] Joshua Fishman, "A Systematization of the Whorfian Hypothesis," *Behavioral Science*, 9 (1960), 323–339.

[10] Eric Lenneberg and John M. Roberts, "The Language of Experience," *Memoir of the International Journal of American Linguistics*, 22 (1956).

[11] DeLee Lantz and Volney Stefflre, "Language and Cognition Revisited," *Journal of Abnormal and Social Psychology*, 69 (1964), 472–481.

[12] Ibid., pp. 480–481.

[13] John B. Carroll and Joseph Casagrande, "The Function of Language Classifications in Behavior," in *Readings in Social Psychology*, Eleanor Maccoby et. al., ed. pp. 23–31. Brown, *Words and Things*, pp. 250–253.

[14] See Harry C. Triandis, "Cultural Influences upon Cognitive Processes," in *Advances in Experimental Social Psychology*, Leonard Berkowitz, ed. (New York: Academic Press, 1964), pp. 25–29.

[15] Brown, *Words and Things*, p. 262.

[16] Charles Hockett, "Chinese versus English: An Exploration of the Whorfian Hypothesis," in *Language in Culture*, Harry Hoijer, ed. (Chicago: University of Chicago Press, 1954), pp. 106–123.

[17] Leonard Schatzman and Anselm Strauss, "Social Class and Modes of Communication," *American Journal of Sociology*, 66 (1955), 329–338.

[18] Basil Bernstein, "Social Class and Linguistic Development: A Theory of Social Learning," *Education, Economy, and Society*, A H. Halsey et. al., ed. (New York: Free Press, 1961), pp. 288–314, and "A Sociolinguistic Approach to Social Learning," *Penguin Survey of the Social Sciences 1965*, Julius Gould, ed. (Baltimore: Penguin Books, 1965), pp. 144–168.

[19] Robert D. Hess and Virginia Shipman, "Early Experience and the Socialization of Cognitive Modes in Children," *Society and Education*, Robert J. Havighurst et. al., ed. (Boston: Allyn and Bacon, 1967), pp. 74–85, and W. P. Robinson and C. D. Creed, "Perceptual and Verbal Discriminations of 'Elaborated' and 'Restricted' Code Users," *Language and Speech*, 11 (1968) 182–193.

PART IV

CLASS

Social stratification is the ranking of individuals (or groups, or associations, or categories of people) according to their possession of some socially valued characteristic. Any such characteristic might serve as criteria—age, race, number of generations in country, beauty, and so on. For an individual's rank within the society at large, sociologists examine three main values—wealth, power, and prestige. In sociological research, income, occupation, and education are the commonly used empirical indicators of these values. When people are placed in categories based on these variables we speak of classes.

The concept of class, however, is useful only to the extent that those whom the sociologist places in a particular category share social characteristics outside of their common socioeconomic standing (SES). That this is indeed the case is attested to by the fact that class is probably the most widely used independent variable in sociological research. A number of studies have found evidence for class differences in attitudes, values, and beliefs as well as behavior patterns. This does not necessarily mean, however, that classes constitute social units as do groups, associations, and societies. The study of the relationship between class and perspective need not be based on the concept of "class consciousness." The sociologist must investigate the specific variations that are implied in class differences, and then relate these differences to variations in perspective. The selections in this section are illustrations of sociological research which describes class differences in perspective.

Social Class and Modes
of Communication [1]

LEONARD SCHATZMAN AND ANSELM STRAUSS

Symbolic interaction provides an important approach to social psychology. The following article by Schatzman and Strauss utilizes this
approach. They see class differences in communication as revealing
differences in modes of thought. Number and scope of perspectives,
cognizance of other's imagery, classificatory thinking, and organizing
frameworks are shown to differ by class. All of these elements are
part of a broad definition of perspective; however, the authors' confine
their use of this concept to "the standpoint from which a description
is made."

The descriptions of lower-class and middle-class communication
types is based on an analysis of extensive interviews with ten respondents from each class. These interviews were conducted with
residents of several rural communities hit by a tornado. Based on the
interview protocols, the authors impute to lower-class members: a
personal perspective (respondent's description is solely from his standpoint); an insensitivity to differences in imagery; concreteness (little
classification of people or events); and limited and segmented organizing frameworks. On the other hand, middle-class communication
recorded on the protocols indicated: a multiple perspective (description from standpoints other than his own); "parallel consciousness of
the other and himself"; classifications; and utilization of a master
framework plus subsidiary frameworks.

Schatzman and Strauss caution the reader about the problems of
cross-class communication analysis and interviewer effect. Nevertheless, they find a distinct difference in perspectives between the lower
and middle classes.

COMMON assumptions suggest that there may be important differences in the thought and communication of social classes. Men live in an
environment which is mediated through symbols. By naming, identifying, and

Reprinted from *The American Journal of Sociology*, Vol. LX, January, 1955, pp. 329–338, by
permission o' the authors and the publisher, The University of Chicago Press.

classifying, the world's objects and events are perceived and handled. Order is imposed through conceptual organization, and this organization embodies not just anybody's rules but the grammatical, logical, and communicative canons of groups. Communication proceeds in terms of social requirements for comprehension, and so does "inner conversation" or thought. Both reasoning and speech meet requirements of criticism, judgment, appreciation, and control. Communication across group boundaries runs the danger—aside from sheer language difficulties—of being blocked by differential rules for the ordering of speech and thought.[2]

If these assumptions are correct, it follows that there should be observable differences in communication according to social class and that these differences should not be merely matters of degree of preciseness, elaboration, vocabulary, and literary style. It follows also that the modes of thought should be revealed by modes of speaking.

Our data are the interview protocols gathered from participants in a disaster. The documents, transcribed from tape, contain a wealth of local speech. Respondents had been given a relatively free hand in reporting their experiences, and the interviews averaged twenty-nine pages. These seemed admirably suited to a study of differences between social classes in modes of communication and in the organization of perception and thought. We used them also to explore the hypothesis that substantial intraclass differences in the organization of stories and accounts existed; hence low-class respondents might fail to satisfy the interviewer's canons of communication.

Approximately 340 interviews were available, representing random sampling of several communities ravaged by a tornado. Cases were selected by extreme position on educational and income continuums. Interviewees were designated as "lower" if education did not go beyond grammar school and if the annual family income was less than two thousand dollars. The "upper" group consisted of persons with one or more years of college education and annual incomes in excess of four thousand dollars. These extremes were purposely chosen for maximum socioeconomic contrast and because it seemed probable that nothing beyond formal or ritual communication would occur between these groups.

Cases were further limited by the following criteria: age (twenty-one to sixty-five years), race (white only), residence (native of Arkansas and more than three years in the community), proximity (either in the disaster area or close by), good co-operation in interview (as rated by interviewer), and less than eight probes per page (to avoid a rigid question-answer style with consequent structuring of interview by the interviewer's questions). The use of these criteria yielded ten upper-group cases, which were then matched randomly with ten from the lower group.[3]

Differences between Classes

Differences between the lower and upper groups were striking; and, once the nature of the difference was grasped, it was astonishing how quickly a characteristic organization of communication could be detected and described from a reading of even a few paragraphs of an interview. The difference is not simply the failure or success—of lower and upper groups, respectively—in communicating clearly and in sufficient detail for the interviewer's purposes. Nor does the difference merely involve correctness or elaborateness of grammar or use of a more precise or colorful vocabulary. The difference is a considerable disparity in (a) the number and kinds of perspectives utilized in communication; (b) the ability to take the listener's role; (c) the handling of classifications; and (d) the frameworks and stylistic devices which order and implement the communication.

Perspective or Centering

By perspective or centering is meant the standpoint from which a description is made.[4] Perspectives may vary in number and scope. The flexibility with which one shifts from perspective to perspective during communication may vary also.

LOWER CLASS

Almost without exception any description offered by a lower-class respondent is a description as seen through his *own* eyes; he offers his own perceptions and images directly to the listener. His best performance is a straight, direct narrative of events as he saw and experienced them. He often locates himself clearly in time and place and indicates by various connective devices a rough progression of events in relation to his activities. But the developmental progression is only in relation to himself. Other persons and their acts come into his narrative more or less as he encountered them. In the clearest interviews other actors are given specific spatial and temporal location, and sometimes the relationships among them or between them and himself are clearly designated.

The speaker's images vary considerably in clarity but are always his own. Although he may occasionally repeat the stories of other persons, he does not tell the story as though he were the other person reconstructing events and feelings. He may describe another person's act and the motive for it, with regard to himself, but this is the extent of his role-taking—he does not assume the role of another toward still others, except occasionally in an implicit fashion: "Some people was helping other people who was hurt."

This limitation is especially pronounced when the behavior of more than two or three persons is being described and related. Here the description becomes confused: At best the speaker reports some reactions, but no clear picture of interaction emerges. The interaction either is not noticed or is implicitly present in the communication ("We run over there to see about them, and they was alright"). Even with careful probing the situation is not clarified much further. The most unintelligible speakers thoroughly confound the interviewer who tries to follow images, acts, persons, and events which seem to come out of nowhere and disappear without warning.

MIDDLE CLASS

The middle class can equal the best performance of the lower class in communicating and elaborating a direct description. However, description is not confined to so narrow a perspective. It may be given from any of several standpoints: for instance, another person, a class of persons, an organization, an organizational role, even the whole town. The middle-class speaker may describe the behavior of others, including classes of others, from their standpoints rather than from his, and he may include sequences of acts as others saw them. Even descriptions of the speaker's own behavior often are portrayed from other points of view.

Correspondence of Imagery between Speaker and Listener

Individuals vary in their ability to see the necessity for mediating linguistically between their own imagery and that of their listeners. The speaker must know the limits within which he may assume a correspondence of imagery. When the context of the item under discussion is in physical view of both, or is shared because of similarity of past experience, or is implicitly present by virtue of a history of former interaction, the problem of context is largely solved.[5] But when the context is neither so provided nor offered by the speaker, the listener is confronted with knotty problems of interpretation. In the accounts of the most unintelligible respondents we found dream-like sets of images with few connective qualifying, explanatory, or other context-providing devices. Thus, the interviewer was hard pressed to make sense of the account and was forced to probe at every turn lest the speaker figuratively run away with the situation. The respondents were willing and often eager to tell their stories, but intention to communicate does not always bring about clear communication. The latter involves, among other requirements, an ability to hear one's words as others hear them.

LOWER CLASS

Lower-class persons displayed a relative insensitivity to disparities in perspective. At best, the respondent corrected himself on the exact time at which he performed an act or became aware that his listener was not present at the scene and so located objects and events for him. On occasion he reached a state of other-consciousness: "You can't imagine if you wasn't there what it was like." However, his assumption of a correspondence in imagery is notable. There is much surnaming of persons without genuine identification, and often terms like "we" and "they" are used without clear referents. The speaker seldom anticipates responses to his communication and seems to feel little need to explain particular features of his account. He seldom qualifies an utterance, presumably because he takes for granted that his perceptions represent reality and are shared by all who were present. Since he is apt to take so much for granted, his narrative lacks depth and richness and contains almost no qualifications and few genuine illustrations. The hearer very often is confronted with a descriptive fragment that supposedly represents a more complete story. The speaker may then add phrases like "and stuff like that" or "and everything." Such phrasing is not genuine summation but a substitute for detail and abstraction. Summary statements are virtually absent, since they signify that speakers are sensitive to the needs of listeners. Certain phrases that appear to be summaries— such as "That's all I know" and "That's the way it was"—merely indicate that the speaker's knowledge is exhausted. Other summary-like phraseologies, like "It was pitiful," appear to be asides, reflective of self-feeling or emotion than that résumés of preceding detail.

MIDDLE CLASS

The middle-class respondent also makes certain assumptions about the correspondence of the other's images with his own. Nevertheless, in contrast with the lower group, he recognizes much more fully that imagery may be diverse and that context must be provided. Hence he uses many devices to supply context and to clarify meaning. He qualifies, summarizes, and sets the stage with rich introductory material, expands themes, frequently illustrates, anticipates disbelief, meticulously locates and identifies places and persons—all with great complexity of detail. He depends less on saying "You know"; he insists upon explaining if he realizes that a point lacks plausibility or force. Hence he rarely fails to locate an image, or series of images, in time or place. Frequent use of qualification is especially noteworthy. This indicates not only multiple centering but a very great sensitivity to listeners, actual and potential—including the speaker himself.

In short, the middle-class respondent has what might be called "communication control," at least in such a semiformal situation as the interview. Figuratively, he stands between his own images and the hearer and says, "Let me introduce you to what I saw and know." It is as though he were directing a movie, having at his command several cameras focused at different perspectives shooting and carefully controlling the effect. By contrast, the lower-class respondent seems himself more like a single camera which unreels the scene to the audience. In the very telling of his story he is more apt to lose himself in his imagery. The middle-class person—by virtue, we would presume, of his greater sensitivity to his listener—stands more outside his experience. He does not so much tell you what he saw as fashion a story about what he saw. The story may be accurate in varying degrees, although, in so far as it is an organized account, it has both the virtues and the defects of organization. The comparative accuracies of middle- and lower-class accounts are not relevant here; the greater objectivity of the former merely reflects greater distance between narrator and event.[6]

In organizing his account, the middle-class respondent displays parallel consciousness of the other and himself. He can stop midstream, take another direction, and, in general, exert great control over the course of his communication. The lower-class respondent seems to have much less foresight, appearing to control only how much he will say to the interviewer, or whether he will say it at all, although presumably he must have some stylistic controls not readily observable by a middle-class reader.

Classifications and Classificatory Relations

LOWER CLASS

Respondents make reference mainly to the acts and persons of particular people, often designating them by proper or family names. This makes for fairly clear denotation and description, but only as long as the account is confined to the experiences of specific individuals. There comes a point when the interviewer wishes to obtain information about classes of persons and entire organizations as well as how they impinged upon the respondent, and here the lower-class respondent becomes relatively or even wholly inarticulate. At worst he cannot talk about categories of people or acts because, apparently, he does not think readily in terms of classes. Questions about organizations, such as the Red Cross, are converted into concrete terms, and he talks about the Red Cross "helping people" and "people helping other people" with no more than the crudest awareness of how organizational activities interlock. At most the respondent categorizes only in a rudimentary fashion: "'Some people were running; other people were looking in the houses." The interviewer receives a sketchy and impressionistic picture. Some idea is conveyed of the confusion that followed upon the tornado, but the organizing of description is very poor. The respondent may mention classes in contrasting juxtaposition (rich and poor, hurt and not-hurt), or list groups of easily perceived, contrasting actions, but he does not otherwise spell out relations between these classes. Neither does he describe a scene systematically in terms of classes that are explicitly or clearly related, a performance which would involve a shifting of viewpoint.

It is apparent that the speakers think mainly in particularistic or concrete terms. Certainly classificatory thought must exist among many or all the respondents; but, in communicating to the interviewer, class terms are rudimentary or absent and class relations implicit: relationships are not spelled out or are left vague. Genuine illustrations are almost totally lacking, either because these require classifications or because we—as middle-class observers —do not recognize that certain details are meant to imply classes.

MIDDLE CLASS

Middle-class speech is richly interlarded with classificatory terms, especially when the narrator is talking about what he saw rather than about himself. Typically, when he describes what other persons are doing, he classifies actions and persons and more often than not explicitly relates class to class. Often his descriptions are artistically organized around what various categories of persons were doing or experiencing. When an illustration is offered, it is clear that the speaker means it to stand for a general category. Relief and other civic organizations are conceived as sets or classes of co-ordinated roles and actions; some persons couch their whole account of the disaster events in organizational terms, hardly deigning to give proper names or personal accounts. In short, concrete imagery in middle-class communication is dwarfed or overshadowed by the prevalence and richness of conceptual terminology. Organization of speech around classifications comes readily, and undoubtedly the speaker is barely conscious of it. It is part and parcel of his formal and informal education. This is not to claim that middle-class persons always think with and use classificatory terms, for doubtless this is not true. Indeed, it may be that the interview exacts from them highly conceptualized descriptions. Nonetheless, we conclude that, in general, the thought and speech of middle-class persons is less concrete than that of the lower group.

Organizing Frameworks and Stylistic Devices

One of the requirements of communication is that utterances be organized. The principle of organization need not be stated explicitly by the speaker or recognized by the listener. Organizing frames can be of various sorts. Thus an ordering of the respondents' description is often set by the interviewer's question, or the speaker may set his own framework ("There is one thing you should know about this"). The frame can be established jointly by both interviewer and respondent, as when the former asks an open-ended question within whose very broad limits the respondent orders his description in ways that strike him as appropriate or interesting. The respondent, indeed, may organize his account much as though he were telling a special kind of story or drama, using the interviewer's questions as hardly more than general cues to what is required. The great number of events, incidents, and images which must be conveyed to the listener may be handled haphazardly, neatly, dramatically, or sequentially; but, if they are to be communicated at all, they must be ordered somehow. Stylistic devices accompany and implement these organizing frames, and the lower and upper groups use them in somewhat different ways.

LOWER CLASS

The interviewer's opening question, "Tell me your story of the tornado," invites the respondent to play an active role in organizing his account; and this he sometimes does. However, with the exception of one person who gave a headlong personal narrative, the respondents did not give long, well-organized, or tightly knit pictures of what happened to them during and after the tornado. This kind of general depiction either did not occur to them or did not strike them as appropriate.

The frames utilized are more segmental or limited in scope than those used by the middle class. They appear to be of several kinds and their centering is personal. One is the personal narrative, with events, acts, images, persons, and places receiving sequential ordering. Stylistic devices further this kind of organization: for instance, crude temporal connectives like "then," "and," and "so" and the reporting of images or events as they are recollected or as they appear in the narrative progression. Asides may specify relationships of kinship or the individuals' location in space. But, unless the line of narrative is compelling to the speaker, he is likely to wander off into detail about a particular incident, where the incident in turn then provides a framework for mentioning further events. Likewise, when a question from the interviewer breaks into the narrative, it may set the stage for an answer composed of a number of images or an incident. Often one incident becomes the trigger for another, and, although some logical or temporal connection between them may exist for the speaker, this can scarcely be perceived by the interviewer. Hence the respondent is likely to move out of frames quickly. The great danger of probes and requests for elaboration is that the speaker will get far away from the life-line of his narrative—and frequently far away from the interviewer's question. As recompense the interviewer may garner useful and unexpectedly rich information from the digressions, although often he needs to probe this material further to bring it into context. General questions are especially likely to divert the speaker, since they suggest only loose frames; or he may answer in general, diffuse, or blurred terms which assume either that the listener was there too or that he will put meaningful content into the words. If a question is asked that concerns abstract classes or is "above" the respondent—a query, say, about relief organizations—then very general answers or concrete listing of images or triggering of images are especially noticeable. When the interviewer probes in an effort to get some elaboration of an occurrence or an expansion of idea, he commonly meets with little more than repetition or with a kind of "buckshot" listing of images or incidents which is supposed to fill out the desired picture. The lack of much genuine elaboration is probably related to the inability to report from multiple perspectives.

One requirement of the interview is that it yield a fairly comprehensive account of the respondent's actions and perceptions. With the lower-class respondent the interviewer, as a rule, must work very hard at building a comprehensive frame directly into the interview. This he does by forcing many subframes upon the respondent. He asks many questions about exact time sequence, placement and identification of persons, expansion of detail, and the like. Especially must he ask pointed questions about the relations of various personages appearing in the account. Left to his own devices, the respondent may give a fairly straightforward narrative or competently reconstruct incidents that seem only partially connected with each other or with his narrative. But the respondent seldom voluntarily gives both linear and cross-sectional pictures.

The devices used to implement communication are rather difficult to isolate, perhaps because we are middle class ourselves. Among the devices most readily observable are the use of crude chronological notations (e.g., "then, . . . and then"), the juxtaposing or direct contrasting of classes (e.g., rich and poor), and the serial locating of events. But the elaborate devices that characterize middle-class interviews are strikingly absent.

MIDDLE CLASS

Without exception middle-class respondents imposed over-all frames of their own upon the entire interview. Although very sensitive generally to the needs of the interviewer, they made the account their own. This is evidenced sometimes from the very outset; many respondents give a lengthy picture in answer to the interviewer's invitation, "Tell me your story." The organizing frame may yield a fluid narrative that engulfs self and others in dense detail; it may give a relatively static but rich picture of a community in distress; or, by dramatic and stage-setting devices, it may show a complicated web of relationships in dramatic motion. The entire town may be taken as the frame of reference and its story portrayed in time and space.

Besides the master-frame, the middle-class respondent utilizes many subsidiary frames. Like the lower-class person, he may take off from a question. But, in doing so—especially where the question gives latitude by its generality or abstractness—he is likely to give an answer organized around a sub-frame which orders his selection and arrangement of items. He may even shift from one image to another, but rarely are these left unrelated to the question which initially provoked them. He is much more likely also to elaborate than to repeat or merely to give a scattered series of percepts.

One prerequisite for the elaboration of a theme is an ability to depart from it while yet holding it in mind. Because he incorporates multiple perspectives, the respondent can add long asides, discuss the parallel acts of other persons in relation to himself, make varied comparisons for the enrichment of detail and comprehension—and then can return to the original point and proceed from there. Often he does this after first preparing his listener for the departure and concludes the circuit with a summary statement or a transitional phrase like "well—anyhow" that marks the end of the digression.

The stylistic devices utilized by any respondent are many and varied. But each speaker uses some devices more frequently than others, since certain ones are more or less appropriate to given frames. There is no point in spelling out the whole range of devices; they are of the sort used in any clear detailed narrative and effective exposition. If the respondent is pressed to the limit of his ability in explaining a complex point or describing a complicated scene, he calls into play resources that are of immensely high order. Sometimes a seemingly simple device will turn out on closer inspection to demand a sophisticated handling of communication—for instance, the frequent and orderly asides that break into exposition or narrative and serve with great economy to add pertinent detail.

Intraclass Differences

MIDDLE CLASS

Although all middle-class accounts were informative, there were considerable differences of construction among them. The frames utilized by any respondent are multiple, but respondents tend to use either a frame emphasizing sequence, human drama, and personal incident or one stressing interlocking classes of civic acts. Each orientation is implemented by somewhat different stylistic techniques. There are of course different ways of narrating; thus one can dwell more upon conditions for activity than upon the acts themselves. Similarly, accounts focused upon town organization vary in such matters as the scope of description and the degree of emphasis upon temporal sequence. Both frameworks are interchangeable, and their use is a function either of the speaker's habitual orientation or of his definition of the interview situation rather than of his ability to use one or the other mode.

LOWER CLASS

Lower-class persons can best be distinguished in terms of ability to meet the minimum requirements of the interview. Some literally cannot tell a straight story or describe a simple incident coherently. At the other extreme we find an adequate self-focused narrative, with considerable detail tightly tied to sequential action, including retrospective observation about the narrator's facts as he develops them. Midway between these extremes are the people who can tell portions of narrative but are easily distracted: either an image suggests some other image, or the interviewer asks a question focusing interest and concentration elsewhere than upon the narrative or he calls for some expansion of detail. Then the interviewer must remind the speaker of the break in narrative. The interviewer constantly must be on the *qui vive* to keep the story going and to fill in gaps.

In the best accounts, also, competent description is handled by linking a variety of perceptions to the narrative. Images then appear to the listener to be in context and thus are fairly comprehensible. At the other extreme, images and incidents are free-floating. Probing improved the quality of this sort of interview but slightly. More frequently, the interviewer was confronted with fragments of the narrative and its related imagery. Then he had to piece together the general lineaments of the story by a barrage of probes: "Who?" "When?" "Where?" Even then the reader of these interviews will come across stray images and be hard pressed to fit them into the context. Competence in recounting narrative generally is accompanied by competence in making understandable departures from the narrative itself, and, lacking both skills, some lower-class respondents gave quite baffling and unintelligible reports. The best accounts are moderately clear, although subject to all the limitations already discussed.

Discussion

Only if the situation in which the respondent spoke is carefully taken into account will we be on safe ground in interpreting class differences. Consider, first, the probable meaning of the interview for the middle-class respondents. Although the interviewer is a stranger, an outsider, he is a well-spoken, educated person. He is seeking information on behalf of some organization, hence his questioning not only has sanction but sets the stage for both a certain freedom of speech and an obligation to give fairly full information. The respondent may never before have been interviewed by a research organization, but he has often talked lengthily, fairly freeely, and responsibly to organizational representatives. At the very least he has had some experience in talking to educated strangers. We may also suppose that the middle-class style of living often compels him to be very careful not to be misunderstood. So he becomes relatively sensitive to communication *per se* and to communication with others who may not exactly share his viewpoints or frames of reference.

Communication with such an audience requires alertness, no less to the meanings of one's own speech than to the possible intent of the other's. Role-taking may be inaccurate, often, but it is markedly active. Assessing and anticipating reactions to what he has said or is about to say, the individual develops flexible and ingenious ways of correcting, qualifying, making more plausible, explaining, rephrasing—in short, he assumes multiple perspectives and communicates in terms of them. A variety of perspectives implies a variety of ways of ordering or framing detail. Moreover, he is able to classify and to relate classes explicitly, which is but another way of saying that he is educated to assume multiple perspectives of rather wide scope.

It would certainly be too much to claim that middle-class persons always react so sensitively. Communication is often routinized, and much of it transpires between and among those who know each other so well or share so much in common that they need not be subtle. Nor is sensitive role-taking called forth in so-called "expressive behavior," as when hurling invective or yelling during a ball game. With the proviso that much middle-class speech is uttered under such conditions, it seems safe enough to say that people of this stratum can, if required, handle the more complex and consciously organized discourse. In addition to skill and perspicacity, this kind of discourse requires a person who can subtly keep a listener at a distance while yet keeping him in some degree informed.

Consider now, even at risk of overstating the case, how the interview appears to the lower group. The interviewer is of higher social class than the respondent, so that the interview is a "conversation between the classes." It is entirely probable that more effort and ability are demanded by cross-class conversation of this sort than between middle-class respondent and middle-class interviewer.[7] It is not surprising that the interviewer is often baffled and that the respondent frequently misinterprets what is wanted. But misunderstanding and misinterpretation are only part of the story.

Cross-class communication, while not rare, probably is fairly formalized or routinized. The communicants know the ritual steps by heart, and can assume much in the way of supporting context for phrase and gesture. The lower-class person in these Arkansas towns infrequently meets a middle-class person in a situation anything like the interview. Here he must talk at great length to a stranger about personal experiences, as well as recall for his listener a tremendous number of details. Presumably he is accustomed to talking about such matters and in such detail only to listeners with whom he shares a great deal of experience and symbolism, so that he need not be very self-conscious about communicative technique. He can, as a rule, safely assume that words, phrases, and gestures are assigned approximately similar meanings by his listeners. But this is not so in the interview or, indeed, in any situation where class converses with class in nontraditional modes.

There still remains the question of whether the descriptions of perceptions and experiences given by the lower-class respondent are merely inadequate or whether this is the way he truly saw and experienced. Does his speech accurately reflect customary "concrete" modes of thought and perception, or is it that he perceives in abstract and classificatory terms, and from multiple perspectives, but is unable to convey his perceptions? [8] Unless one assumes that, when talking in familiar vein to familiar audiences, speech and gesture incorporate multiple perspectives, which is, as we have already indicated, improbable, one concludes that speech does in some sense reflect thought. The reader is perhaps best left at this point to draw his own conclusions, although we shall press upon him certain additional evidence and interpretation arising from examination of the interviews.

In any situation calling for a description of human activities it is necessary to utilize motivational terminology, either explicitly or implicitly, in the very namings of acts.[9] In the speech of those who recognize few disparities of imagery between themselves and their listeners, explicit motivational terms are sparse. The frequent use among the lower class of the expression "of course" followed by something like "They went up to see about their folks" implies that it is almost needless to say what "they" did, much less to give the reason for the act. The motive ("to see about") is implicit and terminal, requiring neither elaboration nor explanation. Where motives are explicit ("They was needin' help, so we went on up there"), they are often gratuitous and could just as well have been omitted. All this is related to preceding discussions of single centering and assumed correspondence of imagery. To the speaker it was quite clear why people did what they did. There was no need to question or elaborate on the grounds for acts. Under probing the respondent did very little better: he used motivational terms but within a quite narrow range. The terms he used ordinarily reflected kinship obligations, concern for property, humanitarian ("help") sentiments, and action from motives of curiosity ("We went down to see"). Such a phrase as "I suppose I went to her house because I wanted reassurance" would rarely occur.

Middle-class persons exhibit familiarity with a host of distinct "reasons" for performing particular acts. Their richness in thinking allows activities to be defined and described in a great variety of ways. Here, indeed, is an instrument for breaking down diffuse images ("They was runnin' all over") into classes of acts and events. The middle-class person is able to do this, for one thing, because he possesses an abstract motivational terminology. Then, too, the fine and subtle distinctions for rationalizing behavior require devices for insuring that they will be grasped by the hearer. In a real sense the need to explain behavior can be linked with the need to communicate well—to give a rational account as well as to be objective. Hence, there is a constant flow of qualifying and generalizing terms linked with motivational phraseology ("I don't know why, but it could be he felt there was no alternative . . .").

It is not surprising to find the middle class as familiar with elements of social structure as with individual behavior. Assuredly, this familiarity rests not only upon contact with institutions but upon the capacity to perceive and talk about abstract classes of acts. The lower-class person, on the other hand, appears to have only rudimentary notions of organizational structure—at least of relief and emergency agencies. Extended contact with representatives of them, no doubt, would familiarize him not only with organizations but with thinking in organizational, or abstract, terms. The propensity of the lower class to state concretely the activities of relief organizations corroborates the observation of Warner that the lowest strata have little knowledge or "feel" for the social structures of their communities.[10] It also suggests the difficulty of conveying to them relatively abstract information through formal media of communication.

It may be that rural townspeople of the lower class are not typical of the national or urban low strata. This raises the question—vital to urban sociology but to which currently there is no adequate answer—of whether pockets of rural-minded folk cannot live encapsulated in the city [11] and, indeed, whether lower-class persons have much opportunity to absorb middle-class culture without themselves beginning the route upward, those remaining behind remaining less urban.[12]

Notes

[1] The writers are greatly indebted to the National Opinion Research Center in Chicago, which allowed them to use data gathered during a study of responses to disaster. The disaster occurred as the result of a tornado which swept through several small Arkansas towns and adjacent rural areas.

[2] Cf. E. Cassirer, *An Essay on Man* (New Haven, 1944); S. Langer, *Philosophy in a New Key* (New York, 1948); A. R. Lindesmith and A. L. Strauss, *Social Psychology* (New York, 1949), pp. 237–52; G. Mead, *Mind, Self, and Society* (Chicago, 1934); C. W. Mills, "Language, Logic, and Culture," *American Sociological Review,* IV (1939), 670–80.

[3] Each document was scrutinized by both authors, and comprehensive notes were taken to help establish categories descriptive of the communicative style and devices of each respondent. From these notes profiles of respondents were constructed. From the notes and case profiles, there emerged the separate profiles for lower and upper groups that will be described. We had expected to code the documents to bring out the degree of overlap between groups, but it turned out that there was literally no overlap; nevertheless, each reader coded separately as he went along. Agreement upon coding scores between readers was virtually perfect.

[4] Cf. J. Piaget, *The Psychology of Intelligence* (London, 1950). See also a suggestive treatment of inadequate thinking analyzed in terms of centering in Max Wertheimer, *Productive Thinking* (New York, 1945), pp. 135–47.

[5] For a good discussion of this see B. Malinowski, "The Problem of Meaning in Primitive Language," in *Magic, Science and Religion and Other Essays* (Boston, 1948), pp. 228–76.

[6] Our discussion of objectivity and of mediation between self and image in communication is reminiscent of some of the literature on child, schizophrenic, and aphasic thought.

[7] Somewhat like this is the I.Q. testing session which involves a middle-class test (and tester) and a lower-class subject. The many and subtle difficulties in this situation are analyzed by Allison Davis in *Social Class Influences upon Learning* (Cambridge, Mass., 1951).

[8] "The lower class is even more concrete in its outlook than the lower-middle class. For example, a question . . . where chewing gum is usually purchased will be answered by an upper-middle person: 'At a cashier's counter or in a grocery store.' By the lower-middle: 'At the National or the corner drugstore.' By the lower class: 'From Tony' " ("Marketing Chewing Gum in New England: A Research Study" [Chicago: Social Research, Inc., 1950]).

[9] Cf. K. Burke, *Grammar of Motives* (New York, 1945).

10 W. L. Warner, *American Life: Dream and Reality* (Chicago: University of Chicago Press, 1953), pp. 193–94.

11 David Riesman, "Urbanity and the Urban Personality," in *Proceedings of the Fourth Annual Symposium, The Human Development Bulletin* (Chicago: University of Chicago, 1953), p. 37.

12 William Henry, of the University of Chicago, has conveyed his impression to us that urban lower-class and middle-class people perform on Thematic Apperception Tests much as our Arkansas respondents did in the interview.

We have also examined interviews about disasters in Brighton, N.Y., a middle-class suburb of Rochester, and Elizabeth, N.J., an urban community near New York City. There are no observable differences between the middle-class respondents of these areas and those of Arkansas. Four interviews with Elizabeth lower-class respondents paralleled the modes of the Arkansas lower class. A fifth exhibited considerable middle-class characteristics.

The Working-Class Woman's Perception of Herself in the World

LEE RAINWATER, RICHARD P. COLEMAN, AND GERALD HANDEL

The starting point of sociological investigation is accurate and adequate description. Rainwater, Coleman, and Handel contribute to our understanding by describing the typical outlook of the American working-class wife. Their data are based on responses to open-ended questions and stories which the housewife subjects made up about the TAT (Thematic Apperception Test) pictures which they were shown.

The working-class woman perceives the world as vast, unfamiliar, and overpowering. Most of this world is seen as outside of her own life —with family and neighborhood constituting, for the most part, her area of experience and understanding. She lacks an organized view of the broader reality and perceives it as unsettling and "potentially catastrophic." Another aspect of this perspective is a pervasive anxiety over possible physical and emotional loss. The authors contrast the working-class women's responses to a TAT picture with those of middle-class women to highlight differences in outlook on this issue. Allied with this phenomenon is the working-class wives' fear of loneliness—again exemplified by their stories about a TAT picture. In each story the possible loss of husband or boyfriend is discussed. Other aspects of the working-class wife's perspective are also presented.

SPECIFIC actions and feelings in any area of life are in one way or another related to the basic guidelines of personality. These refer to *the way in which the person places himself in relation to the world*. The aggressive businessman, for example, often sees the world in terms of the possibilities it offers for expanding and improving his operations. For him, the world consists of resources that he can bring together into a combination that suits his aims and through which he can exert an impact. He sees the external world as amenable to his manipulation. He can see that through his efforts he can change some segment of reality. To take another example, the painter or poet is likely to be more interested in developing and perfecting his perception and understanding of the external world than in manipulating it. For him the external world consists of interesting things to observe, to think about, and portray artistically. For both the businessman and the artist, their own aims and intentions are of at least as much weight and significance as the properties of the world around them.

A central characteristic of the working-class wife is her underlying conviction that most significant action originates from the world external to herself rather than from within herself. For her, the world is largely unchangeable, a kind of massive, immovable apparatus that is simply there. When some feature of it approaches her she responds to it. While not all of these women think of themselves self-consciously as "little" people, a great many of them do and say so. This is well illustrated in the statements which many made in response to the question: "Are you a member of any clubs or other organization?" Some of them say:

> I'm not in any clubs because I don't know anyone who belongs to introduce me.
> I haven't been asked to join any club.
> I'm just not the type to get out and meet people easily.
> I'm not very social myself. I'm too shy and reserved.
> I'm the backward type and I don't like to mix a lot.
> I don't think I'd be very good at it. I'm too self-conscious.
> I've never been asked. Nobody ever talked to me about anything.
> I'd like to join, but I will wait until I'm asked. I'd like to have some place to go.
> No one has ever invited me to join. I'd like to join, but nobody up here bothers with me.
> They don't interest me at all. I'm just an ordinary person, and could never take part in anything and I could never belong. People scare me, and I was always shy even when I went to school.
> I'm just a common ole girl.
> You have to have an interest and I'm no pusher. I like to be told what to do.

In these comments, the women express a certain internal immobility and a *reliance upon the outer world coming to them in terms that are specific, clearly defined, and readily understood.* Lacking such presented stimulation, they do not know how to go about taking suitable action in unfamiliar areas. They do not know where or how to begin. They require, indeed crave, explicit guidance. They feel grateful when it is provided in a form they can use. Without it, they feel self-conscious, painfully conspicuous, and quite uncertain.

This feeling of smallness before the world is not restricted to a specific context, but is pervasive in their outlook. The working-class woman's education and upbringing have acquainted her with a relatively small segment of the world. She knows what is close to home. The rest of the world is not furnished with signs, markers, and guidelines. Consequently, whenever it impinges on her life she is likely to feel that it is at best unsettling. She does not know what governs events and people beyond her ken. With such a meager chart, *she tends to see the world beyond her doorstep and neighborhood as fairly chaotic, and potentially catastrophic.*

She feels she has little ability to influence the larger forces and events which affect her life. She cannot provide for herself an organized view that would help her orient herself in the context of larger happenings around her. In comparison with the middle-class wife, *reality is, in its ordinary presentation to her, flat, unvarnished, and not highly differentiated.*

She would like things to go nicely and smoothly, and her everyday life may often approach such stability, though at the same time, it often feels dull and not adequately rewarding.

A sense of dullness, as well as hope for escape from it, is communicated in these stories to a picture of a young woman who sits with her chin in her hand looking off into space.

> It looks like a mother after a hard day's work. She isn't quite done and wondering what to do next. It is the story of motherhood. There is no outcome. The work just goes on.
>
> This reminds me of a mother after a hard day with the kids. Thinking what's going to happen next, and wondering how she can make them behave better.
>
> Probably a mother that has been working all day. Been wondering about meals, washing, ironing, and just sat down for a rest before starting in again. There is no end. Just work.
>
> Oh, this one. A woman with a large family. Of moderate means. She's just sent her children off to school. She is probably sitting there thinking of all she has to do today. And that's the end of it. (Did she get it done?) Like most women, there's always more to do tomorrow.

Yet always lurking nearby are potential threats. *The working-class wife's outlook is shaded by a fairly pervasive anxiety over possible fundamental deprivations.* She is anxious about her physical safety, stability of affection, dependable income. She sometimes lives in neighborhoods where violence is common, where physical fights between husbands and wives are not unknown, and where tavern brawls are even more frequent. Whether or not she has ever witnessed or been party to such occurrences, she knows about them and knows that they may take place close by. She knows, too, the threat of curtailed income, the loss of dependable funds for necessities through layoffs, strikes, reductions in the hours of work. These are things she knows *may* happen. They may come upon her with no advance warning, the result of larger forces which she has little ability to influence or control. None of these dire events may actually have happened to her, but they are a sufficiently close part of her environment to seem real.

The nature of her anxiety may be illustrated by presenting some stories told to a picture of a little girl sitting in the doorway of a cabin. There are no other details in the picture, so that whatever respondents add to this elementary description is contributed from their own personalities. Experience has taught us that most of the stories told to this picture will be somewhat depressed in tone, so that we do not conclude simply from that fact that the storyteller is deeply concerned. The discriminating features will be pointed out below.

> Looks as though her home is not a very nice one. She looks as though nobody has anything to do with her. Trying to think what she can do to make other kids like her, and what the folks could do to help the place so folks would not think they are so poor. She will get other kids to like her and things will turn out all right.
>
> Looks like a lonely little girl, sitting at the doorway watching for somebody. It looks as if her family have gone away and left her. Well, the somebody who cares for her is not going to show up.

From a picture of a solitary girl, these women conclude that she has been actively rejected, pushed aside, or left behind. This type of story does not appear in the stories from middle-class women. To be sure, they see the girl in a forlorn situation. For example:

> A poor child all by herself. Living conditions don't seem to be too good. Left with too much time, no playmates, nothing to occupy her mind. Could lead to a great deal of trouble. Looks as if the child needs someone to love it and protect it.

This woman construes the situation negatively, as do the working-class women. Her story differs, however, in at least three significant respects:

1. The working-class women identify more completely with the depicted girl than does the middle-class woman. Both of the working-class stories are told almost entirely from the point of view of the little girl, giving her feelings and confining themselves to a description of her situation *vis-à-vis* those who ignore her. The middle-class woman shows more distance from this situation; she steps outside the framework of the girl and gives her own comments upon this situation less in terms of personal relevance than in terms of relevance to an impersonal generalized principle, i.e., idle and solitary children often get into trouble. Thus, she can step back and see this as a meaningful human situation, yet not one which is so directly related to her own life.

2. The middle-class woman does not impute an experience of active rejection, as do the working-class women, suggesting that she does not construe the world in such bruising terms as do the latter.

3. Finally, the middle-class woman proposes a reasonable remedy to the situation. The story of the first working-class woman does indeed indicate a happy ending, but with no indication as to how it is brought about in view of the initial situation she states. It is entirely wishful.

The first working-class woman does give evidence of active effort to cope with her situation. In fact, as we shall point out in greater detail below, many such women show a determination to make their world more satisfactory. However, as illustrated in this particular story, they encounter some difficulty in thinking of specific ways to achieve their resolves.

One further story, this from an upper-middle-class woman, will illustrate how a person relatively free from anxiety can deal with this picture of a solitary girl:

> This is a girl at a summer camp. She sees chipmunks and squirrels near the door and she is sitting real still so as not to frighten them away. If she watches long enough, they will come up and take some food from her.

Not only does she see the log cabin as part of a summer camp instead of as a deprived home (either interpretation is reasonable in view of what is actually depicted) but she is also able to see the girl as being giving—feeding animals, instead of seeing her as deprived. Furthermore, the girl is seen as entirely in control of her own behavior; she is sitting there because she wants to, is able to regulate her conduct in line with her self-chosen aim. The behavior imputed to the girl is realistic and specific in the light of her aim.

In sum, it is not necessary to respond to a picture of a solitary girl sitting in a rude cabin with a story of deprivation and rejection. Nor, if deprivation is seen, is it necessary to respond so directly and immediately as though it related to one's own life. The working-class women tend overwhelmingly to respond to the picture in the latter fashion—reflecting their concerns. The middle-class women tend to show much greater freedom from such concerns.[1] The differences between the working-class women and upper-middle-class women are generally greater than the differences between the former and lower-middle-class women. This is true not only in the area of personality just discussed, but overall.

We have pointed out that the working-class wife is heavily reliant on the external world as it presents itself to her, and that this means further that she is reliant upon her immediate environment. The immediate environment is the source of the stimulation she can respond to and cope with; beyond it lies what is for her an unknown and uncharted realm.

The most important elements in her world are the people in her family. This, of course, is largely true for the middle-class wife as well. But the working-class wife, so overwhelmingly bound up in them, with few significant connections to anything beyond, is faced with the problem of what her life would be like if anything should happen to her family. And we find that *among the working-class wives loneliness is widely feared.* Though it is not necessarily in the forefront of their minds, it looms as a disquieting possibility. This insecurity regarding the stability and dependability of ties to others can be illustrated by these stories to a picture of a young woman standing with downcast head, her face covered with her right hand. Her left is stretched forward against a door.

This looks like there might have been a quarrel between her and her husband. It looks like she's pretty depressed by it. I get the feeling of—wonder if he'll come back or is he definitely gone. Doesn't look like a case of family grief for there would be others around her. It's a quarrel between the two, I guess. She's waiting at the door wondering if he's coming back in, or the door is closed definitely.

Looks like a woman just got some bad news. Maybe her husband left her or died or went away. She's beside herself and heartbroken. She will just have to go on, that's all.

She's crying because her husband left her with two kids. Another woman, yeah, it's another woman. He's no good, anyway. This woman got a divorce in the end. He drank took much—too many times—too often.

That, I don't know. Unless something has happened. Maybe she lost her father. Or her mother. Or her husband. Some sorrow. I don't know how it will come out. You got to look—let it work out for them. That is best.

This one looks like she's been hurt or something. Some tragedy or something and she's crying. Either that or she's just had a fight with her boyfriend. She may have been out on a date and talked to some other boy and her boyfriend didn't like it. (How come out?) Oh, she'll probably make up with him and they'll get along fine until the next time. Could have been a lot of things.

Further evidence of their fear of loneliness and of their desire to remain close to people comes from a projective question in which we asked our respondents to tell us what they would most and least like to be turned into if a magician were to change them into something other than a human being. The most common type of working-class response was along these lines:

> A dog, because it is so faithful.
> A French poodle, it's well fed, brushed and people pet it.
> A house bird because of the love people give it.
> The bed my children lay on so I could still be close to them.
> A house, so I could watch people's lives and be close to home.
> A fairy, so I could watch over the kids and other people.

Two-thirds of the working-class women gave responses which indicate a desire to continue to be with people, to nurture them, to be nurtured by them, or to have power over them. Only one-third of the middle-class women gave such responses. Instead, they were more likely to give responses which represent a desire to escape,[2] or simply for contentment all by one's self:

> A bird because it can fly wherever it wants and see the world.
> A cloud because it is so light and frothy and free.
> A cow so I could just lie around and eat grass.
> A flower that blooms for years.

The middle-class women are able to use this chance to fantasy about what they might otherwise be, and often think only of themselves in such a fantasy. The working-class women still prefer to see themselves closely tied to people and they don't so often want to "get away from it all."

In the life of the working-class wife, the ties that matter can be disrupted for little reasons and for big. Disruption can be final because of death or desertion—or repetitive because of recurrent jealousy or friction. The stories cited (and dozens of similar ones in our data) indicate something of the potentiality for disorganization that hovers close to the lives of these women. This is perhaps nowhere better expressed than in this story to the card depicting the woman with downcast head:

> Oh my I tell you, it reminds me of when I was goin' to have my baby. I didn't know what to do. I was gettin' myself ready, and my two boys ready. And I didn't know what to do. It reminds me of myself. My husband's father was dyin', and he was gone, and I was tryin' to get my uncle.

Looking at the working-class wife's life in terms of her central concerns, we find that *her life has a somewhat elemental character.* Her central concerns are close to the most basic human events: birth, illness, accomplishing the tasks and chores of daily life. Everybody has these concerns to some extent, but they tend to be much more central for the working-class woman than they do for middle-class women and, more generally, women of higher social status.

The personalities of the working-class women tend to be relatively less developed and elaborated, and hence, less involved with more "civilized" concerns such as group life and its ramifications. Their aims and interests tend to be closer to home, less far flung, and to have fewer points of anchorage. Their energy goes into maintaining life and improving it within the framework that is taken for granted, rather than altering the framework.

The life of the working-class wife is characterized by much uncertainty. Though her life is fairly circumscribed, and seems to her often routine and dull, she nonetheless has a sense of uncertainty. This partly derives from the fact that most of her energy goes into day-to-day living. She does not have, or make use of, large time perspectives that give her a sense of on-goingness and a sense of moving through life on an assured course. This shows up, among other ways, in the fairly marked tendency not to give endings to thematic apperception stories, except when pushed by the interviewer, and often not even then. This reflects the uncertainty of these women as a group. They can look at a picture and propose what might be going on, but they do not know how it might come out. At the same time, they do wish to follow the rules set down by the interviewer on the form of story to be told, and they do wish things to work out smoothly and pleasantly. Often, therefore, they attempt to meet both of these requirements by saying simply that everything will work out all right.

The evidence indicates that working-class wives do indeed lead difficult lives. As a group, they tend to find the world an uncomfortable and rather trying place. This is in contrast to other groups of American women we have studied.

However, it would be misleading to suggest that their lives are nothing but hardship and distress. They certainly find occasions for enjoyment and there are situations which give pleasure. This, however, is not the prevailing tone of their lives, but rather a somewhat mitigating circumstance. As we shall point out in more detail in the next section of this chapter, these women have a capacity for accepting a great deal that comes their way. But this acceptance is not the same as genuine contentment or deep satisfaction with their lot.

Notes

[1] To obviate possible misunderstanding, it should be noted that no interpretation rests only on stories presented illustratively, or, in fact, on stories only to one card. Within the compass of this report, it will not be possible always to present detailed story analyses as in this instance. The reader will be able to appraise later illustrative stories in terms of the interpretive procedure exemplified above.

[2] For a discussion of spatial symbolism, see Chapter III, "The Lansons: Equanimity and Its Vicissitudes," in Hess, Robert D. and Handel, Gerald, *Family Worlds,* Chicago: University of Chicago Press, 1959.

Ideological Beliefs about the Distribution of Power in the United States *

WILLIAM H. FORM AND JOAN HUBER RYTINA

Form and Rytina state that an ideology describes how things are (existing beliefs) and how they ought to be (normative beliefs). They circumscribe this rather broad definition by dealing with only one facet of American political ideology—beliefs about political pluralism in this country. Class differences in such beliefs are seen as an important factor in change within the political structure. The authors use income as the most precise and direct indicator of position in the American stratification system. A community study in Muskegon, Michigan, with a sample of 354 respondents provided the data for this study.

    The respondents were asked to choose which of three descriptions —political pluralism, power elite, or big business control—best described the distribution of national power. In each income group, about 60 percent chose the political pluralism model indicating that there is not an overriding consensus in the existing political ideology. In response to the question of what the distribution of power ought to be, however, the rich were least inclined to offer the political pluralism approach. Form and Rytina indicate that those with higher incomes have the least consistent political ideology. Their own study and their reading of others leads them to consider the possibility of "upper-class authoritarianism."

    * We are very grateful to John Pease for a critical reading of the manuscript and for his many suggestions to improve it. The material in this project was prepared under a Grant from the Office of Manpower Policy, Evaluation, and Research, U.S. Department of Labor, under the authority of Title I of the Manpower Development and Training Act of 1962. Researchers undertaking such projects under Government sponsorship are encouraged to express freely their professional judgment. Therefore, points of view or opinions stated in this document do not necessarily represent the official position or policy of the Department of Labor. We are grateful for the Department's support through Grant No. 91-24-66-45.

    Reprinted from the *American Sociological Review*, Vol. 34, No. 1, February, 1969, pp. 19–30, by permission of the authors and the American Sociological Association.

Introduction

STRATIFICATION systems perpetuate inequalities which are maintained by a wide variety of mechanisms. Whatever mechanism is used, every system of stratification develops an ideology to legitimize or justify its presence and persistence. Ideologies presumably describe the world as it is and as it ought to be. In stable societies, where there is little organized opposition to the system of inequalities, existential and normative statements in the ideology are similar and symmetrical, and one ideology predominates. That is, what ought to be, is, and what is, ought to be.

Obviously variations may exist in the symmetry between normative and existential beliefs about a stratification system. Members of some classes may insist that a high symmetry exists, while others may insist that asymmetry is typical. Such situations are potentially revolutionary because some classes may try to restore symmetry either by changing beliefs or conditions, so that existential and normative conceptions in the ideology will be more convergent. Longitudinal studies of ideologies may help us forecast changes which will occur in the stratification system. The present concerns with race and poverty in the United States suggest a situation where normative and existential beliefs of the ideology are in a state of asymmetry. This study explores possible asymmetry in a community situation.

Since an ideology explains and vindicates the unequal distribution of rewards in a society, it follows that those who are the most favored recipients of the rewards support the ideology most fervently and make strongest claims for the convergence of its normative and existential tenets. The "success" of an ideology is measured by the extent that the less favored, if they support the normative aspects, also agree on the convergence.

Rewards in a pecuniary-market society are best measured in monetary terms. In the long run, power and status are converted to income rewards.[1] Yet sociologists have shown little inclination to deal with this stratification variable, preferring less precise variables such as occupation, education, and prestige. It seems appropriate to use annual income as a chief indicator of position in a stratification system since it is the chief reward of that system in the American instance. The purpose of this study is to explore how rich, middle-income, and poor people in a Midwestern, middle-sized city appraise the power tenets of American ideology.

The persistence of any particular allocation of rewards depends upon the distribution of power, or the political structure of the society. The power which maintains the system may be so legitimate, so authoritative, so ubiquitous, and so invisible that it may not be recognized as power. Sociologists are wont to call this type of power "social control." Such mechanisms predominate in a "traditional" stratification system. In a changing industrial society, the political mechanisms which sustain the economic and social structures of inequality become more visible. Politics becomes the means to maintain or change the allocative mechanisms of the society.

The Problem

Therefore what people believe about the political underpinnings of a stratification system is important especially in a relatively "open" society. The purpose of this study is to examine such beliefs from a stratification perspective. The choice of specific political beliefs for study was necessarily arbitrary. We selected beliefs related to democratic mechanisms of *political pluralism* as the major area for investigation. We define a political system as pluralistic when a variety of groups can influence policy in such a way that no single or no small number of groups can control it or, conversely, when all legitimate interest groups have an appreciable share of influence. We made three assumptions: First, people believe that political pluralism is the mechanism which *maintains* an open stratification system. Second, belief in the existence of political pluralism is essentially a belief in the viability of an open opportunity structure; and conversely, a denial of the existence of political pluralism as a system is a rejection of the belief that the ideology of an open stratification society is realized. Third, adherents of political pluralism should, logically, believe that political and governmental actions are necessary to redress any "temporary imbalances," injustices, or inequalities in the opportunity structure of the society.

Since an ideology legitimizes and vindicates a stratification system and therefore a power distribution in a given social order, we propose the following. First, since there are wide differences in distribution of rewards in American society, there will be no overriding consensus among different income strata in the belief that political pluralism accurately describes the distribution of power in the United States. Second, the higher their income, the greater the tendency for people to believe that the dominant ideology of political pluralism more or less accurately describes the way the system really works and, as a corollary, the lower their income, the less symmetry they see between normative and existential aspects of the ideology of political pluralism. Third, the lower their income, the greater the tendency for people to believe that political pluralism *should* be realized by the federal government, acting to restore inequalities produced by the system. Conversely, the higher their income the greater the insistence that government should not act to equalize opportunities. In terms of our frame of reference, higher income groups equate normative and existential statements about political pluralism, while lower income groups tend to deny their symmetry and thus support action to make them more credible. People in all income strata modify or adjust their beliefs about the operation of the political system in accord with their perceived interests.

Together, these hypotheses go beyond the observations commonly found in the literature stating that the poor, less educated and alienated masses reject democratic (pluralistic) philosophy because they do not understand it, feel politically ineffective, and have authoritarian inclinations. (See Kornhauser, 1959; Lipset, 1960; Riesman, 1953; Scheler, 1961; and Milbrath, 1965.) The position taken in this research is that although the rich and better educated express more formal allegiance to the democratic creed of pluralism, like the poor, they do not understand it, nor do they apply it consistently. The authoritarianism of the poor is matched by an authoritarianism of the rich. Both rich and poor *selectively* respond to the ideology of pluralism and adhere to different elements which give support to their situation or aspirations.

The first part of this study focuses on beliefs concerning the actual operation of the political system, and the second part on beliefs about possible changes in the system.

Research Site

The site of the study was Muskegon, Michigan, an industrial community where the Standard Metropolitan Statistical Area (SMSA) population in 1960 was 149,943. Its economy is built principally around metals manufacturing, which is sensitive to fluctuations in economic conditions. According to the 1960 Census, about three-fifths of the labor force were manual workers and about half were employed in manufacturing. Median family income was $6,048, compared to $6,324 for metropolitan areas in the United States (U.S. Census: 1960). Approximately 10 percent of the population were Negro.

The respondents interviewed in this research were heads of households or their spouses who lived in the area included in *Polk's City Directory, 1965*, roughly the Muskegon SMSA. For the larger study, of which this was a part, a systematic sample (N = 186) was drawn. Because such samples typically include few people at income extremes, we drew supplementary samples of rich and poor respondents. They were defined as "rich" if the annual family income was $25,000 or more, which, in the 1960 Census, was the top 1 percent of the income distribution. "Poor" was defined in terms of a scale adjusted for the number of dependents, ranging from less than $2,000 for any number of dependents to $6,000 for eleven or more persons.

The data reported here are based upon an analytic sample (N = 354; the systematic sample, plus the rich and poor samples) which included 37 poor Negroes, 70 poor whites, 48 middle-income Negroes, 152 middle-income whites, and 47 rich whites. The per capita income by households for these categories formed a "scale," the Negroes having lower incomes than the whites, for both poor and middle-income categories.[2] The sex distribution was approximately even in each of these categories. Education was associated with income: three-fifths of the respondents with 0–7 years of education were poor, and three-fifths of college graduates were rich. Although the primary independent variable of this study is income, the data will also be presented by race because recent events indicate that Negroes may have a singular view on political questions. Some responses are also shown in terms of highest grade of education completed. The research design did not justify the use of multivariate analysis; we did control for education but the small number of cases made interpretation risky.

Three Modes of Power Distribution

The main tenet of American political ideology examined here is the idea that power at the national level is distributed pluralistically. Some students of power have concluded that "the struggle for power is largely confined to struggles between the business and government sectors" (D'Antonio and Ehrlich, 1961:147). In this study, respondents were asked to consider only interest groups, not the governmental share in the distribution of power.[3]

The first research problem concerned the respondent's beliefs about the distribution of political power in the country. Two different types of questions were used because of the difficulty in survey research of framing questions that do not differentially elicit a particular response. One type of question suggested implicitly that the distribution of power was in accord with the dominant political ideology of political pluralism, and another suggested implicitly that it was not. At one point in the interview the respondent was read three statements, each purportedly describing a different model of distribution of power in this country, and asked to select what in his opinion was the most accurate description, thus suggesting that one of the descriptions was realistic. At another point in the interview the respondent was given a list of twelve interest groups and asked which one had the most influence over the way things were run in Washington, suggesting that one group was dominant. He was then asked which of these groups was least powerful, and last, which ought to be most powerful.

The three statements describing the distribution of power purportedly represent the positions of David Riesman (political pluralism), C. Wright Mills (the power elite), and the Marxists (big business control).[4] The order in which the three statements were read was rotated in each interview, and the respondent was not advised of their sources. The three statements were presented in this form:

> (Riesman) No one group really runs the government in this country. Instead, important decisions about national policy are made by a lot of different groups such as labor, business, religious, and educational groups, and so on.

These groups influence both political parties, but no single group can dictate to the others, and each group is strong enough to protect its own interests.

(Mills) A small group of men at the top really run the government in this country. These are the heads of the biggest business corporations, the highest officers in the Army, Navy, and Air Force, and a few important senators, congressmen and federal officials in Washington. These men dominate both the Republican and Democratic Parties.

(Marx) Big businessmen really run the government in this country. The heads of the large corporations dominate both the Republican and Democratic Parties. This means that things in Washington go pretty much the way big businessmen want them to.

Table 1—Selection of Societal Models of Power Distribution, by Income and Race (Percents)

MODELS OF POWER DISTRIBUTION

Income	Race	Marx (Economic Dominance)	Mills (Elitist)	Riesman (Pluralistic)	TOTAL %	(N)
Poor	Negro	33	6	61	100	(36)
	White	23	22	55	100	(64)
Middle	Negro	40	16	44	100	(45)
	White	17	20	63	100	(143)
Rich	White	12	23	65	100	(43)
Total, analytic sample	%	22	19	59	100	
	(N)	(74)	(62)	(195)		(331)
Total, systematic sample *	%	18	19	63	100	
	(N)	(32)	(33)	(109)		(174)

* For poor vs. middle and rich, $\chi^2 = 1.80$, d.f. $= 2$, P $= <.50$.
For Negro vs. white, $\chi^2 = 13.08$, d.f. $= 2$, P $= <.01$.

Data in Table 1 reveal that three-fifths of the respondents selected Riesman's model of political pluralism; about one-fifth selected Marx; and one-fifth, Mills. Although pluralism is selected more frequently as the dominant model of political control, the percentage does not represent overwhelming consensus.[5]

Differences in support of the pluralistic model by the income groups are relatively small, although they run in the predicted direction; i.e., the poor and Negroes see less existent pluralism. Although the Mills and the Marx descriptions were selected about equally, Negroes were much more likely to select the Marxian description, while whites were more likely to choose the Millsian position.

Table 2—Selection of Societal Models of Power Distribution, by Years of Education Percents)

MODELS OF POWER DISTRIBUTION

Years of Education		Marx (Economic Dominance)	Mills (Elitist)	Riesman (Pluralistic)	TOTAL %	(N)
0–7		40	26	33	99	(42)
8–11		28	16	57	101	(141)
12–15		14	19	67	100	(108)
16 or more		8	20	73	101	(40)
Total, analytic sample	%	22	19	59	100	
	(N)	(74)	(62)	(195)		(331)
Total, systematic sample *	%	18	19	63	100	
	(N)	(32)	(33)	(109)		(174)

* $\chi^2 = 11.46$, d.f. $= 6$, P $= .10$, when grades 12–15 and 16 years and above are combined.

Perhaps beliefs about power distribution are more affected by years of education than by income. Data in Table 2 show that it does; clearly, in the analytic sample, the higher the education, the greater the belief in the existence of pluralist politics. Thus, almost three-quarters of the college graduates supported the Riesman statement and two-thirds of those having fewer than eight years of schooling rejected it. The Marxist description was more strongly supported than the Millsian among those with less than a high school education.

The data in Table 2 may be explained in at least two ways. First, that since schools teach a pluralistic ideology, the more educated, who also are richer, learn to prefer it. Second, that the pluralistic scheme is more difficult to understand, and that the less educated prefer the conceptually less difficult authoritarian Millsian or Marxist view of the world. Data presented later suggest that the second interpretation should be rejected.

Interest Group Power

For the second question on power, the respondent was given a list of twelve interest groups and asked to indicate which one(s) had most influence in Washington. The interest groups listed were: Protestants, Negroes, labor unions, Jews, farmers, Catholics, big businessmen, university professors, small businessmen, rich people, poor people, and military leaders.

The intent was to include a variety of interest groups that might be considered influential in order to give the respondent a wide choice. No respondent in the 119 interviews completed by the chief interviewer questioned the assumption that some one group or groups must have most influence.

"Big businessmen" and "rich people" were presented separately although it is reasonable to suppose that all big businessmen are rich. We expected that, if respondents named one of these groups, those with higher incomes would tend to choose "big businessmen," and lower income respondents, "rich people." The choice of "rich people" is less in accord with the dominant political ideology than "big businessmen" because being rich does not imply that a man has engaged in a socially fruitful activity. The major differences among respondents occurred between whites and Negroes. Both middle-income and poor Negroes tended to choose "rich people" more often than "big businessmen." Among white respondents, the tendency to choose "big businessmen" more often than "rich people" increased with income.[6] In the subsequent analysis, these two categories are combined.

What is most striking about the response to this question is the high proportion who see "big businessmen and the rich" as most influential (see Table 3). About one-half of the respondents in both the analytic and systematic samples chose "big businessmen" or "rich people" as most influential and about 30 percent chose "labor unions." Less than one-tenth selected "military leaders," and the remaining eight interest groups were chosen by only 10 percent of the respondents. Perhaps significant is the fact that all income strata in the analytic sample saw "the rich" and "big businessmen" as most powerful with the sole exception of the rich, who selected "labor unions" as most powerful. Equally important is the observation that there was more dispersion in the selections of the lower income groups, a situation which seems to refute the alleged categorical authoritarian thinking of the lower classes (Schatzman and Strauss, 1955:329–338). Although the greater dispersion in the lower income group could be interpreted as political fragmentation, it could also be interpreted as behaving according to the norms of political pluralism.

Again, education seems related to the choice of the most powerful group (see Table 4). While the relationship of income strata to perception of "big businessmen" and "the rich" as most powerful is curvilinear, the relationship of income strata to perception of "labor unions" as most powerful is linear. That is, a greater percentage of the middle educational strata see "big businessmen" and "the rich" as most powerful. The percentage seeing "labor unions" as most powerful increases with education to the point that a majority of college graduates take this view.

Comparing the results of Tables 1 and 3 may be fruitful. Thus, although data in Table 1 show that about 60 percent of the respondents believed that "all" interest groups share power, about 75 percent of them in Table 3 focused on just two of these interest groups. This finding does not neces-

Table 3—Interest Group Selected as Most Powerful, by Income and Race (Percents)

Income	Race	Unions	Big Business and Rich	Military	All Others	Don't Know	%	TOTAL (N)
Poor	Negro	32	41	11	14	3	101	(37)
	White	14	46	10	17	12	99	(59)
Middle	Negro	17	54	13	8	8	100	(48)
	White	33	52	8	5	3	101	(150)
Rich	White	54	28	4	13	0	99	(46)
Total, analytic sample	%	30	47	9	10	5	101	
	(N)	(104)	(164)	(31)	(34)	(17)		(350)
Total, systematic sample *	%	26	52	6	10	6	100	
	(N)	(48)	(97)	(13)	(17)	(12)		(183)

* For unions vs. big business and rich vs. all others run against poor vs. middle and rich, $\chi^2 = 8.28$, d.f. = 2, P = <.02.

Table 4—Interest Group Selected as Most Powerful, by Years of Education (Percents)

Years of Education	Unions	Big Business and Rich	Military	All Others	Don't Know	%	TOTAL (N)
0–7	14	38	14	20	14	100	(49)
8–11	27	46	10	11	6	100	(145)
12–15	33	52	6	6	2	99	(113)
16 or more	53	37	5	5	0	100	(43)
Total, analytic sample %	30	47	9	10	5	101	
Total, analytic sample (N)	(104)	(164)	(31)	(34)	(17)		(350)
Total, systematic sample * %	26	52	6	10	6	100	
Total, systematic sample * (N)	(48)	(97)	(13)	(17)	(12)		(183)

* For unions vs. big business and rich vs. all others, $\chi^2 = 15.1$, d.f. = 6, P = <.02.

sarily indicate inconsistency, because respondents might have thought that "big businessmen" or "rich people" were just *slightly* more powerful than other groups, thus "big businessmen" might not necessarily be running everything. Still another interpretation might be that if the belief in political pluralism were strong enough, the question might have been rejected with such statements as "they are all the same," "it depends on the issue," etc. Nevertheless, the results of the two responses indicate that the framing of a survey question makes considerable difference in possible interpretations of the results. Given a specific choice among interest groups, the respondents seem more likely to describe the distribution of political power in somewhat more neo-Marxist terms than in pluralist terms.

Respondents were also asked which group they thought was least powerful in Washington. The results in Table 5 show that there is less consensus on who does not have power than on who does. Interestingly enough, the rich seem to have least consensus on who has least amount of power.

In Table 5, "poor people" were identified as "least influential" oftener than any other group (36 percent). They were followed by "small businessmen" (15 percent), "farmers" (12 percent), and "Negroes" (11 percent). Poor Negroes were most likely to see "poor people" as least influential (46 percent),[7] and rich whites were most likely to choose "small businessmen" as least influential (26 percent); only 20 percent of rich whites chose "poor people" as least influential.

The last question on interest groups shifted to the normative area: which group *ought* to be most influential. Pre-test results had indicated that a number of persons thought that no one interest group should be dominant; so while this response was anticipated, the interviewers were instructed not to let such a response alter their presentation of the question. The responses to this question are presented in Table 6 for income and race, and Table 7 for education. The most striking finding from Table 6 is that 44 percent of the respondents refused to be bound by the question and volunteered the normative response that "all (groups) should be equal." The rich in the sample had highest agreement on who ought to have most power, with 30 percent in the analytic sample naming "big businessmen." The effect of education, seen in Table 7, is generally to reduce variations found by race and income.

To conclude, respondents with highest income and education are most likely to think the Riesman description of the distribution of power best when they hear it, but they are least likely, left to their own devices, to think that this is the way things ought to be. Likewise, those who have the least income and education, and the least convenient skin color, are most likely to respond spontaneously that all interest groups should have equal power. This pattern contradicts some of the literature on political authoritarianism. Presumably, college graduates should be better equipped to think up a free response supporting political pluralism or democratic ideology than those with less than eight grades of education.[8]

Table 5—Interest Group Selected as Least Powerful, by Income and Race (Percents)

Income	Race	Poor	Small Business	Farmers	Negroes	Jews	University Professors	All Others	Don't Know	TOTAL	
										%	(N)
Poor	Negro	46	11	11	19	8	0	3	3	101	(37)
	White	37	11	13	6	11	1	3	17	99	(70)
Middle	Negro	35	6	19	23	4	0	2	10	99	(48)
	White	35	17	12	9	4	6	7	10	100	(151)
Rich	White	20	26	7	9	4	11	24	0	101	(46)
Total, analytic sample	%	35	15	12	11	6	4	7	9	99	
	(N)	(122)	(53)	(42)	(39)	(22)	(15)	(25)	(33)		(352)
Total, systematic sample	%	36	14	15	7	4	5	6	13	100	
	(N)	(67)	(26)	(27)	(13)	(8)	(9)	(11)	(25)		(186)

Table 6—Interest Groups Which Ought to Be Most Powerful, by Income and Race (Percents)

Income	Race	All Should Be Equal	Big Busi-nessmen	Labor Unions	All Others	Don't Know	%	TOTAL (N)
Poor	Negro	64	0	14	8	14	100	(36)
	White	43	6	6	28	17	100	(65)
Middle	Negro	47	4	9	25	15	100	(47)
	White	40	9	13	29	9	100	(149)
Rich	White	39	30	0	27	4	100	(46)
Total, analytic sample	%	44	10	9	26	11	100	
	(N)	(150)	(34)	(32)	(88)	(39)		(343)
Total, systematic sample *	%	41	8	12	29	10	100	
	(N)	(76)	(15)	(22)	(55)	(18)		(186)

* For "all should be equal" vs. all others, and poor vs. middle and rich, $\chi^2 = 30.94$, d.f. $= 1$, $P = <.001$.

Table 7—Interest Groups Which Ought to Be Most Powerful, by Years of Education (Percents)

Years of Education	All Should Be Equal	Big Businessmen	Labor Unions	All Others	Don't Know	TOTAL %	TOTAL (N)
0–7 years	52	2	4	23	19	100	(48)
8–11 years	48	4	13	22	13	100	(141)
12–15 years	38	19	10	25	8	100	(112)
16 years or more	38	14	0	41	7	100	(42)
Total, analytic sample %	44	10	9	26	11		
(N)	(150)	(34)	(32)	(88)	(39)		(343)
Total, systematic sample %	41	8	12	29	10	100	
(N)	(76)	(15)	(22)	(55)	(18)		(186)

* For "all should be equal" vs. all others combined and 12–15 years and 16 years or more combined, $\chi^2 = 7.14$, d.f. = 2, P = <.05.

Government and Opportunity Equalization

According to the dominant ideology, if a man works hard enough, he will get ahead. Getting ahead is defined as social and income mobility. To assure everyone equal opportunity to get ahead regardless of his condition at birth, free public education is provided. Other political action may be necessary (e.g., anti-trust legislation) to prevent *discrepancies* in the American creed (normative tenets) and American practice (existential tenets) from becoming fixed or structured. That is, the government must intervene when the free market and political pluralism have failed to live up to expectations.

Recent evidence suggests that there is some public recognition that the opportunity structure has not been operating according to the American Creed (see Miller and Rein, 1966). Specifically, poverty has become intergenerational, and this condition is more characteristic of Negroes than of whites. Therefore, federal intervention is needed. Three issues were selected which dealt with federal action to help the poor and Negroes: payment of regular wages to adult poor while they attend free schools to learn new skills at government expense, an evaluation of all current federal programs to help the poor, and an evaluation of federal roles in open occupancy.

The third hypothesis of this study was that, since an ideology is a vindication of a system of inequality which benefits those who receive most rewards of the system, there would be an inverse relationship between the amount of income of the respondent and his recognition that political intervention is necessary to help any particular stratum in the society achieve equality of opportunity. For the rich, the system is operating the way it "should," both in terms of distribution of rewards and in terms of its mechanisms (political pluralism). Thus, the political machine does not need repair unless it is operating against those who are receiving most rewards from the system.

Although both major political parties give verbal support to the aspirations of disadvantaged groups, the Democrats are generally thought to be more "liberal." Thus, findings on party preference may be of interest here. First, the analytic sample differed little from the systematic sample. Second, there were no poor Negro Republicans and no rich white Democrats in our samples. Among poor whites, Democrats out-numbered Republicans two to one, but among middle-income whites, the proportions were closer: 34 percent Republicans, 46 percent Democrats, 5 percent independents, and 16 percent no preference. Most of the middle-income Negroes were Democrats.

McClosky and co-workers (1960) offer some reason to doubt that among "ordinary voters" party affiliation is associated with sharp differences concerning government actions in social welfare. Thus, in a national cross-section survey the views of the Republican rank and file were found to be much closer to those of Democratic than those of Republican leaders. Differences between Republican leaders and followers are largest "on those issues which have most sharply separated New Deal-Fair Deal spokesmen from the hard core of Republican opposition—federal aid to education, redistribution of wealth through taxes on business, corporations, and the wealthy; public ownership of natural resources, public housing, regulation of business, Social Security, farm price supports, minimum wages, and trade union regulations" (McClosky, *et al.*, 1960:416).

Similar results can be inferred from a study of an affluent, lower middle class and working class community in the Boston area. Litt (1963) found that leaders in the higher income community showed more support than leaders in the other communities for pluralist beliefs, i.e., the democratic creed, politics as a process, and politics as harmonizing group conflicts. More importantly, the type of political training which high school students received corresponded with differences in support of the creed (ideology). In the poorest community the democratic creed was taught, but no stress was placed on the importance of political participation and political conflict to resolve intergroup differences. "Only in the affluent and politically vibrant community are insights into political processes and function of politics passed on to those . . . (who) will likely man those positions that involve them in influencing or making political decisions" (Litt, 1963:74).

When Muskegon respondents were asked whether the federal government should pay poor people to go to school and get apppropriate job training, the proportion who thought that the government should not do so rose sharply with income and education (see Table 8). Such action was opposed by almost eight-tenths of the rich and three-tenths of Negro poor in the analytic sample.

When asked whether the federal government had not done enough or had done too much for the poor, the proportion of respondents who thought that the government had done too much rose sharply with both income and education. Again, about seven-tenths of the rich and one-tenth of the Negro poor felt the federal government had done too much for the poor.

While open housing is not altogether an issue of economic mobility, it is an issue of racial stratification which has not been resolved by the politics of pluralism. On this issue, political intervention by the state is most highly rejected by rich whites, followed by middle-income whites. Almost all of the rich, 73 percent of the middle-income whites, and 62 percent of the poor whites reject federal intervention, while only 8 percent of both Negro strata did so.

Discussion

Empirical research on the belief systems which comprise an ideology is sorely needed to understand the dynamics of political change. A stratification approach to the study of political ideology is especially fruitful because it reveals how different strata view the mechanisms for distributing rewards

Table 8—Opposition to Federal Help for Disadvantaged Strata (Percents)

Income	Race	Government Should Not Pay Poor to Go to School (a)	Government Has Done Too Much for Poor (b)	Government Should Stay Out of Open Occupancy (c)
Poor	Negro	30	8	8
	White	46	23	62
Middle	Negro	17	15	8
	White	64	32	73
Rich	White	78	72	96
Total, analytic sample	%	52	31	57
	(N)	(350)	(351)	(344)
Total, systematic sample *	%	63	29	64
	(N)	(118)	(54)	(119)

* χ^2's by income categories and (a), (b), and (c) and their residuals are not statistically significant. For race categories and column (a) and its residual, $\chi^2 = 9.06$, d.f.= 1, P = <.01. For race categories and column (b) and its residual, $\chi^2 = 4.14$, d.f. = 1, P = <.05. For race categories and column (c) and its residual, $\chi^2 = 6.67$, d.f.= 1, P = <.01.

in a society. This study probed the verbal adherence of different income strata to the ideology of political pluralism, the mechanism which allegedly maintains an open stratification system in the United States. Although the results of the study are tenuous, certain conclusions are suggested. Perhaps the most important one is that the technique of inquiry clearly affects the observations made about ideological belief systems. Thus, when asked to select one of three general descriptive models of power distribution in the United States, respondents from different income and racial strata did not exhibit overriding consensus on political pluralism, for two-fifths of them accepted an elitist or Marxian view of the political order. Here the data tended to confirm the hypothesis that those who get most rewards from the system, namely those with higher incomes, tend more to see pluralist ideology as a good description of the way the system works.

However, a shift to other techniques of inquiry revealed a different pattern leading to the conclusion that, whatever the income or educational backgrounds of the respondents, few of them possessed a consistent or sophisticated political ideology.[9] Thus, when asked to select which interest group or groups were most powerful in the federal government, very few rejected the task on the grounds that it violated their pluralistic conception of politics. On the contrary, almost four-fifths of the respondents saw two coalitions, "the rich-big businessmen" and "labor unions," as the most powerful groups in federal politics, the poor and middle strata selecting "the rich-big businessmen," and the rich selecting the "labor unions." Some consistency was maintained in identifying the least powerful; a plurality of those at all income levels (the rich excluded) felt the poor were the least powerful.

Finally, the *ideal* of pluralism received least support from the most economically advantaged. In response to the question asking which group ought to be most powerful, the rich educated whites, less than any other category, spontaneously responded that "all interest groups should be equal." In fact, 30 percent felt that "the rich-big businessmen" ought to have most power. Their support of privileged position was maintained in exploring the question whether the federal government should take action to improve the position of the poor and of Negroes. The rich were much more likely than those in other categories to report that no action should be taken.

Although poorer income strata structured their beliefs in a somewhat different pattern, middle-income Negroes were least likely to see the model of political pluralism as an accurate description, and most likely to select the Marxian model, most likely to see the "rich-big businessmen" as most influential in politics, most likely to see Negroes as the least powerful interest group, and most highly supportive of federal action to equalize opportunities.[10] A speculative conclusion is that middle-income Negroes, with rising expectations, may become a new source of the kind of class conflict once associated with the American labor movement.

An overview of these findings suggests that the respondents whose political ideology is least consistent are those who receive most from the economic and political order. The richer and better educated more generally espouse political pluralism as a norm, but are more likely to see business dominance in politics as legitimate, and are least supportive of governmental action to equalize opportunity in the society. These observations support the growing evidence that the higher income groups clearly do not understand the principles of political pluralism, nor do they support them consistently (Prothro and Grigg, 1960:276–294). More than others, they have the most favorable attitude toward sources of power in the community; they have strongest feelings about their beliefs (Haer, 1956); they have the most outgroup antipathy; they are the most class conscious; and they are the most tightly organized to maintain privilege (Glantz, 1958:375–383). A case can be made that the syndrome amounts to an upper-class authoritarianism.

Unfortunately, the recent sociological literature dealing with stratification and politics has not considered ideology systematically. The findings suggest that the resentment of the poor, their feeling of political inefficacy, their low political participation, and their authoritarianism are due to their lack of knowledge and lack of faith in the democratic credo. Our data suggest that this oversimplification is perhaps due to an ideological bias on the part of the researchers and their failure to understand the functions of an ideology generally.

This research suggests that one function of a prevailing ideology, such as political pluralism, is to explain and vindicate the unequal distribution of rewards in a society for its dominant strata. These strata do not recognize conflicts or inconsistencies between their normative beliefs about the society and their view of how the society actually operates, i.e., their existential beliefs. Their collective ideas and sentiments about how power is distributed and *ought* to be distributed in a society are no more systematic, idealistic, or coherent than those of the lower income strata. Other strata, even when they support normative statements in the ideology, are quite knowledgeable about how the society operates when they do not concur with the existential beliefs of the privileged. Students of political movements of any type cannot long ignore the differential adherence of social strata to elements in the dominant ideology. A stratification approach to national studies of political ideologies is sorely needed.

Notes

[1] As Max Weber remarked, "Money increasingly buys—at least on an intergenerational basis —*everything*" (Weber, 1956:179).

[2] The per capita income for the Negro poor was $671; for the white poor, $907; for middle income Negroes, $1,591; for middle income whites, $2,310; for rich whites, over $6,000.

[3] Students of political power distinguish between "power" and "influence," but we did not expect the respondents to be aware of conceptual niceties, and, in this question, "power" and "influence" may be regarded as equivalent concepts.

[4] Abstracted from Riesman (1953); Mills (1956); Feuer (1959). Descriptions of the employee (Peter Drucker) and the managerial (James Burnham) societies were included in the pre-testing, but were later dropped because very few respondents considered them meaningful.

[5] We are not aware of national studies dealing with the degree of popular adherence to various models of power distribution. Community studies of power structure do investigate the views of special populations on elitist or pluralistic models of local decision making. See, for example, Form and Sauer, 1963; Haer, 1956; Horton and Thompson, 1962.

[6] Nineteen percent of poor Negroes, 38 percent of poor whites, 21 percent of middle-income Negroes, 45 percent of middle-income whites, and 45 percent of rich whites chose "big businessmen." Twenty-two percent of poor Negroes, 9 percent of poor whites, 33 percent of middle-income Negroes, 7 percent of middle-income whites, and 4 percent of rich whites chose "the rich." Thirty-five percent of the total sample chose "big businessmen," and 12 percent chose "the rich."

[7] Given the choice of indicating whether poor people or Negroes are least powerful, Negroes in the sample clearly saw poverty as being less powerfully represented than race in Washington.

[8] Lipset has argued that the working class is more authoritarian than other classes (Lipset, 1960). Lipsitz says that when Lipset's data are controlled for education, the greater authoritarianism disappears (Lipsitz, 1965:103–109). Lipset himself has argued that "higher education often makes for greater tolerance, greater regard for due process, and increased tolerance for ambiguity" (Lipset, 1964:399). On the other hand, Key said that "the indoctrination of a high-status, high-income, literate class of persons, seems to be far more feasible than is the mobilization of lesser peoples who are supposedly easy to manipulate" (Key, 1964:125).

[9] Campbell and co-workers found, in a national study, that few respondents employ ideological concepts in a sophisticated way (Campbell, et al., 1964:124–144).

[10] See Goffman's study of the relation of status consistency to preference for change in power distribution (Goffman, 1957:275–281).

References

Campbell, Angus; P. E. Converse; W. E. Miller; D. E. Stokes.
1964   The American Voter, An Abridgement. New York: Wiley.
D'Antonio, William V. and H. J. Ehrlich (eds.).
1961   Power and Democracy in America. Notre Dame: University of Notre Dame Press.
Feuer, Lewis S. (ed.).
1959   Marx and Engels: Basic Writings. Garden City, N.Y.: Doubleday & Co. Pp. 9, 12, 18.
Form, William H. and Warren E. Sauer.
1963   "Labor and community influentials: a comparative study of participation and imagery." Industrial and Labor Relations Review 17 (October).
Glantz, Oscar.
1958   "Class consciousness and political solidarity." American Sociological Review 23 (August), 375–383.
Goffman, Irwin W.
1957   "Status consistency and preference for change in power distribution." American Sociological Review 22 (June), 275–281.
Haer, John L.
1956   "Social stratification in relation to attitude toward sources of power in the community." Social Forces 34 (December), 37–42.
Horton, John E. and Wayne E. Thompson.
1962   "Powerlessness and political negativism: a study of defeated local referendums." American Journal of Sociology 47 (March), 485–493.
Key, V. O., Jr.
1964   Politics, Parties and Pressure Groups. P. 125. New York: Crowell.

Kornhauser, William.
1959   Politics of Mass Society. Glencoe, Illinois: The Free Press.
Lipset, Seymour Martin.
1960   Political Man. Garden City: Doubleday.
1964   "Three decades of the radical right: Coughlinites, McCarthyites, and
        Birchers." P. 399 in Daniel Bell (ed.), The Radical Right. Garden City:
        Doubleday.
Lipsitz, Lewis.
1965   "Working class authoritarianism: a reevaluation." American Sociological
        Review 30 (February), 103–109.
Litt, Edgar.
1963   "Civic education, community norms and political indoctrination." Ameri-
        can Sociological Review 28 (February), p. 74.
McClosky, Herbert; P. J. Hoffman; R. O'Hara.
1960   "Issue conflict and consensus among party leaders and followers." Ameri-
        can Political Science Review 54 (June), 416.
Milbrath, Lester W.
1965   Political Participation. Chicago: Rand McNally.
Miller, S. M. and Martin Rein.
1966   "Poverty, inequality and policy." In Howard S. Becker (ed.), Social
        Problems. New York: Wiley.
Mills, C. Wright.
1956   The Power Elite. Pp. 269–297. New York: Oxford University Press.
Prothro, James W. and Charles M. Grigg.
1960   "Fundamental principles of democracy: Bases of agreement and dis-
        agreement." Journal of Politics 22 (May), 276–294.
Riesman, David.
1953   The Lonely Crowd. Pp. 242–258. Garden City: Doubleday.
Schatzman, Leonard and Anselm Strauss.
1955   "Social class and modes of communication." American Journal of Sociol-
        ogy 60 (January), 329–338.
Scheler, Max.
1961   Ressentiment. Lewis Coser (trans.). Glencoe, Illinois: The Free Press.
U.S. Census of Population.
1960   General Summary, Social and Economic Characteristics. Washington:
        U.S. Government Printing Office.
Weber, Max.
1956   Wirtschaft und Gesellschaft: Grundiss der Verstehenden Soziologie I. P.
        179. Johannes Winckelman (ed.), Tübingen: J. C. B. Mohr.

PART V

OCCUPATIONS

When we ask someone "who he is" or "what he does," we expect to be told his occupation. In American society, and other complex industrial societies, occupation is probably the most salient aspect of individual identity. More and more people are spending more and more years preparing for their occupational life; and the typical American male spends most of the days of his life engaged in an occupation. From the societal standpoint, the occupational structure is one of the most important aspects of social life. Durkheim chose to study society in terms of the division of labor; Marx saw man's relation to the means of production as the basis of social life. One does not have to be an economic determinist to see the fundamental and pervasive role that the world of work plays in social life, both from the individual and societal standpoint. The sociology of work and occupations has contributed significantly to our understanding of the world.

An occupation places one in interaction with others in that occupation and with people in other jobs in an organization. It therefore determines to a large extent with whom one comes in contact. Inherent in any occupation is a set of norms and values which must be adhered to if one is to function on the job. These factors affect what and how a person thinks in the performance of his occupational role; they also affect his more general perspective. Some occupations necessitate contact with many types of people in various situations. They present a diversity of problems and challenge an individual's intellectual potential. Some occupations also expose a person to various beliefs, values, and behavior patterns. On the other hand, many occupations are relatively devoid of these characteristics. They provide little interest or challenge and narrow or dull the perspective of those who work at them. The selections in this section discuss some of the many ways in which one's occupation affects the individual in society.

Bureaucratic Structure and Personality

ROBERT K. MERTON

In this classic article Merton analyzes the effect of bureaucracy on the personality of the career official or bureaucrat. Bureaucratic social structure is seen as inextricably related to the bureaucrat's perspective. Merton describes the process by which the official develops this "orientation" making him incapable of handling clients' problems. Specific features of the bureaucratic structure are related to the "sentiments" that constitute this perspective. The bureaucrat's career is based on occupational steps or grades. To reach the next step calls for reliability and strict conformity to the rules. This career pattern leads to "timidity, conservatism, and technicism." Furthermore, since the official rules are so important to him, the means become ends in themselves (he develops an "absolutist" conception of them). Since there is relatively little competition when promotion is based on seniority, bureaucrats often develop a tight informal group with strong esprit de corps. They come to see noncareer officials and clientele as potential, if not actual, threats to their ingroup. Merton also discusses the categorizing tendency and attitude of impersonality as dimensions of the bureaucrat's perspective.

This selection emphasizes the negative aspects of bureaucracy and the bureaucrat's perspective. The reader should also consider whether bureaucratic norms and values have useful aspects as well.

A FORMAL, rationally organized social structure involves clearly defined patterns of activity in which, ideally, every series of actions is functionally related to the purposes of the organization.[1] In such an organization there is integrated a series of offices, of hierarchized statuses, in which inhere a number of obligations and privileges closely defined by limited and specific rules. Each of these offices contains an area of imputed competence and responsibility. Authority, the power of control which derives from an acknowledged status, inheres in the office and not in the particular person who performs the official role. Official action ordinarily occurs within the framework of preexisting rules of the organization. The system of prescribed rela-

Reprinted with permission of The Macmillan Company from *Social Theory and Social Structure*, revised edition, pp. 197–205, by Robert K. Merton. Copyright 1949 by The Free Press. Copyright © by The Free Press, a corporation, 1957.

tions between the various offices involves a considerable degree of formality and clearly defined social distance between the occupants of these positions. Formality is manifested by means of a more or less complicated social ritual which symbolizes and supports the pecking order of the various offices. Such formality, which is integrated with the distribution of authority within the system, serves to minimize friction by largely restricting (official) contact to modes which are previously defined by the rules of the organization. Ready calculability of others' behavior and a stable set of mutual expectations is thus built up. Moreover, formality facilitates the interaction of the occupants of offices despite their (possibly hostile) private attitudes toward one another. In this way, the subordinate is protected from the arbitrary action of his superior, since the actions of both are constrained by a mutually recognized set of rules. Specific procedural devices foster objectivity and restrain the "quick passage of impulse into action." [2]

The Structure of Bureaucracy

The ideal type of such formal organization is bureaucracy and, in many respects, the classical analysis of bureaucracy is that by Max Weber.[3] As Weber indicates, bureaucracy involves a clear-cut division of integrated activities which are regarded as duties inherent in the office. A system of differentiated controls and sanctions is stated in the regulations. The assignment of roles occurs on the basis of technical qualifications which are ascertained through formalized, impersonal procedures (*e.g.,* examinations). Within the structure of hierarchically arranged authority, the activities of "trained and salaried experts" are governed by general, abstract, and clearly defined rules which preclude the necessity for the issuance of specific instructions for each specific case. The generality of the rules requires the constant use of *categorization,* whereby individual problems and cases are classified on the basis of designated criteria and are treated accordingly. The pure type of bureaucratic official is appointed, either by a superior or through the exercise of impersonal competition; he is not elected. A measure of flexibility in the bureaucracy is attained by electing higher functionaries who presumably express the will of the electorate (*e.g.,* a body of citizens or a board of directors). The election of higher officials is designed to affect the purposes of the organization, but the technical procedures for attaining these ends are carried out by continuing bureaucratic personnel.[4]

Most bureaucratic offices involve the expectation of life-long tenure, in the absence of disturbing factors which may decrease the size of the organization. Bureaucracy maximizes vocational security.[5] The function of security of tenure, pensions, incremental salaries and regularized procedures for promotion is to ensure the devoted performance of official duties, without regard for extraneous pressures.[6] The chief merit of bureaucracy is its technical efficiency, with a premium placed on precision, speed, expert control, continuity, discretion, and optimal returns on input. The structure is one which approaches the complete elimination of personalized relationships and non-rational considerations (hostility, anxiety, affectual involvements, etc.).

With increasing bureaucratization, it becomes plain to all who would see that man is to a very important degree controlled by his social relations to the instruments of production. This can no longer seem only a tenet of Marxism, but a stubborn fact to be acknowledged by all, quite apart from their ideological persuasion. Bureaucratization makes readily visible what was previously dim and obscure. More and more people discover that to work, they must be employed. For to work, one must have tools and equipment. And the tools and equipment are increasingly available only in bureaucracies, private or public. Consequently, one must be employed by the bureaucracies in order to have access to tools in order to work in order to live. It is in this sense that bureaucratization entails separation of individuals from the instruments of production, as in modern capitalistic enterprise or in state communistic enterprise (of the midcentury variety), just as in the post-feudal army, bureaucratization entailed complete separation from the instruments of destruction. Typically, the worker no longer owns his tools nor the soldier, his weapons. And in this special sense, more and more people become workers, either blue collar or white collar or stiff shirt. So develops, for example, the new type of scientific worker, as the scientist is "separated" from his technical equipment—after all, the physicist does not ordinarily own his cyclotron. To work at his research, he must be employed by a bureaucracy with laboratory resources.

Bureaucracy is administration which almost completely avoids public discussion of its techniques, although there may occur public discussion of its policies.[7] This secrecy is confined neither to public nor to private bureaucracies. It is held to be necessary to keep valuable information from private economic competitors or from foreign and potentially hostile political groups. And though it is not often so called, espionage among competitors is perhaps as common, if not as intricately organized, in systems of private economic enterprise as in systems of national states. Cost figures, lists of clients, new technical processes, plans for production—all these are typically regarded as essential secrets of private economic bureaucracies which might be revealed if the bases of all decisions and policies had to be publicly defended.

The Dysfunctions of Bureaucracy

In these bold outlines, the positive attainments and functions of bureaucratic organization are emphasized and the internal stresses and strains of such structures are almost wholly neglected. The community at large, however, evidently emphasizes the imperfections of bureaucracy, as is suggested by the fact that the "horrid hybrid," bureaucrat, has become an epithet, a *Schimpfwort.*

The transition to a study of the negative aspects of bureaucracy is afforded by the application of Veblen's concept of "trained incapacity," Dewey's notion of "occupational psychosis" or Warnotte's view of "professional deformation." Trained incapacity refers to that state of affairs in which one's abilities function as inadequacies or blind spots. Actions based upon training and skills which have been successfully applied in the past may result in inappropriate responses *under changed conditions.* An inadequate flexibility in the application of skills, will, in a changing milieu, result in more or less serious maladjustments.[8] Thus, to adopt a barnyard illustration used in this connection by Burke, chickens may be readily conditioned to interpret the sound of a bell as a signal for food. The same bell may now be used to summon the trained chickens to their doom as they are assembled to suffer decapitation. In general, one adopts measures in keeping with one's past training and, under new conditions which are not recognized as *significantly* different, the very soundness of this training may lead to the adoption of the wrong procedures. Again, in Burke's almost echolalic phrase, "people may be unfitted by being fit in an unfit fitness"; their training may become an incapacity.

Dewey's concept of occupational psychosis rests upon much the same observations. As a result of their day to day routines, people develop special preferences, antipathies, discriminations and emphases.[9] (The term psychosis is used by Dewey to denote a "pronounced character of the mind.") These psychoses develop through demands put upon the individual by the particular organization of his occupational role.

The concepts of both Veblen and Dewey refer to a fundamental ambivalence. Any action can be considered in terms of what it attains or what it fails to attain. "A way of seeing is also a way of not seeing—a focus upon object A involves a neglect of object B." [10] In his discussion, Weber is almost exclusively concerned with what the bureaucratic structure attains: precision, reliability, efficiency. This same structure may be examined from another perspective provided by the ambivalence. What are the limitations of the organizations designed to attain these goals?

For reasons which we have already noted, the bureaucratic structure exerts a constant pressure upon the official to be "methodical, prudent, disciplined." If the bureaucracy is to operate successfully, it must attain a high degree of reliability of behavior, an unusual degree of conformity with prescribed patterns of action. Hence, the fundamental importance of discipline which may be as highly developed in a religious or economic bureaucracy as in the army. Discipline can be effective only if the ideal patterns are buttressed by strong sentiments which entail devotion to one's duties, a keen sense of the limitation of one's authority and competence, and methodical performance of routine activities. The efficacy of social structure depends ultimately upon infusing group participants with appropriate attitudes and sentiments. As we shall see, there are definite arrangements in the bureaucracy for inculcating and reinforcing these sentiments.

At the moment, it suffices to observe that in order to ensure discipline (the necessary reliability of response), these sentiments are often more intense than is technically necessary. There is a margin of safety, so to speak, in the pressure exerted by these sentiments upon the bureaucrat to conform to his patterned obligations, in much the same sense that added allowances (precautionary overestimations) are made by the engineer in designing the supports for a bridge. But this very emphasis leads to a transference of the sentiments from the *aims* of the organization onto the particular details of behavior required by the rules. Adherence to the rules, originally conceived as a means, becomes transformed into an end-in-itself; there occurs the familiar process of *displacement of goals* whereby "an instrumental value becomes a terminal value." [11] Discipline, readily interpreted as conformance with regulations, whatever the situation, is seen not as a measure designed for specific purposes but becomes an immediate value in the life-organization of the bureaucrat. This emphasis, resulting from the displacement of the original goals, develops into rigidities and an inability to adjust readily. Formalism, even ritualism, ensues with an unchallenged insistence upon punctilious adherence to formalized procedures.[12] This may be exaggerated to the point where primary concern with conformity to the rules interferes with the achievement of the purposes of the organization, in which case we have the familiar phenomenon of the technicism or red tape of the official. An extreme product of this process of displacement of goals is the bureaucratic virtuoso, who never forgets a single rule binding his action and hence is unable to assist many of his clients.[13] A case in point, where strict recognition of the limits of authority and literal adherence to rules produced this result, is the pathetic plight of Bernt Balchen, Admiral Byrd's pilot in the flight over the South Pole.

> According to a ruling of the department of labor Bernt Balchen . . . cannot receive his citizenship papers. Balchen, a native of Norway, declared his intention in 1927. It is held that he has failed to meet the condition of five years' continuous residence in the United States. The Byrd antarctic voyage took him out of the country, although he was on a ship carrying the American flag, was an invaluable member of the American expedition, and in a region to which there is an American claim because of the exploration and occupation of it by Americans, this region being Little America.
>
> The bureau of naturalization explains that it cannot proceed on the assumption that Little America is American soil. That would be *trespass on international questions* where it has no sanction. So far as the bureau is concerned, Balchen was out of the country and *technically* has not complied with the law of naturalization.[14]

Structural Sources of Overconformity

Such inadequacies in orientation which involve trained incapacity clearly derive from structural sources. The process may be briefly recapitulated. (1) An effective bureaucracy demands reliability of response and strict devotion to regulations. (2) Such devotion to the rules leads to their transformation into absolutes; they are no longer conceived as relative to a set of purposes. (3) This interferes with ready adaptation under special conditions not clearly envisaged by those who drew up the general rules. (4) Thus, the very elements which conduce toward efficiency in general produce inefficiency in specific instances. Full realization of the inadequacy is seldom attained by members of the group who have not divorced themselves from the meanings which the rules have for them. These rules in time become symbolic in cast, rather than strictly utilitarian.

Thus far, we have treated the ingrained sentiments making for rigorous discipline simply as data, as given. However, definite features of the bureaucratic structure may be seen to conduce to these sentiments. The bureaucrat's official life is planned for him in terms of a graded career, through the organizational devices of promotion by seniority, pensions, incremental salaries, *etc.,* all of which are designed to provide incentives for disciplined action and conformity to the official regulations.[15] The official is tacitly expected to and largely does adapt his thoughts, feelings and actions to the prospect of his career. But *these very devices* which increase the probability of conformance also lead to an over-concern with strict adherence to regulations which induces timidity, conservatism, and technicism. Displacement of sentiments from goals onto means is fostered by the tremendous symbolic significance of the means (rules).

Another feature of the bureaucratic structure tends to produce much the same result. Functionaries have the sense of a common destiny for all those who work together. They share the same interests, especially since there is relatively little competition in so far as promotion is in terms of seniority. In-group aggression is thus minimized and this arrangement is therefore conceived to be positively functional for the bureaucracy. However, the *esprit de corps* and informal social organization which typically develops in such situations often leads the personnel to defend their entrenched interests rather than to assist their clientele and elected higher officials. As President Lowell reports, if the bureaucrats believe that their status is not adequately recognized by an incoming elected official, detailed information will be withheld from him, leading him to errors for which he is held responsible. Or, if he seeks to dominate fully, and thus violates the sentiment of self-integrity of the bureaucrats, he may have documents brought to him in such numbers that he cannot manage to sign them all, let alone read them.[16] This illustrates the defensive informal organization which tends to arise whenever there is an apparent threat to the integrity of the group.[17]

It would be much too facile and partly erroneous to attribute such resistance by bureaucrats simply to vested interests. Vested interests oppose any new order which either eliminates or at least makes uncertain their differential advantage deriving from the current arrangements. This is undoubtedly involved in part in bureaucratic resistance to change but another process is perhaps more significant. As we have seen, bureaucratic officials affectively identify themselves with their way of life. They have a pride of craft which leads them to resist change in established routines; at least, those changes which are felt to be imposed by others. This nonlogical pride of craft is a familiar pattern found even, to judge from Sutherland's *Professional Thief,* among pickpockets who, despite the risk, delight in mastering the prestige-bearing feat of "beating a left breech" (picking the left front trousers pocket).

In a stimulating paper, Hughes has applied the concepts of "secular" and "sacred" to various types of division of labor; "the sacredness" of caste and *Stände* prerogatives contrasts sharply with the increasing secularism of occupational differentiation in our society.[18] However, as our discussion suggests, there may ensue, in particular vocations and in particular types of organization, the *process of sanctification* (viewed as the counterpart of the process of secularization). This is to say that through sentiment-formation, emotional dependence upon bureaucratic symbols and status, and affective involvement in spheres of competence and authority, there develop prerogatives involving attitudes of moral legitimacy which are established as values in their own right, and are no longer viewed as merely technical means for expediting administration. One may note a tendency for certain bureaucratic norms, originally introduced for technical reasons, to become rigidified and sacred, although, as Durkheim would say, they are *laïque en apparence.*[19] Durkheim has touched on this general process in his description of the attitudes and values which persist in the organic solidarity of a highly differentiated society.

Primary vs. Secondary Relations

Another feature of the bureaucratic structure, the stress on depersonalization of relationships, also plays its part in the bureaucrat's trained incapacity. The personality pattern of the bureaucrat is nucleated about this norm of impersonality. Both this and the categorizing tendency, which develops from the dominant role of general, abstract rules, tend to produce conflict in the bureaucrat's contacts with the public or clientele. Since functionaries minimize personal relations and resort to categorization, the peculiarities of individual cases are often ignored. But the client who, quite understandably, is convinced of the special features of *his* own problem often objects to such categorical treatment. Stereotyped behavior is not adapted to the exigencies of individual problems. The impersonal treatment of affairs which are at times of great personal significance to the client gives rise to the charge of "arrrogance" and "haughtiness" of the bureaucrat. Thus, at the Greenwich Employment Exchange, the unemployed worker who is securing his insurance payment resents what he deems to be "the impersonality and, at times, the apparent abruptness and even harshness of his treatment by the clerks. . . . Some men complain of the superior attitude which the clerks have." [20]

Still another source of conflict with the public derives from the bureaucratic structure. The bureaucrat, in part irrespective of his position with*in* the hierarchy, acts as a representative of the power and prestige of the entire structure. In his official role he is vested with definite authority. This often leads to an actually or apparently domineering attitude, which may only be exaggerated by a discrepancy between his position within the hierarchy and his position with reference to the public.[21] Protest and recourse to other officials on the part of the client are often ineffective or largely precluded by the previously mentioned *esprit de corps* which joins the officials into a more or less solidary in-group. This source of conflict *may* be minimized in private enterprise since the client can register an effective protest by transferring his trade to another organization within the competitive system. But with the monopolistic nature of the public organization, no such alternative is possible. Moreover, in this case, tension is increased because of a discrepancy between ideology and fact: the governmental personnel are held to be "servants of the people," but in fact they are often superordinate, and release of tension can seldom be afforded by turning to other agencies for the necessary service.[22] This tension is in part attributable to the confusion of the status of bureaucrat and client; the client may consider himself socially superior to the official who is at the moment dominant.[23]

Thus, with respect to the relations between officials and clientele, one structural source of conflict is the pressure for formal and impersonal treatment when individual, personalized consideration is desired by the client. The conflict may be viewed, then, as deriving from the introduction of inappropriate attitudes and relationships. Conflict with*in* the bureaucratic structure arises from the converse situation, namely, when personalized relationships are substituted for the structurally required impersonal relationships. This type of conflict may be characterized as follows.

The bureaucracy, as we have seen, is organized as a secondary, formal group. The normal responses involved in this organized network of social expectations are supported by affective attitudes of members of the group. Since the group is oriented toward secondary norms of impersonality, any failure to conform to these norms will arouse antagonism from those who have identified themselves with the legitimacy of these rules. Hence, the substitution of personal for impersonal treatment within the structure is met with widespread disapproval and is characterized by such epithets as graft, favoritism, nepotism, apple-polishing, etc. These epithets are clearly manifestations of injured sentiments.[24] The function of such virtually automatic resentment can be clearly seen in terms of the requirements of bureaucratic structure.

Bureaucracy is a secondary group structure designed to carry on certain activities which cannot be satisfactorily performed on the basis of primary group criteria.[25] Hence behavior which runs counter to these formalized norms becomes the object of emotionalized disapproval. This constitutes a functionally significant defense set up against tendencies which jeopardize the performance of socially necessary activities. To be sure, these reactions are not rationally determined practices explicitly designed for the fulfillment of this function. Rather, viewed in terms of the individual's interpretation of the situation, such resentment is simply an immediate response opposing the "dishonesty" of those who violate the rules of the game. However, this subjective frame of reference notwithstanding, these reactions serve the latent function of maintaining the essential structural elements of bureaucracy by reaffirming the necessity for formalized, secondary relations and by helping to prevent the disintegration of the bureaucratic structure which would occur should these be supplanted by personalized relations. This type of conflict may be generically described as the intrusion of primary group attitudes when secondary group attitudes are institutionally demanded, just as the bureaucrat-client conflict often derives from interaction on impersonal terms when personal treatment is individually demanded.[26]

Notes

[1] For a development of the concept of "rational organization," see Karl Mannheim, *Mensch und Gesellschaft im Zeitalter des Umbaus* (Leiden: A. W. Sijthoff, 1935), esp. 28 ff.

[2] H. D. Lasswell, *Politics* (New York: McGraw-Hill, 1936), 120–21.

[3] Max Weber, *Wirtschaft und Gesellschaft* (Tübingen: J. C. B. Mohr, 1922), Pt. III, chap. 6; 650–678. For a brief summary of Weber's discussion, see Talcott Parsons, *The Structure of Social Action*, esp. 506 ff. For a description, which is not a caricature, of the bureaucrat as a personality type, see C. Rabany, "Les types sociaux: le fonctionnaire," *Revue générale d'administration*, 1907, 88, 5–28.

[4] Karl Mannheim, *Ideology and Utopia* (New York: Harcourt, Brace, 1936), 18n., 105 ff. See also Ramsay Muir, *Peers and Bureaucrats* (London: Constable, 1910), 12–13.

[5] E. G. Cahen-Salvador suggests that the personnel of bureaucracies is largely constituted by those who values security above all else. See his "La situation matérielle et morale des fonctionnaires," *Revue politique et parlementaire* (1926), 319.

[6] H. J. Laski, "Bureaucracy," *Encyclopedia of the Social Sciences*. This article is written primarily from the standpoint of the political scientist rather than that of the sociologist.

[7] Weber, *op. cit.*, 671.

[8] For a stimulating discussion and application of these concepts, see Kenneth Burke, *Permanence and Change* (New York: New Republic, 1935), pp. 50 ff.; Daniel Warnotte, "Bureaucratie et Fonctionnarisme," *Revue de l'Institut de Sociologie*, 1937, 17, 245.

[9] *Ibid.*, 58–59.

[10] *Ibid.*, 70.

[11] This process has often been observed in various connections. Wundt's *heterogony of ends* is a case in point; Max Weber's *Paradoxie der Folgen* is another. See also MacIver's observations on the transformation of civilization into culture and Lasswell's remark that "the human animal distinguishes himself by his infinite capacity for making ends of his means." See Merton, "The unanticipated consequences of purposive social action," *American Sociological Review,* 1936, 1, 894–904. In terms of the psychological mechanisms involved, this process has been analyzed most fully by Gordon W. Allport, in his discussion of what he calls "the functional autonomy of motives." Allport emends the earlier formulations of Woodworth, Tolman, and William Stern, and arrives at a statement of the process from the standpoint of individual motivation. He does not consider those phases of the social structure which conduce toward the "transformation of motives." The formulation adopted in this paper is thus complementary to Allport's analysis; the one stressing the psychological mechanisms involved, the other considering the constraints of the social structure. The convergence of psychology and sociology toward this central concept suggests that it may well constitute one of the conceptual bridges between the two disciplines. See Gordon W. Allport, *Personality* (New York: Henry Holt & Co., 1937), chap. 7.

[12] See E. C. Hughes, "Institutional office and the person," *American Journal of Sociology,* 1937, 43, 404–413; E. T. Hiller, "Social structure in relation to the person," *Social Forces,* 1937, 16, 34 ff.

[13] Mannheim, *Ideology and Utopia,* 106.

[14] Quoted from the *Chicago Tribune* (June 24, 1931, p. 10) by Thurman Arnold, *The Symbols of Government* (New Haven: Yale University Press, 1935), 201–2. (My italics.)

[15] Mannheim, *Mensch und Gesellschaft,* 32–33. Mannheim stresses the importance of the "Lebensplan" and the "Amtskarriere." See the comments by Hughes, *op. cit.,* 413.

[16] A. L. Lowell, *The Government of England* (New York, 1908), I, 189 ff.

[17] For an instructive description of the development of such a defensive organization in a group of workers, see F. J. Roethlisberger and W. J. Dickson, *Management and the Worker* (Boston: Harvard School of Business Administration, 1934).

[18] E. C. Hughes, "Personality types and the division of labor," *American Journal of Sociology,* 1928, 33, 754–768. Much the same distinction is drawn by Leopold von Wiese and Howard Becker, *Systematic Sociology* (New York: John Wiley & Sons, 1932), 222–25 *et passim.*

[19] Hughes recognizes one phase of this process of sanctification when he writes that professional training "carries with it as a by-product assimilation of the candidate to a set of professional attitudes and controls, *a professional conscience and solidarity. The profession claims and aims to become a moral unit.*" Hughes, *op. cit.,* 762 (italics inserted). In this same connection, Sumner's concept of *pathos,* as the halo of sentiment which protects a social value from criticism, is particularly relevant, inasmuch as it affords a clue to the mechanism involved in the process of sanctification. See his *Folkways,* 180–181.

[20] " 'They treat you like a lump of dirt they do. I see a navvy reach across the counter and shake one of them by the collar the other day. The rest of us felt like cheering. Of course he lost his benefit over it. . . . But the clerk deserved it for his sassy way.' " (E. W. Bakke, *The Unemployed Man,* 79–80). Note that the domineering attitude was *imputed* by the unemployed client who is in a state of tension due to his loss of status and self-esteem in a society where the ideology is still current that an "able man" can always find a job. That the imputation of arrogance stems largely from the client's state of mind is seen from Bakke's own observation that "the clerks were rushed, and had no time for pleasantries, but there was little sign of harshness or a superiority feeling in their treatment of the men." In so far as there is an objective basis for the imputation of arrogant behavior to bureaucrats, it may possibly be explained by the following juxtaposed statements. "Auch der moderne, sei es öffentliche, sei es private, Beamte erstrebt immer und geniesst meist den Beherrschten gegenüber eine spezifisch gehobene, 'ständische' soziale Schätzung." (Weber, *op. cit.,* 652.) "In persons in whom the craving for prestige is uppermost, hostility usually takes the form of a desire to humiliate others." K. Horney, *The Neurotic Personality of Our Time,* 178–79.

[21] In this connection, note the relevance of Koffka's comments on certain features of the pecking-order of birds. "If one compares the behavior of the bird at the top of the pecking list, the despot, with that of one very far down, the second or third from the last, then one finds the latter much more cruel to the few others over whom he lords it than the former in his treatment of all members. As soon as one removes from the group all members above the penultimate, his behavior becomes milder and may even become very friendly. . . . It is not difficult to find analogies to this in human societies, and therefore one side of such behavior must be primarily the effects of the social groupings, and not of individual characteristics." K. Koffka, *Principles of Gestalt Psychology* (New York: Harcourt, Brace, 1935), 668–9.

[22] At this point the political machine often becomes functionally significant. As Steffens and others have shown, highly personalized relations and the abrogation of formal rules (red tape) by the machine often satisfy the needs of individual "clients" more fully than the formalized mechanism of governmental bureaucracy. See the slight elaboration of this as set forth in Chapter I.

[23] As one of the unemployed men remarked about the clerks at the Greenwich Employment Exchange: " 'And the bloody blokes wouldn't have their jobs if it wasn't for us men out of a job either. That's what gets me about their holding their noses up.' " Bakke, *op. cit.*, 80. See also H. D. Lasswell and G. Almond, "Aggressive behavior by clients towards public relief administrators," *American Political Science Review*, 1934, 28, 643–55.

[24] The diagnostic significance of such linguistic indices as epithets has scarcely been explored by the sociologist. Sumner properly observes that epithets produce "summary criticisms" and definitions of social situations. Dollard also notes that "epithets frequently define the central issues in a society," and Sapir has rightly emphasized the importance of context of situations in appraising the significance of epithets. Of equal relevance is Linton's observation that "in case histories the way in which the community felt about a particular episode is, if anything, more important to our study than the actual behavior. . . ." A sociological study of "vocabularies of encomium and opprobrium" should lead to valuable findings.

[25] *Cf.* Ellsworth Faris, *The Nature of Human Nature* (New York: McGraw-Hill, 1937), 41 ff.

[26] Community disapproval of many forms of behavior may be analyzed in terms of one or the other of these patterns of substitution of culturally inappropriate types of relationship. Thus, prostitution constitutes a type-case where coitus, a form of intimacy which is institutionally defined as symbolic of the most "sacred" primary group relationship, is placed within a contractual context, symbolized by the exchange of that most impersonal of all symbols, money. See Kingsley Davis, "The sociology of prostitution," *American Sociological Review*, 1937, 2, 744–55.

Industrial Workers' Worlds *

ROBERT DUBIN

"Industrial Workers' Worlds" by Dubin appears here since it focuses on the worker's occupational life. Dubin is concerned with the work and workplace of industrial workers as areas of experience. He introduces the concept of "central life interest" to articulate his research problem. Besides studying work as a central life interest, he also assesses the importance of primary relations on the job and explores sources of organizational attachment.

In order to learn about these problems he constructed the Central Life Interests questionnaire which provided data on four categories of workers' experiences: formal aspects of membership and behavior in organizations; technological aspects of the environment; informal group life; and general everyday experiences. His scoring technique allows him to classify workers as job-oriented or nonjob-oriented in each of these areas. Dubin's assumptions and propositions lead him to propose a series of hypotheses which state that work and workplace do *not* provide central life interests for industrial workers. His data support these hypotheses. On the basis of their responses to the Central Life Interest questionnaire, only 24 percent of all workers were classified as job-oriented in their life interests, only 9 percent indicated that they preferred the informal group life that centered on the job, and only 15 percent gave job-oriented preferences to the general experiences section of the schedule.

This study indicates that the industrial workers' personal relationships and attitudes have their center outside of work and workplace. Community rather than occupation is the central area of personal and interpersonal experience for the industrial worker.

IN an urban industrial society it seems more than pertinent to inquire into the world of industrial workers. We are here concerned with defining this world in terms of the significant areas of social experience. For each area of experience our basic object is to determine whether it represents a life

* This article was one of two presented with the Helen L. DeRoy Award in 1955.

Originally published as "Industrial Workers' Worlds: A Study of the 'Central Life Interests' of Industrial Workers," in *Social Problems,* Vol. 3, No. 3, January, 1956, pp. 131–141. Reprinted by permission of the author and the publisher, The Society for the Study of Social Problems.

interest of importance to the worker. In particular, we will focus attention on work and the workplace to determine its standing as a central life interest to workers in industry.

The impact of industrialization and urbanization on human behavior is empirically noted and theoretically accounted for in the general sociological literature. Microscopic studies of industrial organizations and of "human relations" within them are producing their own observations and generalizations. The bodies of knowledge in general sociology and in industrial sociology are at variance on critical points. This study presents one part of a larger research linking general and industrial sociology. The linkage is made through an intensive study of the "central life interests" of industrial workers.

Introduction

It is a commonplace to note that work has long been considered a central life interest for adults in most societies, and certainly in the Western world. Indeed, the capitalist system itself is asserted to rest upon the moral and religious justification that the Reformation gave to work, as Weber[1] and Tawney[2] have pointed out. Our research shows that for almost three out of every four industrial workers studied, work and the workplace *are not* central life interests.

This result is surely not startling to the general sociologist. He has already noted that the social world of urban man is continuously subdivided into areas of activity and interest, with each social segment lived out more or less independently of the rest. It seems highly plausible that the urban world, with its emphasis upon secondary and instrumental social relations, might indeed be one in which work has become secondary as a life interest.

The one large subject matter illuminated by industrial sociologists in the past decade has been the human relationships that surround job and task performance in the formal organizations of modern life.[3,4,5] We are generally led to believe that informal human relationships at work are important to the individual industrial man—he finds that the informal work society presents opportunities for intimate and primary human interaction. Our research indicates that only about 10 percent of the industrial workers perceived their important primary social relationships as taking place at work. The other 90 percent preferred primary interactions with fellowmen elsewhere than on the job!

This finding should jolt the industrial sociologist, if duplicated in subsequent studies. The result will be an important corrective to the naive assumption that complex and rational organizations of modern society, through which most of the society's business gets done, are effective or not as the human relations of their members are "good" or "bad."

In an era when loyalty is in the vocabulary of even the common man, the ways in which members become attached to and thereby loyal toward an organization are of central interest. Our research findings indicate that more than three out of five industrial workers have strong job-oriented preferences for those sectors of their experience that involve either a formal organization or technological aspects of their personal environment. This result (again perhaps surprising to the human relations expert) suggests that strong bonds of organization may be forged out of the impersonal aspects of work experience that attach the individual more or less firmly to his company or workplace.

These three problems taken together, then, are the subject of this report: (*a*) work as a central life interest; (*b*) the role and importance of primary social relations on the job; and (*c*) some sources of organizational attachment.

Theory

The theory underlying this study involves five basic points: (*a*) the axiom that social experience is inevitably segmented; (*b*) the assumption that an individual's social participation may be necessary in one or more sectors of his social experience but may not be important to him; (*c*) the logical conclusion that adequate social behavior will occur in sectors of social experience which are mandatory for social participation by the individual but not important to him; (*d*) the second conclusion that in situations of necessary but unimportant social participation the most direct and obvious features of the situation become bases for the individual's attachment to that situation; and (*e*) the third conclusion that primary social relations take place only in situations where the social experience is valued by the individual.

The axiom with which we start scarcely needs elaboration. The segmented character of experience is revealed in the round of daily activities where one kind of activity succeeds another; in the succession of days, and particularly the weekend days when leisure-time activity replaces remunerative work, in the physical separation of such significant locales as place of residence and place of work; and in the numerous autonomous organizations that serve special, and sometimes very esoteric, interests in our lives. This by no means exhausts the illustrations of ways in which social experience is divided into discrete parts, but it should serve adequately to demonstrate the reasonableness of our initial axiom.

It is equally obvious that participation in some segments or sectors of social experience may be necessary but not important to an individual. The significance of this assumption rests on the definition of important social experience. We are here concerned with a subjective state of mind. Some social experience is important because it is valued by its participants; some is important because it is necessary as a means towards an end, though slightly valued in itself. The ceremonial banquet for awarding football letters to the college team may be valued as public recognition of achievement. The meal eaten at the banquet is important, too, but only as the justification for naming the ceremony, not for its nutritive value or esthetic appeal. The kind of importance we are concerned with is illustrated by the ceremony, not the meal.

This assumption tells us that social experience is differentially valued. The form in which it is stated emphasizes the fact that participation takes place in some experiences because it is necessary and not because the activity is itself valued. We could equally well state the axiom as follows: only a portion of all social experience is important or valued by its participants. We have chosen the first formulation because it gives greater emphasis to the subject matter of this research—the fact that remunerative work may be required by the society but that this does not guarantee that it will be viewed as important or valued by workers.

Three propositions or generalized predictions follow from our two axioms. The first is that individuals will exhibit adequate social behavior in sectors of social experience in which participation is mandatory but not valued. This proposition, when converted to hypothesis form, becomes empirically testable. In its proposition form it makes a general prediction for any and all individuals. In the form of a hypothesis the prediction is limited to the particular data of the study and the actual empirical indicators used. For example, this proposition in our study becomes the following hypothesis: a significant proportion of industrial workers will rate non-job interests high in their value orientation on the Central Life Interests questionnaire. Our hypothesis as a prediction is completely consonant with the general proposition, but it is also directly related to the data of our study. The hypothesis is the bridge between the general proposition and the empirical data marshaled in testing the proposition. Any proposition can be converted to an indefinite number of hypotheses. Consequently, no confirmation of a single hypothesis can establish any proposition. The confirmed hypothesis does, however, lend support to the proposition. Our research findings lend support to the three propositions set forth. We are not, of course, asserting that the propositions are thereby proven.

The second proposition or general prediction is that an individual's attachment to a situation in which his social experience is not valued by him will be to the most physically and directly obvious characteristics of that situation. The pertinent hypotheses that flow from this proposition will be set forth below.

The third general prediction in proposition form is that primary human relations take place only in situations where the social experience is valued by the individual. By "primary human relations" we mean, of course, the relationships that occur in groups where the interaction is face-to-face, continuous, intimate, and shared over a wide range of subjects. The directly related hypotheses will be stated below.

Research Procedure

This study was conducted in 1952–53 in three Midwestern plants employing a total of approximately 1,200 workers. The companies are located in different communities ranging in size from 35,000 to 125,000, all clearly urban units. The largest company makes industrial equipment, employing about 600 workers on two shifts in a wide and typical range of metal manufacturing and equipment assembly operations. The smallest company manufactures industrial, dress, and novelty gloves of cloth and leather with a work force of approximately 200 employees, who were represented by an A.F. of L. union. The third company produces printed and novelty advertising items and employs about 400 people.

Active cooperation was secured in each plant to carry on the total study, which included observation of work performance and work behavior, the anonymous completion of a series of separate questionnaires administered over a period of time and completed by 491 workers, and intensive recorded interviews with a sample of 120 selected employees.

We will report here the results of the Central Life Interests questionnaire only. This questionnaire was designed to determine whether the job and workplace were central life interests of workers or whether other areas of their social experience were important to them. We defined "central life interest" as the expressed preference for a given locale or situation in carrying out an activity. After a pretest, forty questions were selected for the Central Life Interests (CLI) schedule.

Each question represented an activity that had an approximately equal likelihood of occurring in connection with some aspect of the job or workplace, or at some definite point in the community outside of work. A third choice was added that represented an indifferent or neutral response to the question. An example of a typical question is the following:

I would most hate
.... missing a day's work
.... missing a meeting of an organization I belong to
.... missing almost anything I usually do

The forty questions used dealt with the formal aspects of membership and behavior in organizations, the technological aspects of the environment, the informal group life experiences, and general everyday experiences. Each question was individually scored as a job-oriented response, as a non-job-oriented response, or as an indifferent response. The questions that applied to each of the four areas were then scored as separate groups by summing the responses to the individual questions in each group. Those workers who chose a work-related response on at least half the questions in each group and answered the remaining ones with a non-job or indifferent response, or who had at least 70 percent of their answers made up of a combination of job-oriented and indifferent responses, were designated job-oriented workers. The remaining workers were designated non-job in their outlook because they responded with more emphasis upon non-job and indifferent choices. The indifferent response is not utilized as a separate category in this report.

By the same scoring procedure and using the same criteria a total classification was secured for each worker. This indicated whether he was job-oriented or non-job-oriented in his total pattern of responses on all forty questions.

Work as a Central Life Interest

Previous researchers have generally assumed that work must be a central life interest because so many are engaged in it. We make quite a different assumption about work. We assume that holding a job is simply evidence of adequate performance above some minimal level that justifies continued employment by the company. In short, we assume that social behavior is adequate in this sector of social experience. For us the research question becomes one of determining to what extent the job and its locale are central life interests to workers.

It will be recalled that our first proposition is that individuals will exhibit adequate social behavior in sectors of social experience in which participation is mandatory but not valued. Remunerative work is mandatory both in the general sense that most male adults (or female heads of households) are expected to work for a living and in the specific sense that each job is surrounded by many imperatives and requirements for its performance. We have thus assumed that continued employment is evidence of adequacy of social behavior and that holding a paying job is evidence of mandatory participation in the two senses mentioned.

Our hypothesis can now be stated as follows: a significant proportion of industrial workers will be classified as non-job-oriented when central life interest is measured with the CLI questionnaire.

Considering the pattern of responses to all the questions, we found that only 24 percent of all the workers [6] studied could be labelled job-oriented in their life interests. Thus, three out of four of this group of industrial workers did not see their jobs and workplaces as central life interests for themselves. They found their preferred human associations and preferred areas of behavior outside of employment.

If this finding holds generally, the role and significance of work in American society has departed from its presumed historical position. Factory work may now very well be viewed by industrial workers as a means to an end—a way of acquiring income for life in the community. The factory as a locale for living out a lifetime seems clearly secondary to other areas of central life interest. The factory and factory work as sources of personal satisfaction, pride, satisfying human associations, perhaps even of pleasure in expressing what Veblen called the "instinct of workmanship," seem clearly subordinated in the American scene. The general and specific implications of this finding will be examined in the last section of this report.

Work and Informal Social Relations

Our third general prediction of human behavior in proposition form was that primary human relations take place only in situations where social experience is valued by the individual. From the test of our first hypothesis we have strong evidence that the workplace does not provide social experience that is valued more highly than other experiences. It would follow, then, that we may expect a significant proportion of industrial workers to be non-job-oriented with respect specifically to informal group experiences when measured on the relevant portion of the CLI questionnaire. This is the hypothesis derived from the above proposition.

Informal group experiences are those relations between people that are not directly a product of an official relationship in an organization or related positions in a division of labor. Illustrative of informal social relations are those involving small talk, leisure-time behavior, friendship interactions, and affectional attachments. Questions such as the following were asked:

I would rather take my vacation
.... with my family
.... with some friends from work
.... by myself

The people I would be most likely to borrow money from are
.... the people I know around town   ·
.... anyone who would lend it to me
.... the people I know here in the plant

It hurts me more if I am disliked
.... by the people at work
.... by the people around town
.... by anyone I know

In all a total of fourteen questions were used to sample informal group experiences. A job-oriented or non-job-oriented score was secured for each worker for the informal group experience sector in accordance with the procedure set forth above.

Only 9 percent of the industrial workers in the sample prefer the informal group life that is centered in the job. Nine out of ten of those studied clearly indicated that their preferred informal human associations and contacts were found in the community, among friends, and in the family.

The industrial sociologist has been impressive in demonstrating the informal group life of people associated together at work. But the relative significance of this kind of human experience in relation to the full round of life has never before been considered. If our findings are at all typical—and general sociology theory would predict the findings to be of this sort—then the workplace is not very congenial to the development of preferred informal human relationships.

Much action research and some company policy has implicitly or explicitly been grounded in the simple-minded assumption that improving, enriching, or facilitating the development of informal group life is both desirable as a goal (to develop "happy" workers) and necessary as a means (to improve production, decrease turnover, etc.). Now it can perhaps be suggested that, on balance, such well-intended efforts may be misdirected. The workplace is not the breeding ground of preferred informal human relationships; deliberate efforts to make it so may be relatively ineffectual. The possible exception, perhaps, is the one worker in ten who sees the job environment as his most likely source of desired informal group life.

The immediately preceding hypothesis tested its underlying proposition by asking questions directly about primary or informal social relations. We can make another test of the proposition by focusing upon the part of it that deals with valued social experience. One of the direct ways of getting at valued social experience is to ask questions that deal with activities giving pleasure, satisfaction, or general rewards, which may be pursued in varying places and at varying times. For questions dealing with this area we have used the designation of "general experience." In terms of this approach to our third proposition, the hypothesis becomes: a significant proportion of industrial workers will not respond to work as a valued social experience when this is tested by the general experience section of the CLI questionnaire. Questions dealing with general experience include those concerning "the most important things I do," "the most pleasant things I do," "my ideas about getting ahead," "my worries," and "my interests." General experience was sampled in a total of nine questions on the basis of which each worker was classified as job-oriented or non-job-oriented in this area.

Only 15 percent of the workers give job-oriented preferences. The rest—about eleven in thirteen—saw experiences of theirs that were sampled in the study as taking place somewhere away from the workplace.

It is immediately suggested that the emotional impact of work and the work environment seems to be remarkably low in terms of general life experiences. Not only is the workplace relatively unimportant as a place of preferred primary human relationships, but it cannot even evoke significant sentiments and emotions in its occupants. These two conclusions may, of course, be related. A large proportion of emotionally significant experience takes place in primary group relationships. If the informal work group is a matter of relative indifference to workers, then it is reasonable that general social experiences of emotional importance will not take place with high frequency in the workplace.

It seems fair to conclude that our hypotheses have been supported. When measured in terms of valued social experience, the workplace is preferred by only 15 percent of the workers studied. When measured in terms of primary human relations, only 9 percent of the workers report that the workplace provides their preferred associations. Thus, in terms of the workplace as a testing ground, we can conclude that the underlying proposition may well be valid: primary human relations take place only in situations where social experience is valued by the individual. Obviously, many more tests of this proposition must be made, but the present tests encourage its future exploration.

Some Bases of Organizational Attachment

Max Weber has pointed out that, in formal organizations based upon rational authority with staff units organized in bureaucracies, the staff members are loyal to the legally established impersonal order of the organization.[7] By implicit extension of this idea we can see immediately the possibilities of other sources of organizational attachment for members. In particular, we can examine the possibility that organizational attachment can be a product of the formal organization and its operations, and of the technology which surrounds work.

Our second general proposition was set forth in the following manner: an individual's attachment to a situation in which his social experience is not valued by him will be to the most physically and directly obvious characteristics of that situation. From our data we propose to test this in terms of experience in formal organizations and experience with technology.

The choice of these two kinds of experiences is based on clear grounds. Both kinds of experiences are direct and obvious. We have many daily evidences of our participation in an organization. We arrive at its building from home, enter into a specified location, do required jobs under the direction of organization supervisors, work with machines and equipment under operating conditions that are special to the work, and have our time spent and output measured and recorded as a basis for remuneration.

We know from the first portion of this study that a significantly large percentage of the industrial workers studied do not value the work situation in terms of its opportunities for informal group experiences and for general affective experiences. This suggests that the workplace provides an excellent opportunity to test our second proposition, because it generally meets the condition that it does not provide valued social experience for a large proportion of its participants. We can derive the following hypothesis from that proposition: a significant proportion of industrial workers will score job-oriented for their organizational experience when measured on the organizational section of the CLI schedule.

A sampling was made of typical relationships between members and organizations. Experience in the formal sector includes a number of different relationships between an organization, its officials, and its members. Hiring, joining, firing, disciplining, rewarding, directing, and ordering are illustrative of relationships of this sort. Some of these relationships were covered in the study and on the basis of his responses to seven questions, each worker was rated as job-oriented or non-job-oriented in the formal sector.

More than three out of five of the workers were scored as job-oriented with respect to their experiences in organizations: 61 percent chose their companies as the most meaningful context to them when their life experiences in organizations were brought into their focus. Put another way, the most significant formal organization when judged in terms of standard and typical organizational ties and bonds is the employing one, the industrial company.

This conclusion should not be confused with the notion that these workers are saying they necessarily like their employer or the company for which they work. No such questions were included. The questions asked placed emphasis only upon choosing that situation or organizational context in which a particular behavior was best carried out, or in which the worker would most like to have it happen. Thus, he was asked to choose between getting a job promotion or "becoming a more important member in my club, church, or lodge"; between workplace or "an organization I belong to" as the locale where praise received produces greater happiness; between regretting most "missing a day's work" or "missing a meeting of an organization I belong to." These choices serve to illustrate the questions asked in order to seek information on attachment to the formal organizations in workers' lives. Like all the questions asked, those in the formal sector were designed to determine the central life interests of workers.

We may conclude, then, that the workers studied were not confusing a liking for their company or its officials with a preference for their workplace as the most important formal organization in their lives. It seems reasonably clear that a significant majority of these workers believed that the companies in which they worked provided the important or preferred opportunities for organizational experience. Further important implications of this finding will be examined below.

The second test of the general proposition underlying this section can be made through the following hypothesis: a significant proportion of industrial workers will be job-oriented for their experiences with technological aspects of their environments when measured on the technological section of the CLI questionnaire.

A sampling was made of experiences involving the relations between people and the technical aspects of their environment. The questions probing this aspect of experience gave the workers the opportunity to select the place or situation most preferred or desired for behavior directly involving relations with machines or technical operating conditions. The technical sector of experience was defined as that involving the relationships between an individual and his actual work operations. Tool, equipment, and machine maintenance; concern with job and operating techniques; overcoming operating problems; minimizing waste; accuracy of operations; quality of materials; and cleanliness and care of operations are illustrative of the kinds of relationships between an individual and technical aspects of his environment. These relations were sampled and another score on job vs. non-job orientation was secured for each worker for the technological sector of experience, based on a total of ten questions.

In the technological sector, 63 percent of the respondents were scored as job-oriented. This is the highest proportion of job-oriented responses for any of the sectors of experience examined. It certainly seems notable that almost two out of every three of the workers studied identified their workplace as the locale of their preferred relationships with the purely technical aspects of their environment.

The meaning of this finding can, perhaps, be made clearer when we examine some of the kinds of questions asked. For the statement, "I don't mind getting dirty," the alternative responses were: "while working at home," "at anytime if I can wash up afterwards," "while working at the plant." The introductory phrase, "I most enjoy keeping," was followed by these choices of response: "my things around the house in good shape," "my hand tools and workspace on the job in good shape," "my mind off such things." Additional questions in this area included:

Noise bothers me most
. . . . when working at home
. . . . when working at the plant
. . . . hardly ever

When I am doing some work
. . . . I am usually most accurate working at home
. . . . I seldom think about being accurate
. . . . I am usually most accurate working at the plant

It will be noted that an attempt was made to select those kinds of technical considerations that would have an equal likelihood of being relevant to the non-job and job environments. We feel certain that the high percentage of job-oriented responses is not the product of a bias in the questions asked that tended to favor the job environment.

The fact that the technological sector of experience is the most clearly job-oriented one suggests the desirability of a fresh appraisal of this dimension of social experience. In the past there has been considerable concern with the general meaninglessness of industrial work derived directly from a technology that makes work itself monotonous, repetitive, mechanical, and fragmentary. The human consequence of this has been generally assumed to be indifference, alienation, rebellion, or even personal disorganization and possibly mental disorder.

We can, however, return to one of Durkheim's important theoretical points and see another possible analytical approach to the problem of technology.[8] It will be recalled that Durkheim stressed the organic solidarity that made whole the individual units, tasks, and jobs in a given division of labor. He was emphasizing, of course, the necessary unity and integration that must bind together the divided and separate tasks and functions constituting the given division of labor. Without such unity the parts cannot mesh properly with each other with the result that the planned-for outcome (product or service) will not be forthcoming.

To Durkheim, this organic solidarity was a non-consensual one. People who were part of a given division of labor did not necessarily share with other members of it either a sense of common enterprise or a body of common values. To be sure, Durkheim clearly saw that consensus was essential to social unity, as his concept of mechanical solidarity illustrates. The connections between the two forms of social bond were a central research interest of his, but remain even to this day a set of mooted issues.

It may now be possible to suggest that industrial employment is one of the important focal points in our society for experiences with technical environments. This kind of experience has meaning in a sociological sense because it signifies the interdependence of man with man even where there is no necessary common ground of values shared between them. The urban environment is heterogeneous—in values, in the backgrounds of its residents, and in their daily experiences. Diversity is one of the hallmarks of urban life. But underpinning this heterogeneity and diversity is a fundamental human interdependence that flows from the far-flung division of labor. The real experiencing of this interdependence and sensing of it comes from the daily job. On the job the urbanite learns more directly and acutely than anywhere else how dependent he is upon those about him. There may follow from this the unity of interdependent action that is such an impressive feature of industrial work. This can often be achieved even in spite of lack of consensus, as Goode and Fowler neatly demonstrated in their study of an industrial plant.[9]

The characteristics of industrial work that are alleged to be disturbing to the individual (monotony, repetitiveness, mechanistic character, and over-specialization) are the very features that make obvious to its participants the nature of symbiotic or technological interdependence. In short, industrial work may be functional for the society because it sharply etches for the individual some awareness of the division of labor and its resultant interdependence.

Both of the hypotheses derived from our second proposition have been supported. This suggests that the proposition has merit. It certainly must be subjected to further test, but we now have some prospect that the tests will continue to sustain the general prediction about human behavior that it represents.

Conclusions

The industrial workers' world is one in which work and the workplace are not central life interests for a vast majority. In particular, work is not a central life interest for industrial workers when we study the informal group experiences and the general social experiences that have some affective value for them. Industrial man seems to perceive his life history as having its center outside of work for his intimate human relationships and for his feelings of enjoyment, happiness, and worth. On the other hand, for his experiences with the technological aspects of his life space and for his participation in formal organizations, he clearly recognizes the primacy of the workplace. In short, he has a well-developed sense of attachment to his work and workplace without a corresponding sense of total commitment to it.

In a more general sense this study has been designed to provide empirical tests for three propositions. We have evidence to believe that these propositions are worthy of further testing. It now seems reasonable to believe that individuals will exhibit adequate social behavior in sectors of social experience in which participation is mandatory but not valued. Where the social experience is not valued, the individual may still become attached to the situation of the experience in terms of the most physically and directly obvious features of that situation (as we examined it, the formal organization and its technology). Finally, we would predict that primary human relationships develop only in situations where the social experience is valued by the individual.

Implications and Speculations

Several years ago the Corning Glass Company celebrated its centennial with a conference whose proceedings have been published under the title of *Creating an Industrial Civilization*.[10] This suggests a theme for drawing implications from this study in a speculative vein. The emphasis is upon the future and the creative task that lies ahead.

Viewed from the standpoint of industrial management there are two broad and contradictory influences at work in the society. Work is no longer a central life interest for workers. These life interests have moved out into the community. Yet work was presumably once a central life interest. Much management activity in personnel and industrial relations is implicitly directed at restoring work to the status of a central life interest. Management's efforts and the main drift of social developments work at directly contrary purposes.

The second contradictory influence centers on the location of primary human relationships in the total social fabric. Some groups in management have accepted a philosophy and developed social engineering practices summed up in the phrase "human relations in industry." The major purpose of this movement is to center primary human relationships in work and make it functional for productivity. At the same time it seems evident that primary human relations are much more likely to be located at some place out in the community. The management efforts again seem to be at odds with social reality.

The first dilemma is perhaps best highlighted in the pronounced frustration that management practitioners experience with the relative failure of their efforts to engender a sense of participation in their work forces. Many have become convinced that it's all a matter of communication and semantics. If simple language is chosen, comic-book presentation is used, and volume of impact is raised, then employees will feel they are part of the "company team," a phrase commonly used. Other efforts have been directed at "participant management" and its latter-day descendant, "group dynamics." Here the chief goal seems to be to make a central life interest out of work by permitting some sharing by employees of decisions affecting their work routines.

None of these efforts has been crowned by remarkable success. Indeed, the group dynamics technique, which has much research background and a number of practical applications, seems singularly sterile. When the research findings indicate that the technique has not produced a material change in the output of an experimental group over an "old-fashioned" control group, the group dynamics approach is justified on the ground that it is easier on the emotional hide of those who are subjected to it.

Perhaps the issue is really not one of human manipulation after all. All the communication effort and group dynamics in the world will not alter the basic drift in our society away from a central life interest in work. Some of the older personnel techniques of supporting after-work activities, bowling leagues and bird-watching clubs, may really be more sensible. Company involvement in a constructive way in community affairs, in the non-work activities of its own employees as well as in a general sense, might be a more significant way to enhance attachment of employees to their company. Perhaps the basic problem is not one of central life interest in work after all, but one of enhancing the sense of attachment of participants to social organizations in which participation is necessary but not important to them. These are all questions that are suggestively derived from this study. They may be examined with profit.

The second dilemma has an interesting intellectual history in which theorizers and researchers, having established the concept of primary group and primary social relations,[11,12] proceeded to apply it indiscriminately to all kinds of social organizations. Whyte in his finest study [13] gave us a magnificent picture of primary relations in boys' gangs (community, not work, organizations). He has since attempted to discover the same primary group life in industry,[14] with much less certainty of the results obtained. At least in this writer's opinion we have a good deal of evidence that there are non-official as well as official, or informal along with formal, relations in a business organization. But to call these "primary social relationships" may do grave injustice to a perfectly good concept.

It may very well be that those efforts of any managerial group in any kind of organization to center primary group life for a majority of employees in the workplace are misplaced. If our evidence is substantiated in other studies, the community is the locale of preferred primary social relations. To attempt to shift the locale to the workplace may be trying to reverse a social development that is not alterable in that direction.

This may not be an entirely undesirable prospect. Weber emphasized the impersonality and efficiency of modern bureaucratic organization. The efficiency can remain along with the impersonality, providing there are other points in the society where the primary social relations can be experienced.

The general conclusion of the Corning Glass Conference was that the problem of creating an industrial civilization is essentially a problem of social invention and creativity in the non-work aspects of life. Our great social inventions will probably not come in connection with work life; they will center in community life. This research certainly suggests the importance of this insight.

Notes

[1] Max Weber, *The Protestant Ethic and the Spirit of Capitalism* (London: Geo. Allen and Unwin, Ltd., 1930).

[2] R. H. Tawney, *Religion and the Rise of Capitalism* (New York: Harcourt, 1926).

[3] George C. Homans, *The Human Group* (New York: Harcourt, Brace and Co., 1950).

[4] F. J. Roethlisberger and W. J. Dickson, *Management and the Worker* (Cambridge: Harvard University Press, 1934).

[5] W. F. Whyte, *Human Relations in the Restaurant Industry* (New York: McGraw-Hill Book Co., 1948).

[6] $N = 491$, for this and all other percentages reported here.

[7] Max Weber, *Theory of Social and Economic Organization* (New York: Oxford University Press, 1947).

[8] Émile Durkheim, *Division of Labor in Society* (Glencoe, Ill.: Free Press, 1947).

[9] W. J. Goode and I. Fowler, "Incentive Factors in a Low Morale Plant," *American Sociological Review*, 14 (October, 1949), pp. 619–24.

[10] *Creating an Industrial Civilization*, Eugene A. Staley, ed. (New York: Harper Bros., 1952).

[11] C. H. Cooley, *Social Organization* (New York: Scribner, 1924).

[12] Georg Simmel, *The Sociology of Georg Simmel*, K. H. Wolff ed. (Glencoe, Ill.: Free Press, 1950).

[13] W. F. Whyte, *Street Corner Society* (Chicago: University of Chicago Press, 1943).

[14] Whyte, *Human Relations in the Restaurant Industry, op. cit.*

PART VI

EDUCATION

The mass media throughout the world has been filled in the last few years with news of campus strikes, sit-ins of administration offices, and other forms of student collective behavior. The issue of school desegregation in the United States also regularly makes the front pages and the network news. These as well as other events draw our attention to the educational institution as a focal point for the study of many large-scale social processes including politi-cal-economic change. The sociology of education, however, is concerned with a myriad of social phenomena on many different levels—from dyadic inter-action (the student-teacher relationship) to interinstitutional analyses (the relationship between economy and education). In complex industrial societies where many people spend a significant portion of their life as students (in some cases "student" is the most salient societal role for a third of one's life), an understanding of the educational system is necessary for understanding social life. Schools are prime socializing agents both through the learning processes they provide, and through the effect of peer groups which grow up within the formal educational structure.

How Children Fail

JOHN HOLT

In this selection the author, an outspoken critic of American education, contends that our schools adversely affect a child's intelligence by helping to destroy his natural inquisitiveness and creative initiative. The child is taught that there is one answer and one right way which he must know; he learns to be afraid of failure. Furthermore, the educational institution compartmentalizes the world into arbitrary units using words and symbols which often have little relation to the child's view of reality. He is told what is important to know rather than allowed to investigate and discover for himself. Therefore, the child forgets all but a small part of what he learns.

The process of education emphasizes memorization of a certain subject matter. Conformity and correctness are supported and rewarded. Children are forced to please others, rather than themselves, and, therefore, become unable to direct their own learning. The educational institution thereby creates "unintelligence." We should add that to the extent this analysis is correct, its effects on an individual are relatively permanent and pervasive. Not only can such "unintelligence" be seen as an integral part of many children's perspective, but it also becomes a factor in determining the effect of all their subsequent experiences.

WHEN we talk about intelligence, we do not mean the ability to get a good score on a certain kind of test, or even the ability to do well in school; these are at best only indicators of something larger, deeper, and far more important. By intelligence we mean a style of life, a way of behaving in various situations, and particularly in new, strange, and perplexing situations. The true test of intelligence is not how much we know how to do, but how we behave when we don't know what to do.

The intelligent person, young or old, meeting a new situation or problem, opens himself up to it; he tries to take in with mind and senses everything he can about it; he thinks about *it,* instead of about himself or what it might cause to happen to him; he grapples with it boldly, imaginatively, resourcefully, and if not confidently at least hopefully; if he fails to master it, he looks without shame or fear at his mistakes and learns what he can from them. This is intelligence. Clearly its roots lie in a certain feeling about life, and one's self with respect to life. Just as clearly, unintelligence is not what most psychologists seem to suppose, the same thing as intelligence only less of it. It is an entirely different style of behavior, arising out of an entirely different set of attitudes.

Years of watching and comparing bright children and the not-bright, or less bright, have shown that they are very different kinds of people. The bright child is curious about life and reality, eager to get in touch with it, embrace it, unite himself with it. There is no wall, no barrier between him and life. The dull child is far less curious, far less interested in what goes on and what is real, more inclined to live in worlds of fantasy. The bright child likes to experiment, to try things out. He lives by the maxim that there is more than one way to skin a cat. If he can't do something one way, he'll try another. The dull child is usually afraid to try at all. It takes a good deal of urging to get him to try even once; if that try fails, he is through.

The bright child is patient. He can tolerate uncertainty and failure, and will keep trying until he gets an answer. When all his experiments fail, he can even admit to himself and others that for the time being he is not going to get an answer. This may annoy him, but he can wait. Very often, he does not want to be told how to do the problem or solve the puzzle he has struggled with, because he does not want to be cheated out of the chance to figure it out for himself in the future. Not so the dull child. He cannot stand uncertainty or failure. To him, an unanswered question is not a challenge or an opportunity, but a threat. If he can't find the answer quickly, it must be given to him, and quickly; and he must have answers for everything. Such are the children of whom a second-grade teacher once said, "But my children *like* to have questions for which there is only one answer." They did; and by a mysterious coincidence, so did she.

The bright child is willing to go ahead on the basis of incomplete understanding and information. He will take risks, sail uncharted seas, explore when the landscape is dim, the landmarks few, the light poor. To give only one example, he will often read books he does not understand in the hope that after a while enough understanding will emerge to make it worth while to go on. In this spirit some of my fifth graders tried to read *Moby Dick*. But the dull child will go ahead only when he thinks he knows exactly where he stands and exactly what is ahead of him. If he does not feel he knows exactly what an experience will be like, and if it will not be exactly like other experiences he already knows, he wants no part of it. For while the bright child feels that the universe is, on the whole, a sensible, reasonable, and trustworthy place, the dull child feels that it is senseless, unpredictable, and treacherous. He feels that he can never tell what may happen, particularly in a new situation, except that it will probably be bad.

Nobody starts off stupid. You have only to watch babies and infants, and think seriously about what all of them learn and do, to see that, except for the most grossly retarded, they show a style of life, and a desire and ability to learn that in an older person we might well call genius. Hardly an adult in a thousand, or ten thousand, could in any three years of his life learn as much, grow as much in his understanding of the world around him, as every infant learns and grows in his first three years. But what happens, as we get older, to this extraordinary capacity for learning and intellectual growth?

What happens is that it is destroyed, and more than by any other one thing, by the process that we misname education—a process that goes on in most homes and schools. We adults destroy most of the intellectual and creative capacity of children by the things we do to them or make them do. We destroy this capacity above all by making them afraid, afraid of not doing what other people want, of not pleasing, of making mistakes, of failing, of being *wrong*. Thus we make them afraid to gamble, afraid to experiment, afraid to try the difficult and the unknown. Even when we do not create children's fears, when they come to us with fears ready-made and built-in, we use these fears as handles to manipulate them and get them to do what we want. Instead of trying to whittle down their fears, we build them up, often to monstrous size. For we like chlidren who are a little afraid of us, docile, deferential children, though not, of course, if they are so obviously afraid that they threaten our image of ourselves as kind, lovable people whom there is no reason to fear. We find ideal the kind of "good" cihldren who are just enough afraid of us to do everything we want, without making us feel that fear of us is what is making them do it.

We destroy the disinterested (I do *not* mean *un*interested) love of learning in children, which is so strong when they are small, by encouraging and compelling them to work for petty and contemptible rewards—gold stars, or papers marked 100 and tacked to the wall, or *A*'s on report cards, or honor rolls, or dean's lists, or Phi Beta Kappa keys—in short, for the ignoble satisfaction of feeling that they are better than someone else. We encourage them to feel that the end and aim of all they do in school is nothing more than to get a good mark on a test, or to impress someone with what they seem to know. We kill, not only their curiosity, but their feeling that it is a good and admirable thing to be curious, so that by the age of ten most of them will not ask questions, and will show a good deal of scorn for the few who do.

In many ways, we break down children's convictions that things make sense, or their hope that things may prove to make sense. We do it, first of all, by breaking up life into arbitrary and disconnected hunks of subject matter, which we then try to "integrate" by such artificial and irrelevant devices as having children sing Swiss folk songs while they are studying the geography of Switzerland, or do arithmetic problems about rail-splitting while they are studying the boyhood of Lincoln. Furthermore, we continually confront them with what is senseless, ambiguous, and contradictory; worse, we do it without knowing that we are doing it, so that, hearing nonsense shoved at them as if it were sense, they come to feel that the source of their confusion lies not in the material but in their own stupidity. Still further, we cut children off from their own common sense and the world of reality by requiring them to play with and shove around words and symbols that have little or no meaning to them. Thus we turn the vast majority of our students into the kind of people for whom all symbols are meaningless; who cannot use symbols as a way of learning about and dealing with reality; who cannot understand written instructions; who, even if they read books, come out knowing no more than when they went in; who may have a few new words rattling around in their heads, but whose mental models of the world remain unchanged and, indeed, impervious to change. The minority, the able and successful students, we are very likely to turn into something different but just as dangerous: the kind of people who can manipulate words and symbols fluently while keeping themselves largely divorced from the reality for which they stand; the kind of people who like to speak in large generalities but grow silent or indignant if someone asks for an example of what they are talking about; the kind of people who, in their discussions of world affairs, coin and use such words as megadeaths and megacorpses, with scarcely a thought to the blood and suffering these words imply.

We encourage children to act stupidly, not only by scaring and confusing them, but by boring them, by filling up their days with dull, repetitive tasks that make little or no claim on their attention or demands on their intelligence. Our hearts leap for joy at the sight of a roomful of children all slogging away at some imposed task, and we are all the more pleased and satisfied if someone tells us that the children don't really like what they are doing. We tell ourselves that this drudgery, this endless busywork, is good preparation for life, and we fear that without it children would be hard to "control." But why must this busywork be so dull? Why not give tasks that are interesting and demanding? Because, in schools where every task must be completed and every answer must be right, if we give children more demanding tasks they will be fearful and will instantly insist that we show them how to do the job. When you have acres of paper to fill up with pencil marks, you have no time to waste on the luxury of thinking. By such means children are firmly established in the habit of using only a small part of their thinking capacity. They feel that school is a place where they must spend most of their time doing dull tasks in a dull way. Before long they are deeply settled in a rut of unintelligent behavior from which most of them could not escape even if they wanted to.

School tends to be a dishonest as well as a nervous place. We adults are not often honest with children, least of all in school. We tell them, not what we think, but what we feel they ought to think; or what other people feel or tell us they ought to think. Pressure groups find it easy to weed out of our classrooms, texts, and libraries whatever facts, truths, and ideas they happen to find unpleasant or inconvenient. And we are not even as truthful with children as we could safely be, as the parents, politicians, and pressure groups would let us be. Even in the most non-controversial areas our teaching, the books, and the textbooks we give children present a dishonest and distorted picture of the world.

The fact is that we do not feel an obligation to be truthful to children. We are like the managers and manipulators of news in Washington, Moscow, London, Peking, and Paris, and all the other capitals of the world. We think it our right and our duty, not to tell the truth, but to say whatever will best serve our cause—in this case, the cause of making children grow up into the kind of people we want them to be, thinking whatever we want them to think. We have only to convince ourselves (and we are very easily convinced) that a lie will be "better" for the children than the truth, and we will lie. We don't always need even that excuse; we often lie only for our own convenience.

Worse yet, we are not honest about ourselves, our own fears, limitations, weaknesses, prejudices, motives. We present ourselves to children as if we were gods, all-knowing, all-powerful, always rational, always just, always right. This is worse than any lie we could tell about ourselves. I have more than once shocked teachers by telling them that when kids ask me a question to which I don't know the answer, I say, "I haven't the faintest idea"; or that when I make a mistake, as I often do, I say, "I goofed again"; or that when I am trying to do something I am no good at, like paint in water colors or play a clarinet or bugle, I do it in front of them so they can see me struggling with it, and can realize that not all adults are good at everything. If a child asks me to do something that I don't want to do, I tell him that I won't do it because I don't want to do it, instead of giving him a list of "good" reasons sounding as if they had come down from the Supreme Court. Interestingly enough, this rather open way of dealing with children works quite well. If you tell a child that you won't do something because you don't want to, he is very likely to accept that as a fact which he cannot change; if you ask him to stop doing something because it drives you crazy, there is a very good chance that, without further talk, he will stop, because he knows what that is like. . . .

Behind much of what we do in school lie some ideas, that could be expressed roughly as follows: (1) Of the vast body of human knowledge, there are certain bits and pieces that can be called essential, that everyone should know; (2) the extent to which a person can be considered educated, qualified to live intelligently in today's world and be a useful member of society, depends on the amount of this essential knowledge that he carries about with him; (3) it is the duty of schools, therefore, to get as much of this essential knowledge as possible into the minds of children. Thus we find ourselves trying to poke certain facts, recipes, and ideas down the gullets of every child in school, whether the morsel interests him or not, even if it frightens him or sickens him, and even if there are other things that he is much more interested in learning.

These ideas are absurd and harmful nonsense. We will not begin to have true education or real learning in our schools until we sweep this nonsense out of the way. Schools should be a place where children learn what they most want to know, instead of what we think they ought to know. The child who wants to know something remembers it and uses it once he has it; the child who learns something to please or appease someone else forgets it when the need for pleasing or the danger of not appeasing is past. This is why children quickly forget all but a small part of what they learn in school. It is of no use or interest to them; they do not want, or expect, or even intend to remember it. The only difference between bad and good students in this respect is that the bad students forget right away, while the good students are careful to wait until after the exam. If for no other reason, we could well afford to throw out most of what we teach in school because the children throw out almost all of it anyway. . . .

Learning is not everything, and certainly one piece of learning is as good as another. One of my brightest and boldest fifth graders was deeply interested in snakes. He knew more about snakes than anyone I've ever known. The school did not offer herpetology; snakes were not in the curriculum; but as far as I was concerned, any time he spent learning about snakes was better spent than in ways I could think of to spend it; not least of all because, in the process of learning about snakes, he learned a great deal more about many other things than I was ever able to "teach" those unfortunates in my class who were not interested in anything at all. In another fifth-grade class, studying Romans in Britain, I saw a boy trying to read a science book behind the cover of his desk. He was spotted, and made to put the book away, and listen to the teacher; with a heavy sigh he did so. What was gained here? She traded a chance for an hour's real learning about science for, at best, an hour's temporary learning about history—much more probably no learning at all, just an hour's worth of daydreaming and resentful thoughts about school.

It is not subject matter that makes some learning more valuable than others, but the spirit in which the work is done. If a child is doing the kind of learning that most children do in school, when they learn at all—swallowing words, to spit back at the teacher on demand—he is wasting his time, or rather, we are wasting it for him. This learning will not be permanent, or relevant, or useful. But a child who is learning naturally, following his curiosity where it leads him, adding to his mental model of reality whatever he needs and can find a place for, and rejecting without fear or guilt what he does not need, is growing—in knowledge, in the love of learning, and in the ability to learn. He is on his way to becoming the kind of person we need in our society, and that our "best" schools and colleges are *not* turning out, the kind of person who, in Whitney Griswold's words, seeks and finds meaning, truth, and enjoyment in everything he does. All his life he will go on learning. Every experience will make his mental model of reality more complete and more true to life, and thus make him more able to deal realistically, imaginatively, and constructively with whatever new experience life thows his way.

We cannot have real learning in school if we think it is our duty and our right to tell children what they must learn. We cannot know, at any moment, what particular bit of knowledge or understanding a child needs most, will most strengthen and best fit his model of reality. Only he can do this. He may not do it very well, but he can do it a hundred times better than we can. The most we can do is try to help, by letting him know roughly what is available and where he can look for it. Choosing what he wants to learn and what he does not is something he must do for himself.

There is one more reason, and the most important one, why we must reject the idea of school and classroom as places where, most of the time, children are doing what some adult tells them to do. The reason is that there is no way to coerce children without making them afraid, or more afraid. We must not try to fool ourselves into thinking that this is not so. The would-be progressives, who until recently had great influence over most American public school education, did not recognize this—and still do not. They thought, or at least talked and wrote as if they thought, that there were good ways and bad ways to coerce children (the bad ones mean, harsh, cruel; the good ones gentle, persuasive, subtle, kindly), and that if they avoided the bad and stuck to the good they would do no harm. This was one of their greatest mistakes, and the main reason why the revolution they hoped to accomplish never took hold.

The idea of painless, non-threatening coercion is an illusion. Fear is the inseparable companion of coercion, and its inescapable consequence. If you think it your duty to make children do what you want, whether they will or not, then it follows inexorably that you must make them afraid of what will happen to them if they don't do what you want. You can do this in the old-fashioned way, openly and avowedly, with the threat of harsh words, infringement of liberty, or physical punishment. Or you can do it in the modern way, subtly, smoothly, quietly, by withholding the acceptance and approval which you and others have trained the children to depend on; or by making them feel that some retribution awaits them in the future, too vague to imagine but too implacable to escape. You can, as many skilled teachers do, learn to tap with a word, a gesture, a look, even a smile, the great reservoir of fear, shame, and guilt that today's children carry around inside them. Or you can simply let your own fears, about what will happen to you if the children don't do what you want, reach out and infect them. Thus the children will feel more and more that life is full of dangers from which only the goodwill of adults like you can protect them, and that this goodwill is perishable and must be earned anew each day.

The alternative—I can see no other—is to have schools and classrooms in which each child in his own way can satisfy his curiosity, develop his abilities and talents, pursue his interests, and from the adults and older children around him get a glimpse of the great variety and richness of life. In short, the school should be a great smörgåsbord of intellectual, artistic, creative, and athletic activities, from which each child could take whatever he wanted, and as much as he wanted, or as little. When Anna was in the sixth grade, the year after she was in my class, I mentioned this idea to her. After describing very sketchily how such a school might be run, and what the children might do, I said, "Tell me, what do you think of it? Do you think it would work? Do you think the kids would learn anything?" She said, with utmost conviction, "Oh, yes, it would be wonderful!" She was silent for a minute or two, perhaps remembering her own generally unhappy schooling. Then she said thoughtfully, "You know, kids really like to learn; we just don't like being pushed around."

No, they don't; and we should be grateful for that. So let's stop pushing them around, and give them a chance.

Learning the Norms of Adult Life

ROBERT DREEBEN

In this excerpt from his book *On What Is Learned in School,* Dreeben discusses the ways in which school contributes to the learning of certain norms which are basic to adult life in contemporary industrial society. He points out that family experience does not function in terms of these principles, and that it is largely in the schools that people learn "to participate competently in the public realm."

In school, children learn that others can legitimately expect them to do certain things, in a certain way, and do them alone. Dreeben cites cheating and testing as two aspects of classroom experience that bear on learning the norm of independence. Paradoxically, these aspects proscribe cooperative behavior which is encouraged in the occupational realm, and in other adult areas. The rules on cheating and testing, however, affirm the primacy of independence as a cultural value. Achievement orientation is also learned in school, both within the classroom and in extracurricular activities. Most children learn to cope with successes and failures in such activities, and this prepares them for adult life in industrial society which is based in large part on achievement principles. Dreeben uses the concepts of universalism and specificity developed by Talcott Parsons to indicate two other basic norms that are learned in school. By universalism, Dreeben means viewing someone in terms of his membership in a category or set of categories rather than in terms of his particular personal attributes. Universalism is the prevailing norm in school since children see themselves and their teachers in terms of categories and social positions. Specificity refers to how narrow or broad one's interest is in the person with whom he is interacting. In school, associations between teachers and students revolve about specific issues, particularly when the child reaches secondary school.

In sum, Dreeben shows that other things are learned in school besides reading, writing, and 'rithmetic. Children also learn the norms and values upon which adult life in industrial society is based.

Generally speaking . . . a teacher must balance a concern with specific accomplishments with some concern for a state of well-being: he has to keep a relatively "happy" class which "learns." But a class is more than a collection of

Originally published as "The Contribution of Schooling to the Learning of Norms: Independence, Achievement, Universalism, and Specificity" in *On What Is Learned in School,* pp. 63–79, by Robert Dreeben, Addison-Wesley Publishing Co., Inc., Reading, Mass. Copyright © 1968.

individuals. The teacher always has to manage children in groups. His acts towards individuals must somehow be interpreted either as expressions of general rules or of a particular circumstance. In the latter case he must draw the further line between legitimate special treatment and favouritism. He must teach the relegation of private needs as well as their occasional relevance.

—Kaspar D. Naegele, "Clergymen, Teachers, and Psychiatrists: . . ."

IN speaking of these four ideas as norms, I mean that individuals accept them as legitimate standards for governing their own conduct in the appropriate situations. Specifically, they accept the obligations to (1) act by themselves (unless collaborative effort is called for), and accept personal responsibility for their conduct and accountability for its consequences; (2) perform tasks actively and master the environment according to certain standards of excellence; and (3) acknowledge the rights of others to treat them as members of categories (4) on the basis of a few discrete characteristics rather than on the full constellation of them that represent the whole person. I treat these four norms because they are integral parts of public and occupational life in industrial societies, or institutional realms adjacent to the school.

In earlier parts of this book, I have discussed only the pre-adult phases of socialization, which occur in the family of orientation and in the school. In one sense, at least for men, full adult status requires occupational employment, and one of the outcomes of schooling is employability. The capacity to hold a job involves not only adequate physical capacities (in part the outcome of biological maturation), but also the appropriate intellectual and psychological skills to cope with the demands of work. The requirements of job-holding are multifarious; however, most occupations require, among other things, that individuals take personal responsibility for the completion and quality of their work and individual accountability for its shortcomings, and that they perform their tasks to the best of their ability.

Public life extends beyond occupational employment. Even though people work as members of occupational categories, and in association with others as clients, patients, customers, parishioners, students, and so on, they also have nonoccupational identities as voters, communicants, petitioners, depositors, applicants, and creditors (to name just a few), in which people are similarly classified according to one primary characteristic, irrespective of how they differ otherwise.

Goode observes:

The prime social characteristic of modern industrial enterprise is that the individual is ideally given a job on the basis of his ability to fulfill its demands, and that this achievement is evaluated universalistically; the same standards apply *to all who hold the same job*.[1]

Industrially oriented societies tend to have occupational systems based on normative principles different from those of kinship units. Many observers, recognizing that individuals must undergo psychological changes of considerable magnitude in order to make the transition from family of orientation to economic employment,[2] have noted (but at the same time understated) the contribution of schooling. Eisenstadt, for example, in an otherwise penetrating analysis of age-grouping, restricts his treatment of the school's contribution to that of ". . . *adapting the psychological (and to some extent also physiological) learning potential of the child to the various skills and knowledges which must be acquired by him.*"[3] Eistenstadt's emphasis is too narrowly limited to those cognitive outcomes of schooling related to instrumental knowledge.

Furthermore, while stressing the transition between family and occupation, most writers have largely ignored the contribution of schooling to the development of psychological capacities necessary for participating in other (noneconomic) segments of society. It is my contention that the social experiences available to pupils in schools, by virtue of the nature and sequence of their structural arrangements, provide opportunities for children to learn norms characteristic of several facets of adult public life, occupation being but one.

The social properties of schools are such that pupils, by coping with the sequence of classroom tasks and situations, are more likely to learn the principles (i.e., social norms) of independence, achievement, universalism, and specificity than if they had remained full-time members of the household. Although I have spoken thus far only of the similarities and differences between the family and the school, the nature of that comparison is largely determined by the character of public institutions, in particular the economy and the polity. Schools, that is to say, form one of several institutional linkages between the household and the public sphere of adult life, a linkage organized around stages of the life cycle in industrial societies. There is substantial evidence that conduct in the family and conduct on the job are governed by contrasting normative principles. From this we can imply that if the education of children were carried on primarily within the jurisdiction of the family, the nature of experiences available in that setting would not provide conditions appropriate for acquiring those capacities that enable people to participate competently in the public realm.

It is not inevitable that schools should provide such an institutional linkage, but the fact of the matter is that they do, even though there are other candidates for the job. Mass media, for example, might perform a comparable knowledge-dispensing function, and if their potentialities for effecting more profound psychological changes were plumbed, they might constitute an agency sufficiently potent to bring about changes in principles of conduct. The media have not yet proved up to the job, however, perhaps in part because children's early experiences in the family predispose them to be responsive to human agents, and the media do not provide such agents. In fact, much research on the impact of mass media points to the importance of human links in the chain from source to audience. Occupational apprenticeship might be an acceptable substitute for the schools; it has the human element and is directly related to occupational employment, one of the main locations of men's engagement in the public sphere of industrial society. Apprenticeship, however, like the media, has its own liabilities, one of which is that it continues relationships of dependency (not of child on parent, but of worker on employer), and those relationships are often found to be incompatible with many of the institutional demands of public life. Since the media and apprenticeship arrangements do not exhaust the possibilities, and since I am not trying to demonstrate the inevitability of schools, the impact of schooling remains to be explained, because schools are what we have. I turn, then, to a discussion of how the experiences of schooling contribute to the acquisition of the four norms in question.

Independence

One answer to the question, "What is learned in school?" is that pupils learn to acknowledge that there are tasks they must do alone, and to do them that way. Along with this self-imposed obligation goes the idea that others have a legitimate right to expect such independent behavior under certain circumstances.[4] Independence has a widely acknowledged though not unequivocal meaning. In using it here I refer to a cluster of meanings: doing things on one's own, being self-reliant, accepting personal responsibility for one's behavior, acting self-sufficiently,[5] and handling tasks with which, *under different circumstances,* one can rightfully expect the help of others. The pupil, when in school, is separated from family members who have customarily provided help, support, and sustenance—persons on whom he has long been dependent.

A constellation of classroom characteristics, teacher actions, and pupil actions shape experiences in which the norm of independence is learned. In addition to the fact that school children are removed from persons with whom they have already formed strong relationships of dependency, the sheer size of a classroom assemblage limits each pupil's claim to personal contact with the teacher, and more so at the secondary levels than at the elementary. This numerical property of classrooms reduces pupils' opportunities for establishing new relationships of dependency with adults and for receiving help from them.

Parents expect their children to act independently in many situations, but teachers are more systematic in expecting pupils to adhere to standards of independence in performing academic tasks. There are at least two additional aspects of classroom operation that bear directly on learning the norm of independence: rules about cheating and formal testing. Let us consider cheating first. The word itself is condemnatory in its reference to illegal and immoral acts. Most commonly, attention turns to how much cheating occurs, who cheats, and why. But these questions, while of great importance elsewhere, are of no concern here. My interest is in a different problem: to what types of conduct is the pejorative "cheating" assigned?

In school, cheating pertains primarily to instructional activities and usually refers to acts in which two or more parties participate when the unaided action of only one is expected. Illegal or immoral acts such as stealing and vandalism, whether carried out by individuals or groups, are not considered cheating because they have no direct connection with the central academic core of school activities. Nor is joint participation categorically proscribed; joint effort is called cooperation or collusion depending on the teacher's prior definition of the task.

Cheating takes many forms, most of which involve collective effort. A parent and a child may collaborate to produce homework; two pupils can pool their wisdom (or ignorance, as the case may be) in the interest of passing an examination. In both cases the parties join deliberately, although deliberateness is not essential to the definition; one pupil can copy from another without the latter knowing. In the case of plagiarism, of course, the second party is not a person at all, but information compiled by another. The use of crib notes, perhaps a limiting case, involves no collusion; it consists, rather, of an illegitimate form of help. These are the main forms of school cheating, but there are many variations, routine to exotic. Thus actions called cheating are those closely tied to the instructional goals of the school and usually involve assisted performance when unaided performance is expected. As one observer put it: Pupils ". . . *must learn to distinguish between cooperating and cheating.*" [6]

The irony of cheating *in school* is that the same kinds of acts are considered morally acceptable and even commendable in other situations. It is praiseworthy for one friend to assist another in distress, or for a parent to help a child; and if one lacks the information to do a job, the resourceful thing is to look it up. In effect, many school activities called cheating are the customary forms of support and assistance in the family and among friends.

In one obvious sense, school rules against cheating are designed to establish the content of moral standards. In another sense, the school attaches the stigma of immorality to certain types of behavior for social as distinct from ethical reasons; namely, to change the character of prevailing social relationships in which children are involved. In the case of homework, the school, in effect, attempts to redefine the relationship between parents and children by proscribing one kind of parental support, which is not a problem in other circumstances. The teacher has no direct control over parents but tries to influence them at a distance by asking their adherence to a principle clothed in moral language whose violations are punishable. The line between legitimate parental support (encouraged when it takes the form of parents stressing the importance of school and urging their children to do well) and collusion is unclear, but by morally proscribing parental intervention beyond a certain point, the teacher attempts to limit the child's dependence on family members in doing his school work. In other words, he expects the pupil to work independently. The same argument applies to pupils and their friends; the teacher attempts to eliminate those parts of friendship that make it difficult or impossible for him to discover what a pupil can do on his own. In relationships with kin and friends, the customary sources of support in times of adversity, the school intervenes by restricting solidarity and, in the process, determines what the pupil can accomplish unaided. The pupil, for his part, discovers which of his actions he is held accountable for individually within the confines of tasks set by the school.

This argument is indirectly supported by the comparison between schooling and the occupational employment for which school is intended as preparation. The question here is the sense in which school experience is preparatory. Usually workers are not restricted in seeking help on problems confronting them; on the contrary, many occupations provide resources specifically intended to be helpful: arrangements for consultation, libraries, access to more experienced colleagues, and so on. Only in rare situations are people expected not to enlist the aid of family and friends in matters pertaining to work where that aid is appropriate. In other words, activities on the job, directly analogous to school work, do not carry comparable restrictions. However, people in their occupational activities are required to accept individual responsibility and accountability for the performance of assigned and self-initiated tasks. To the extent that the school contributes to the development of independence, the preparation lies more in the development of a psychological disposition to act independently than to perform a certain range of tasks without help.

Second, as to testing, and particularly the use of achievement tests; most important for independence are the social conditions designed for the *administration* of tests, not their content or format. By and large, pupils are tested under more or less rigorously controlled conditions. At one end of the spectrum, formal standardized tests are administered most stringently; pupils are physically separated, and the testing room is patrolled by proctors whose job is to discover contraband and to guarantee that no communication occurs, these arrangements being designed so that each examination paper represents independent work. At the other end, some testing situations are more informal, less elaborately staged, although there is almost always some provision to ensure that each pupil's work represents the product of only his own efforts.

Testing represents an approach to establishing the norm of independence, which is different from the proscription against cheating even though both are designed to reduce the likelihood of joint effort. Whereas the rules against cheating are directed toward delineating the form of appropriate behavior, the restrictions built into the testing situation provide physical constraints intended to guarantee that teachers will receive samples of the work pupils do unassisted. Actually, unless they stipulate otherwise, teachers expect pupils to do most of their everyday work by themselves; daily assignments provide the opportunity for and practice in independent work. Tests, because they occur at less frequent intervals than ordinary assignments, cannot provide comparably frequent opportunities; by the elaborate trappings of their administration, particularly with college entrance exams, and the anxiety they provoke, they symbolize the magnitude of the stakes.

It may be objected that in emphasizing independence I have ignored cooperation, since an important item on the school agenda is the instruction of pupils in the skills of working with others. Teachers do assign work to groups and expect a collaborative product, and to this extent they require the subordination of individual to collective efforts, but judging the product according to collective standards is another question.

To evaluate the contribution of each member of a working team, the teacher must either judge the quality of each one's work, in effect relying on the standard of independence, or rate each contribution according to the quality of the total product. The latter procedure rests on the assumption that each member has contributed equally, an untenable assumption if one member has carried the rest or if a few members have carried a weak sister. That occurrences of this kind are usually considered "unfair" suggests the normative priority of independence and the simple fact of life in industrial societies, i.e., that institutions of higher learning and employers want to know how well each person can do and put constraints on the school in order to find out. Thus, although the school provides opportunities for pupils to gain experience in cooperative situations, in the last analysis it is the individual assessment that counts.

Achievement

Pupils come to accept the premise that they should perform their tasks the best they can, and act accordingly. The concept of achievement, like independence, has several referents. It usually denotes activity and mastery, making an impact on the environment rather than fatalistically accepting it, and competing against some standard of excellence. Analytically, the concept should be distinguished from independence, since, among other differences, achievement criteria can apply to activities performed collectively.

Much of the recent literature treats achievement in the context of child-rearing within the family as if achievement motivation were primarily a product of parental behavior.[7] Even though there is reason to believe that early childhood experiences in the family do contribute to its development, classroom experiences also contribute through teachers' use of resources beyond those ordinarily at the command of family members.

Classrooms are organized around a set of core activities in which a teacher assigns tasks to pupils and evaluates and compares the quality of their work. In the course of time, pupils differentiate themselves according to how well they perform a variety of tasks, most of which require the use of symbolic skills. Achievement standards are not limited in applicability to the classroom nor is their content restricted to the cognitive areas. Schools afford opportunities for participation in a variety of extra-curricular activities, most conspicuously athletics, but also music, dramatics, and a bewildering array of club and small group activities serving individual interests and talents.

The direct relevance of classroom work in providing task experience judged by achievement criteria is almost self-evident; the experience is built into the assignment-performance-evaluation sequence of the work. Less evident, however, is the fact that these activities force pupils to cope with various degrees of success and failure, both of which can be psychologically problematic. Consistently successful performance requires that pupils deal with the consequences of their own excellence in a context of peer equality in nonacademic areas. For example, they confront the dilemma inherent in having surpassed their age-mates in some respects while depending on their friendship and support in others, particularly in out-of-school social activities. The classroom provides not only the achievement experience itself but by-products of it, taking the form of the dilemma just described.

Similarly, pupils whose work is consistently poor not only must participate in achievement activities leading to their failure, they must also experience living with that failure. They adopt various modes of coping with this, most of which center around maintaining personal self-respect in the face of continuing assaults upon it. Probably a minority succeed or fail consistently; a majority, most likely, do neither one consistently, but nonetheless worry about not doing well. Schooling, then, assures most pupils the experiences of both winning and losing, and to the extent that they gain some modicum of gratification from academic activities, it teaches them to approach their work in a frame of mind conducive to achievement. At the same time they learn how to cope, in a variety of ways and more or less well, with success and failure.

Failure is perhaps the more difficult condition with which to cope because it requires acknowledgment that the premise of achievement, to which failure itself can be attributed in part, is a legitimate principle by which to govern one's actions. Yet situations that constrain people to live with personal failure are endemic to industrial societies in which many facets of public life are based on achievement principles; political defeat and occupational nonpromotion being two cases in point.

As suggested earlier, the school provides a broad range of experiences other than those restricted to the classroom and academic in nature; these experiences are also based on achievement criteria but differ in several important respects. Alternatives to academic performance give the pupil a chance to succeed in achievement-oriented activities even though he may not be able to do well in the classroom.

How these alternative activities differ from those of the classroom is as important as the fact that they do so differ, as evidenced by the case of athletics. Competitive sports resemble classroom activities in that both provide participants with the chance to demonstrate individual excellence. However, the former—and this is more true of team than individual sports— permit collective responsibility for defeat, whereas the latter by and large allow only individual responsibility for failure. That is to say, the chances of receiving personal gratification for success are at least as great in sports as in the classroom, while the assault on personal self-respect for failure is potentially less intense. Athletics should not be written off as a manifestation of mere adolescent nonintellectualism, as recent writers have treated it.[8] I do not suggest that athletics has an as yet undiscovered intellectual richness; rather that its contribution should not be viewed simply in terms of intellectuality. Wilkinson, in talking about athletics in the British public schools, makes a similar argument, not so much in terms of mitigating the psychological consequences of achievement for individuals as in striking a balance between competition and social cooperation:

> On the football field and on the river, the public school taught its boys to compete, not so much in personal contests, as in struggles between groups—between teams, houses, and schools. . . . They preserved middle-class morality and energy, but they adapted these to the needs of the public servant,[9]

so important, according to Wilkinson, in establishing the ethic that private privilege meant public duty.

A similar contention holds for music and dramatics; both provide the potentiality for individual accomplishment and recognition without the persistent, systematic, and potentially corrosive evaluation typical of the classroom. Finally, in various club activities based on interest and talent, a pupil can do the things he is good at in the company of others who share an appreciation for them. In all these situations, either the rigors of competition and judgment characteristic of the classroom are mitigated, or the activity in question has its own built-in source of support and personal protection, not to the same extent as in the family, but more than is available in the crucible of the classroom.

The school provides a wider variety of achievement experiences than does the family, but it also has fewer resources for supporting and protecting pupils' self-respect in the face of failure. As pupils proceed through successive school levels, the rigors of achievement increase, at least for those who continue along the main academic line. Moreover, at the secondary levels the number of activities governed according to achievement principles increases as does the variety of these activities. As preparation for adult public life in which the application of these principles is widespread, schooling contributes to personal development in assuring that the majority of pupils not only will have performed tasks according to the achievement standard, but that they will have had experience in an expanding number of situations in which activities are organized according to it.

Universalism and Specificity

Unlike independence and achievement, universalism and specificity are not commonly regarded as good things. Parents and teachers admonish children to act independently and do their work well; few of them support the idea that people should willingly acknowledge their similarity to one another in specifically categorical terms while ignoring their obvious differences; that is, in a sense, denying their own individuality.

Ideologically, social critics have deplored the impersonal, ostensibly dehumanizing, aspects of categorization, a principle widely believed to lie at the heart of the problem of human alienation; the attachment of man to machine, the detachment of man from man. Often ignored, however, is the connection between this principle and the idea of fairness, or equity. Seen from this vantage point, categorization is widely regarded as a good thing, especially when contrasted to nepotism, favoritism, and arbitrariness. People resent the principle when they think they have a legitimate reason to receive special consideration, and when their individuality appears to vanish by being "processed." Yet when a newcomer breaks into a long queue of patiently waiting people instead of proceeding to the end of the line, they usually condemn him for acting unfairly (for not following the standard rule for all newcomers to a line). They do *not* react by expressing any sense of their own alienation, since they accept the same categorical principle as binding on themselves. In other words, this is not the occasion to proclaim one's individuality, but to act like everybody else and be sure they do likewise. The contrasts between the two dualities (individuality and dehumanization, fairness and special privilege) are similarly predicated on the principles of universalism and specificity; people differ in their posture toward each duality according to ideological position, situation, and, more cynically, in their conception of self-interest.

The concepts of universalism and specificity have been formulated most comprehensively by Parsons, though only part of his formulation is directly germane to this discussion. As part of his concern with social systems, Parsons views universalism as one horn of a dilemma (the other being particularism) in role definition; under what circumstances does the occupant of one social position govern his actions by adopting one standard or another when dealing with the occupant of another social position? My concern, however, is not with a selection among alternative, conflicting standards, but with the conditions under which individuals learn to impose the standards of universalism and specificity on themselves and to act accordingly.

Defining the central theme of universalism raises problems because the term has been assigned a variety of meanings, not all of them clear.[10] The relevant distinction here is whether individuals are treated in terms of their membership in categories or as special cases. In one respect or another an individual can always be viewed as a member of one or more categories, universalistically; he is viewed particularistically if, considering his similarity to others in the same category, he still receives special treatment. As Blau puts it:

> An attribute is defined as a universalistic standard if persons, regardless of their own characteristics, direct a disproportionate number of their positive (or negative) evaluations to others with a certain characteristic. An attribute is defined as a particularistic standard if persons tend to direct their positive (or, in special cases, negative) evaluations to others whose characteristics are like their own.[11]

The treatment of others does not become more particularistic as an increasing number of categories is taken into account. If age, sex, religion, ethnicity, and the like are considered, all examples of general categories, treatment is still categorical in nature because it is oriented to categorical similarities and not to what is special about the person. Thus, *"A man's orientation toward his family,"* according to Blau, *"is considered particularistic because it* singles out for special attention *the members of an ingroup, rather than persons with a certain attribute regardless of whether it makes them part of his ingroup or not."* [12]

The norm of specificity is easily confused with universalism despite its distinctiveness. It refers to the scope of one person's interest in another; to the obligation to confine one's interest to a narrow range of characteristics and concerns, or to extend them to include a broad range.[13] The notion of relevance is implicit; the characteristics and concerns that should be included within the range, whether broad or narrow, are those considered relevant in terms of the activities in which the persons in question are involved. Doctors and storekeepers, for example, differ in the scope of the interest they have in the persons seeking their services, but the content of their interests also varies according to the nature of the needs and desires of those persons.

It is my contention that what the school contributes to the acceptance by children of those norms that penetrate many areas of public life is critical, because children's pre-school experience in the family is weighted heavily on the side of special treatment and parental consideration of the whole child. To say that children learn the norm of universalism means that they come to accept being treated by others as members of categories (in addition to being treated as special cases, as in the family).

CATEGORIZATION

Schools provide a number of experiences that families cannot readily provide because of limitations in their social composition and structure. One such experience is the systematic establishment and demarcation of membership categories. First, by assigning all pupils in a classroom the same or similar tasks to perform, teachers in effect make them confront the same set of demands. Even if there are variations in task content, class members still confront the same teacher and the obligations he imposes. Second, parity of age creates a condition of homogeneity according to developmental stage, a rough equalization of pupil capacities making it possible for teachers to assign similar tasks. Third, through the process of yearly promotion from grade to grade, pupils cross the boundaries separating one age category from another. With successive boundary crossings comes the knowledge that each age-grade category is associated with a particular set of circumstances (e.g., teachers, difficulty of tasks, subject matter studied). Moreover, pupils learn the relationship between categories and how their present position relates to past and future positions by virtue of having experienced the transitions between them. In these three ways, the grade (more specifically the classroom within the grade) with its age-homogeneous membership and clearly demarcated boundaries provides a basis for categorical grouping that the family cannot readily duplicate. Most important, the experiences of membership in a group of age-equals and repeated boundary crossings makes it possible for pupils to acquire a relativity of perspective, a capacity to view their own circumstances from other vantage points that they themselves have occupied.[14]

Although each child holds membership in the category "children" at home, parents, in raising them, tend to take age differences into account and thereby accentuate the uniqueness of each child's circumstances, thus belying in some measure the categorical aspects of "childhood." However, even if the category "children" breaks into its age-related components within the family, it remains intact when children compare themselves with friends and neighbors of similar age. In typical situations of this kind, children inform their parents that friends of the same age have greater privileges or fewer responsibilities than they. Parents, if they cannot actually equalize the circumstances, often explain or justify the disparity by pointing to the special situation of the neighbor family; they have more money, fewer children, a bigger house. Whatever the reason, that is, parents point out the uniqueness of family circumstances and thereby emphasize the particularities of each child's situation. The school, in contrast, provides the requisite circumstances for making comparisons among pupils in categorical rather than particular terms.

Another school experience fostering the establishment of social categories is the re-equalization of pupils by means of the high school track system after they have differentiated themselves through academic achievement in the lower grades, a mechanism that minimizes the likelihood of teachers having to deal with special cases. Teachers with a variegated batch of pupils must adopt more individualized methods of instruction than those whose pupils are similar in their level of achievement. In so doing, they partially recreate a kinship-type of relationship with pupils, treating segments of the class differently according to differences in capacity, much as parents treat their children differently according to age-related capacities.

As far as level is concerned, the high school is a better place to acquire the principle of universalism than the lower school levels because pupils within each track, who are of roughly similar capacity, move from classroom to classroom, in each one receiving instruction in a different subject area by a different teacher. They discover that over a range of activities, they are treated alike and that relatively uniform demands and criteria of evaluation are applied to them. Thus they learn which differences in experience are subordinated to the principle of categorization. The elementary classroom, oriented more to instruction in different subjects by a single teacher, does not provide the necessary variations in persons and subjects for a clear-cut demonstration of the categorical principle.

PERSONS AND POSITIONS

Although the idea of categorization is central to the norm of universalism, it has additional and derivative aspects. One is the crucial distinction, widely relevant in industrial societies, between the person and the social position he occupies. Individuals are often expected to treat one another according to their social position, rather than according to their individual identity. Schooling contributes to the capacity to make the distinction (and to the obligation to do so) by making it possible for pupils to discover that different individuals occupying a single social position often act in ways that are attached to the position rather than to the different persons filling it. Even though all members of a given classroom find themselves in the same circumstances (they are about equal in age and roughly resemble each other in social characteristics related to residence), they still differ in many respects: sex, race, religion, ethnicity, and physical characteristics being among the most obvious. Their situation, therefore, provides the experience of finding that common interests and shared circumstances are assigned a priority that submerges obvious personal differences. The same contention holds for adults. Male and female adults are found in both school and family settings; in school, pupils can discover that an increasingly large number of different adults of both sexes can occupy the same position, that of "teacher." This discovery is not as easily made in the family because it is not possible to determine definitively whether "parent" represents two positions, one occupied by a male, the other by a female, or a single position with two occupants differing in sex. Children are not left completely without clues in this matter since they do have other adult relatives who can be seen as distinct persons occupying the same position: aunts, uncles, grandparents, and the like. Yet even extended families do not provide the frequent and systematic comparisons characteristic of the schools. Schooling, in other words, enables pupils to distinguish between persons and the social positions they occupy (a capacity crucially important in both occupational and political life) by placing them in situations in which the membership of each position is varied in its composition and the similarities between persons in a single position are made evident.

SPECIFICITY

The school provides structural arrangements more conducive to the acquisition of the norm of specificity than does the family. First, since the number of persons and the ratio between adults and nonadults is much larger in classrooms than in the household, the school provides large social aggregates in which pupils can form many casual associations (in addition to their close friendships) in which they invest but a small portion of themselves. As both the size and heterogeneity of the student body increase at each successive level, the opportunities for these somewhat fragmented social contacts increase and diversify. The relative shallowness and transiency of these relationships increase the likelihood that pupils will have experiences in which the fullness of their individuality is *not* involved, as it tends to be in their relationships among kin and close friends.

Second, on leaving the elementary school and proceeding through the departmentalized secondary levels, pupils form associations with teachers who have a progressively narrowing and specialized interest in them. (This comes about both because of subject matter specialization itself and because the number of pupils each teacher faces in the course of a day grows larger.) Although it is true that children, as they grow older, tend to form more specific relationships with their parents (symptomatically, this trend manifests itself in adolescents' complaints of parental invasions of privacy), the resources of the school far exceed those of the family in providing the social basis for the establishment of relationships in which only narrow segments of personality are invested.

Notes

1 William J. Goode, *World Revolution and Family Patterns,* p. 11, Free Press of Glencoe, New York (1963).
2 See, for example, Ruth Benedict, "Continuities and Discontinuities in Cultural Conditioning," in Clyde Kluckhohn, Henry A. Murray, and David M. Schneider (eds.), *Personality,* pp. 522–531, Alfred A. Knopf, New York (1953); Talcott Parsons, "The School Class as a Social System: Some of its Functions in American Society," *Harvard Educational Review* **29,**

No. 4, 297–318 (1959); and S. N. Eisenstadt, *From Generation to Generation*, pp. 115–185, Free Press, Glencoe, Ill. (1956).

[3] S. N. Eisenstadt, *ibid.*, p. 164.

[4] My emphasis here differs from Parsons' in that he views independence primarily as a personal resource: ". . . it may be said that the most important single predispositional factor with which the child enters the school is his level of *independence.*" Talcott Parsons, *op. cit.*, p. 300. Although independence is very likely such a predisposition—whether it is the most important single one is debatable—it is part of the school's agenda to further the development of independence to a point beyond the level at which family resources become inadequate to do so.

[5] Winterbottom, for example, lumps independence and mastery together; the indices she uses to measure them, however, involve ostensibly different phenomena in that the mastery items refer to tendencies toward activity rather than to independence. Marian R. Winterbottom, "The Relation of Need for Achievement to Learning Experiences in Independence and Mastery," in John T. Atkinson (ed.), *Motives in Fantasy, Action, and Society*, pp. 453–478, Van Nostrand, Princeton (1958). As a definitional guideline for this discussion, I have followed the usage of Bernard C. Rosen and Roy D'Andrade, "The Psychosocial Origins of Achievement Motivation," *Sociometry* 22, No. 3, 186 (1959) in their discussion of independence training; and of McClelland and his colleagues in a study of independence training, David C. McClelland, A. Rindlisbacher, and Richard DeCharms, "Religious and Other Sources of Parental Attitudes toward Independence Training," in David C. McClelland (ed.), *Studies in Motivation*, pp. 389–397, Appleton-Century-Crofts, New York (1955).

[6] Kaspar D. Naegele, "Clergymen, Teachers, and Psychiatrists: A Study in Roles and Socialization," *Canadian Journal of Economics and Political Science* 22, No. 1, 53 (1956).

[7] See, for example, Marian R. Winterbottom, *ibid.*; Bernard C. Rosen and Roy D'Andrade, *op. cit.*, pp. 185–218; and Fred L. Strodtbeck, "Family Interaction, Values, and Achievement," in David C. McClelland *et al.*, *Talent and Society*, pp. 135–191, Van Nostrand, Princeton (1958).

[8] For one attempt to treat athletics condescendingly as nonintellectualism, see James S. Coleman, *The Adolescent Society*, Free Press of Glencoe, New York (1961).

[9] Rupert Wilkinson, *Gentlemanly Power*, p. 21, Oxford University Press, London (1964).

[10] Although Parsons considers universalism-particularism to be a dichotomy, they are distinguished on at least two dimensions: cognitive and cathectic. "The primacy of cognitive values may be said to imply a *universalistic* standard, while that of appreciative values implies a *particularistic* standard. In the former case the standard is derived from the validity of a set of existential ideas, or the generality of a normative rule, in the latter from the particularity of the cathectic significance of an object or of the status of the object in a relational system." Talcott Parsons, *The Social System*, p. 62, Free Press, Glencoe, Ill. (1951).

[11] Peter M. Blau, "Operationalizing a Conceptual Scheme: The Universalism-Particularism Pattern Variable," *American Sociological Review* 27, No. 2, 169 (1962). The permission of Peter M. Blau to quote from his paper is gratefully acknowledged.

[12] Peter M. Blau, *ibid.*, p. 164; my emphasis.

[13] In the case of specificity, ". . . the burden of proof rests on him who would suggest that ego has obligations vis-à-vis the object in question which transcend this specificity of relevance." Talcott Parsons, *The Social System*, p. 65. In the case of diffuseness, ". . . the burden of proof is on the side of the exclusion of an interest or mode of orientation as outside the range of obligations defined by the role-expectation." Parsons, *ibid.*, p. 66.

[14] For a discussion of relativity of perspective, see Daniel Lerner, *The Passing of Traditional Society*, pp. 43–75, Free Press of Glencoe, Glencoe, Ill. (1958). See also Chapter 6, below.

The Impact of Higher Education

on Student Attitudes, Values,

and Critical Thinking Abilities

PAUL L. DRESSEL AND IRVIN J. LEHMANN

Dressel and Lehmann find that research on college experience shows changes in students' perspectives ("attitudes, values, interests, and beliefs") between the freshman and senior years. Their own study explores the nature of this change by utilizing a comprehensive, relatively large (in sample size), longitudinal research design. This design allowed the analysis of changes from year to year. Furthermore, the researchers were able to compare people in college with those who had withdrawn after a varying number of terms. They define three categories—stereotypic, dogmatic, and traditional values, which can be construed as aspects of perspective.

The data indicate "a lessening of stereotypic beliefs, and a movement away from the traditional value orientation" during the four years of college. No change in value orientation appears, however, between junior and senior years. Students also appear to become less dogmatic during the course of four years in college. These changes were found to be most pronounced during the first two years. Those who attended for four years became less traditional value oriented than those who had withdrawn. However, "there was no significant relationship between length of college attendance and changes in dogmatism." For males this was also the case in stereotypic beliefs. Females, on the other hand, showed a decrease in such beliefs as length of college attendance increased. Data on the relationship between college attendance and other values and attitudes important to our understanding of changes in students' perspectives are also presented in this article. Dressel and Lehmann conclude by considering some of the implications of their findings for higher education.

Reprinted by permission from the *Educational Record,* Summer 1965, pp. 248–258. Copyright 1965 by the American Council on Education.

IN 1957, Philip Jacob [10] started a continuing controversy about the impact of higher education on student values by systematically reviewing a wide range of data from unrelated research projects and interpreting them to indicate that:

1. "the impetus to change does not come from the formal educational process";
2. students are "unabashedly self-centered" and greatly value the "material" aspects of life;
3. colleges produced no great changes in values, but increased conformity— "more homogeneity and greater consistency of values among students at the end of their four years than when they begin."

Jacob's statements were variously viewed as unjustified (by social scientists who criticized his basic sources and methodology); as irrationally cynical (by administrators convinced that the major contribution of colleges resides in their molding of youthful lives around time-tested values); and with indifference (by the large majority of college teachers who view their responsibility as limited to the inculcation of factual knowledge).

Jacob, of course, was not the first researcher in this area. Most previous researchers, however, focused their attention on *specific changes* in student attitudes and opinions about current social, religious, economic, or political issues [1, 9, 19]. Many studies, too, had been concerned with limited personality characteristics, such as authoritarianism, ethnocentrism, rigidity, and so on. Most of these investigations were cross-sectional rather than longitudinal, and few involved large numbers of students. On the whole, such restricted studies contributed little to the understanding of the impact of the four-year college experience on the student.

There have been a few studies of the total impact of college, carried out in relatively small, selective colleges, such as Vassar, Bennington, and Sarah Lawrence. These more inclusive studies have focused attention on the need to study the student's total environmental matrix in attempting to determine and explain changes in attitudes and values. Two comprehensive reviews in this area are: *Impact of College,* by Freedman [7], and *The American College,* by Sanford [22]. In his brief survey, Freedman has highlighted the important research reports, including those with controversial results. Reporting upon the longitudinal study at Vassar College, Freedman concluded that there are substantial personality changes between the time the student enters as a freshman and when she leaves college four years later. (Seniors tend to be more mature but less stable; they tend to be less "feminine"; they are less authoritarian, more tolerant, and display greater religious liberalism; they demonstrate greater acceptance of intellectual values and greater internal conflict than freshmen.)

In a chapter of *The American College,* Webster, Freedman, and Heist [25] discuss in a most illuminating manner the problem of change in students' attitudes and values. Reviewing the studies conducted before World War II, the authors conclude that: "in general, students in college changed in the direction of greater liberalism and sophistication in their political, social, and religious outlooks." They report similar trends evident in the subsequent research on college student populations.

The part played by the "campus climate" in changing the attitudes and values of college students is explored in the works of Eddy [5, 6], and Brown and Bystrym [2]. Eddy feels that "perhaps the best way to transmit values is to create an 'atmosphere' on the campus." By visitation and interview of faculty, administrators, and students at twenty colleges and universities of various types throughout the United States, Eddy [6] found that experiences outside the classroom were a factor of paramount significance in the development of *character,* and that particular aspects of the environment, such as attitudes, surroundings, extra activities, manners, and morals, have the power either to reinforce or to negate all that the college has to offer. Furthermore, he contends that "the best environment for the development of character is the result of unity in common goals, a communicated tradition to which all phases of campus life make their particular contribution."

Eddy found further that the "level of expectancy" in all matters concerning and involving the student in the college environment is a highly important determinant of *what happens* to him. The level of expectancy controls not just academic situations but social relationships, group life, and, in fact, all that happens to the student. He concluded, again, that "the level [of expectancy] is established most successfully in the acceptance by all of a common task, a common goal. It is reached only by the mutual assumption of particular responsibilities. Beyond what the college expects of itself, it must maintain a high but realistic level of expectations of its faculty."

In summary, the results of both longitudinal and cross-sectional studies of college students have demonstrated that significant changes in the attitudes, values, interests, and beliefs of college students *do* occur between the freshman and senior years. There has been very little evidence, however, that any one factor from the multitude of college experiences explains changes in attitudes and values. Changes in personality characteristics during school and college years may be a function of the person's maturity or personality, a function of "the times we live in," the direct result of college experiences, or a combination of one or more such factors [10, 14, 24].

Individuals adopt only those attitudes and values which will help them achieve desired ends [13, 16] and which are normally sanctioned by the community in which they live [4, 8]. In addition, the extent to which attitudes and values are modifiable depends upon the nature of the modifying experience, [23] the type of contact, [11, 15] the personality make-up of the individual, [17] the group's approval of new attitudes, [21] and the subject's perception of the outcome [3, 12]. Because of the continual interaction of these variables, it is difficult indeed to conclude, as did Jacob [10], that neither courses, nor instructors, nor instructional methods have a marked impact upon student values.

Holding our conclusions in abeyance for the moment, however, we may agree with Raushenbush [20]:

> If student mores and the influence of the peer group and the experiences outside the classroom are as important as all this research has indicated, the conclusion we should come to is, not the pessimistic one that education does not matter at all, but rather that education as another job to do, perhaps beyond the one educators have felt was their job. Colleges must take responsibility for creating a *climate of values* that will give some direction to student mores. [Emphasis supplied.]

The Michigan State University Study

The prior research, briefly and inadequately reviewed in the previous paragraphs, left us with the confused impression that college students do change, but that no one knows quite how, or why. The studies available, limited in numbers and types of institutions, lacked meaning for a large, complex university. The tendency to divorce attitudes and values from development of critical thinking abilities seemed, too, to savor of interest in changes wrought through indoctrination or unconscious assimilation of values, rather than through conscious modification by the student as a result of forthright consideration of the implications of espousal of alternative values. Moreover, the fact of change in college-going students does not establish the role of the college as effector of the change.

Although comparison of changes in values of college-going and non-college-going youth presents—because of the selective factors involved in college attendance—insurmountable difficulties, it seemed to us that some of the deficiencies of most studies could be reduced by noting changes *at intervals* over the four college years, and by comparing changes of those remaining for the full four years with changes in those individuals withdrawing from college after varying lengths of stay. Finally, we felt that, by judicious combination of objective evidence from a number of instruments—including a test of critical thinking, a number of questionnaires developed specifically in relation to student experiences and student phraseology, and interview materials from both students and faculty—a more student-oriented assessment of changes and probable effecting factors might be possible.

We wanted to learn something of the *degree* and *direction* of change in critical thinking, in attitudes, and in values at various stages of progress through college; and, having done this, to compare the changes over a four-year span for those individuals completing a degree with those who withdrew at various stages. We were unwilling to delimit the study to any particular set of values deemed *a priori* desirable, although we were inclined to expect that the majority of the student population would improve in critical thinking, and would become less stereotypic in beliefs and more receptive to new ideas.

From previous studies, we concluded that sex, religious beliefs, socioeconomic backgrounds, courses, instruction, the gamut of college-related experiences, and maturation would all be influential factors in determining the nature and extent of changes in individuals.

From these admitted preconceptions flowed many specific questions to be investigated and many hypotheses to be tested. The range and types of data are suggested by the list of data collection instruments and procedures used:

Major battery:
   Test of Critical Thinking, Form G
   Inventory of Beliefs, Form I
   Prince's Differential Values Inventory
   Rokeach's Dogmatism Scale
   College Objectives Checklist (locally developed)
   College Qualification Test (Psychological Corporation)
   MSU Reading Test
   MSU English Test
   Experience Inventories, I and II (locally developed)

Minor battery:
   Allport-Vernon-Lindzey Study of Values
   Wesley's Rigidity Scale
   Sophomore and Junior Year Interviews
   Interviews with academic personnel

It was not possible to accumulate all of this information on all students, but initial testing of freshmen and repetition at the end of the freshman year and at the end of the senior year were nearly complete on the five items of the major battery. Other instruments and procedures were used, with samples so chosen as to be reasonably representative of the total student body. Discontinuing students were asked by mail to take a reduced set of tests and to return questionnaires that had been so selected as to permit comparisons with those students who were surveyed in more detail. The cooperation of two small liberal arts colleges in administering many of the instruments in a pattern paralleling that at M.S.U. was also obtained. The study involved nearly 3,000 freshmen initially, repetitions of data collection with groups of from 500 to 1,000, and follow-up data from over 600 withdrawals. In sheer numbers of individuals involved and range of information collected, this study is very likely the most extensive one of its kind carried on by any single institution. The analyses of the data included variance and covariance analyses, multiple discriminant function analyses, factor analyses, content analyses, and various subjective judgmental assessments. In recording these facts, the intent is not to claim perfection in design, data collection, or analytical procedures; rather, it is to say that the findings reported here are based upon a comprehensive program of research.

Observations and Reflections Generated by the Study

One of the obvious problems in such a comprehensive project was that of analyzing and interpreting the massive accumulation of data. The possible interrelationships were too numerous to pursue exhaustively. Problems of terminology and definition continually beset us in attempting to interpret seemingly inconsistent results and in stating conclusions in an objective manner. To what extent, for example, are stereotypy, rigidity, and dogmatism really distinct? Can one use such terms without making, or at least appearing to make, some value judgment regarding them? For whom are "traditional" values traditional? Are apparent changes really changes, or simply a result of increased sophistication and precision in interpretation of words and statements? With students who have not consciously confronted and assessed their attitudes and values, can inventories or interviews get at their convictions?

There is great diversity in the experiences of students in a large university, and perhaps even greater diversity in the extent of personal involvement in and reaction to any given experience. Instructors with no recollection of contact with certain students were credited as having marked impact on the attitudes and values of these students. Some students, apparently, are attracted only to teachers and to student associates whose attitudes and values correspond closely to their own and, in them, consequently, they find reinforcement rather than incentive for self-examination and change.

There are violently contrasting views current among both students and faculty as to the responsibility of a college for promoting changes in attitudes and values. In interviews, numerous students expressed resentment at the implication that their basic beliefs and values would in any way be influenced by their college experiences. Instructors, interviewed to ascertain their intent and their observations in respect to value change, often disavowed any interest in or concern for such change. Thus, the study seemed to be seeking value changes in a milieu in which conscious concern for value change was disavowed by all parties!

Although higher education seems obviously committed to exposing students to some set of broad (though not always clearly expressed) values, the assumption of many of the faculty members and students seemed to be that presence in an institution involves an *a priori* acceptance of these values rather than participation in a planned program of experiences which highlight and may encourage assimilation of these values.

There are also very different views about what changes in attitudes and values are desirable. When evidence accrued that many seniors, though not

necessarily less religious than they were as freshmen, no longer accepted specific tenets or dogma of their particular church affiliation, it was repeatedly
pointed out that such a finding should be reported with great discretion, since
it would be construed by some groups as evidence that college experiences
were deleterious rather than constructive. Similarly, many students, as seniors,
viewed the vocational significance of a college education as much less important than the acquiring of a broad liberal education. Such a finding is simply
not accepted by some vocationally oriented segments of the faculty, who
aspire to increase vocationally oriented education at the expense of the liberal.
In some cases, such adverse reactions or doubts may lead to the accusation
that the investigator, either by unconscious bias or malicious intent, forced
the unhappy finding.

College attendance commonly involves some weakening of the dependence
of youth on home and parents, and is paralleled for the non-college-attending
youth by acceptance of full-time employment. Thus, the years immediately
following completion of secondary school are closely related to the assumption by youth of a greater degree of freedom and responsibility—a heady and
maturing experience. How much, then, of any change which takes place during
the college years is really a result of college experiences, and how much is a
result simply of the freedom to question and doubt values imposed by parents
and the home community? The college should not claim credit for, nor should
it be blamed for, changes which are a normal part of the maturation process.
As our report of findings will indicate, we found the distinction not an easy one
to make. Plant [18] had previously hypothesized that the function of a college
is simply to accelerate the process of change already in operation in the society
at large. Even this hypothesis, on closer examination, involves the highly debatable issue of whether higher education should only reinforce existing social
norms or undertake to improve them. In actuality, our study was undertaken
only to determine what, if anything, happens to students, but we have found
this a difficult position to sustain and interpret. Any approach to values generates emotional and irrational reactions, both from some of those studied and
from some who learn of the findings.

Changes in Attitudes, Values, and Critical Thinking

When changes in attitudes, values, and in critical thinking abilities are
reported for a group of students, it should be understood what such a reported
change means and does not mean. To state, for example, that students became
"more liberal" from the freshman to the senior year does *not* mean that *all*
students became more liberal. What is meant is that, on the average, the percentage of a group of students responding to one or more statements in a
manner somewhat arbitrarily designated as liberal or conservative was greater
for these students as seniors than it was as freshmen. Some students may have

become more conservative; others may not have changed; but more students accepted the liberal view at the second than at the first response. Despite the *increase* in liberal point of view, the majority response to a statement may still be in the conservative direction. Some few students may have moved from a consistently conservative view on many matters to a consistently liberal one; others may have shifted on only a few items.

In brief, the statement of a statistically significant change in a certain direction must be taken as only an indication that changes were observed, and that they tend, on the average, to be in the stated direction. The change, even though statistically significant, may not be sufficiently great in any one individual that it would be apparent to a friend or interviewer. Furthermore, it is difficult to say whether change in attitudes or values in a given direction is desirable or undesirable. An extremist or dogmatic liberal on a given issue may well become somewhat more conservative, while the extreme conservative becomes more liberal on the same issue. The composite result of such contrasting changes may be equally viewed as an undesirable conformity or as general acceptance of a more moderate position, conducive to constructive compromise. Whereas *improvement* in critical thinking can be accepted as the desirable and unambiguous direction of change, the same cannot be said of changes in attitudes and values. Accordingly, the following statements of results must be viewed as that and as nothing more than that. Judgments as to desirability or undesirability of the results must be left to those more dogmatic than ourselves.

Major Findings

Since certain terms occur repeatedly in these statements of findings, the following brief definitions will be helpful:

Stereotypic—The stereotypic personality accepts pseudorational clichés, is rigid in attitudes and values, and is compulsive and authoritarian in relationship with others.

Dogmatic—The dogmatic personality has fixed views and is unreceptive to new ideas.

Traditional values—Traditional values include belief in personal responsibility, Puritan morality, the work-success ethic, and future-time orientation in contrast to the "emergent" values of sociability, security, group-determined moral standards, and present-time orientation.

BIOGRAPHICAL AND DEMOGRAPHIC DIFFERENCES

1. Male undergraduates were significantly more stereotypic, dogmatic, and unreceptive to new ideas than females. Males also were significantly more traditional-value oriented than females.

2. Catholic students were the most stereotypic and dogmatic and had the

highest traditional-value scores. Jewish students were the least traditional-value oriented.

3. There were significant differences in attitudes and values of Protestant students coming from the liberal and fundamentalist sects. The latter were significantly more stereotypic and dogmatic.

4. There was no significant difference in attitudes and values between those students whose parents were native-born Americans and those students whose parents were foreign-born.

5. Students from the rural areas had higher mean traditional-value scores than those from urban areas.

6. Students from the lower socioeconomic levels tended to be more stereotypic and have higher traditional-value scores than students from the upper-middle or upper social levels.

7. Females majoring in the nontechnical curricula were less stereotypic and dogmatic than those in vocationally-oriented programs. Males in the physical and biological sciences were less stereotypic in their beliefs than males enrolled in other fields.

CHANGES FROM FRESHMAN TO SENIOR YEAR

1. In nearly all instances there was a significant improvement in critical thinking ability, a lessening of stereotypic beliefs, and a movement away from the traditional-value orientation in each of the freshman, sophomore, junior, and senior years. The only exception was for changes in value orientation for both males and females during the senior year. Although the previous college years demonstrated a trend from "inner" to "outer-or-other" directedness, the senior year did not evidence such a change. In fact, it would appear that, after the junior year, a plateau is reached with respect to value orientation of college students.

2. Students, in general, became more flexible and less authoritarian from their freshman to senior year; more receptive of people of different races, creeds, and religions; more liberal in their views and opinions about standards of behavior; more aware of their own goals in life; more confident of their ability to deal with new problems; more realistic in outlook toward the future; and more likely to question the absolutes in life insofar as they pertain to moral and religious conduct.

3. Although the changes were found each year from the freshman to the senior year, the major changes took place during the first two years of college. In fact, the changes in critical thinking ability and in value orientation were of greatest magnitude in the freshman year.

4. With only one exception (dogmatism for males), there was greater homogeneity at the end of the senior year than there was at the beginning of the freshman year.

5. Although college freshmen were concerned with obtaining good grades, as seniors they attached even more importance to grades.

6. College freshmen were concerned with preparation for a specific vocation, but as seniors they attached increased significance to a well-rounded education.

7. Seniors, to a greater extent than freshmen, felt that college professors should be allowed to subscribe to any political or ideological belief they wish. However, these same students felt that the faculty should not interfere with the students' behavior or beliefs.

8. A sizable percentage of students indicated that they felt they had undergone no marked change in their attitudes, values, beliefs, and interests while at college.

9. A small percentage of students changed in what might be termed a negative direction; that is, they became more stereotypic and prejudiced in their views, became less tolerant of others, became less receptive to new ideas, and became more authoritarian.

10. Although many students felt that during their college career they became less attached rather than more attached to a particular religious orientation, they reported no diminution of belief in the value of religion in a mature life.

11. For the males, those who enrolled at Michigan State and attended for four years became less traditional-value oriented than their counterparts who enrolled at the same time but withdrew from college during their freshman, sophomore, or junior year. In fact, for the male withdrawals, those males who attended college for 0–3 terms became more traditional-value oriented (between 1958 and 1962) than their withdrawal counterparts who attended for 4–6 or 7–10 terms. A somewhat similar trend was evident for the change in value orientation for females.

12. For both males and females, there was no significant relationship between length of college attendance and changes in dogmatism, receptivity to new ideas, or an attitude of open-mindedness. All groups moved toward a more open-minded and flexible attitude.

13. For both males and females, there was a significant decrease in stereotypic beliefs between 1958 and 1962 regardless of amount of education. For the females only, the intensity of the decrease was related to length of college attendance; that is, the longer a girl attended college, the more likely was she to become less stereotypic in her beliefs in comparison to her counterparts who withdrew before graduation.

INTERRELATIONSHIPS OF VARIOUS FACTORS WITH CONTINUING IN COLLEGE

1. The analysis of data on freshman year withdrawals suggests that collegiate persistence depends primarily upon intellectual ability, but that certain

affective factors, such as attitudes, motivation, and interest, have a definite but individually variable influence.

2. For both males and females, the inclusion of a battery of affective variables contributed very little to the over-all prediction of academic success. This was so whether the measure of academic success is in terms of grade-point average or grades in specific general education courses.

3. Students who were highly stereotypic and dogmatic tended to receive higher grades from their instructors than were apparently warranted by their general academic aptitude.

4. There was no significant relationship between amount of college education and certainty of plans for the immediate future. Over 50 percent of the females and over 45 percent of the males, regardless of length of college attendance, felt that they were uncertain regarding their future plans.

5. Over 60 percent of the males and females in each of the groups felt that all college students should be required to take a series of general education courses. Although the period of time in college made no difference among the males in their responses to this item, female seniors were somewhat less favorably inclined toward general education courses than were female freshman and sophomore withdrawals.

6. The majority of those in the study, regardless of sex and amount of college education, felt that a college education should place equal emphasis on both academic and social aspects of development.

7. There was no clear-cut pattern evident in regard to the relationship between the amount of college education and opinions on selected social, economic, and political issues. On some issues, the findings were in the expected direction (more liberal in accord with the general trend), while in others they were contrary to what would be expected.

8. Regardless of sex and amount of college education, the majority of subjects felt that Red China should not be admitted to the U.N., that medical care for the aged should be provided by the Federal Government, that the United States should continue nuclear testing in the atmosphere, that petting and deep kissing are appropriate sex outlets for unmarried college students, and that a person in a skilled trade is worth as much to society as one in a profession.

9. Anticipated participation in community activities was greater for those completing more years of college.

10. Although students in general, regardless of sex and amount of college education, changed in their attitudes, values, beliefs, and opinions between 1958 and 1962, the females underwent a more marked change during this period than did the males. Changes were greater for those completing college than for any of the withdrawal groups.

IMPACT OF COLLEGE

1. Students, in general, felt that the most significant thing that had happened to them or that they learned while at college was to get along with all types of people. Although many do not necessarily agree with the views and opinions of their peers, they have developed, or at least adopted, a "live and let live" outlook.

2. College students, regardless of level, were highly resentful of any rules and regulations which they felt interfered with their independence.

3. The most significant reported experience in the collegiate lives of these students was their association with differing personalities in their living unit. The analysis of interview and questionnaire data also strongly suggested that discussions and bull sessions were a potent factor in shaping the attitudes and values of these college students.

4. Before the junior year, courses and instructors were rarely mentioned as having a marked impact upon student attitudes and values. From the junior year on, however, the formal, academic experiences (especially courses and instructors in the student's major) began to assume an increased, although not predominant, importance. One might conclude that, whereas the formal, academic experiences prior to the junior year were subordinate to the informal nonacademic experiences, the converse was true after the sophomore year.

5. Courses and instructors in the general education area were frequently characterized by both juniors and seniors as having had a reinforcing rather than a modifying effect on their personality development.

6. Of all the course or instructional experiences mentioned by juniors and seniors (both males and females) as having had a reinforcing or modifying effect, instructors and courses in the humanities were most frequently chosen.

7. Both senior students and former students who had withdrawn felt that the academic values should be of utmost importance to both faculty and students. Being original and creative, demonstrating scholarly capacity, and dedicating one's self to his studies were factors thought to be important by all, regardless of sex and amount of college education.

COMPARISONS OF M.S.U. STUDENTS WITH STUDENTS
IN TWO SMALL LIBERAL ARTS COLLEGES

1. There did not appear to be an atypical or unique personality characteristic or set of characteristics that distinguished students at the three colleges surveyed. However, the students at the university had higher critical thinking ability scores.

2. After controlling for differences in critical thinking ability among students at three Midwestern colleges (two church-affiliated liberal arts colleges and Michigan State University), there was no significant difference in dog-

matism or in traditional-value orientation for either males or females. There was, however, a significant difference in stereotypic beliefs among the males at the three colleges, with such beliefs being more common in the liberal arts colleges.

Some Implications of the Study

College students *do* change during the period of college attendance and, generally speaking, the amount and nature of change are related to the period of time spent at college. However, individual students and identifiable subgroups change in varying degrees and even in different directions. In a large university, there is such a variety of experiences and subcultures that the experiences of individuals may be very different, either by chance or by choice. Some students apparently seek new experiences which induce changes, while others seek contacts and experiences which reinforce their present views and prejudices. The reactions of students to experiences also vary. Some, disturbed by their experiences, withdraw from them and from the university; others, equally disturbed, find a challenge and seek a new accommodation to a new world; still others, with restricted patterns of experience, withdraw from sheer boredom.

Affective factors are involved in college success and are changed by college, but the factors themselves are complex and unclear; they are neither unidimensional nor unidirectional in nature and development. Hence, generalizations as specific and as generally applicable as those which can be made about academic aptitude or critical thinking abilities are not possible. Furthermore, the changes in attitudes and values are the result of the interaction of so many factors, including maturation, that it is not possible to say with any certainty what experiences, either in general or in specific cases, have been most productive of change.

Although courses and instructors do seem to have some impact on students' attitudes and values—especially in the last two years—peer-group contacts and nonacademic experiences are regarded by students as being more important. Although the results may be, in part, an artifact of the instruments and appraisal procedures, it also seems clear that the major impact of the college on critical thinking, attitudes, and values is made within the first years. Students increase in homogeneity over the four years and, at least in part, they do so by accommodating to prevailing mores or withdrawing entirely. The enrollment disparity between lower and upper division, coupled with widely prevalent faculty emphasis on majors and specialization, tends to focus concern on the junior and senior years—a situation defensible only if a very limited purview is taken of the objectives of higher education. The first two years appear, in many ways, to be more critical than the last two.

There is some indication that students characterized by stereotypic beliefs, rigidity, and an authoritarian orientation receive from some instructors better grades than they deserve, while the critically minded nonauthoritarian may suffer because he makes his own judgments rather than reflects those of the instructor. This tendency is not of catastrophic proportion, but it is an illustration that an institution may harbor practices and personalities which have an impact contradictory to its announced intent. A college which presumes to have a desirable impact on the critical thinking abilities, attitudes, and values of its students may find that its grading practices, regulations, and policy-making procedures have an undesirable impact controverting the changes sought in students.

Change in college students, as in all human beings, is inevitable over a four-year period. However, change in any specific set of attitudes or values is not necessarily to be found in all students, and probably should not be. A college program so structured as to force acceptance of certain attitudes or values molds a student into a pattern instead of permitting him to develop. Such enforced molding, whatever the techniques used, has no place in higher education. Some students may evince deviant and disconcerting attitudes and values, but, unless these are completely disruptive, we must accept them, for such variations provide evidence that education is developmental and that it encourages individuality in attitude and originality in thinking. We noted that many students seemed to resent the implication that college experiences should change their attitudes and values. Although some students saw little change in themselves, others admitted to change while in college, but objected to relating these changes to specific experiences. We interpret this to mean that students, rightfully, will resent the implication that they are being changed in particular ways without their knowledge or consent. On the other hand, students do agree that the college environment should provide opportunity for *examination* of one's attitudes, values, and thought processes. Change may then occur if the individual so wills it.

Higher education involves a continuing search for answers, not the dissemination of answers. Thus the attitudes, values, and the methods characteristic of the scholar in his continuing search for more and better answers must be the concern of higher education. These attitudes, values, and methods may be collectively termed "process values," since they are essential in the process of collecting and organizing knowledge and of making judgments about what decisions or courses of action most likely contribute to securing freedom, justice, beauty, or whatever other values an individual desires to promote.

If the student is to examine his values and internalize a set of attitudes, values, and capabilities of judgment, his total college experience must be considered. The scholarly approach of the classroom must be paralleled by a deliberative approach to all other phases of campus activity. The student must see that his mentors have recourse to the views they espouse, the methods they present, and the values they hold in the decisions required in the planning and operation of the college and, by extension, to the decisions involved in all phases of living. Only then does the student have an interrelated or integrated educational experience in which the significance and necessity of a value is made evident. Such an educational experience is integrative also, for it forces the student to examine his own values in reference to each decision he makes.

The impact of higher education in the area of values, then, should be found in: (a) increased consciousness of one's own values; (b) increased awareness of value differences and conflicts among individuals and groups; (c) re-examination and possibly modification of one's values; and (d) increased ability to make decisions and take actions which witness and reinforce the values in which one believes.

Our study suggested that these changes, at least in some small measure, took place in many of our students. Unfortunately, this study, like others, was designed more to look for specific changes than for a change in value orientation. Thus research to date reveals something of value change, but it tells very little of the effectiveness of colleges in fostering a value orientation and value-based decisions and actions on the part of our students.

References

1. Arsenian, Seth. "Changes in Evaluative Attitude," *Journal of Applied Psychology,* August 1943, pp. 338–49.
2. Brown, Donald R., and Bystrym, Denise. "College Environment, Personality, and Social Ideology of Three Ethnic Groups," *Journal of Social Psychology,* November 1956, pp. 279–88.
3. Carlson, Earl R. "Attitude Change through Modification of Attitude Structure," *Journal of Abnormal and Social Psychology,* March 1956, pp. 256–61.
4. Dameron, Lawrence E. "Mother-Child Interaction in the Development of Self-Restraint," *Journal of Genetic Psychology,* June 1955, pp. 289–308.
5. Eddy, Edward D., Jr. "Changing Values and Attitudes on the Campus," in *Long-Range Planning for Education,* ed. Arthur E. Traxler. Washington: American Council on Education, 1958.
6. ———. *The College Influence on Student Character.* Washington: American Council on Education, 1959.
7. Freedman, Mervin B. *The Impact of College,* New Dimensions in Higher Education, No. 4, U.S. Office of Education. Washington: Government Printing Office, 1960.
8. Hemming, James. "Some Aspects of Moral Development in a Changing Society," *British Journal of Educational Psychology,* June 1957, pp. 77–78.
9. Hunter, E. C. "Changes in General Attitudes of Women Students during Four Years of College," *Journal of Social Psychology,* November 1942, pp. 243–57.
10. Jacob, Philip E. *Changing Values in College.* New York: Harper & Bros., 1957.

11. James, H. E. O. "Personal Contact in School and Change in Intergroup Attitudes," *International Social Science Bulletin,* January 1955, pp. 55–60.

12. Katz, Daniel; McClintoc, Charles; and Sarnoff, Irving. "The Measurement of Ego-Defense as Related to Attitude Change," *Journal of Personality,* June 1957, pp. 465–74.

13. Kurtz, Paul W. "Human Nature, Homeostasis, and Value," *Philosophy and Phenomenological Research,* September 1956, pp. 36–55.

14. Mayhew, Lewis B. "And in Attitudes," in *Evaluation in the Basic College,* ed. Paul L. Dressel. New York: Harper & Bros., 1958.

15. McGuigan, F. Joseph. "Psychological Changes Related to Intercultural Experiences," *Psychological Reports,* March 1958, pp. 55–60.

16. Morris, Charles. *Varieties of Human Value.* Chicago: University of Chicago Press, 1958.

17. Nelson, Erland N. P. "Patterns of Religious Attitude Shift from College to Fourteen Years Later," *Psychological Monographs,* No. 424. Washington: American Psychological Association, 1956.

18. Plant, Walter T. *Personality Changes Associated with a College Education.* San Jose, Calif.: San Jose State College, 1962.

19. Pressey, S. L. "Changes from 1923 to 1943 in the Attitudes of Public School and University Students," *Journal of Psychology,* January 1946, pp. 173–88.

20. Raushenbush, Esther. "Changing Values and Attitudes on the Campus—A Look to the Future," in *Long-Range Planning for Education,* ed. Arthur E. Traxler. Washington: American Council on Education, 1957.

21. Rosenberg, Morris. "Psychological Depression and Educational Attitudes." *Student Medicine,* January 1956, pp. 5–20.

22. Sanford, Nevitt (ed). *The American College.* New York: John Wiley & Sons, 1962.

23. Smith, Howard P. "Do Intercultural Experiences Affect Attitudes?" *Journal of Abnormal and Social Psychology,* November 1955, pp. 469–77.

24. Wagman, Morton. "Attitude Change and Authoritarian Personality," *Journal of Psychology,* July 1955, pp. 3–24.

25. Webster, Harold; Freedman, Mervin B.; and Heist, Paul. "Personality Changes in College Students," in *The American College,* ed. Nevitt Sanford. New York: John Wiley & Sons, 1962.

PART VII

THE FAMILY

The sociology of the family deals with a number of issues from a variety of approaches. One approach is the study of cultural norms, attitudes, values, and so on, regarding how people live together, have sexual relations, procreate, raise children, and relate to members of their kinship group. (This is the "institutional" approach to the family.) Other sociologists study the structure and function of the primary and extended groups called families. They analyze the patterns of interaction that exist within such groups and the effects of this interaction on individual family members. Although many students of social life believe that the family is of decreasing importance in modern industrialized societies, we contend that family positions and experiences within the family are still a principal aspect of life within contemporary societies. From the point of view of the development of sociological knowledge, the family is a crucial unit of analysis for our understanding of such areas as socialization, reference groups, interpersonal interaction, and group dynamics.

Child-rearing Patterns
and Supernatural Beings[1]

WILLIAM W. LAMBERT, LEIGH MINTURN TRIANDIS,
AND MARGERY WOLF

Socialization is an important area of sociology. This study, using data
from sixty-two ethnographies, investigates the relationship between
child-rearing practice and "aspects of the formal beliefs systems of a
society." The major hypothesis posited a relationship between nurturant infant and child socialization, and a societal belief in the
benevolence of supernatural beings. Punitive socialization was hypothesized to be related to a belief in their malevolence. In regard to
childhood socialization the authors found a number of significant relationships which supported their hypothesis. Their interpretation which
is "derived from conditioning theory, reinforcement theory, and conflict theory" is basically a functional one. The child's conception of a
malevolent supernatural being reduces his psychological conflict
caused by primitive child-rearing practices. Where there is considerable nurture and less "hurt," the child has a conception of a benevolent deity. This is only a part of their interpretation; however, the
reader should recognize the necessary "leap" which the authors make
between data and explanation. Certainly not all of their interpretations
are based on what the data in this article reveals.

A STUDY of some of the social psychological functions of "primitive"
religious beliefs, this paper tests cross-societally some hypotheses about how
general anticipations of pain develop in children, and the relation of these
to aspects of the formal belief systems of a society. The major hypothesis
was that beliefs in the *malevolence* of the supernatural world reflect punitive
practices in infant and child rearing, while beliefs in the *benevolence* of the
supernatural world reflect nurturant practices in infant and child training.
The research program in which the present study is included investigated

Originally published as "Some Correlates of Belief in the Malevolence and Benevolence of
Supernatural Beings: A Cross-Societal Study," in the *Journal of Abnormal and Social Psychol-
ogy*, Vol. 58, No. 2, March 1959, pp. 162–169. Copyright 1959 by the American Psychological
Association, and reproduced by permission.

antecedents of aggression by means both of direct field study (8) (not reported here) and of ratings derived from ethnographic reports of 62 societies.

Method

The societies rated for the present paper include a wide range of geographic settings. Thirty-one of Murdock's[2] 61 world culture areas are represented by at least one society. Our sources were necessarily limited to those affording adequate descriptions of child training practices. Most of the ethnographic sources were selected from the bibliography of Heinicke and Whiting (5). The geographical distribution of our "sample" is shown in Table 1.[3] None of the tables of results includes all these cultures because

Table 1—Geographical Distribution of Societies in Sample

Polynesia	Micronesia	Melanesia	Indonesia
6	3	7	7
Africa	Eurasia	North Amer.	South Amer.
11	5	17	6

in each case the available sources provided inadequate information for some of the ratings. Table 2 lists most of the societies studied. We attempted ratings that would reflect the *general* benevolence and aggressiveness of the supernatural belief system, on the assumption that there is some basic coherence in the "traits" underlying the various representations that the gods and spirits may take within the belief systems of a culture. The raters had therefore to consider the ethnographer's report of all situations in adult life in which the supernatural appears in any form; and specific beliefs in supernatural intervention in formal religion, ritual, witchcraft, and sorcery were thus all of some importance in making the judgments.

The ratings on socialization practices and on beliefs about gods were made independently, the former under the direction of Irvin Child at Yale University and the latter by members of a research seminal under the direction of Lambert and Triandis at Cornell. A recent analysis of the Yale data has been presented in two papers by Child et al. (3) and Barry et al. (1).

SOCIALIZATION SCALES [4]

Independent ratings of socialization measures were made by two judges on a 7-point scale, the sum of the two ratings being the score.

Infancy. Ratings were made on several variables covering the first year of a child's life and as long thereafter as the treatment of the infant remains approximately constant. The nine scales used were: *protection from environmental discomforts, absence of pain inflicted by nurturant agent, over-all in-*

Table 2—Relation Between Absence of Pain from Nurturing Agent in Infancy and Properties of the Supernaturals

High Pain (Low Absence of Pain)	Low Pain (High Absence of Pain)
Supernaturals—mainly aggressive	
Alor	Andaman
Aymara	Bena
BaVenda	Lepcha
Chagga	Lesu
Chirricahua Apache	Manus
Dahomey	Wogeo
Kurtachi	Yagua
Kwakiutl	
Kwoma	
Maori	
Navaho	
Ojibwa	
Lovedo	
Siriono	
Tenetehara	
Tepotztlan	
Thonga	
Supernaturals—mainly benevolent	
Arapesh	Ashanti
Chamorro	Chenchu
Klamath	Cheyenne
Ontonga-Java	Comanche
Ovimbundu	Fiji
Puka Puka	Hopi
Tallensi	Papago
	Samoa
	Teton
	Tikopia
	Winnegago
	Zuñi

NOTE.—$p = .05$. 95% confidence limits for the relative frequency $(29/14 = .68) = .51 - .81$ (4, pp. 66–69)

dulgence, diffusion of nurturance, display of affection, consistency of drive reduction, immediacy of drive reduction, degree of drive reduction, and *constancy of presence of nurturing agent.* The scale on over-all indulgence covers all the data on which the other infancy scales were rated, except diffusion of nurturance, in addition to other general statements on the topic made by the ethnographer. In regard to the scale of environmental discomforts, raters considered the extent to which these were not experienced, were usually prevented, or were quickly eliminated. Pain inflicted by nurturant agent included such things as cold baths, depilation, and so on, as well as physical punishment. In considering diffusion of nurturance, raters judged the degree to which nurturance is shared by others than the mother, who was thus used as reference point.

Childhood. Ratings were made for the period between infancy and puberty (roughly 5–12 years). Scales for six behavior areas were rated: *nurturance, responsibility, self-reliance, achievement, obedience,* and *general independence.* For each of the scales, ratings were made on the basis of "positive training" (both reward for presence and punishment for absence of the behavior), punishment for nonperformance only, punishment for performance, and frequency of performance. In scoring "positive training," raters considered frequency, degree, consistency, and immediacy of reward for performance and of punishment for nonperformance. Examples of rewards are adult approval, approval of contemporaries, status gain, basic drive reduction, material gain, and anxiety avoidance. In scoring punishment, raters considered severity and frequency. Examples of punishments are corporal punishment, disapproval, deprivation (of freedom, food, etc.), threats, and natural consequences (such as curtailed freedom, food, etc.).

SCALES ON PROPERTIES OF THE DEITIES [5]

A god or spirit was defined as any supernatural being who was capable in principle of responding to the actions of tribal members. The definition was designed to include diverse kinds of gods and spirits and to exclude such impersonal life forces as *mana.* In scoring aggressive behavior by the gods, judges were instructed to consider the frequency with which gods were considered responsible for such occurrences as famines, plagues, weather disturbances, personal mishaps, etc. Examples of benevolent behavior ascribed to the gods include protection from enemies, granting personal favors, curing, growing good crops, good hunting, etc. The bad things and good things that happen to people in a primitive society are much the same everywhere—sickness, death, love, birth, good hunting, or good crops cover most of the instances, and in terms of frequency the weight probably lies with the first four. Our procedure amounted to asking what proportion of these good or bad "things" are referred to the supernatural.

Two ratings were made of benevolence and aggressiveness with regard both to frequency of benevolent or aggressive action and to intensity of the modal action. The frequency scales were stated as the proportion of all the acts of the gods which were aggressive or benevolent. Any act could be considered as benevolent or aggressive, as both benevolent and aggressive, or as neither benevolent nor aggressive. The intensity measures were an over-all rating of the intensity of the gods' benevolent or aggressive actions. A culture was termed either "mainly aggressive" or "mainly benevolent" on the basis of the arithmetic relation between the two frequency scales, with the intensity scales being used to determine ties. Seven-point scales were used. If the ratings obtained independently by two raters diverged by more than two points, the raters conferred on the evidence involved in their judgments, and where agreement was not reached the score was omitted. Ratings with a disagreement of two points or less were averaged. In 85% of all the cases, the independent original ratings differed from each other by two points or less.

We report the following socialization data, knowing that the various measures of both infancy and childhood treatment are statistically and sometimes definitionally related. Our argument outlines one way of explaining some of the common variance.

Results

INFANCY

A clear relationship between absence of pain from nurturing agent in infancy and properties of the supernaturals is shown in Table 2. This relationship is significant at the .05 level.

The relationship of other infancy variables to the aggressive or benevolent properties of the deities is displayed in Table 3. Although none of these additional relationships emerges as significant, all of them are similar in direction in the sense that the children in societies with predominantly aggressive gods and spirits are less cosseted. The only exception to this generalization is that the nurturant agent tends to be more constantly present in the societies with aggressive deities. Even when only those societies are considered where little pain is inflicted by the nurturant agent, there is still a tendency for the nurturant agent to be present less often in benevolent cultures. This result may perhaps mean that what is done to the child by caretakers is more closely related to the properties of the deities than is the mere fact of the presence of the caretaker.

If we combine the diffusion of nurturance ratings with the over-all indulgence ratings, the pattern of low diffusion–low indulgence characterizes the societies with aggressive deities to at least the .04 point of significance, employing the exact χ^2 solution.

In summary, there is a general tendency for less indulgent treatment in infancy to be related to predominantly aggressive deities in the cultural belief system, and for more indulgent treatment to be related to benevolent deities. The clearest relationship has to do with pain caused by the nurturing agents.

CHILDHOOD

The relations between the ratings of childhood variables and those of supernaturals are examined in Table 4, which lists first "positive training" for the various systems of behavior, then punishments for failure to behave, then the reported actual frequency of children's behavior in the various systems. These relationships are followed by some compound indices of

Table 3—Relationships Between Infancy Treatment Variables and the Aggressiveness and Benevolence of the Supernaturals

Infancy Training Variable	SUPERNATURALS PREDOMINANTLY:		Significance Tests [a]
	Aggres-sive	Benev-olent	
High Protection from Environmental Discomforts	36% (8/22)[b]	61% (11/18)	NS
High Absence of Pain Inflicted by Nur-turant Agent	29% (7/24)	63% (12/19)	$p = <.05$; c.l. for 29/43 = .51–.81
High Over-all Indulgence	39% (11/28)	60% (12/20)	NS
High Diffusion of Nurturance	44% (12/27)	68% (13/19)	NS
High Display of Affection	33% (8/24)	50% (10/20)	NS
High Consistency of Drive Reduction	39% (9/23)	53% (10/19)	NS
High Immediacy of Drive Reduction	35% (8/23)	47% (9/19)	NS
High Degree of Drive Reduction	37% (10/27)	44% (8/18)	NS
High Constancy of Presence of Nurtur-ing Agent	52% (14/27)	37% (7/19)	NS

[a] We report significance level by χ^2 test, usually as .05 level with no further refinement. We also report 95% confidence limits for either the proportion of "successful" cases or of "unsuccessful" cases.

[b] The figures in parentheses show the numbers on which the percentages are based. The numerator is the number of tribes showing the characteristic at the left out of the number of tribes classified as having either predominantly aggressive or benevolent gods (the denominator).

"pressure" (which combine the ratings of "positive training" and punishment for failure) and an index of "rigidity" of childhood training (the total score for punishment for nonperformance of all these behaviors).

The table shows that high self-reliance and independence training are related to the aggressiveness of the deities. This relationship holds for positive training, for punishment for nonperformance, for pressure, and for frequency of actual behavior. Despite an empirical relationship between the systems of self-reliance and independence training, we have retained them as separate because of differences in meanings of the ratings.

The nurturance behavior system appears generally to be positively related to the benevolence of the supernaturals. This relationship is significant at beyond the .05 level for frequency of actual behavior, and the trend is main-

Table 4—Relationships Between Childhood Training Variables and the Aggressiveness and Benevolence of the Supernaturals

Childhood Training Variables	SUPERNATURALS PREDOMINANTLY		Significance Tests [a]
	Aggressive	Benevolent	
High Positive Training for Self-Reliance	62% (16/26)[b]	16% (3/19)	$p = <.05$; c.l. for 32/45 = .54–.83
High Positive Training for Independence	61% (17/28)	20% (4/20)	$p = <.05$; c.l. for 33/48 = .55–.82
High Positive Training for Nurturance	40% (8/20)	73% (11/15)	NS
High Positive Training for Responsibility	46% (12/26)	65% (13/20)	NS
High Positive Training for Obedience	33% (8/24)	44% (8/18)	NS
High Positive Training for Achievement	50% (11/22)	53% (8/15)	NS
High Punishment for Nonperf. Self-Reliance	73% (19/26)	31% (6/19)	$p = <.05$; c.l. for 32/45 = .54–.83
High Punishment for Nonperf. Independence	57% (16/28)	20% (4/20)	$p = <.05$; c.l. for 32/48 = .52–.80
High Punishment for Nonperf. Nurturance	60% (12/20)	71% (10/14)	NS
High Punishment for Nonperf. Responsibility	63% (15/24)	30% (6/20)	$p = <.10$; c.l. for 29/44 = .51–.80
High Punishment for Nonperf. Obedience	60% (15/25)	50% (9/18)	NS
High Punishment for Nonperf. Achievement	48% (10/21)	47% (7/15)	NS
High Frequency of Child's Self-Reliance	67% (18/27)	26% (5/19)	$p = <.05$; c.l. for 32/46 = .53–.82
High Frequency of Child's Independence	64% (18/28)	30% (6/20)	$p = <.05$; c.l. for 32/48 = .50–.59
High Frequency of Child's Nurturance	24% (5/21)	67% (10/15)	$p = <.02$; c.l. for 25/36 = .54–.85
High Frequency of Child's Responsibility	54% (13/24)	45% (9/20)	NS
High Frequency of Child's Obedience	44% (11/25)	56% (10/18)	NS

[a] We report significance level by χ^2 test, usually as .05 level with no further refinement. We also report 95% confidence limits for either the proportion of "successful" cases or of "unsuccessful" cases.

[b] The figures in parentheses show the numbers on which the percentages are based. The numerator is the number of tribes showing the characteristic at the left out of the number of tribes classified as having either predominantly aggressive or benevolent gods (the denominator). All "high-low" breaks reported in this paper are the closest possible to the median.

Table 4—(Cont'd)

Childhood Training Variables	SUPERNATURALS PREDOMINANTLY		Significance Tests [a]
	Aggressive	Benevolent	
High Frequency of	45%	44%	
Achievement Behavior	(10/22)	(7/16)	NS
High Pressure for	73%	32%	$p = <.05$;
Self-Reliance	(19/26)	(6/19)	c.l. for $32/45 = .54-.83$
High Pressure for	71%	35%	$p = <.05$;
Independence	(20/28)	(7/20)	c.l. for $33/48 = .55-.82$
High Pressure for	58%	57%	
Achievement	(11/19)	(8/14)	NS
High Rigidity Score	71%	18%	$p = <.01$;
	(12/17)	(2/11)	c.l. for $21/28 = .55-.89$

tained at levels short of statistical significance for positive training and punishment for nonperformance.

There appears to be more positive training for responsibility behavior in societies with benevolent deities and more punishment for nonperformance in societies with aggressive deities, although neither of these relationships quite reaches statistical significance. There is also a suggestive trend for the frequency of responsibility behavior to be somewhat higher in societies with aggressive deities. Thus responsibility training through reward may characterize societies with benevolent deities, and responsibility training through threat of punishment, those with aggressive deities. The obedience behavior system follows the same pattern as that for responsibility, except that the frequency of children's performance of obedience behavior tends (nonsignificantly) to be greater in societies with benevolent deities.

The achievement behavior system appears to be least related of any of the systems to these properties of the deities. In no case is there any discernible trend.

There is a tendency for societies with benevolent deities to be higher in positive training for four of the behavior systems, but with a very strong reversal on the remaining two—self-reliance and independence. The societies with aggressive deities, however, tend to use relatively more punishment for failure to perform in all but one of the systems—nurturance. This tendency in societies with aggressive deities toward control of behavior of children through punishment is most clearly highlighted in the rigidity score. Despite the general characterization of societies with aggressive deities as ones that make more use of punishment and less use of reward in socialization, it must be kept in mind that typical practices with respect to the various behavioral systems do differ. Societies with aggressive deities do reward self-reliance and independence (although this may be accompanied by some neglect), and societies with benevolent deities do tend to punish lapses from nurturance (although not significantly more than in the other kind of culture). To be ready to punish lapses does not necessarily betoken less attentiveness to children—it may require even more.

As far as children's actual performance of behavior in these systems is concerned, it appears to be clearly related to the properties of the supernaturals in three of the six systems. Children in societies with aggressive deities are more self-reliant, more independent, and less nurturant than those in societies with benevolent deities. The other directional tendencies in children's behavior have already been noted.

Discussion

The relationships that have been presented are useful in evaluating theories of the culture-personality relationship but are not decisive with regard to any of the major causal assumptions that such theory may take. One may, like McClelland (7), view the religious belief system as the independent factor, or one may see it as a projection of parental behavior. Another approach would view both the religious system and the child training system as controlled by some other aspect of the culture or personality of the people. And one may also see these relationships as specific historical accidents of no theoretical interest.

Our own interpretation of these data draws upon conditioning theory, reinforcement theory, and conflict theory (2). Let us trace in these terms the interrelations between the factual, psychological, and belief levels in societies with predominantly aggressive deities and those with predominantly benevolent deities. In societies with predominantly aggressive deities, we begin with the facts of hurt and pain in infancy, along with some nurture. On the psychological level, these facts should lead to anxiety in the child, because of his conflicting anticipations of hurt and of nurture. The resulting conflict, and attendant conflict drive, is reduced by a conception of the deity as more angry than kind and thus consonant with human anticipations of hurt. Concurrently with this resolution, we find on the psychological level a reduction in the tension of ambivalence in the child's anticipations and, in addition, a vicarious anxiety on the part of the parent for the child's welfare in a hurtful world. Returning to the factual level, we find the parent reinforcing independent and self-reliant behavior in his child to prepare him for the adult world, thus reducing the parent's own anxiety for the child.

Our interpretation of socialization in societies with predominantly benevolent deities starts in much the same way. We begin in infancy with the fact of considerable nurture, along with some hurt. The psychological conflict between anticipations of nurture and of hurt is resolved here in the notion of a deity more kind than angry. Along with this belief we find, on the psychological level, a reduction in the tension arising from the ambivalence of the child's anticipations, and, in addition, vicarious anticipations in the parent of a probably pleasant future life for the child. On the factual level we find no pressures by the parent toward any particular behavior systems in the child but we do find considerable use of reward in child training, and we find the child, through identification or imitation, taking on such nurturant behavior.

An additional relationship that seems to require a different interpretation, though one not inconsistent with the foregoing, concerns the "capriciousness" of the gods. We assume that in societies with aggressive deities, the infant would not be able, particularly at the preverbal level, to understand or to predict the occasions of his receiving pain, and a property of capriciousness would thus accrue to the agent bestowing pain and nurture. A conception of the deities as capricious would therefore be seen as resolving the human anxiety deriving from inability to predict or foresee one's pains and woes. In another study, our raters were asked to judge whether a theme of "capriciousness" was present in the religious beliefs of a number of the same cultures as those analyzed in this study. A strong but nonsignificant tendency was found for the capricious deities to be the same as the aggressive ones, a relationship that becomes clearly significant when the variable of pain in infancy is controlled. Societies with predominantly aggressive deities and with high pain in the treatment of infants have capricious gods and spirits in six out of seven cases, and the societies with predominantly benevolent deities and with low pain in infant treatment lack capricious gods and spirits in seven out of seven cases ($p = <.004$).

We have considered two radically different interpretations of our data. The first of these would view the factual level of parents' training behavior toward infant and child as stemming from the religious belief system. That is, societies characterized by beliefs in predominantly aggressive deities would regulate their infant and child training practices along compatibly aggressive lines. This view does not seem to us as fruitful of testable consequences as the interpretation proposed above, and there seems to be little evidence for or against it. We were able to make a minor check on it concerning the possibility that the pain involved in infant care would be explained or rationalized in the culture along explicitly religious lines. In none of the six societies with preponderantly aggressive deities for which data were easily available was the hurting of infants reported as done for religious purposes. This result is, of course, not conclusive, nor does it bear on the possibility of a "latent" religious theme as the psychological mediator of the practice of inflicting pain in infant care.

A second major interpretation would have its causal base in what we might call "nature." The aggressiveness of the deity, the amount of pain inflicted during infant care, and the emphasis or lack of emphasis in child training on particular behavior systems would all derive from the physical setting of the society. Unfortunately no satisfactory index is available that combines for each society the relevant aspects of climate, diet, energy and work levels, natural hazards, frequency of natural "calamities," etc. Lacking such an index that would permit a more definitive test, we used Horton's data (5) in a preliminary test of the hypothesis that both the aggressive properties of the supernaturals and the infancy and child training practices arise from the low subsistence level of a society. A small number of our societies also fall in Horton's sample, and his categorization of the level of subsistence "insecurity" is available for these cultures. There was no apparent relationship between subsistence insecurity and the properties of the deities. Another partial test employed some indices of aspects of natural phenomena in a number of our cultures provided by Whiting.[6] One might entertain the possibility that belief in aggressive supernaturals is in part an outcome of extreme cold or of extreme heat conditions. No analyses that we have made to date show any clear relationships of this kind. The only trend is a weak directional one in which low mean temperatures ($30°$–$75°$) go with aggressive supernaturals in seven out of ten cases, whereas high mean temperatures ($81°$ and up) tend to go with benevolent supernaturals in six out of eight cases. Temperature *variation* appears to have no trend of relationship with our data on the properties of the supernaturals.

Still additional explanatory hypotheses have been explored without appreciable support. According to one such hypothesis, mothers visit pain upon children as a displaced aggression arising from the frustrations of particularly low status. In a different study, our raters judged the status of women on such dimensions as ownership of property, inheritance of status, control of arrangements for love affairs and marriage, exercise of family authority, and so on. None of these, nor these in combination, predict the position of the societies on the variable of pain in infancy. The only suggestive trend is a tendency for the nurturant agent to inflict less pain on the infant in societies where the property is owned by women.

Summary

The belief systems concerning supernatural beings of 62 societies with a wide geographic spread were characterized as being mainly aggressive or hurtful, or mainly benevolent. Other, often interrelated, factors in the socialization of the infant (approximately to a year and a half) or child (up to ten years) were related to the benevolence of the supernatural.

Societies with beliefs in aggressive supernaturals were significantly more likely than those with beliefs in benevolent gods and spirits to be described as having generally punitive or hurtful practices in treating infants. At levels short of statistical significance, such cultures had fewer nurturant agents, protected the infant less from environmental discomforts, showed him less affection, were more inconsistent in caring for his needs, and took less care of his needs. Societies with beliefs in aggressive supernaturals also tended to see their supernaturals as "capricious" in hurting people.

In regard to childhood, parents in societies with beliefs in aggressive supernaturals were found to be more likely to reward their children for self-reliance and independence and to punish them for absence of these behaviors. They are generally more "rigid" in their training in the sense of depending more heavily on punishments than on rewards. Beliefs in benevolent gods and spirits are significantly related to the rated frequency of nurturant behavior shown by children in these cultures.

Several hypotheses according to which the obtained relationships might be explained were considered. The interpretation favored is derived from conditioning theory, reinforcement theory, and conflict theory. According to this view, the frequent hurt and pain in infancy in societies with aggressive deities causes anxiety in the child because of his conflicting anticipations of hurt and of nurture. His conflict is reduced by a conception of the deity as aggressive and thus compatible with human anticipations of hurt. The resulting reduction in the tension of ambivalence in the child's anticipations is accompanied by vicarious anxiety on the part of the parent concerning the child's future. The parent's anxiety is in turn reduced by following practices that reinforce independent and self-reliant behavior in his child to prepare him for the hurtful world he will encounter as an adult. In societies with benevolent deities there are no specific pressures toward training the child in particular behavior systems, but there is considerable reward used in child training. In result the child takes on such nurturant behavior through identification or imitation.

Notes

[1] The present study was facilitated by grants from the Social Science Research Council and from the Ford Foundation (Cornell-Harvard-Yale Socialization Study) as well as by the facilities of the Center for Advanced Study in the Behavioral Sciences. The authors are indebted for data and suggestions to Irvin Child (and his collaborators), Elisabeth Lambert, Wallace E. Lambert, Charles Morris, Morris E. Opler, and John W. M. Whiting. We are also indebted to William and Corinne Nydegger, Florence Rosenberg, and to members of two Seminars at Cornell University who helped develop the scales and did many of the ratings.

[2] Murdock, G. P., World Ethnographic Sample. (Mimeographed paper)

[3] It might be argued that only one culture from each of Murdock's culture areas should be represented in our "sample." We considered this, but the plan was dropped when we noted that in all areas there was at least one culture from each area which had a different pattern of relationship on the deities scale and infant pain scale from the others, and in four of the nine areas there were no repetitions of patterns on the two variables.

[4] In this study, only the infancy and childhood ratings related to boys are used. Ratings for girls were also available. Ratings for boys were chosen because another study (in preparation) on the role of women for these same cultures found that women very rarely develop high status in those power roles that *may* tend to determine some changes in culture. Their child training, where it differs, may have different functions in cultural integration. This problem has been set aside for later analysis.

[5] Roberts et al. provide a relationship that gives further meaning to our interpretation of this scale. They related this scale to the presence or absence of games of chance in a society and found that where the supernaturals were judged to be aggressive more than half the time the people did not play chance games, but that where the supernaturals were benevolent more than half the time games of chance were played. (Roberts, J., Bush, R., & Arth, M. J. Mastery in games: A cross-cultural study. [Mimeo.])

[6] Whiting, J. W. M. Personal communication.

References

1. Barry, H., Bacon, Margaret K., & Child, I. L. A cross-cultural survey of some sex differences in socialization. *J. abnorm. soc. Psychol.,* 1957, **55,** 327–332.
2. Berlyne, D. E. Uncertainty and conflict: A point of contact between information theory and behavior theory. *Psychol. Rev.,* 1957, **64,** 329–389.
3. Child, I. L., Storm, T., & Veroff, J. An analysis of folk tales in relation to socialization practices. In J. W. Atkinson, *Motives in fantasy, action, and society: A method of assessment and study.* Princeton: D. Van Nostrand, 1958.
4. Hald, A., *Statistical tables and formulas.* New York: Wiley, 1952.
5. Heinicke, C., & Whiting, B. B. *Bibliographies on personality and social development of the child.* New York: Social Science Research Council, Pamphlet 10, 1953.
6. Horton, D. The functions of alcohol in primitive societies. *Quart. Jour. Stud. Alcohol,* 1943, **4,** 292–303.
7. McClelland, D. C. Some social consequences of achievement motivation. In M. Jones (Ed.), *Nebraska symposium on motivation.* Lincoln: Univer. Nebraska Press, 1955.
8. Whiting, J. W. M., Child, I. L., Lambert, W. W., et al. *Field guide for a study of socialization in five societies.* Laboratory of Human Development, 1955. (Mimeo.)

Received October 21, 1957.

A Theory for Relating Family Interaction to Individual Thinking

DAVID REISS

In this article Reiss presents some basic conceptualizations and hypotheses for a theory of family interaction and individual thinking. The key concept relating these two areas is "consensual experience" which means the shared and distinctive world view that develops within each family. Using evidence based on experiments with groups of clinical population families, three types of consensual experience families were identified. "Consensual-sensitive" families shared a view of the world as threatening and hostile where each member needed to protect the family from the outside environment. When engaged in problem solving, members of this type of family were very successful in using cues from other family members while being relatively impervious to cues from the wider environment. "Environment-sensitive" families had a common perception of the world as basically knowable with the help of other family members. People in this type of family successfully used cues from within their families and from the outside world. Members of "interpersonal distance-sensitive" families shared a view of the world as existing in disparate pieces each applying to only one member. In this type of family cues from other family members were viewed as irrelevant, and each member attempted to function in the wider environment by himself. The author finds support for his typology in the findings of others who investigated nonclinical families with a variety of approaches.

Reiss suggests that the characteristics which identify these three types can be reduced to three attributes—problem-solving effectiveness, coordination, and a penchant for closure. He hypothesizes how his various family types stand on each dimension. In the final section he links each of these dimensions to a particular characteristic of individual thinking.

Originally published as "Varieties of Consensual Experience I. A Theory for Relating Family Interaction to Individual Thinking," in *Family Process*, Vol. 10, No. 1, March, 1971, pp. 1–28. Reprinted by permission of the author and the publisher, The Mental Research Institute and The Family Institute.

Mrs. Loann Drake assisted in the design of the procedure, conduct of the experiment, and analysis of the results. Dr. Lyman C. Wynne made many useful suggestions for the planning of the project and interpretations of findings. Dr. Robert Ryder assisted with the statistical analysis. Dr. John Zinner assisted in clinical diagnosis. Mr. Leonard Montgomery and Mr. George Shakarji assisted in computer programming. Mr. Leo Leitner assisted in the design and construction of the apparatus.

BACKGROUND

THE theory of consensual experience has been developed primarily to explain, relate, and predict observations made simultaneously on a) family interaction and b) the thinking and perception of individual members as these two processes unfold together through time. The theory has attempted to develop concepts that embrace both phenomena. Therefore, it has been required to draw upon sociologic concepts of family functioning and individual psychologic concepts of thinking and perception and to integrate these two domains. The notion of "consensual experience" is assigned a primary role as a relational concept. Briefly, the notion is that each family develops its own shared and distinctive view or explanation of its environment and the patterns or principles that govern its people and events. On one hand, *perceptual and cognitive abilities of individual members* are hypothesized as playing a major role in the formation and perpetuation of these family constructs. On the other hand, the family constructs are seen as determining how *family members interact* with each other in response to stimuli from the environment. Thus, the notion of family construct serves to relate individual thinking and family interaction.

The present investigation has some of its roots in the clinical investigations of Lidz (18) and Wynne (39, 45, 46). These investigators, in separate studies of the family's role in the development of schizophrenia, postulated that family interaction had a direct effect on the thinking of its individuals; the individual of most interest for them was the schizophrenic-to-be. The problem of verifying their entire hypothesis on schizophrenia in a single series of experimental studies seemed impossible. Part of the problem arises from the lack in current theory and method for the direct study of the relationship between family interaction and individual thinking. We began the study of this problem by designing procedures that at the same time elicited from families a variety of interactional patterns as well as complex perceptual and cognitive activity in individual members. These procedures were designed to objectively measure processes at both levels, family interaction and individual thinking, as they occurred simultaneously. In the first stage of building our theory on these observations, we have sought to develop concepts that relate these two domains of functioning as they occur simultaneously. We have given comparatively little emphasis, in contrast to Wynne, Lidz and other clinical theorists, to the questions of ultimate or long range causality: what style of family interaction may determine cognitive styles or cognitive defects in its members, or vice versa. Hopefully, when our empirical findings are more complete, we will be able to address directly these major questions of causality.

Our first experiments compared the performance of groups of families of normals, hospitalized character disorders, and schizophrenics (24, 25, 26). The psychopathology of the index child was used only as a sampling criterion. The major focus of these studies continues to be the identification of varieties of family interaction and their relationship to individual thinking, rather than the pathogenesis or familial correlates of a particular syndrome. The striking finding was that members in families of schizophrenics showed a great ability to utilize cues coming from each other. They appeared to infer from these cues the ideas, objectives, questions, and needs of the other members. However, these same family members did not effectively utilize cues coming from the non-family environment. Their inferences were inaccurate, unstable and internally inconsistent. Their ability to use cues from each other permitted a good deal of similarity and agreement on approaches to solutions of the experimental problems, but these solutions were usually poor. Members in normal families, on the other hand, could utilize cues from both the non-family environment and others in the family. Families of patients with character disorders effectively utilized cues from the environment but not from each other.

In order to explain these findings we proposed that members of the same family had shared experiences of the relationship of their family to the non-family environment as represented by the laboratory and its procedures. Members in families of schizophrenics, we proposed, shared the experience of the environment as threatening, chaotic and unknowable; the family's role was to protect each other. Thus, cues from the family were attended to and successfully used and integrated; those from the environment were not. These families can be termed "consensus-sensitive." Members in families of normals, we suggested, shared the experience that interacting with each other was a way of enlarging their already developing knowledge and mastery of the environment. Thus, cues from the environment and family received much attention. These can be termed "environment-sensitive" families. Families of patients with character disorders were seen as sharing a perception that the environment was split into as many pieces as there were family members; each member had access to his own piece and therefore attended to environmental cues from his piece only. It would follow that the ideas, opinions and observations of others would be valueless on the presumption of an environment so uniquely split. Thus, cues from others concerning their opinions and ideas could safely be neglected. We termed these "interpersonal distance-sensitive" families.

Our theory of consensual variety uses these experimental findings and the interpretations derived from them as a conceptual point of departure. Broader theoretical notions are developed as follows: *First,* we assume that the three types of families, two of which had been drawn from a clinical sample, might be found fairly frequently in a non-clinical sample. Although this assumption raises several problems which will be considered later, it did justify expanding our concepts of the three family types and making them, very provisionally, a basis for a more general typology of families. It must be emphasized that the typology is elaborated primarily in the service of developing our theory. Each type is distinguished by its characteristic orientation towards the environment. The shared orientation is posited as a major regulator of the style or mode by which the family interacts with its environment. We use data and concepts from a variety of clinical, sociologic, and anthropologic sources to develop this typology of family orientation (42).

Second, we postulate three basic dimensions of family orientation to the environment. They are conceptualized so that a profile of scores on all three dimensions would give an adequate characterization of a family's shared consensual experience of the environment and would clearly distinguish environment-, consensus- and interpersonal distance-sensitive family types (42).

Third, we propose that these dimensions could provide a clear conceptual link between family interaction and individual thinking. From a variety of models, or conceptualizations of individual thinking and perception, we selected Riley Gardner's notions of "cognitive controls" (8). Gardner's notions were developed to characterize the variety of an individual's orientation to his perceptual world by detailed studies of individual differences in perception and thinking. The fundamental orientation of Gardner's ideas is an attempt to characterize the ways in which individuals differ in their subjective grasp and understanding of their experiential world. This is very congenial with our theory of families, which explores differences between families with respect to shared perception and structuring of the environment. As we developed our dimensions of shared family orientation towards the environment, we noted that they had a strong formal similarity to three dimensions of cognitive control. In its current development, our theory hypothesizes that if we know a family's profile on the three dimensions of its shared orientation towards the environment, as determined from observing an episode of its interaction with the environment, we can predict the style or type of thinking, in terms of cognitive controls, employed by its individual members during that episode.

Exposition of Theory

In accord with this overall logic, the explication of our theory is in three parts: I. A more detailed description of our basic typology of families; II. A description of dimensions of consensual experience that can distinguish between our types of families and III. Hypotheses on the counterparts of these family dimensions in the cognitive and perceptual styles of individual members.

THREE TYPES OF FAMILIES

1. Environment-sensitive variety. In most situations, when a problem is presented to them, family members jointly perceive the problem as "out there," and its analysis and solution have no personal relevance for the family. The search for a solution can be governed by general principles of logic. This fundamental consensus on the nature of the problem has two consequences. First, the family jointly experiences the necessity to observe as many cues as possible. Each individual recognizes that the others' percepts and thoughts are a response to or an understanding of the externally-given problem. Therefore, if they are different from his own, he will include them among the various approaches or solutions he is considering. He will accept them or reject them based on their objective accuracy—not simply because the other has made a strong case for them. Because individuals share their observations and ideas completely, they have a broad and common base of cues and provisional solutions upon which to base their final conclusions. Thus, the family will agree on the final solution to the problem because it is based on a fully shared set of cues and hypotheses. Since each member depends exclusively on information from the environment, gained by his own efforts or vicariously through another member, the family will delay closure until it has examined as much evidence as possible. Each individual recognizes that the solution he agrees to is a result of sharing ideas with his family as well as of his own efforts to analyze and solve the problem.

2. *Interpersonal distance-sensitive variety.* In these families there is a joint perception that problem analysis and solution are simply a means by which each individual can demonstrate to the others his independence from the family and his own decisiveness and mastery. Each individual experiences accepting suggestions, observations, or ideas of others as a sign of his own weakness. At the extreme, each member sees the externally-given problem as a segment of his own personal universe, which operates according to laws and values unique for him. According to this formulation, his actions and their consequences simply cannot be useful to or evaluated by others in the family. In order to demonstrate their independence, individuals may reach decisions quickly based on little information, or they may accumulate information indefinitely refusing to come to closure until long after others do.

3. *Consensus-sensitive variety.* In this kind of family there is a joint perception that the analysis and solution of the problem are simply a means to maintain a close and uninterrupted agreement at all times. Even transient dissent is not tolerated. This is a consequence of viewing the laboratory and its tasks as potentially harmful and disruptive of inter-member ties. It is postulated that the problem is experienced "in here." Family members will quickly surrender their ideas or have others accept them without reference to the externally-given clues concerning problem solution. Thus, each individual's personal experience with the externally-given problem and its cues is not fully expressed in the family nor fully developed by the individual on his own. The family reaches its hastily-forged consensus early in the task. If cues and information continue to be provided, the family distorts or oversimplifies them in order to justify its initial collective solution. Each individual may continue to respond to this inflow of cues. When working

with his family, however, he is likely to regard cues from without as unpredictable, indecipherable, and unknowable. His sense of regularity and structure will be derived from the perdictability of his family's response to each new piece of information, not from his own scheme for ordering and patterning the cues themselves.

From a clinical perspective there is some evidence that this typology may clarify some important distinctions among characteristics of families frequently encountered in treatment. For example, in an experimental study, Mishler and Waxler compared families free of serious psychopathology with those in which an offspring was schizophrenic (20). Their data suggested that the former permitted the continuous influx, in the family's shared awareness, of new observations and ideas in contrast to the latter who showed over-control of ideas and premature closure. The picture of the former is in accord with several aspects of our environment-sensitive type. A reasonably good fit between other findings on families without psychopathology and our environment-sensitive type can also be made (15, 23, 41). Likewise, there is a fit between data on families of delinquents and our characterization of interpersonal distance-sensitive families. In clinical studies, Kaufman (13) and Minuchin (19) suggested that there is a pervasive sense of isolation and subjectively experienced interpersonal distance in these families. In an experimental study of families of delinquents, Stabenau et al. (40) provided data suggesting open conflict between family members, each preoccupied with obtaining his own "self-centered satisfaction."

Again, a reasonable fit can be made between features of consensus-sensitive families and families of schizophrenics. A large clinical literature has emphasized that families of schizophrenic patients experience themselves as estranged from their community or their immediate social environment. The most dramatic accounts are exemplified by Fleck's description of a family that collectively believed in an oriental-like cult they experienced as setting them apart from and in a superior position to their neighbors (7). For these kinds of shared, delusional experiences Fleck and Lidz offered the term *folie en famille*. More subtle but equally pervasive boundaries between the family of the schizophrenic and its social environment were described by Wynne et al. as a "rubber fence" which enforced for each family member the experience of his family as all encompassing (44). The extraordinary mutual "involvement" (Scott and Askworth 36) and "embroilment" (Hoover, 12) among members in these families have been widely described. It may be generated or intensified by a pervasive fear of the environment as threatening or potentially disruptive of inter-member bonds (Hill, 11). A paradox has been the repeated experimental finding that communication between members in these families is "poor" (17, 5, 21). These findings are widely accepted. However, the paradox is explained when one considers how delicately members of the family must be tuned to each other's experience in order to maintain a vivid and precisely-shared *folie en famille*. Searles (37) has suggested, in contrast to the prevailing view, that a schizophrenic patient and his mother are exquisitely sensitive to each other's unconscious experiences. Elsewhere (27) we have attempted to resolve this paradox by providing evidence that suggests that families of schizophrenics may communicate effectively when information is being exchanged about matters that require no attention to stimuli from the non-family environment.

Other evidence suggests that these families become preoccupied with their idiosyncratic experiences and filter out or foreclose the possibility of extensively or intensively experiencing stimuli from outside the family. For example, Mishler andd Waxler (20) showed that verbal communication in families of good pre-morbid schizophrenics is monotonous and invariant. They suggested that this makes the family unable to shift or adapt itself to changing environmental situations; in effect it has maintained premature closure in response to a continually changing environment.

This brief review of clinically-oriented literature suggests that clinicians and clinical researchers have already noted the kinds of distinctions among families our theory is specifying. The clinician's distinctions have been made piecemeal, a few at a time by different observers, often with a view towards establishing etiology or designing treatment for the several clinical syndromes. Our initial theoretical work ties these separate observations into a more coherent whole for the purpose of building a more comprehensive theory of interaction and thinking, not for specifying etiology or treatment. However, since the initial theorizing is clearly based in clinical research, it is useful to inquire, at least briefly, whether this typology is related to findings in research on non-clinical populations.

Distinctions analogous to those we make between environment and consensus-sensitive families have indeed been made in non-clinical research. For example, Strodtbeck (41), in his study of family values and achievement, summarizes a world-view typical of Jewish families in Eastern European *shtetl* culture.

"The external world for the Jews was hostile, to be sure, but it was by nature solvable . . . Old culture Jewish beliefs appear to be congruent in many, if not all, respects with such a belief in a rational mastery of the world." (p. 151)

In addition to other aspects, Strodtbeck stresses that the families were intensely aware of and open to the wider community and the technical, impersonal aspects of culture. In contrast, families in Southern Italy often view the external world as unpredictable and unmasterable:

"The unpredictable intervention of fate may be for good or for evil, but *Destino* is omnipresent. If a man works all his life for something which *Destino* may deny him, well then, why should men look so far ahead?" (p. 151)

Describing the boundedness of the Southern Italian family Strodtbeck writes:

"*La famiglia* in the Southern Italian culture was an inclusive social world. The basic mores of this world were primarily family mores; everyone outside the family was viewed with suspicion. Where the basic code was family solidarity, there was a strong feeling that the family should stay together—physically close together." (p. 150)

These distinctions, in terms of beliefs about order and mastery of the external world and solidarity between members, bear a strong similarity to our own: Jewish families from the "old culture" being environment-sensitive and, to a degree, Southern Italians being consensus-sensitive. There are some respects in which there is not a specific similarity in formulations. For example, we discuss the interdependence among members as a prime constituent of the family world-view whereas Strodtbeck discusses power relations as instrumental in maintaining such collective views. These differing formulations are not logically incompatible and might profitably be combined in future theoretical work.

It is significant that Strodtbeck formulated the distinctions between Jewish and Italian families in an effort to explain the ingredients of success and upward social mobility in the American culture. Indeed, similar distinctions have been made in another study relating the experience of family membership to success in the American culture, where success is broadly defined in terms of attained socioeconomic class. In two large-scale questionnaire survey studies Kohn (16) has found that working-class-parents typically view the outside world as unchangeable. Middle-class parents view the world as masterable by their own efforts. This orientation is expressed in the parents' attitudes towards their children. For example, working-class mothers more highly value obedience in their children and punish them when their behavior violates standards of society no matter what the intent of child. These standards are uncontrollable by the family. Middle-class mothers more highly value curiosity in their children and punish them according to the intent of their misbehavior. In effect, working-class parents value conformity, middle-class parents value initiative, and each punishes accordingly. Here, Kohn appears to be characterizing two groups of families: working-class families behave in accord with a view of the world as unchangeable and to which they must conform; middle-class families see the world as changeable by their own efforts and encourage exploratory behavior in their children.

In their study of *Family Worlds,* Hess and Handel (10) developed concepts that overlap ours. Their conceptions of dimensions of family experience will be discussed in connection with presenting our own concepts of dimensions below. Here we wish to note correspondence between our concepts of interpersonal distance-sensitive families and a group of families alluded to as "disconnected" by Hess and Handel. Using the case study method, supplemented by several psychological tests, these investigators intensively studied 33 families drawn from a non-clinical population and presented five families in detail because each "represented in its interactional aspects a cluster of

families of the total group." The family selected, as representative of the disconnected group, is described in part as follows:

"The Littletons offer a fragmented pattern of family goals and standards.
Preferences and ambitions affecting the family do not constitute an image
upon which the group has achieved consensus. The image is lacking in
clarity; it is not explicit; it is not shared . . . the family feels it is not
working together as a unit towards group objectives." (p. 129)

And continuing about the same family:

"The avoidance of intimacy which characterizes the Littletons springs
from a basic mistrust of the reciprocity and stability of affectional intimate
exchange." (p. 161)

In our formulation concerning the interpersonal distance-sensitive family, we
proposed the dominant family experience as arising from each member's wish
to demonstrate independence and mastery. This dynamic is not as central in
Hess and Handel's formulations. However, there is a most important similarity
in the existential description of family *ambience:* the existence of separate
experiential universes, one for each member.

In sum, several studies of non-clinical populations—using experimental,
survey, and case study methods—have also made many of the same distinctions emphasized by our typology. The data suggest a variety of ways in which
dominant family consensual experiences may be indexed. For example, we
may be able to locate families with the consensus-sensitive orientation in a
sample of families of schizophrenics, in a group of working-class families, or
in the Southern Italian subculture. Environment-sensitive families may be most
frequent in a sample free of serious psychopathology in any member, a
middle-class family, and Jewish families of Eastern European origin. Interpersonal distance-sensitive families may not be confined to families where
offspring are overtly delinquent but may also appear in a more general sample, although we have a less clear notion of how they may be indexed.

DIMENSIONS OF FAMILY CONSENSUAL EXPERIENCE

Our typology attempts to distinguish between groups of families by giving
an array or profile of characteristics for each group. The next theoretical step
is to propose that, for each group of families, this array can be simplified
into just three attributes and that a family can be typed if we know whether
it is low or high on each of three attributes or dimensions. These dimensions
characterize the shared consensual experiences of families in problem-solving
situations. Although they refer conceptually to shared, subjective experiences
of families, their names are more closely related to a class of behaviors by
which they may be objectively assessed in problem-solving situations.

Family Problem-solving Effectiveness. This dimension refers to the contribution that the family, working as a group, makes to the problem's solution. It is conceptualized as independent from the problem-solving skills each

individual may be able to apply, by himself, towards the problem. For example, consider a family moving into a strange neighborhood. Each member might make some exploration of the neighborhood on his own to develop his notions of the structure of human relationships and non-human resources in the new location. This individual exploration would reflect a range of cognitive, perceptual, and interpersonal skills. Family problem-solving effectiveness would represent the additional contribution the family group makes to whatever the individuals, acting separately, could achieve on their own. In some cases the family's "contribution" is negative, *i.e.*, the family may interfere with exploration.

In the experimental setting we can present problems of various kinds to individual members and measure or assess their solutions. Then we can present the same or similar problems to the family group. The difference between the average solution of the individuals and the solution of the family is the measure of family problem-solving effectiveness. Roman (33) designed such a study using the WAIS, giving it first to each member of a marital pair and then asking the couple to respond jointly. Several of our previous experiments have had an analogous design.

Unlike Roman, we would not equate an *effective* problem solution with an *accurate* one. We conceive everyday problems as soluble by a variety of alternative solutions. It is relatively uncommon that there is a clear standard of accuracy against which an individual's or a family's solution may be judged. Therefore, rather than view the poles of this dimension as *accurate versus inaccurate,* we conceive of them as *subtle, detailed,* and *highly structured versus coarse, simple* or *chaotic.* In the former, the family construes events and people as complex, and their relationship to each other is seen as conditional on many factors. In the latter, events and people are classed according to simple and coarse attributes, and their perceived relationship to each other is incomprehensible or is very stylized.

Hess and Handel (10) have conceptualized five "processes that give shape to the flux of family life, coherence to the extended array of events, perceptions, emotions, actions, learnings, and changes which the members experience or undertake." Among these notions is one of "establishing boundaries of the family's world of experience"; it is similar to our concept of family problem-solving effectiveness. Some aspects of their very broad concept are expressed as follows:

"The family maps its domain of acceptable and desirable experience, its life space . . . Limits to experience—broad or narrow—are established in a variety of ways and along several dimensions . . . (The family determines) how deep or how shallow experience . . . how many kinds of life and action are conceived of, known of, or understood." (p. 14)

According to our definitions we would expect environment-sensitive families to score high on measures of this dimension and consensus-sensitive families should score in the low range. Interpersonal distance-sensitive families, lacking the richness and stimulation inherent in cooperative problem solving, would also have low scores although perhaps not as low as consensus-sensitive families.

Coordination. This dimension refers to the family members' ability and willingness to develop problem solutions similar to each other. It is a distinctly different dimension from problem-solving effectiveness, since family members may effectively share solutions that are either coarse and simple, or subtle and detailed. The concept refers to those situations in which the family is working as a group and extends beyond the notion of simple agreement. It refers to a more pervasive experience by all members that they are, for the moment, in the same experiential universe, and its principles and patterns are equally true and equally relevant for all members. In this sense, agreement on a problem's solution follows from a more basic experience in the family that consensus is possible. Therefore, in our attempts to assess coordination, we would measure more than agreement within the family. We shall also require evidence of a more basic or primary sharing process both in formulating solutions and believing in them.

Interpersonal distance-sensitive families should clearly score very low on this dimension. Interestingly, consensus-sensitives and environment-sensitives should be high but for very different reasons. Environment-sensitives will effectively and collaboratively explore the problem and its relative context in the environment. Because of continuous sharing of percepts and ideas, their solutions should be in good agreement. Supporting this process is the family's shared belief that the problem's solution is governed by general, impersonal laws of logic. This sense of the problem as impersonal emphasizes the belief that the laws are applicable to and discoverable by all members of the family. As apparent in our description of them, consensus-sensitive families have a shared view of the environment arising from a more fundamental need to cohere in the face of uncertain, unmasterable, and at times threatening environment.

Penchant for Closure. This dimension refers to the family's proclivity for suspending or applying ordered and coherent concepts to raw sensory experience. On one extreme are families who rapidly apply structured explanations to all incoming stimuli. Not only may the world be experienced as ordered and patterned; it may be experienced as *continuously* ordered and patterned, and the current structure is experienced as derivative from the past in a smooth or uninterrupted way. In families, each individual has a clear experience of how his family has responded to similar input in the recent or remote past. This remembrance of things past forms a central basis for the structuring of current experience. These families struggle to apply past explanations to new data, or failing that, apply new explanations as quickly as possible; they avoid periods or episodes where stimuli seem uncanny, inexplicable, or mysterious. On the other extreme are families, who, for the most part, experience stimuli as continuously novel and, at times, chaotic. They cannot utilize or cannot remember the family's previous approaches or solutions to similar problems. Their sense of the present is very intense and, experientially, time seems very fleeting. Stimuli are experienced as very immediate and very transient.

The present concept is meant to refer to continuity of experience over short-time spans such as the hour or two a family might spend in a laboratory. At one extreme would be families who have a clear sense of how they might have solved the problem previously and hold to a similar solution, without change, throughout the task. At the other extreme might be families who experience the problem as entirely novel and continuously change their solution in response to every slight variation in the quality of stimuli or information relevant to the problem. However, continuity of structure and interpretation in families may be conceptualized as occurring over much longer periods of time. Bossard and Boll (2), in a study of family ritual, showed how patterned group practices provide a family with a sense of permanence and durability through many phases of its development. We also have fragmentary reports of eminent families, most with unusual political or literary gifts, who experience a clear sense of how their forebears would have responded to a great range of problems in the environment (35). Indeed the members could often say "I see the world through the eyes of my ancestors." However, the experience of continuity over these much greater time spans requires considerable theoretical and empirical work before it can be related to that hypothesized for comparatively brief intervals.

Our characterization of "environment-sensitive" families implies they show a good deal of delayed or suspended closure. Most important, they experience the problem as "out there." The sought-after solution will be a product of logical connections perceived in a psychological space outside the family; there is no necessity to experience them as continuous with the family's own previous solutions, in the recent or remote past. There is a prime valuation on evidence rather than explanation, and so a maximum exposure to ambiguity and uncertainty is sought in order to strengthen and generalize any tentatively-held hypotheses. In sharp contrast, are consensus-sensitive families who experience and utilize explanation and solution itself as major mechanisms to maintain family coherence. Thus, they strive to sustain unbroken continuity in their explanation of events; closure is early and often premature even when they are confronted with the most novel or unusual problems. The situation is much more complex for interpersonal distance-sensitive families. Here, there is no sense of a common family universe of explanations and viewpoints. The isolation of each individual provides him with little family "heritage," even in the short term, to permit him to build his present concept on his notions of his family's previous explanations. Nonetheless, each member may show a good deal of premature closure when operating in relative isolation. This is one good way to shut the others out of one's own personal world: "my mind's made up; I don't need to listen to you." On the other hand, in the same families, there may be a tendency for some individuals to delay closure. Paradoxically, delaying closure when others in the family have come to it prematurely is another way of marking out an individual universe. So, we would expect great variability within interpersonal distance-sensitive families with perhaps a tendency to the premature.

The three types of families described and their hypothesized position on our three dimensions are shown in Table 1.

Table 1—Summary of Predictions, for Each of Three Putative Basic Dimensions, for Environment-, Distance- and Consensus-sensitive Families

	DIMENSIONS		
Type of Family	Problem Solving	Coordination	Penchant for Closure
Environment-sensitive (Normal)	High	High	Low
Interpersonal-distance-sensitive (Delinquent)	Moderate to low	Low	Variable
Consensus-sensitive (Schizophrenic)	Moderate to low	High	High

COUNTERPARTS OF FAMILY DIMENSIONS IN INDIVIDUAL EXPERIENCE

We shall attempt to show that our dimensions of family consensual experience provide specific conceptual links between patterns of observable family interaction and measurable cognitive and perceptual styles in individuals. The relationship between these two domains must rest largely on theoretical grounds, although there is some empirical evidence to guide us.

Problem-solving Effectiveness and Field Articulation. Our concept of problem-solving effectiveness focuses on the comprehensiveness, detail, and structure perceived in the environment by the family as a group. Families located on the upper extreme effectively perceive highly articulated structure in complex and variegated stimulus fields. This capacity, on the family level, bears a distinct, formal relationship to the concept of field articulation developed by Witkin (43) and Gardner (8). Witkin has said:

"The person who experiences in articulated fashion has the ability to perceive items as discrete from their backgrounds, or to reorganize a field, when the field is organized; and to impose structure on a field, and so perceive it as organized, when the field has relatively little inherent structure. In this view the ability to analyze experience and the ability to structure experience are both aspects of increasing articulation." (p. 14)

We hypothesize that families whose individuals are typically excellent field articulators will, when they interact or work on problems together, develop shared concepts of their environment that are profoundly and complexly structured. However, effective family problem solving, in this sense, is not construed as a simple product or sum of the field-articulating abilities of individual members. Rather, it is a more complex, reciprocal process directly involving family interaction patterns. For example, a family composed of high field articulators will establish interaction patterns that permit each individual maximum opportunity to examine and re-examine the stimulus field free from coercive pressures from others, that might operate to restrict the range of his attention. Indeed, in small laboratory *ad hoc* groups, high field articulators successfully resist the pressure of group opinion (34). The family group would, we predict, maintain interaction patterns that permitted individuals to alert each other to relevant or hidden aspects of the environment's structure. Moreover, the relationship being reciprocal, such interaction patterns would support and shape more refined field articulation in its members. The latter effect may be particularly true for children whose emerging capacity to articulate stimulus fields may be a direct product of such family experience.

The empirical evidence linking family problem-solving effectiveness to high field articulation in its members is, to our knowledge, fragmentary. Two studies from our laboratory are suggestive. In the first, cited above, a group of families was tested by three very different kinds of problem-solving procedures (24, 25, 26, 27). These procedures permitted the simultaneous monitoring of family interaction and individual thinking, as they occurred concurrently. A correlational analysis (27) suggested that at the time a family was interacting to produce effective problem solutions, its individuals were processing information as would high field articulators; *i.e.* they were systematically setting aside irrelevant cues and developing an increasingly articulated picture of the relevant aspects of the stimulus field. However, our measures of individual information processing did not include any of the criterial procedures of Witkin and Gardner so that these data are merely suggestive. A second fragment, also from our own laboratory, suggests that families of psychiatric patients, parents and children alike, have lower scores on the Embedded Figures Test, a criterial measure of field articulation, than normals studied by other investigators (32). Since these families often show ineffective problem solving, these data again are suggestive of a link.

Coordination and Leveling Sharpening. In our terms coordination in families refers to a fundamental experience of sharing the same universe of experience. Each person perceives the structure of his environment the way his family does because each has a strong sense that the environment is the same for all. Thus, coordination in the problem-solving situation is manifested by agreement on the problem's solution. But the agreement does not represent coercion; instead, it arises from a shared process of formulating and believing in solutions. In order for a member to remain responsively in tune with his coordinated family, he must remain continuously in touch with their changing percepts. Each cue from others must serve as a pregnant and highly interpretable epigram of the others' percepts and ideas. Because each cue is so precious, all cues must be attended to and understood. In particular, successive changes in cues must be carefully noted to recognize successive changes in the others. Unlike building up structured concepts of relatively static external stimulus situations, individuals cannot systematically set aside irrelevant or peripheral cues, nor can they, in a stepwise fashion, develop their articulated impressions. Indeed, it is often seemingly irrelevant or peripheral cues that inform about a significant change in the other; high field articulation may involve setting aside just those crucial cues. We may regard high field articulation as representing a systematic pursuit and test of one's *own* developing and structuring notions of a relatively *static environment,* whereas quite a different ability is required for keeping pace with *changes* in *others'* notions.

Silverman (38), in a lengthy review, posited that field dependence, the polar opposite of field articulation (measured by low scores on the Embedded Figures and Rod and Frame Tests) was the likely perceptual basis for social sensitivity, particularly the moment-by-moment responsiveness to peripheral cues. He argues that being influenced by peripheral cues can be construed as a positive ability when an individual attempts to grasp subtleties and changes in others. We have argued the merits of this attractive hypothesis in a prior publication (27), but, nonetheless, it presents at least two problems. First, we have studied a number of families that appear to develop *simultaneously* structured and articulated concepts of their environment as well as displaying great interpersonal sensitivity and responsiveness among its members; as explained above, we have called these "environment-sensitive" families. According to the formulations presented so far, this would require family members to be both high and low field articulators. But field articulation has been conceived, by all leading theorists, as a bi-polar dimension separating individuals; one cannot be both high and low at the same time. (It is possible that, in environment-sensitive families, some members are high and others low and the total family "product" contains both articulated problem solutions and interpersonal sensitivity, but evidence from our previous experiments does not support this.) Second, although low field articulators (field-dependent individuals) are responsive to peripheral cues, they are not necessarily able to distinguish between *successive changes* in cues. For example, several studies show that performance on the Rod and Frame and Embedded Figures Tests is unrelated to the ability to make fine discriminations between successive stimuli on the Schematizing Test, in which subjects estimate the size of successively presented squares whose objective size changes slightly from trial to trial. (8)

It seems most parsimonious, therefore, to regard the underlying perceptual dimension related to coordination as a dimension entirely uncorrelated with field articulation. The construct of "leveling/sharpening" as formulated by Gardner (8) and others meets many of our requirements. Its criterial measure, the Schematizing Test, seems to assess an entirely different perceptual dimension than do the measures of field articulation. The concept has been used to relate a number of findings in the study of memory. In general, levelers "formed relatively undifferentiated memory schemata in a variety of situations involving temporal sequences of stimuli. Subjects at the sharpening extreme seemed to register discrete memories of successive stimulation. In general, sharpener's impressions of past experiences were "recoverable" in relatively unaltered form, e.g., for purposes of comparison with new stimulation." (7, p. 67)

We hypothesize that levelers, placed in social situations, would fail to discriminate temporal changes in cues coming from others. Present cues would "assimilate" with memories of previous cues and be indistinguishable from them. We hypothesize that families high in coordination contain sharpeners who are sensitive to minute changes in the constant flow of stimuli—including those from other members.

Penchant for Closure and Tolerance of Unrealistic Experience. Our concept of closure emphasized for each member in a problem-solving family a balance between his raw, unstructured experience and the explanation and structure derived from a family heritage. A family showing suspended closure frequently sets aside its shared notions of how the environment is structured in favor of directly considering the novel, ambiguous, and uncanny aspects of the direct or raw sensory experience of its members. As we have suggested, this results in a discontinuity of experienced structure in favor of an interweaving over time of explained experience and inexplicable sensation. Klein *et al.* (14) have formulated the concept of "tolerance of unrealistic experiences," which we believe to be an individual counterpart to this phenomenon on the family level. The criterial measure is the subject's readiness to perceive movement in two alternating static pictures (*e.g.,* a running horse where one picture has its legs outstretched and the second has them drawn in, both in a running posture). In order to perceive movement at low rates of alternation, the subject has to be willing or able to set aside his conventional notion of what is true (he has been told the image does not move) in favor of the direct and uncanny sensory experience of movement. Readiness to perceive apparent movement correlates highly with the perception of frequent perspective reversals in the Schroeder staircase and great freedom to "perceive" a variety of images based on many different kinds of determinants on the Rorschach cards.

In a separate series of investigations, Feirstein (4) demonstrated that individuals tolerant of unrealistic experiences, as measured by the procedures of Klein, were better able to *integrate* such experiences into a more conventional framework for socially understandable expression or into their own defensive operations. He used a measure of Rorschach responses which assessed "the effectiveness with which *S* made the unrealistic aspect (of his Rorschach response) . . . in a more understandable and acceptable communication." Moreover, his tolerant subjects were clearly able to set aside convention in their productions on a word association test and showed responses more reflective of their own drives rather than conventional tastes (as in preferences for pictures connoting sexual, anal, or oral themes). Individual differences in preference for non-conventional and deeply personal experiences have also been studied by Fitzgerald under the rubric "openness to experience" (6). He used a questionnaire to explore not only subjects' tolerance for unrealistic experiences but also for logical inconsistencies, regressive experiences (fantasy, daydreaming), and altered states (inspirational, numbed, serene, and ecstatic states). Fitzgerald's subjects, who showed "openness" on his questionnaire, also produced unconventional word associations. Thus, they may be similar to the tolerant subjects of Feirstein who also produced unconventional associations. When the cross correlations between Klein's and Feirstein's measures and Fitzgerald's questionnaire are fully studied, it may be possible to broaden our conception of this dimension as a general *openness* to *personal* experience rather than the more restricted concept of *tolerance* of *unrealistic* experience.

Our proposal is that individual members must be able to tolerate unrealistic experiences—indeed seek them out—in order for families to periodically suspend closure in their search for problem solutions. The "unreality" is construed in Klein's original terms, *i.e.* setting aside explanations that are conventional. As part of the experience of family membership, conventionality refers most specifically to what the family, as a group, holds to be true. In other words, individuals who can set aside a large variety of conventional explanations in the kinds of experimental situations used by Klein, we propose, can also set aside or are likely to set aside, explanations they have conventionally shared with their family. The two types of "convention" are related because both depend, in the eyes of the subject, on views of a reference group or a set of beliefs generally held by others. In Klein's experimental situation the subject intolerant of unreality accepts and applies the experimenter's explanation of the mechanical workings of the apparent movement tachistoscope or the generally held notions about the most "obvious" forms on the inkblots. In this sense, the intolerant subject sees the stimulus through the eyes of a specific or general other. We hold that this self-willed imposition on private perception bears crucial formal similarity to premature closure in family problem solving; here the member perceives stimuli and solutions "through the eyes of his family."

Delayed closure in the problem-solving situation, as we have said, should show itself by frequent changes and alterations of the family's solution in response to new stimuli. Detailed inspection of concurrent family interaction should show periods during which individuals are released or permitted private access to the content of their own sensations. According to Feirstein's work, we would expect such individuals to be able to integrate such personal experiences into communicable and understandable framework. However, the coherence, understandings, explanations, or structure derived from this personal experience ought to be highly individualistic or idiosyncratic rather than commonplace and conventional. These periods of personal experiences may be followed by intense interjection of novel percepts and concepts by all individuals into the stream of family interaction. It was this latter variable of family interaction that clearly distinguished families of normals from those of families of good pre-morbid schizophrenics in Mishler and Waxler's study (20). Members of normal families could frequently interject material into the onward flow of family interaction.

It is also of considerable interest that we have found that parents and children in families of schizophrenics show extremely low rates for figure reversal, *i.e.* they were intolerant of unrealistic experiences (32). We have postulated that families of schizophrenics are consensus sensitive (one experiment (29) has already shown this to be true). Since consensus-sensitive families show premature closure, our reversible figure data support the relationship between intolerance of unrealistic experience and premature closure.

The question arises, if delayed closure—and its associate private experience of "unreality"—requires a periodic separation or release of the individual from his family, then isn't low coordination required in order to accomplish it? If this were the case, delayed closure might be construed as another aspect of low coordination rather than a separate dimension with its own underpinnings in the perceptual style of the individual members. However, the kind of "perceptual privacy," which we are suggesting is crucial to delayed closure, is entirely different from low coordination. Consider an individual who tolerates or even searches for native, raw, and inexplicable experiences. If he is in a coordinated family, he will continue to believe that he shares the same experiential universe with his family. Therefore, he will feel it imperative to report the contents of his own sensory experience to his family and to stay in touch with those of other members. If he is in an uncoordinated family, he will retain his private, uncanny experiences to elaborate or embroider his personal universe. In this sense there is no necessary relationship between coordination and closure; the former refers to the balance between a personal or shared experiental universe, the latter refers to the balance between a continuously structured and familiar, or an uncanny and novel experiental universe.

SUMMARY AND PROSPECT

We have begun to sketch a theory that, as it presently stands, has three major components. *First,* we have postulated a *typology of family constructs.* Here we have suggested that a crucial component of the subjective experience of being-in-a-family is to share with other members a common construction of the environment and the family's place in it. We have described three types of constructs or orientations, although, presumably, there are others. *Second,* we have conceptualized three basic *dimensions* of this shared, consensual experience in families that adequately characterize and distinguish these types. *Third,* we have hypothesized that each dimension of *shared family* experience corresponds to a dimension of *individual* perceptual orientation in each member. The primary objective of this theory building has been to provide conceptual links between observations of individual thinking and family interaction. We are interested in knowing the ways in which family interaction shapes the development of cognitive styles in its members and the ways in which individuals use their cognitive resources in their most intimate relationships in family groups. Also we have provided some concepts for understanding the ways in which families relate to the non-family world; *i.e.* a theory of interaction between the family and its environment (rather than among members within a family). In a general sense this may strengthen our understanding of the relationship between family systems and the broader social systems of community, sub-culture, and nation. In a more specific clinical sense, these notions may help understand and predict a family's response to various therapeutic interventions. For example, the clinic becomes a crucial part of the family's environment when one of its members becomes an identified patient. The family's response to the clinic may be heavily conditioned by its typical response to other events, people, and agencies in its more usual experiential universe.

This theory cannot be tested all at once and small portions of it must be elaborated and then tested piece by piece. For example, in the companion paper (30) we describe an experimental procedure designed to explore the notion of separate, uncorrelated dimensions of consensual experience. The procedure is designed to provide, simultaneously, variables whose face validity suggests they should be good measures of family problem-solving effectiveness, coordination, and closure. A study is run to see if, indeed, such dimensions emerge and are separable from each other. The same experimental procedure has also been used to test our notion of a typology of consensual experiences. As we have explained, we expect middle-class normal families to be environment-sensitive, families of delinquents to be interpersonal distance-sensitive and families of schizophrenics, consensus-sensitive. Our theory specifies a *pattern* of findings for each of these three clinical groups. Indeed, in a study reported elsewhere (29), the predicted patterns were found. Another crucial piece is the assertion that the family solution is not the simple sum of the problem-solving abilities of its members; *i.e.* that family interaction patterns, representing the experience of being-in-the-family, make their own, unique contribution to the problem solution. Evidence from a carefully-controlled, computer-automated experiment supports this view (28, 31). Finally, we have alluded to our direct measures of the individual cognitive and perceptual resources of clinical family groups which support but do not by themselves prove aspects of our overall theory (32).

Experimental methods being developed or in actual use offer the promise of effectively testing pieces of our theory in the future. For example, we should like to know whether experiences in *ad hoc* laboratory groups could be made to simulate those in established families. Data suggest that several investigators have apparently been able to shape *ad hoc* groups that resemble our consensus-sensitive and environment-sensitive families by altering experimental instructions (22, 42). Therapy groups, containing unrelated persons, also appear to develop shared experiences of the leader and the non-group environment that bear distinct resemblances to our characterizations of the family construct. Indeed, Bion's (1) notions of "basic assumptions" and "group culture" have a clear formal relationship to many of our own ideas. The use of *ad hoc* groups may permit us to explore the various conditions under which consensual experiences of various types develop. A particularly stiff challenge will come in relating family interaction to individual cognitive style. It will not be enough simply to correlate scores on batteries of cognitive style tests now in use and scores on family interaction procedures of subjects so tested. These correlations relate individual perceptual functioning measured at time x with family interaction measured at time y. First, what we really want to know is: what perceptual and cognitive resources a member is using when he is actually engaged in interaction with his family? In other words what are the perceptual and cognitive processes going on *simultaneously* with family interaction at time y? This question is clearly answerable only by sophisticated experimental techniques. We believe we have come close, especially with our computer-automated procedures, to the necessary sophistication for measuring family interaction variables. As to the perceptual variables, recent developments in the experimental psychology of perception, particularly with automated recording of individual differences in subtle perceptual variables, suggest that it will soon be possible to "read out" perceptual activity of individual members while they are interacting with their families in the kinds of family problem-solving procedures we have designed. Moreover, we want to study systematically the "chicken and egg" problem: how much impact does a particular variety of consensual experience have on the development of cognitive style in individuals exposed to it and participating in it? Conversely, how much is the family consensual experience itself shaped by the cognitive styles of its members? Simulation experiments, using *ad hoc* groups, may help provide leads. Ultimately more comprehensive designs using real families will probably be necessary.

References

1. Bion, W. R., *Experiences in Groups,* New York, Basic Books, Inc., 1959.
2. Bossard, J. H. S. and Boll, E. S., *Ritual in Family Living,* Philadelphia, University of Pennsylvania Press, 1950.
3. Buchsbaum, M. and Silverman, J., "Average Evoked Response and Perception of the Vertical," *J. Exp. Res. Pers., 4:* 79–83, 1970.
4. Feirstein, A., "Personality Correlates of Tolerance for Unrealistic Experiences," *J. Consulting Psychol., 31:* 387–395, 1967.

5. Fisher, S., Boyd, I., Walker, D., and Sheer, D., "Parents of Schizophrenics, Neurotics, and Normals," *Arch. Gen. Psychiat., 1:* 149–166, 1959.

6. Fitzgerald, E. T., "Measurement of Openness to Experience: A Study of Regression in the Service of the Ego," *J. Personality Soc. Psychol., 4:* 655–663, 1966.

7. Fleck, S., Lidz, T., and Cornelison, A. R., "The Understanding of Symptomatology through the Study of Family Interaction," *Schizophrenia and the Family,* New York, International Universities Press, Inc., 1965, pp. 163–170.

8. Gardner, R. W., Holzman, P. S., Klein, G. S., Linton, H. B., and Spence, D. P., "Cognitive Control: A Study of Individual Consistencies in Cognitive Behavior," *Psychological Issues, 1* (4), New York, International Universities Press, 1959.

9. Gardner, R. W., Jackson, D. N., and Messick, S. J., "Personality Organization in Cognitive Controls and Intellectual Abilities," *Psychological Issues, 2:* (4), New York, International Universities Press, 1960.

10. Hess, R. D., and Handel, G., *Family Worlds,* Chicago, University of Chicago Press, 1959.

11. Hill, L. B., *Psychotherapeutic Intervention in Schizophrenia,* Chicago, University of Chicago Press, 1955.

12. Hoover, C. F., "The Embroiled Family: A Blueprint for Schizophrenia," *Family Process, 4:* 291–310, 1965.

13. Kaufman, I., Durkin, H., Frank, T., Heims, L. W., Jones, D. B., Ryter, Z., Stone, E., and Zilbach, J., "Delineation of Two Diagnostic Groups Among Juvenile Delinquents: The Schizophrenic and the Impulse-Ridden Character Disorder," *J. Am. Acad. Child. Psychiat., 2:* 292–318, 1963.

14. Klein, G. S., Gardner, R. W., and Schlesinger, H. J., "Tolerance for Unrealistic Experiences: A Study of the Generality of a Cognitive Control," *Brit. J. Psychol., 53:* 41–55, 1962.

15. Kluckhohn, F. R., "Variations in the Basic Values of Family Systems," in Bell, N. W., and Vogel, E. F. (Eds.), *A Modern Introduction to the Family,* Glencoe, Ill., The Free Press, 1960.

16. Kohn, M. L., *Class and Conformity,* Homewood, Ill., The Dorsey Press, 1969.

17. Lerner, P. M., "Resolution of Intrafamilial Role Conflict in Families of Schizophrenic Patients—I. Thought Disturbance," *J. Nerv. Ment. Dis., 141:* 342–351, 1965.

18. Lidz, T., Cornelison, A., Terry, D., and Fleck, S., "Intrafamilial Environment of the Schizophrenic Patient: VI. The Transmission of Irrationality," *Arch. Neurol. Psychiat., 79:* 305–316, 1958.

19. Minuchin, S. Auerswald, E., King, C., and Rabinowitz, C., "The Study of Treatment of Families That Produce Multiple Acting Out Boys," *Am. J. Orthopsychiat., 34:* 125–133, 1964.

20. Mishler, E. G. and Waxler, N. E., *Interaction in Families. An Experimental Study of Family Processes and Schizophrenia,* New York, John Wiley, Inc., 1968.

21. Morris, G. O., and Wynne, L. C., "Schizophrenic Offspring and Parental Styles of Communication. A Predictive Study Utilizing Excerpts of Family Therapy Recordings," *Psychiatry, 28:* 19–44, 1965.

22. Olmstead, M. S., "Orientation and Role in the Small Group," *Amer. Sociol. Rev., 19:* 741–751, 1954.
23. Parsons, T., "The Normal American Family," in Farber, S. M., Mustacchi, P., and Wilson, R. H. L. (Eds.), *Man and Civilization: The Family's Search for Survival,* New York, McGraw Hill, 1965.
24. Reiss, D., "Individual Thinking and Family Interaction, II. A Study of Pattern Recognition and Hypothesis Testing in Families of Normals, Character Disorders and Schizophrenics," *J. Psychiat. Res., 5:* 193–211, 1967.
25. Reiss, D., "Individual Thinking and Family Interaction, III. An Experimental Study of Categorization Performance in Families of Normals, Those with Character Disorders, and Schizophrenics," *J. Nerv. Ment. Dis., 146:* 384–403, 1968.
26. Reiss, D., "Individual Thinking and Family Interaction, IV. A Study of Information Exchange in Families of Normals, Those with Character Disorders, and Schizophrenics," *J. Nerv. Ment. Dis., 149:* 473–490, 1969.
27. Reiss, D., "Individual Thinking and Family Interaction, V. Proposals for the Contrasting Character of Experiential Sensitivity and Expressive Form in Families," *J. Nerv. Ment. Dis., 151:* 187–202, 1970.
28. Reiss, D., "Intimacy and Problem Solving: An Automated Procedure for Testing a Theory of Consensual Experience in Families," *Arch. Gen. Psychiat.,* in press.
29. Reiss, D., "Varieties of Consensual Experience III. Contrast Between Families of Normals, Delinquents, and Schizophrenics," *J. Nerv. Ment. Dis., 152:* 73–95, 1971.
30. Reiss, D., "Varieties of Consensual Experience II: Dimensions of a Family's Experience of Its Environment," *Family Process, 10:* 28–35, 1971.
31. Reiss, D., and Sheriff, W. H., Jr., "A Computer-Automated Procedure for Testing Some Experiences of Family Membership," *Behav. Sci., 15:* 431–443, 1970.
32. Reiss, D., and Elstein, A., "Perceptual and Cognitive Resources of Family Members: Contrasts Between Families of Paranoid and Non-paranoid Schizophrenics and Non-schizophrenic Psychiatric Patients," *Arch. Gen. Psychiat., 24:* 121–134, 1971.
33. Roman, M., Bauman, G., Borello, J., and Meltzer, B., "Interaction Testing in the Measurement of Marital Intelligence," *J. Abnor. Psychol., 72:* 489–495, 1967.
34. Rosner, S., "Consistency in Response to Group Pressures," *J. Abnor. Soc. Psychol., 55:* 145–146, 1957.
35. Saveth, E. N., "The American Patrician Class: A Field of Research," in Farber, B. (Ed.), *Kinship and Family Organization,* New York, John Wiley, Inc., 1966.
36. Scott, R. D., and Askworth, P. L., " 'Closure' at the First Schizophrenic Breakdown: A Family Study," *Brit. J. Med. Psychol., 40:* 109–145, 1967.
37. Searles, H., "The Effort to Drive the Other Person Crazy—An Element in the Aetiology and Psychotherapy of Schizophrenia," *Brit. J. Med. Psychol.,* Part 1, *32:* 1–18 (a), 1959.
38. Silverman, J., "Personality Trait and 'Perceptual Style' of the Psychotherapists of Schizophrenic Patients," *J. Nerv. Ment. Dis., 145:* 5–17, 1967.

39. Singer, M. T., and Wynne, L. C., "Thought Disorder and Family Relations of Schizophrenics: III. Methodology Using Projective Techniques," *Arch. Gen. Psychiat., 12:* 187–200, 1965.
40. Stabenau, J. R., Tupin, J., Werner, M., and Rollin, W. A., "A Comparative Study of Families of Schizophrenics, Delinquents, and Normals," *Psychiatry, 28:* 45–59, 1965.
41. Strodtbeck, F. L., "Family Interaction, Values, and Achievement," in McClelland, D. C., Baldwin, A. L., and Bronfenbrenner, U. (Eds.), *Talent and Society,* Princeton, N.J., D. Van Nostrand Co., 1958, pp. 135–194.
42. Thibaut, J. W., and Strickland, L. H., "Psychological Set and Social Conformity," *J. Pers. 25:* 115–129, 1956.
43. Witkin, H. A., Dyk, R. B., Fatherson, H. F., Goodenough, D. R., and Karp, S. A., *Psychological Differentiation,* New York, John Wiley, Inc., 1962.
44. Wynne, L. C., Ryckoff, I. M., Day, J., and Hirsch, S. I., "Pseudo-mutuality in the Family Relations of Schizophrenics," *Psychiatry, 21:* 205–222, 1958.
45. Wynne, L. C., and Singer, M. T., "Thought Disorder and Family Relations of Schizophrenics: II. A Classification of Forms of Thinking," *Arch. Gen. Psychiat., 9:* 199–206, 1963.
46. Wynne, L. C., and Singer, M. T., "Thought Disorder and Family Relations of Schizophrenics: IV. Results and Implications," *Arch. Gen. Psychiat., 12:* 201–212, 1965.

Training the Woman To Know Her Place:
The Power of a Nonconscious Ideology

SANDRA L. BEM AND DARYL J. BEM *

On some issues our perspective is so deeply held that we cannot even imagine alternative beliefs and attitudes. Bem and Bem call this a nonconscious ideology and cite as the example par excellence the perspective which most Americans have about women and sex roles. They show that this ideology pervades the society—including "radicals" and educated females.

There appears to be a wide chasm between the ideals of most American students and their actual views toward sex roles Although contemporary student values stress self-fulfillment, American women nevertheless undergo a socialization process whereby most of them become full-time homemakers. (The male socialization process is also a major factor in this outcome since men come to expect women to enact this role.) The authors debunk three arguments which claim that this situation does not violate the value of self-fulfillment. The refuted arguments are: (1) free will—after 21 years of socialization a woman is "free" to choose her role; (2) biology—sex-linked biological differences account for the "natural" woman's role, although women in the Soviet Union have much different roles, and variations in personality because of biological differences *among* women are not even considered; (3) complementarity—the role of the woman as homemaker is complementary but equal, which as the authors infer is a fraud and a hoax similar to the "separate but equal" slogan of school segregationists. Bem and Bem's hypothetical example of the "progressive" academic couple's views toward sex roles shows the extent and subtlety of this perspective. The application of their "roommate test" to the expectations of a typical white male college student for his black male roommate as well as the expectations of this same student for his female marriage partner (and, indeed, *her* expectations for her role) exemplifies the power of this nonconscious ideology.

* Order of authorship determined by the flip of a coin.

From *Beliefs, Attitudes, and Human Affairs* by Daryl J. Bem. © 1970 by Wadsworth Publishing Company, Inc., Belmont, California 94002. Reprinted by permission of the publisher, Brooks/Cole Publishing Company.

This selection should stimulate us to consider the contemporary American culture concerning not only sex roles as they relate to occupational differences, but also concerning our attitudes toward such related issues as family rights and obligations and sexual expression.

In the beginning God created the heaven and the earth. . . . And God said, Let us make man in our image, after our likeness; and let them have dominion over the fish of the sea, and over the fowl of the air, and over the cattle, and over all the earth. . . . And the rib, which the Lord God had taken from man, made he a woman and brought her unto the man. . . . And the Lord God said unto the woman, What is this that thou has done? And the woman said, The serpent beguiled me, and I did eat. . . . Unto the woman He said, I will greatly multiply thy sorrow and thy conception; in sorrow thou shalt bring forth children; and thy desire shall be to thy husband, and he shall rule over thee. (Gen. 1, 2, 3)

AND lest anyone fail to grasp the moral of this story, Saint Paul provides further clarification:

For a man . . . is the image and glory of God; but the woman is the glory of the man. For the man is not of the woman, but the woman of the man. Neither was the man created for the woman, but the woman for the man. (1 Cor. 11)

Let the woman learn in silence with all subjection. But I suffer not a woman to teach, nor to usurp authority over the man, but to be in silence. For Adam was formed, then Eve. And Adam was not deceived, but the woman, being deceived, was in the transgression. Notwithstanding, she shall be saved in childbearing, if they continue in faith and charity and holiness with sobriety. (1 Tim. 2)

And lest it be thought that only Christians have this rich heritage of ideology about women, consider the morning prayer of the Orthodox Jew:

Blessed art Thou, oh Lord our God, King of the Universe, that I was not born a gentile.

Blessed art Thou, oh Lord our God, King of the Universe, that I was not born a slave.

Blessed art Thou, oh Lord our God, King of the Universe, that I was not born a woman.

Or the Koran, the sacred text of Islam:

Men are superior to women on account of the qualities in which God has given them pre-eminence.

Because they think they sense a decline in feminine "faith, charity, and holiness with sobriety," many people today jump to the conclusion that the ideology expressed in these passages is a relic of the past. Not so. It has simply been obscured by an equalitarian veneer, and the ideology has now become nonconscious. That is, we remain unaware of it because alternative beliefs and attitudes about women go unimagined. We are like the fish who is unaware that his environment is wet. After all, what else could it be? Such is the nature of all nonconscious ideologies. Such is the nature of America's ideology about women. For even those Americans who agree that a black skin should not uniquely qualify its owner for janitorial or domestic service continue to act as if the possession of a uterus uniquely qualifies *its* owner for precisely that.

Consider, for example, the 1968 student rebellion at Columbia University. Students from the radical left took over some administration buildings in the name of equalitarian principles which they accused the university of flouting. Here were the most militant spokesmen one could hope to find in the cause of equalitarian ideals. But no sooner had they occupied the buildings than the male militants blandly turned to their sisters-in-arms and assigned them the task of preparing the food, while they—the menfolk—would presumably plan further strategy. The reply these males received was the reply they deserved, and the fact that domestic tasks behind the barricades were desegregated across the sex line that day is an everlasting tribute to the class consciousness of the ladies of the left.

But these conscious coeds are not typical, for the nonconscious assumptions about a woman's "natural" talents (or lack of them) are at least as prevalent among women as they are among men. A psychologist named Philip Goldberg (1968) demonstrated this by asking female college students to rate a number of professional articles from each of six fields. The articles were collated into two equal sets of booklets, and the names of the authors were changed so that the identical article was attributed to a male author (e.g., John T. McKay) in one set of booklets and to a female author (e.g., Joan T. McKay) in the other set. Each student was asked to read the articles in her booklet and to rate them for value, competence, persuasiveness, writing style, and so forth.

As he had anticipated, Goldberg found that the identical article received significantly lower ratings when it was attributed to a female author than when it was attributed to a male author. He had predicted this result for articles from professional fields generally considered the province of men, like law and city planning, but to his surprise, these coeds also downgraded articles from the fields of dietetics and elementary school education when they were attributed to female authors. In other words, these students rated the male authors as better at everything, agreeing with Aristotle that "we should regard the female nature as afflicted with a natural defectiveness." We repeated this experiment informally in our own classrooms and discovered that male students show the same implicit prejudice against female authors that Goldberg's female students showed. Such is the nature of a nonconscious ideology!

It is significant that examples like these can be drawn from the college world, for today's students have challenged the established ways of looking at almost every other issue, and they have been quick to reject those practices of our society which conflict explicitly with their major values. But as the above examples suggest, they will find it far more difficult to shed the more subtle aspects of a sex-role ideology which—as we shall now attempt to demonstrate—conflicts just as surely with their existential values as any of the other societal practices to which they have so effectively raised objection. And as we shall see, there is no better way to appreciate the power of a society's nonconscious ideology than to examine it within the framework of values held by that society's avant-garde.

Individuality and Self-Fulfillment

The dominant values of today's students concern personal growth on the one hand, and interpersonal relationships on the other. The first of these emphasizes individuality and self-fulfillment; the second stresses openness, honesty, and equality in all human relationships.

The values of individuality and self-fulfillment imply that each human being, male or female, is to be encouraged to "do his own thing." Men and women are no longer to be stereotyped by society's definitions. If sensitivity, emotionality, and warmth are desirable human characteristics, then they are desirable for men as well as for women. (John Wayne is no longer an idol of the young, but their pop-art satire.) If independence, assertiveness, and serious intellectual commitment are desirable human characteristics, then they are desirable for women as well as for men. The major prescription of this college generation is that each individual should be encouraged to discover and fulfill his own unique potential and identity, unfettered by society s presumptions.

But society's presumptions enter the scene much earlier than most people suspect, for parents begin to raise their children in accord with the popular stereotypes from the very first. Boys are encouraged to be aggressive, competitive, and independent, whereas girls are rewarded for being passive and dependent (Barry, Bacon, & Child, 1957; Sears, Maccoby, & Levin, 1957). In one study, six-month-old infant girls were already being touched and spoken to more by their mothers while they were playing than were infant boys. When they were thirteen months old, these same girls were more reluctant than the boys to leave their mothers; they returned more quickly and more frequently to them; and they remained closer to them throughout the entire play period. When a physical barrier was placed between mother and child, the girls tended to cry and motion for help; the boys made more active attempts to get around the barrier (Goldberg & Lewis, 1969). No one knows to what extent these sex differences at the age of thirteen months can be attributed to the mothers' behavior at the age of six months, but it is hard to believe that the two are unconnected.

As children grow older, more explicit sex-role training is introduced. Boys are encouraged to take more of an interest in mathematics and science. Boys, not girls, are given chemistry sets and microscopes for Christmas. Moreover, all children quickly learn that mommy is proud to be a moron when it comes to mathematics and science, whereas daddy knows all about those things. When a young boy returns from school all excited about biology, he is almost certain to be encouraged to think of becoming a physician. A girl with similar enthusiasm is told that she might want to consider nurse's training later so she can have "an interesting job to fall back upon in case—God forbid—she ever needs to support herself." A very different kind of encouragement. And any girl who doggedly persists in her enthusiasm for science is likely to find her parents as horrified by the prospect of a permanent love affair with physics as they would be by the prospect of an interracial marriage.

These socialization practices quickly take their toll. By nursery school age, for example, boys are already asking more questions about how and why things work (Smith, 1933). In first and second grade, when asked to suggest ways of improving various toys, boys do better on the fire truck and girls do better on the nurse's kit, but by the third grade, boys do better regardless of the toy presented (Torrance, 1962). By the ninth grade, 25% of the boys, but only 3% of the girls, are considering careers in science or engineering (Flanagan, unpublished; cited by Kagan, 1964). When they apply for college, boys and girls are about equal on verbal aptitude tests, but boys score significantly higher on mathematical aptitude tests—about 60 points higher on the College Board examinations, for example (Brown, 1965, p. 162). Moreover, girls improve their mathematical performance if problems are reworded so that they deal with cooking and gardening, even though the abstract reasoning required for their solutions remains the same (Milton, 1958). Clearly, not just ability, but motivation too, has been affected.

But these effects in mathematics and science are only part of the story. A girl's long training in passivity and dependence appears to exact an even higher toll from her overall motivation to achieve, to search for new and independent ways of doing things, and to welcome the challenge of new and unsolved problems. In one study, for example, elementary school girls were more likely to try solving a puzzle by imitating an adult, whereas the boys were more likely to search for a novel solution not provided by the adult (McDavid, 1959). In another puzzle-solving study, young girls asked for help and approval from adults more frequently than the boys; and, when given the opportunity to return to the puzzles a second time, the girls were more likely to rework those they had already solved, whereas the boys were more likely to try puzzles they had been unable to solve previously (Crandall

& Rabson, 1960). A girl's sigh of relief is almost audible when she marries and retires from the outside world of novel and unsolved problems. This, of course, is the most conspicuous outcome of all: the majority of American women become full-time homemakers. Such are the consequences of a non-conscious ideology.

But why does this process violate the values of individuality and self-fulfillment? It is *not* because some people may regard the role of homemaker as inferior to other roles. That is not the point. Rather, the point is that our society is managing to consign a large segment of its population to the role of homemaker solely on the basis of sex just as inexorably as it has in the past consigned the individual with a black skin to the role of janitor or domestic. It is not the quality of the role itself which is at issue here, but the fact that in spite of their unique identities, the majority of America's women end up in the *same* role.

Even so, however, several arguments are typically advanced to counter the claim that America's homogenization of its women subverts individuality and self-fulfillment. The three most common arguments invoke, respectively, (1) free will, (2) biology, and (3) complementarity.

1. The free will argument proposes that a 21-year-old woman is perfectly free to choose some other role if she cares to do so; no one is standing in her way. But this argument conveniently overlooks the fact that the society which has spent twenty years carefully marking the woman's ballot for her has nothing to lose in that twenty-first year by pretending to let her cast it for the alternative of her choice. Society has controlled not her alternatives, but her motivation to choose any but one of these alternatives. The so-called freedom to choose is illusory and cannot be evoked to justify the society which controls the motivation to choose.

2. The biological argument suggests that there may really be inborn differences between men and women in, say, independence or mathematical ability. Or that there may be biological factors beyond the fact that women can become pregnant and nurse children which uniquely dictate that they, but not men, should stay home all day and shun serious outside commitment. Maybe female hormones really are responsible somehow. One difficulty with this argument, of course, is that female hormones would have to be different in the Soviet Union, where one-third of the engineers and 75% of the physicians are women. In America, women constitute less than 1% of the engineers and only 7% of the physicians (Dodge, 1966). Female physiology *is* different, and it may account for some of the psychological differences between the sexes, but America's sex-role ideology still seems primarily responsible for the fact that so few women emerge from childhood with the motivation to seek out any role beyond the one that our society dictates.

But even if there really were biological differences between the sexes along these lines, the biological argument would still be irrelevant. The reason can best be illustrated with an analogy.

Suppose that every black American boy were to be socialized to become a jazz musician on the assumption that he has a "natural" talent in that direction, or suppose that his parents should subtly discourage him from other pursuits because it is considered "inappropriate" for black men to become physicians or physicists. Most liberal Americans, we submit, would disapprove. But suppose that it *could* be demonstrated that black Americans, *on the average,* did possess an inborn better sense of rhythm than white Americans. Would *that* justify ignoring the unique characteristics of a *particular* black youngster from the very beginning and specifically socializing him to become a musician? We don't think so. Similarly, as long as a woman's socialization does not nurture her uniqueness, but treats her only as a member of a group on the basis of some assumed *average* characteristic, she will not be prepared to realize her own potential in the way that the values of individuality and self-fulfillment imply she should.

The irony of the biological argument is that it does not take biological differences seriously enough. That is, it fails to recognize the range of biological differences between individuals within the same sex. Thus, recent research has revealed that biological factors help determine many personality traits. Dominance and submissiveness, for example, have been found to have large inheritable components; in other words, biological factors *do* have the potential for partially determining how dominant or submissive an individual, male or female, will turn out to be. But the effects of this biological potential could be detected only in males (Gottesman, 1963). This implies that only the males in our culture are raised with sufficient flexibility, with sufficient latitude given to their biological differences, for their "natural" or biologically determined potential to shine through. Females, on the other hand, are subjected to a socialization which so ignores their unique attributes that even the effects of biology seem to be swamped. In sum, the biological argument for continuing America's homogenization of its women gets hoist with its own petard.

3. Many people recognize that most women do end up as full-time homemakers because of their socialization and that these women do exemplify the failure of our society to raise girls as unique individuals. But, they point out, the role of the homemaker is not inferior to the role of the professional man: it is complementary but equal.

This argument is usually bolstered by pointing to the joys and importance of taking care of small children. Indeed, mothers *and* fathers find childrearing rewarding, and it is certainly important. But this argument becomes insufficient when one considers that the average American woman now lives to age 74 and has her *last* child at about age 26; thus, by the time the woman is 33 or so, her children all have more important things to do with their daytime hours than to spend them entertaining an adult woman who has nothing to do during the second half of her lifespan. As for the other "joys" of homemaking, many writers (e.g., Friedan, 1963) have persuasively argued that the role of the homemaker has been glamorized far beyond its intrinsic worth. This charge becomes plausible when one considers that the average American homemaker spends the equivalent of a man's working day, 7.1 hours, in preparing meals, cleaning house, laundering, mending, shopping, and doing other household tasks. In other words, 43% of her waking time is spent in activity that would command an hourly wage on the open market well below the federally-set minimum for menial industrial work.

The point is not how little she would earn if she did these things in someone else's home, but that this use of time is virtually the same for homemakers with college degrees and for those with less than a grade school education, for women married to professional men and for women married to blue-collar workers. Talent, education, ability, interests, motivations: all are irrelevant. In our society, being female uniquely qualifies an individual for domestic work.

It is true, of course, that the American homemaker has, on the average, 5.1 hours of leisure time per day, and it is here, we are told, that each woman can express her unique identity. Thus, politically interested women can join the League of Women Voters; women with humane interests can become part-time Gray Ladies; women who love music can raise money for the symphony. Protestant woman play Canasta; Jewish women play Mah-Jongg; brighter women of all denominations and faculty wives play bridge; and so forth.

But politically interested *men* serve in legislatures; *men* with humane interests become physicians or clinical psychologists; *men* who love music play in the symphony; and so forth. In other words, why should a woman's unique identity determine only the periphery of her life rather than its central core?

Again, the important point is not that the role of homemaker is necessarily inferior, but that the woman's unique identity has been rendered irrelevant. Consider the following "predictability test." When a boy is born, it is difficult to predict what he will be doing 25 years later. We cannot say whether he will be an artist, a doctor, or college professor because he will be permitted to develop and to fulfill his own unique potential, particularly if he is white and middle-class. But if the newborn child is a girl, we can usually predict with confidence how she will be spending her time 25 years later. Her individuality doesn't have to be considered; it is irrelevant.

The socialization of the American male has closed off certain options for him too. Men are discouraged from developing certain desirable traits such as tenderness and sensitivity just as surely as women are discouraged from being assertive and, alas, "too bright." Young boys are encouraged to be incompetent at cooking and child care just as surely as young girls are urged to be incompetent at mathematics and science.

Indeed, one of the errors of the early feminist movement in this country was that it assumed that men had all the goodies and that women could attain self-fulfillment merely by being like men. But that is hardly the utopia implied by the values of individuality and self-fulfillment. Rather, these values would require society to raise its children so flexibly and with sufficient respect for the integrity of individual uniqueness that some men might emerge with the motivation, the ability, and the opportunity to stay home and raise children without bearing the stigma of being peculiar. If homemaking is as glamorous as the women's magazines and television commercials portray it, then men, too, should have that option. Even if home-making isn't all that glamorous, it would probably still be more fulfilling for some men than the jobs in which they now find themselves.

And if biological differences really do exist between men and women in "nurturance," in their inborn motivations to care for children, then this will show up automatically in the final distribution of men and women across the various roles: relatively fewer men will choose to stay at home. The values of individuality and self-fulfillment do not imply that there must be equality of outcome, an equal number of men and women in each role, but that there should be the widest possible variation in outcome consistent with the range of individual differences among people, regardless of sex. At the very least, these values imply that society should raise its males so that they could freely engage in activities that might pay less than those being pursued by their wives without feeling that they were "living off their wives." One rarely hears it said of a woman that she is "living off her husband."

Thus, it is true that a man's options are limited by our society's sex-role ideology, but as the "predictability test" reveals, it is still the woman in our society whose identity is rendered irrelevant by America's socialization practices. In 1954, the United States Supreme Court declared that a fraud and hoax lay behind the slogan "separate but equal." It is unlikely that any court will ever do the same for the more subtle motto that successfully keeps the woman in her place: "complementary but equal."

Interpersonal Equality

> Wives, submit yourselves unto your own husbands, as unto the lord. For the husband is the head of the wife, even as Christ is the head of the church; and he is the savior of the body. Therefore, as the church is subject unto Christ, so let the wives be to their own husbands in everything. (Eph. 5)

As this passage reveals, the ideological rationalization that men and women hold complementary but equal positions is a recent invention of our modern "liberal" society, part of the equalitarian veneer which helps to keep today's version of the ideology nonconscious. Certainly those Americans who value open, honest, and equalitarian relationships generally are quick to reject this traditional view of the male-female relationship; and, an increasing number of young people even plan to enter "utopian" marriages very much like the following hypothetical example:

> Both my wife and I earned Ph.D. degrees in our respective disciplines. I turned down a superior academic post in Oregon and accepted a slightly less desirable position in New York where my wife could obtain a part-time teaching job and do research at one of the several other colleges in the area. Although I would have preferred to live in a suburb, we purchased a home near my wife's college so that she could have an office at home where she would be when the children returned from school. Because my wife earns a good salary, she can easily afford to pay a maid to do her major household chores. My wife and I share all other tasks around the house equally. For example, she cooks the meals, but I do the laundry for her and help her with many of her other household tasks.

Without questioning the basic happiness of such a marriage or its appropriateness for many couples, we can legitimately ask if such a marriage is, in fact, an instance of interpersonal equality. Have all the hidden assumptions about the woman's "natural" role really been eliminated? Has the traditional ideology really been exorcised? There is a very simple test. If the marriage is truly equalitarian, then its description should retain the same flavor and tone even if the roles of the husband and wife were to be reversed:

> Both my husband and I earned Ph.D. degrees in our respective disciplines. I turned down a superior academic post in Oregon and accepted a slightly less desirable position in New York where my husband could obtain a part-time teaching job and do research at one of the several other colleges in the area. Although I would have preferred to live in a suburb, we purchased a home near my husband's college so that he could have an office at home where he would be when the children returned from school. Because my husband earns a good salary, he can easily afford to pay a maid to do his major household chores. My husband and I share all other tasks around the house equally. For example, he cooks the meals, but I do the laundry for him and help him with many of his other household tasks.

It seems unlikely that many men or women in our society would mistake the marriage *just* described as either equalitarian or desirable, and thus it becomes apparent that the ideology about the woman's "natural" role nonconsciously permeates the entire fabric of such "utopian" marriages. It is true that the wife gains some measure of equality when her career can influence the final place of residence, but why is it the unquestioned assumption that the husband's career solely determines the initial set of alternatives that are to be considered? Why is it the wife who automatically seeks the part-time position? Why is it *her* maid instead of *their* maid? Why *her* laundry? Why *her* household tasks? And so forth throughout the entire relationship.

The important point here is not that such marriages are bad or that their basic assumptions of inequality produce unhappy, frustrated women. Quite the contrary. It is the very happiness of the wives in such marriages that reveals society's smashing success in socializing its women. It is a measure of the distance our society must yet traverse toward the goals of self-fulfillment and interpersonal equality that such marriages are widely characterized as utopian and fully equalitarian. It is a mark of how well the woman has been kept in her place that the husband in such a marriage is often idolized by women, including his wife, for "permitting" her to squeeze a career into the interstices of their marriage as long as his own career is not unduly inconvenienced. Thus is the white man blessed for exercising his power benignly while his "natural" right to that power forever remains unquestioned.

Such is the subtlety of a nonconscious ideology!

A truly equalitarian marriage would permit both partners to pursue careers or outside commitments which carry equal weight when all important decisions are to be made. It is here, of course, that the "problem" of children arises. People often assume that the woman who seeks a role beyond home and family would not care to have children. They assume that if she wants a career or serious outside commitment, then children must be unimportant to her. But of course no one makes this assumption about her husband. No one assumes that a father's interest in his career necessarily precludes a deep and abiding affection for his children or a vital interest in their development. Once again America applies a double standard of judgment. Suppose that a father of small children suddenly lost his wife. No matter how much he loved his children, no one would expect him to sacrifice his career in order to stay home with them on a full-time basis—*even if he had an independent source of income.* No one would charge him with selfishness or lack of parental feeling if he sought professional care for his children during the day. An equalitarian marriage simply abolishes this double standard and extends the same freedom to the mother, while also providing the framework for the father to enter more fully into the pleasures and responsibilities of childrearing. In fact, it is the equalitarian marriage which has the most potential for giving children the love and concern of two parents rather than one.

But few women are prepared to make use of this freedom. Even those women who have managed to finesse society's attempt to rob them of their career motivations are likely to find themselves blocked by society's trump card: the feeling that the raising of the children is their unique responsibility and—in time of crisis—ultimately theirs alone. Such is the emotional power of a nonconscious ideology.

In addition to providing this potential for equalized child care, a truly equalitarian marriage embraces a more general division of labor which satisfies what might be called "the roommate test." That is, the labor is divided just as it is when two men or two women room together in college or set up a bachelor apartment together. Errands and domestic chores are assigned by preference, agreement, flipping a coin, given to hired help, or— as is sometimes the case—left undone.

It is significant that today's young people, many of whom live this way prior to marriage, find this kind of arrangement within marriage so foreign to their thinking. Consider an analogy. Suppose that a white male college student decided to room or set up a bachelor apartment with a black male friend. Surely the typical white student would not blithely assume that his black roommate was to handle all the domestic chores. Nor would his conscience allow him to do so even in the unlikely event that his roommate would say: "No, that's okay. I like doing housework. I'd be happy to do it." We suspect that the typical white student would still not be comfortable if he took advantage of this offer, if he took advantage of the fact that his roommate had been socialized to be "happy" with such an arrangement. But change this hypothetical black roommate to a female marriage partner, and somehow the student's conscience goes to sleep. At most it is quickly tranquilized by the thought that "she is happiest when she is ironing for her loved one." Such is the power of a nonconscious ideology.

Of course, it may well be that she *is* happiest when she is ironing for her loved one.

Such, indeed, is the power of a nonconscious ideology!

References

Barry, H., III, Bacon, M. K., & Child, I. L. A cross-cultural survey of some sex differences in socialization. *Journal of Abnormal and Social Psychology,* 1957, *55,* 327–332.

Brown, R. *Social Psychology.* New York: Free Press, 1965.

Crandall, V. J., & Rabson, A. Children's repetition choices in an intellectual achievement situation following success and failure. *Journal of Genetic Psychology,* 1960, *97,* 161–168.

Dodge, N. D. *Women in the Soviet Economy.* Baltimore: The Johns Hopkins Press, 1966.

Flanagan, J. C. Project talent. Unpublished manuscript.

Friedan, B. *The feminine mystique.* New York: Norton, 1963.

Goldberg, P. Are women prejudiced against women? *Transaction,* April 1968, *5,* 28–30.

Goldberg, S. & Lewis, M. Play behavior in the year-old infant: early sex differences. *Child Development,* 1969, *40,* 21–31.

Gottesman, I. I. Heritability of personality: a demonstration. *Psychological Monographs,* 1963, *77* (Whole No. 572).

Kagan, J. Acquisition and significance of sex typing and sex role identity. In M. L. Hoffman & L. W. Hoffman (Eds.). *Review of child development research, Vol. 1.* New York: Russell Sage Foundation, 1964. Pp. 137–167.

McDavid, J. W. Imitative behavior in preschool children. *Psychological Monographs,* 1959, *73* (Whole No. 486).

Milton, G. A. Five studies of the relation between sex role identification and achievement in problem solving. Technical Report No. 3, Department of

Industrial Administration, Department of Psychology, Yale University, December, 1958.

Sears, R. R., Maccoby, E. E., & Levin, H. *Patterns of child rearing.* Evanston, Ill.: Row, Peterson, 1957.

Smith, M. E. The influence of age, sex, and situation on the frequency of form and functions of questions asked by preschool children. *Child Development,* 1933, *3,* 201–213.

Torrance, E. P. *Guilding creative talent.* Englewood Cliffs, N.J.: Prentice-Hall, 1962.

PART VIII

RELIGION

Religion has been a powerful force throughout human history. In most societies it has been a major institutional determinant of behavior, beliefs, and values. The sociology of religion includes the study of small groups (cults and sects), bureaucracy (ecclesia and church hierarchies), and community (for instance, the Amish), as well as studies on the societal level. In our analyses of social cohesion and of culture, the study of religion occupies a central place. The functional approach in sociology focuses on religion as the socially instituted response to crisis situations, to periods of transition, and to man's need for order and purpose in his life. It focuses on religion as an integrating, stabilizing factor contributing to the maintenance of the social order. The symbol-oriented sociologist concentrates on the creation and perpetuation of the sacred within religion. That is, he considers the social processes by which certain objects, gestures, and words come to be regarded as outside the realm of everyday life and in contact with the supernatural. Finally, in the study of ritual, we find that religion contains, in bold relief, routinized, normative patterns of behavior—a central concern of the sociologist. Since religion usually encompasses a belief-value system, its part in the determination of perspective is important. Furthermore, religion has an important effect on other institutions such as family, economy, and government.

The Protestant Ethic
and the Spirit of Capitalism

MAX WEBER

In "The Protestant Ethic and the Spirit of Capitalism" Weber proposed one of the most widely used ideas in the sociological literature. He argued that Calvinism was an influential factor in the rise of modern capitalism. Christian asceticism demanded rational conduct and self-control. In the Catholic church this was manifested largely in monasticism. The Reformation approach was that asceticism be practiced by all Christians in the everyday world. Calvinism added the "necessity of proving one's faith in worldly activity." Calvinists believed that those who were among God's elect found proof of salvation in their economic success. This sanctified economic life coupled with worldly asceticism provided the essential elements for a particular perspective known as the spirit of capitalism.

Capitalism no longer rests on such theological underpinnings. Our modern economic system has developed its own institutions and its own rationale. Weber refers to this result as "an iron cage," condemning the economic order as the determinant of men's lives rather than the result of their beliefs and values. He concludes by noting some of the other areas in which the Protestant ethic has been significant. Of course, Weber was far too sophisticated a sociologist to consider a monocausal theory of economic existence or to see only one of the influences of religion.

WITHOUT doubt Christian asceticism, both outwardly and in its inner meaning, contains many different things. But it has had a definitely rational character in its highest Occidental forms as early as the Middle Ages, and in several forms even in antiquity. The great historical significance of Western monasticism, as contrasted with that of the Orient, is based on this fact, not in all cases, but in its general type. In the rules of St. Benedict, still more with the monks of Cluny, again with the Cistercians, and most strongly the

Reprinted with the permission of Charles Scribner's Sons and George Allen & Unwin Ltd. from *The Protestant Ethic and the Spirit of Capitalism*, pp. 118–125, 180–183, by Max Weber, translated by Talcott Parsons.

Jesuits, it has become emancipated from planless otherworldliness and irrational self-torture. It had developed a systematic method of rational conduct with the purpose of overcoming the *status naturæ,* to free man from the power of irrational impulses and his dependence on the world and on nature. It attempted to subject man to the supremacy of a purposeful will, to bring his actions under constant self-control with a careful consideration of their ethical consequences. Thus it trained the monk, objectively, as a worker in the service of the kingdom of God, and thereby further, subjectively, assured the salvation of his soul. This active self-control, which formed the end of the *exercitia* of St. Ignatius and of the rational monastic virtues everywhere, was also the most important practical ideal of Puritanism. In the deep contempt with which the cool reserve of its adherents is contrasted, in the reports of the trials of its martyrs, with the undisciplined blustering of the noble prelates and officials can be seen that respect for quiet self-control which still distinguishes the best type of English or American gentleman today. To put it in our terms: The Puritan, like every rational type of asceticism, tried to enable a man to maintain and act upon his constant motives, especially those which it taught him itself, against the emotions. In this formal psychological sense of the term it tried to make him into a personality. Contrary to many popular ideas, the end of this asceticism was to be able to lead an alert, intelligent life: the most urgent task the destruction of spontaneous, impulsive enjoyment, the most important means was to bring order into the conduct of its adherents. All these important points are emphasized in the rules of Catholic monasticism as strongly as in the principles of conduct of the Calvinists. On this methodical control over the whole man rests the enormous expansive power of both, especially the ability of Calvinism as against Lutheranism to defend the cause of Protestantism as the Church militant.

On the other hand, the difference of the Calvinistic from the mediæval asceticism is evident. It consisted in the disappearance of the *consilia evangelica* and the accompanying transformation of asceticism to activity within the world. It is not as though Catholicism had restricted the methodical life to monastic cells. This was by no means the case either in theory or in practice. On the contrary, it has already been pointed out that, in spite of the greater ethical moderation of Catholicism, an ethically unsystematic life did not satisfy the highest ideals which it had set up even for the life of the layman. The tertiary order of St. Francis was, for instance, a powerful attempt in the direction of an ascetic penetration of everyday life, and, as we know, by no means the only one. But, in fact, works like the *Nachfolge Christi* show, through the manner in which their strong influence was exerted, that the way of life preached in them was felt to be something higher than the everyday morality which sufficed as a minimum, and that this latter was not measured by such standards as Puritanism demanded. Moreover, the practical use made of certain institutions of the Church, above all of indulgences inevitably counteracted the tendencies toward systematic worldly asceticism. For that reason it was not felt at the time of the Reformation to be merely an unessential abuse, but one of the most fundamental evils of the Church.

But the most important thing was the fact that the man who, *par excellence,* lived a rational life in the religious sense was, and remained, alone the monk. Thus asceticism, the more strongly it gripped an individual, simply served to drive him farther away from everyday life, because the holiest task was definitely to surpass all worldly morality. Luther, who was not in any sense fulfilling any law of development, but acting upon his quite personal experience, which was, though at first somewhat uncertain in its practical consequences, later pushed farther by the political situation, had repudiated that tendency, and Calvinism simply took this over from him. Sebastian Franck struck the central characteristic of this type of religion when he saw the significance of the Reformation in the fact that now every Christian had to be a monk all his life. The drain of asceticism from everyday worldly life had been stopped by a dam, and those passionately spiritual natures which had formerly supplied the highest type of monk were now forced to pursue their ascetic ideals within mundane occupations.

But in the course of its development Calvinism added something positive to this, the idea of the necessity of proving one's faith in worldly activity. Therein it gave the broader groups of religiously inclined people a positive incentive to asceticism. By founding its ethic in the doctrine of predestination, it substituted for the spiritual aristocracy of monks outside of and above the world the spiritual aristocracy of the predestined saints of God within the world. It was an aristocracy which, with its *character indelebilis,* was divided from the eternally damned remainder of humanity by a more impassable and in its invisibility more terrifying gulf, than separated the monk of the Middle Ages from the rest of the world about him, a gulf which penetrated all social relations with its sharp brutality. This consciousness of divine grace of the elect and holy was accompanied by an attitude toward the sin of one's neighbor, not of sympathetic understanding based on consciousness of one's own weakness, but of hatred and contempt for him as an enemy of God bearing the signs of eternal damnation. This sort of feeling was capable of such intensity that it sometimes resulted in the formation of sects. This was the case when, as in the Independent movement of the seventeenth century, the genuine Calvinist doctrine that the glory of God required the Church to bring the damned under the law, was outweighed by the conviction that it was an insult to God if an unregenerate soul should be admitted to His house and partake in the sacraments, or even, as a minister, administer them. Thus, as a consequence of the doctrine of proof, the Donatist idea of the Church appeared, as in the case of the Calvinistic Baptists. The full logical consequence of the demand for a pure Church, a community of those proved to be in a state of grace, was not often drawn by forming sects. Modifications in the constitution of the Church resulted from the attempt to separate regenerate from unregenerate Christians, those who were from those who were not prepared for the sacrament, to keep the government of the Church or some other privilege in the hands of the former, and only to ordain ministers of whom there was no question.

The norm by which it could always measure itself, of which it was evidently in need, this asceticism naturally found in the Bible. It is important to note that the well-known bibliocracy of the Calvinists held the moral precepts of the Old Testament, since it was fully as authentically revealed, on the same level of esteem as those of the New. It was only necessary that they should not obviously be applicable only to the historical circumstances of the Hebrews, or have been specifically denied by Christ. For the believer, the law was an ideal though never quite attainable norm while Luther, on the other hand, originally had prized freedom from subjugation to the law as a divine privilege of the believer. The influence of the God-fearing but perfectly unemotional wisdom of the Hebrews, which is expressed in the books most read by the Puritans, the Proverbs and the Psalms, can be felt in their whole attitude toward life. In particular, its rational suppression of the mystical, in fact the whole emotional side of religion, has rightly been attributed by Sanford to the influence of the Old Testament. But this Old Testament rationalism was as such essentially of a small bourgeois, traditionalistic type, and was mixed not only with the powerful pathos of the prophets, but also with elements which encouraged the development of a peculiarly emotional type of religion even in the Middle Ages. It was thus in the last analysis the peculiar, fundamentally ascetic, character of Calvinism itself which made it select and assimilate those elements of Old Testament religion which suited it best.

Now that systematization of ethical conduct which the asceticism of Calvinistic Protestantism had in common with the rational forms of life in the Catholic orders is expressed quite superficially in the way in which the conscientious Puritan continually supervised his own state of grace. To be sure, the religious account-books in which sins, temptations, and progress made in grace were entered or tabulated were common to both the most enthusiastic Reformed circles and some parts of modern Catholicism (especially in France), above all under the influence of the Jesuits. But in Catholicism it served the purpose of completeness of the confession, or gave the *directeur de l'âme* a basis for his authoritarian guidance of the Christian (mostly female). The Reformed Christian, however, felt his own pulse with its aid. It is mentioned by all the moralists and theologians, while Benjamin Franklin's tabulated statistical book-keeping on his progress in the different virtues is a classic example. On the other hand, the old mediæval (even ancient) idea of God's book-keeping is carried by Bunyan to the characteristically tasteless extreme of comparing the relation of a sinner to his God with that of customer and shopkeeper. One who has once got into debt may well, by the product of all his virtuous acts, succeed in paying off the accumulated interest but never the principal.

As he observed his own conduct, the later Puritan also observed that of God and saw His finger in all the details of life. And, contrary to the strict doctrine of Calvin, he always knew why God took this or that measure. The process of sanctifying life could thus almost take on the character of a business enterprise. A thoroughgoing Christianization of the whole life was the consequence of this methodical quality of ethical conduct into which Calvinism as distinct from Lutheranism forced men. That this rationality was decisive in its influence on practical life must always be borne in mind in order rightly to understand the influence of Calvinism. On the one hand we can see that it took this element to exercise such an influence at all. But other faiths as well necessarily had a similar influence when their ethical motives were the same in this decisive point, the doctrine of proof. . . .

One of the fundamental elements of the spirit of modern capitalism, and not only of that but of all modern culture: rational conduct on the basis of the idea of the calling, was born—that is what this discussion has sought to demonstrate—from the spirit of Christian asceticism. One has only to re-read the passage from Franklin, quoted at the beginning of this essay, in order to see that the essential elements of the attitude which was there called the spirit of capitalism are the same as what we have just shown to be the content of the Puritan worldly asceticism, only without the religious basis, which by Franklin's time had died away. The idea that modern labor has as ascetic character is of course not new. Limitation to specialized work, with a renunciation of the Faustian universality of man which it involves, is a condition of any valuable work in the modern world; hence deeds and renunciation inevitably condition each other today. This fundamentally ascetic trait of middle-class life, if it attempts to be a way of life at all, and not simply the absence of any, was what Goethe wanted to teach, at the height of his wisdom, in the *Wanderjahren,* and in the end which he gave to the life of his *Faust.* For him the realization meant a renunciation, a departure from an age of full and beautiful humanity, which can no more be repeated in the course of our cultural development than can the flower of the Athenian culture of antiquity.

The Puritan wanted to work in a calling; we are forced to do so. For when asceticism was carried out of monastic cells into everyday life, and began to dominate worldly morality, it did its part in building the tremendous cosmos of the modern economic order. This order is now bound to the technical and economic conditions of machine production which today determine the lives of all the individuals who are born into this mechanism, not only those directly concerned with economic acquisition, with irresistible force. Perhaps it will so determine them until the last ton of fossilized coal is burnt.

In Baxter's view the care for external goods should only lie on the shoulders of the "saint like a light cloak, which can be thrown aside at any moment." But fate decreed that the cloak should become an iron cage.

Since asceticism undertook to remodel the world and to work out its ideals in the world, material goods have gained an increasing and finally an inexorable power over the lives of men as at no previous period in history. Today the spirit of religious asceticism—whether finally, who knows?—has escaped from the cage. But victorious capitalism, since it rests on mechanical foundations, needs its support no longer. The rosy blush of its laughing heir, the Enlightenment, seems also to be irretrievably fading, and the idea of duty in one's calling prowls about in our lives like the ghost of dead religious beliefs. Where the fulfilment of the calling cannot directly be related to the highest spiritual and cultural values, or when, on the other hand, it need not be felt simply as economic compulsion, the individual generally abandons the attempt to justify it at all. In the field of its highest development, in the United States, the pursuit of wealth, stripped of its religious and ethical meaning, tends to become associated with purely mundane passions, which often actually give it the character of sport.

No one knows who will live in this cage in the future, or whether at the end of this tremendous development entirely new prophets will arise, or there will be a great rebirth of old ideas and ideals, or, if neither, mechanized petrification, embellished with a sort of convulsive self-importance. For of the last stage of this cultural development, it might well be truly said: "Specialists without spirit, sensualists without heart; this nullity imagines that it has attained a level of civilization never before achieved."

But this brings us to the world of judgments of value and of faith, with which this purely historical discussion need not be burdened. The next task would be rather to show the significance of ascetic rationalism, which has only been touched in the foregoing sketch, for the content of practical social ethics, thus for the types of organization and the functions of social groups from the conventicle to the State. Then its relations to humanistic rationalism, its ideals of life and cultural influence; further to the development of philosophical and scientific empiricism, to technical development and to spiritual ideals would have to be analyzed. Then its historical development from the mediæval beginnings of worldly asceticism to its dissolution into pure utilitarianism would have to be traced out through all the areas of ascetic religion. Only then could the quantitative cultural significance of ascetic Protestantism in its relation to the other plastic elements of modern culture be estimated.

Here we have only attempted to trace the fact and the direction of its influence to their motives in one, though a very important point. But it would also further be necessary to investigate how Protestant Asceticism was in turn influenced in its development and its character by the totality of social conditions, especially economic. The modern man is in general, even with the best will, unable to give religious ideas a significance for culture and national character which they deserve. But it is, of course, not my aim to substitute for a one-sided materialistic an equally one-sided spiritualistic causal interpretation of culture and of history. Each is equally possible, but each, if it does not serve as the preparation, but as the conclusion of an investigation, accomplishes equally little in the interest of historical truth.

Political Values and Religious Cultures: Jews, Catholics, and Protestants*

MICHAEL PARENTI

The political orientations of certain groups appear to be inconsistent with their rational self-interest. This inconsistency may indicate an adherence by those groups to their religious belief systems. In this article, Parenti describes such systems and relates them to conservative and liberal political orientations. He asserts that the Jewish belief system leads to liberalism because: (1) faith and intellect coexist and support one another; (2) Judaic morality obliges one to be concerned with social betterment and justice; and (3) a high value is placed on life in this world. The Catholic belief system leads to conservatism since: (1) it emphasizes the unchanging truth of sacred dogmas and distrust of secular scholarship; (2) the theology is concerned with personal salvation and individual rather than collective responsibility; and (3) this system emphasizes man's natural propensity to sin and, therefore, demands the avoidance of worldly temptations. Parenti finds a basic similarity of underlying belief systems between modernist Protestantism and Judaism, and between fundamentalist Protestantism and Catholicism. The liberal denominations have for the most part abandoned the concepts of "hell" and "devil." They focus on social, economic, and political conditions and have a humanistic and reformist view. The fundamentalists have a distrust of intellectuality, an abiding faith in their dogma, an emphasis on salvation in the afterlife, and an ascetic rejection of secularity. The political orientations of the former groups tend to be liberal; the latter groups are inclined toward conservatism. Parenti shows that the religious belief system transcends sectarian issues in its influence on perspective.

THE literature on pressure groups and voting behavior demonstrates that American politics are, for the most part, "rational." That is to say: group attitudes and actions are generally directed toward promoting some kind of sub-

* A revised version of a paper presented at the annual meeting of the Society for the Scientific Study of Religion, New York, October 29, 1965; Benjamin Nelson, program chairman.

Reprinted from the *Journal for the Scientific Study of Religion*, Vol. VI, No. 2, Fall, 1967, pp. 259–269, by permission of the author and publisher.

stantive measure which the group deems beneficial to its interests. Thus we can observe party-class voting correlations, union support of the closed shop, business opposition to certain state regulations, rural opposition to reapportionment, Negro support of civil rights, Catholic support of parochial school aid, etc. The objective position an individual or group occupies in the social structure, and the material conditions operating therein, determine much about individual or group perceptions and evaluations of life, including political life.

Corresponding to the above definition of "rational," "*irrational*" political behavior would be that kind of action or attitude which is intended to minimize rather than maximize socio-economic self-interest (for instance, unions opposing the closed shop and Negroes supporting an inferior status for themselves). Are there such instances of political behavior, and if so, how might they be explained?

In the Wilson and Banfield study [1] of twenty referenda elections for bond issues to pay for public services such as hospitals, schools and parks, it was found that the groups which because of their income level would pay little or nothing at all and yet benefit most from the services were also the groups which were most opposed to such services. These were the Poles, Czechs, Italians, Irish and other Catholic ethnic groups. Conversely, upper income white Protestants and Jews, the very groups that would be paying the costs while benefitting least, were the strongest supporters of the proposed expenditures. (The only group acting according to rational self interest was the low-income Negroes, who were supporters of public services.) The correlations were too compelling to assume that the voters of all groups were acting out of ignorance of their actual material interests; such ignorance would have produced more random results. It might be that upper-income groups place less value on the dollar or are better schooled civically, but these appear to be, at best, only partial explanations. More likely, the authors conclude, the WASP and Jewish sub-cultures tend "to be more public-regarding and less private-(self or family) regarding" than are the Catholic ethnic sub-cultural groups.[2]

While no delineation of these cultural ingredients was attempted by Wilson and Banfield, their findings do lead us directly to Max Weber's consideration of culture as a force operating independently of the objective or material factors, an understanding Weber submitted not to confound but to complement the usually recognized materialist interpretations of causality.[3] According to Weber, different social groups possess some kind of "style of life" and operate under the influence of distinct, albeit sometimes implicit, moral ideas, among which are those associated (or originally associated) with religion. These ideas or values, while frequently a response to material conditions, are also often the product of other ideas which persist in the face of drastically changing material conditions.[4] Ideas, for Weber, are also an expression of human aspirations and longings that seem to transcend a particular material environment, frequently in response to some deep-seated spiritual challenge.[5] Religious belief systems possess both the inspirational and the durable traditional qualities and through much of history have played a key role in the determination of moral and normative codes. While not all religions afford guidance on the many particulars of secular life (some are relatively indifferent to certain economic and political questions), the belief systems of all do provide principles and assumptions that shape many of the basic orientations toward worldly activity.

Herein, I shall attempt to trace the religio-political value derivatives of the major American denominations. Despite the allegedly growing "Americanization," "homogenization" and secularization of religions in this society,[6] there exist significant differences in the ideational content of sectarian systems, especially in regard to beliefs about man's nature, his redemption and his commitments to the temporal world. These beliefs may produce, or help explain, political orientations that cannot readily be explained as manifestations of rational material self-interest.

The following discussion is to be considered suggestive rather than exhaustive in its scope. At no time is it being contended that socio-economic interests are of no importance for the shaping of group political attitudes. Nor is it to be assumed that there may not be normative persuasions other than those of a religious origin that lead to responses counter to rational self-interest (*e.g.*, some of those propagated in the name of "patriotism"). Our concern here, however, is with certain of the key components of religious sub-cultures.

Jewish Liberalism

One of the more striking examples of the influence of religious sub-culture is to be found in American Jewry. By most objective measures of class level, Jews occupy as high a status as the more well-to-do white Protestants. Yet support of civil rights and civil liberties, and, more significantly, support of welfare expenditures and reforms on behalf of lower strata groups (along with an addiction to the Democratic Party) remains characteristic of Jewish political behavior.[7]

It may be that Jews, despite high income and occupational status, still suffer many of the social disabilities of an "underdog" group, as evidenced by the exclusionist practices of an unofficial but quite prevalent upper-class anti-Semitism.[8] Nor is this underdog sensitivity weakened by a history of ruthless oppression. Thus, it might be said that Jewish liberalism is a reaction to the marginality that challenges a seemingly solid economic position.

Without denying what was affirmed at the onset, *viz.*, the importance of the group's position in the social system in determining its perspectives, we might still wonder whether such explanations take all factors into account. First, it might be noted that Catholic ethnic groups such as the Irish, Italians, and Poles have had somewhat comparable centuries of hardship behind them. Starvation, oppression, and harsh military occupation is the history of Ireland, Poland and Southern Italy. Similarly, the discrimination and exploitation accorded the Catholic newcomers in America were at least as severe as anything the Jewish immigrants encountered. Yet among the Catholic groups we find few traces of that liberal reform-mindedness which seems a substantial sentiment in the Jewish community.[9]

If oppression and marginality have been, then, the common lot of many, it may be said that the various groups have defined and reacted to such historical experiences in accordance with their respective value systems. Is there anything in the Judaic view of life that might help explain Jewish liberalism? Fuchs and others have observed several distinct themes: [10]

(1) The usual tension between faith and intellect does not grip Judaism. If anything, the spiritual leader in the Jewish community was traditionally not one who cultivated an inner-worldly asceticism or other-worldly spirituality, but one who was expert in the interpretation and application of the law. The synagogue was also the *shul,* a place of study as well as a place of worship. Given this intimate connection between learning and religion, "the religious virtuoso was not the saint but the scholar." [11] Historically, for Jews, the intellectual has not been an object of scorn, but a man to be esteemed and entrusted with the responsibilities of leadership and power.[12]

(2) In modern times, Judaism has been less an other-worldly theology and formulated creed than a system of practices, observances and moral commitments. An important component of the morality of Judaism is the continuing obligation to live with some dedication to social betterment and justice. Prayer and personal piety alone do not make one a Jew. Redemption is to be found in the worldly enactment of God's love and charity as evidenced by one's efforts on behalf of his fellow men and his community: one must be "a Jew for the world." Closely associated with the idea of social justice is the belief that the Jews, as the chosen people, serve a distinct missionary purpose in the world. Exile is not seen as the punishment of a wrathful Yahweh, but as fulfillment of the divine purpose: they are to serve God by working for social righteousness wherever Jews be found. "Our secret weapon as a people," David Ben-Gurion instructs, "is our moral, intellectual and spiritual superiority which we inherited from the Bible." [13]

(3) Whatever may be said of orthodox Old Testament strictures, Judaism does not, like traditional Christianity, teach ascetic renunciation as the prime means to personal salvation. A high value is placed on life in this world. Bodily appetites are understood to be natural and acceptable rather than sinful, and one does not face the world in a chronic state of antagonistic, guilt-ridden self-denial. Liberal reforms designed to maximize man's well-being and happiness on earth are part of a noble quest untainted by a fear of worldliness, sin, or loss of salvation. Life is reaffirmed rather than renounced.

Even if we were to grant Nathan Glazer's contention that contemporary Jewish liberalism derives more from nineteenth century liberalism and socialism than from the Judaic religious tradition,[14] we might still wonder why Jews of that day responded to and initiated such political traditions rather than electing any one of several other alternatives open to them. Jewish liberalism today may be an example of how the value commitments of a religion persist as an "idea of life" well after the specific theological underpinnings are discarded. This is what Weber meant when he spoke of the "ghost of dead religious beliefs." To the extent that Jews today are concerned with questions like "What examples of Jewish life shall we present to the world?" and "What are the special ethical demands made upon a man who calls himself a Jew?", they are still involved in a distinct ethno-religious tradition.

Catholic Conservatism

In contrast to Jewish political behavior, the Catholic tradition in America could hardly be characterized as liberal-reformist. Democratic party affiliations among Catholic voters reflect their urban working class background and status interests (*viz.,* the status attractions of Democratic Catholic candidates for high office), rather than any commitment to liberalism. And their loyalty to the Democratic party, especially in the postwar years, has been markedly less stable than that of Jews and Negroes.[15]

The special popularity enjoyed by Father Coughlin and Senator Joseph McCarthy and the lukewarm response to civil rights among the Catholic lay public, along with somewhat conservative attitudes toward civil liberties, censorship and Communism, place American Catholics decidedly further from the liberal side of the political spectrum than might be supposed, were judgments made solely on the basis of voting returns.[16] Among lower middle-class Catholics there is growing evidence of an ultra-conservatism at least as virulent as any found among middle-class urban Protestants, and certainly of a kind alien to middle-class Jews. One Catholic writer suggests that the conservatism of William Buckley is probably preferred to the liberalism of *Commonweal* by most of the rank and file faithful "and the less articulate of the clergy." [17]

An explanation may be found in the fact that the American Catholic belief system contrasts sharply with the Judaic orientation on each of the major value areas previously discussed.

(1) There is a wealth of evidence, most of it from the pens of devout Catholics, suggesting the existence of a strong anti-intellectual strain in the Catholic constituency. A religious system which stresses the unchanging truth and purity of its sacred dogma and lay obedience to hierarchical teachings is prone to view the secular and sometimes irreverent scholarship of the modern age with something less than unmitigated enthusiasm. "[In the minds of many Catholics] . . . 'Science' is irretrievably allied with 'atheism'," observes one Catholic sociologist, "and to ask why we have so few Catholic scientists of note is equivalent to asking why we have so few Catholic atheists." [18]

This "censorship mentality" has been a long-standing trait of Catholic America. In his study of nineteenth century Irish immigrants in Boston, Handlin notes that books and public schools were considered instruments of heresy, licentiousness, and secularity.[19] The heroic Catholic effort in parochial education can be seen not as any commitment to worldly intellectuality, but rather as a protection against it.

The effects of this education tell us something about Catholic value orientations: Lenski finds, after controlling for income level and family party affiliation, that parochially educated Catholics rank obedience ahead of intellectual autonomy and tend to be more doctrinally orthodox and politically conservative than publicly educated Catholics.[20] A survey of midwestern Catholic students yielded the following results: only 53 percent agreed that "love of neighbor is more important than fasting on Friday." Only 55 percent thought that "the heart of the race question is moral and religious." Fifty-eight percent declared that they would not "share our food with people of Communist countries if their need is great." And in choosing between "a comfortable life" and "a job which enabled you to do good to others," 77 percent voted for personal comfort.[21]

(2) Catholicism is essentially a theology of personal salvation. Good works are acts of personal faith directed toward the propagation of spiritual rather than earthly values. Catholic concern for the poor traditionally has confined itself to charity work and rarely includes reformist attacks upon the abuses of the existing social system. The American hierarchy has issued statements reaffirming the necessity for individual responsibility in social and economic life and less reliance on the "inordinate demand" for benefits that arise from the pressures of organized social action.[22] It is felt that by relying on temporal rather than spiritual agencies, liberals propagate worldly values and obscure the far greater task of saving one's eternal soul.[23]

(3) "One often has the impression," observes a noted French Dominican, "that American Catholics are more Puritan than anybody else and that they are very close to setting themselves up as the Champions of Puritanism." [24] (The same writer conjectures that it was this Puritan mentality of "either virtue or the reign of terror" that made Catholics so responsive to McCarthyism.) The Catholic Church, while not as ascetic as many Protestant fundamentalist sects (dancing, drinking, and gambling in moderation are not sinful), contains within it a strong antagonism toward the erotic and pleasurable components of life. The orientation is "puritanical" insofar as it emphasizes the inherent propensity for sin in man's nature, the dangers of fleshly temptation, the proximity of hell, and the pitfalls of "too much freedom." Evil is willed and individually, rather than socially, caused. Viewed from this perspective, liberalism frequently appears as an invitation to self-indulgence, license and concupiscence. What are, for the liberal, social problems calling for social solutions (e.g., juvenile delinquency and crime) are, for many Catholics, problems of discipline, authority, and personal rectitude.[25] Lacking true religious com-

mitment, and suffering under the illusion that man is perfectible without divine intervention, the liberal coddles the evil-doers while encouraging moral irresponsibility. He strives too hard for happiness in this world because he does not believe in the happiness of the next.

In conclusion, it might be observed that much of American Catholic sociopolitical conservatism might be ascribed to the peasant ethnic cultures of the various Catholic groups rather than to religious belief systems *per se*.

Yet, lest undue reliance be placed on the secular antecedents of immigrant life, it should be remembered that the Old World peasant values themselves emanated from, and were heavily influenced by, Catholicism. This is certainly true of the group that has shaped and dominated the American Church—the Irish Catholics.[26] Finally, it should be kept in mind that whatever the peculiarities of Jansenist-Irish or Italian and Polish peasant conservative influences, the Catholic belief orientations described above are not exclusively American. It need only be noted that liberal English Catholics have observed in English Catholicism the same elements of insularity, "censorship mentality" and want of liberal social commitment.[27]

Protestant Fundamentalism and Modernism

The particulars of historical origin, name and ecclesiology that distinguish the many Protestant churches are less crucial for the purposes of this analysis than the differences between fundamentalists and modernists which, even while separating one sect from another, also tend to cut across denominational lines.[28] One should take exception to the presumption that every theological conservative is a political conservative, but one cannot deny the existence in Protestantism of a congruence between religious belief and political orientation.

What is especially interesting is the striking resemblance in underlying belief orientations between fundamentalist Protestantism and Catholicism on the one hand,[29] and liberal Protestantism and Judaism on the other. Most sects of a predominantly fundamentalist hue eschew hierarchical control, priest administered sacramental grace, and elaborate liturgy and canon doctrine; there does exist, however, a distrust of intellectuality, a strong faith in sacred dogma, an other-worldly emphasis on salvation, and an ascetic rejection of secularity, of the kind represented in Catholicism. For the fundamentalist, the Bible is the unchallengeable source of Christian faith and the font of all sacred wisdom. The truth is final, fixed and revealed, something to be learned and obeyed; the intellectual search, therefore, can only lead one astray. As with many Catholics, the fundamentalists often consider secular intellectuality to be a potential threat to faith; at best, it is a form of excessive worldliness, and at worst, an open invitation to heresy.

For the fundamentalist, it is God alone who rewards and punishes and who will deliver final judgment at the Second Coming. Man is guilty of hubris in thinking that he can solve the world's ills through secular effort. One's real task is to attend to personal faith and piety and wait for the day when God will decide that righteousness shall prevail in His universe. The fundamentalist ethos has little concern for social, racial, and international justice, for it "denies the existence of this world and its woes" and substitutes a "putative society in the Kingdom of God," wherein the underprivileged, by virtue of their piety and special religious endowment, will be the elite.[30]

Rejection of worldliness, however, means neither withdrawal from the world, nor protest against the established structure of society. Thrift and industriousness which foster steadiness in work and individual achievement are, as in Calvin's day, traits of the good Christian.[31] The faithful must believe in the avoidance of worldly pleasures, amusements and esthetic frivolities and must be, in Weber's phrase, devoted to "the destruction of spontaneous, impulsive enjoyment." [32]

There is substantial evidence to support the proposition that fundamentalism may lead to certain kinds of conservative political derivatives. One only has to note, as have Liston Pope and others, the affinity between the values of ascetic Protestantism and the ideals and interests of the business community, or the nature of fundamentalist political attacks upon the liberal National Council of Churches, or the response of fundamentalist populations to rightwing candidates (especially discernible during the 1964 elections), or the prominence of fundamentalist preachers in those movements preoccupied both with the "devil influence" of Communism and with apocalyptic anticipations of an East-West conflagration—a kind of political rendition of the Last Judgment.[33]

Theologically liberal Protestantism, in contrast to fundamentalism, does not place exclusive reliance on the Bible as the source of spiritual guidance and faith; rather it entertains the proposition that the Scriptures contain historical errors and occasional ethical contradictions and aberrations which are open to the challenge of modern scholarship and the human intellect. Emphasis is on God's immanence in Nature and the present world. Like the Jews, and in contrast to Catholics and fundamentalists, modernist Protestants have largely discarded the ideas of hell and devil. Personal sin is not the cause of all the world's ills; rather, attention should be focused on social, economic and political forces.[34] The Christian ethic, then, must be applied not only to private conduct but to the public sphere as well. Redemption is achieved by participation in the kind of social commitment that will lead to the Christianizing of the economic, political and social order, the true fulfillment of the Church's mission in this world. With its antecedents in the Social Gospel movement of the early part of this century, liberal Protestantism represents a decisive gravitation away from the theistic and traditional elements of Christianity and toward the humanistic and reformist.[35]

The political effects of this kind of belief orientation are perhaps most visible in the "irrational" positions held by articulate elements of the mainstream Protestant ministry and by organizations like the National Council of Churches on such issues as race relations, international affairs, and social welfare—especially when these positions are compared to those assumed by fundamentalist groups.[36] Rational responses to material self-interest, however, are still evident among the faithful rank and file. Thus, Benton Johnson finds that parishioners among the liberal denominations tend, in accordance with their higher socio-economic status, to be more Republican than are fundamentalist believers,[37] and most studies support the impression that modernist Protestant clergy are usually more liberal than their followers. Nevertheless, the influence of the Church's orientation on the political predispositions of the faithful is not to be discounted. Johnson also discovers that upper income mainstream Protestants who attend church frequently are less Republican than those who seldom attend. The converse holds true for fundamentalists. When comparing frequent attenders of all denominations, it was found that fundamentalists are more Republican than those attending the modernist Protestant churches, even when occupational class is controlled.

Conclusion

This investigation has not focused on those political issues usually identified in the public mind with denominational controversies (*e.g.,* divorce laws, sabbath observances, parochial school aid, etc.), but rather on the less readily observable political derivatives of religious belief systems—specifically liberal-conservative orientations.

The differences in ecclesiology and social origin that usually distinguish sect from church are less pertinent to an understanding of religiously based political valuations than are the similarities and disparities among the belief systems of the major faiths. Thus, the Roman church and the Protestant sects, while polar extremes on the church-sect spectrum, bear a striking resemblance to each other in certain crucial underlying beliefs. By the same token, the semblances that Episcopalianism bears to Catholicism in liturgy, rites, services, conditions for membership and church organization, should not hide from view the differences in religious and political belief.

The key components of belief that seem best to distinguish the politically conservative from the liberal may be summarized as follows:

(a) The extent to which divine teaching is considered fixed, final and unchallengeable, as opposed to being susceptible to rational investigation and modification, and consequently, the extent to which intellectualism, and many of the values associated with it, are opposed or welcomed.

(b) The extent to which the drama of redemption and atonement is defined as a personal battle one wages for one's soul for the sake of eternal salvation, rather than as a moral commitment to a this-worldly social betterment of mankind.

(c) The extent to which sin and evil are defined as inherent in man's nature (*e.g.*, original sin) and inevitable in his behavior (*e.g.*, concupiscence), rather than as social effects of widespread environmental causes.

(d) The extent to which human well-being and natural pleasures are manifestations of a "lower," corrupting realm of nature, something to be repressed as the contamination of the spiritual, rather than responsibly cultivated as the fulfillment of God's beneficence.

We return to Weber's view that the cultural (or subcultural) ethic is rarely exclusively a response to "objective" factors shaped by the productive forces. An individual or group might give any one of a variety of ideational constructions to any particular material condition before reacting to it; therefore, the question is not *whether* a people are responding to their material conditions, but rather, *why* they are responding in this way rather than in some other way. The evidence offered herein suggests that certain political predispositions which ordinarily might be defined as "irrational" as measured against narrowly defined rational material self-interest might better be understood as reflections of subcultural religious matrices. Despite the alleged secularistic dilution of religious devotion, the beliefs held regarding man's nature, his redemption and his commitments to this and the next world compose a crucial component of that ideational environment which defines responses toward political conditions.

Notes

[1] James Q. Wilson and Edward C. Banfield, "Public Regardingness As a Value Premise in Voting Behavior," *American Political Science Review*, 58 (1964), 876–887. These elections were held in seven major cities between 1956 and 1963.

[2] *Ibid.*, 882–885. Wilson's study of the Democratic reform movement in New York shows a similar division between liberal-activist-reformist Jews and WASPs on the one hand, and conservative, non-ideological, politically traditional Irish and Italian Democrats on the other. See James Q. Wilson, *The Amateur Democrat* (Chicago: University of Chicago Press, 1962).

[3] Weber's best known and probably most pertinent work on this question is *The Protestant Ethic and the Spirit of Capitalism* (New York: Charles Scribner's Sons, 1958).

[4] For application of this proposition to the American scene, see Seymour Martin Lipset, *The First New Nation* (New York: Basic Books, 1963), especially the sections entitled "The Unchanging American Values and Their Connection with American Character" and "The Inadequacy of a Materialistic Interpretation of Change," pp. 110–129.

[5] See Reinhard Bendix's discussion of these points in *Max Weber, an Intellectual Portrait* (Garden City, New York: Doubleday, 1962), pp. 59 ff. For a broader statement on the transcendent quest, see Benjamin Nelson, "The Future of Illusions," in Contemporary Civilization Staff, Columbia University (eds.), *Man in Contemporary Society* (New York: Columbia University Press, 1956), II, 958–976. I wish to acknowledge a personal debt to my former colleague, Nelson, for much of my own interest in, and understanding of, Weber's work.

[6] Representation of this homogenization theme may be found in Will Herberg, *Protestant-Catholic-Jew* (Garden City, New York: Doubleday, rev. ed. 1960); Martin E. Marty, *Varieties of Unbelief* (New York: Holt, Rinehart & Winston, 1964). For a discussion of the theological and material factors that foster denominational consensus in America, see Talcott Parsons, "The Cultural Background of American Religious Organization," in Harlan Cleveland & Harold D. Lasswell, *Ethics and Bigness, Scientific, Academic, Religious, Political and Military* (New York: Harper & Brothers, 1962), pp. 141–167.

7 The Allinsmiths find that while Jews are like Presbyterians and Congregationalists in their professional and white collar SES level, their opinions on policies affecting job security are like those of the Baptist and Catholic urban workers. Wesley and Beverly Allinsmith, "Religious Affiliation and Politico-Economic Attitude," *Public Opinion Quarterly*, XII (1948), 377–389. See also Lawrence Fuchs, *The Political Behavior of the American Jews* (Glencoe, Ill.: The Free Press, 1956).

8 *Cf.* E. Digby Baltzell, *The Protestant Establishment, Aristocracy and Caste in America* (New York: Random House, 1964). On the distinction between the Jews' high economic status and their social "subordination," see W. Lloyd Warner and Leo Srole, *The Social System of American Ethnic Groups* (New Haven: Yale University Press, 1945), p. 96.

9 See Allinsmith, *op. cit.;* also Milton Himmelfarb, "The Jew: Subject or Object?" *Commentary*, XL (1965), 54–57.

10 Fuchs, *op. cit.*, pp. 171–203; also Himmelfarb, *op. cit.;* Werner J. Cahnman, "The Cultural Consciousness of Jewish Youth," *Jewish Social Studies*, XIV (1952), 198–199; Israel S. Chipin, "Judaism and Social Welfare," in Louis Finkelstein, *The Jews, Their History, Culture and Religion* (New York: Harper & Brothers, 1949), Vol. I, Chapter 16.

11 Marshall Sklare, *Conservative Judaism: An American Religious Movement* (Glencoe, Ill.: The Free Press, 1955).

12 The Israeli "Knesset is as packed with historians and economists as our Congress is studded with lawyers." Fuchs, *op. cit.*, p. 180 fn.

13 Quoted in the *New York Times*, May 26, 1965, "Ben-Gurion Urges Jewish Renewal." See also Oscar Handlin, "Judaism in the United States," in James Ward Smith and A. Leland Jamison, *The Shaping of American Religion* (Princeton: Princeton University Press, 1961), pp. 122–161.

14 Nathan Glazer, *American Judaism* (Chicago: University of Chicago Press, 1957), Chapter 8.

15 Catholic attachments to the Democratic party have been evident at all income levels. However, unlike the Jews, Democratic affiliation decreases as income rises. See P. F. Lazarsfeld *et al.*, *The People's Choice* (New York: Duell, Sloan and Pearce, 1944). See Angus Campbell *et al.*, *The American Voter* (New York: John Wiley & Sons, 1960), pp. 301–306. The Catholic vote in 1956 actually went Republican despite the low Catholic SES level. The appearance of John Kennedy brought this group's vote back into the Democratic column in 1960.

16 *Cf.* Gary Wade Marx, *The Social Basis of the Support of a Depression Era Extremist: Father Coughlin* (Berkeley, California: Survey Research Center, University of California, 1962); Alan F. Westin, "The John Birch Society," in Daniel Bell (ed.), *The Radical Right* (Garden City, New York: Doubleday, 1964), pp. 239–268; Seymour Martin Lipset, "Three Decades of the Radical Right: Coughlinites, McCarthyites and Birchers," *ibid.*, pp. 344–373.

17 Henry J. Browne, "Catholicism," in Smith and Jamison, *op. cit.*, p. 107; Lipset, *op. cit.*, p. 431, shows that the John Birch Society appeals somewhat more to Catholics than to Protestants among well-to-do Republicans; Robert D. Cross concludes that the Church's liberal element has long been "conscious that the majority of Catholics in America were indifferent if not actually hostile to their program . . . ," *The Emergence of Liberal Catholicism in America* (Cambridge, Mass.: Harvard University Press, 1958), p. 50.

18 Thomas F. O'Dea, *American Catholic Dilemma* (New York: New American Library, 1962), p. 23; see also John Tracy Ellis, "The American Catholic & The Intellectual Life," *Thought*, XXX (Autumn, 1955). For a discussion of the hostility of Catholic culture toward Catholic intellectuals see Daniel P. Moynihan, "The Irish," in N. Glazer and D. Moynihan, *Beyond the Melting Pot* (Boston: M.I.T. Press, 1963), pp. 276–286.

19 Oscar Handlin, *Boston's Immigrants* (Cambridge, Mass.: Belknap Press, 1959), pp. 130–144.

20 Gehard Lenski, *The Religious Factor* (Garden City, New York: Doubleday, 1963, rev. ed.), pp. 268–270.

21 Cited in Emmet John Hughes, "God, Man and Holy Cross," *Newsweek*, May 3, 1965, p. 21.

22 Quoted in Roger A. Freeman, "Big Government and the Moral Order," *The Catholic World*, May, 1962, p. 88.

23 William A. Osborne, "The Catholic Church and the Desegregation Process" (a paper presented at the 1965 Conference of the Society for the Scientific Study of Religion), notes the dysfunction effects of such a theology with respect to the civil rights struggle.

24 Rev. R. L. Bruckberger, O. P., "The American Catholics as a Minority," in Thomas T. McAvoy (ed.), *Roman Catholicism and the American Way of Life* (Notre Dame, Indiana: University of Notre Dame Press, 1960), pp. 46–47.

25 See Leo Pfeffer, "Changing Relationships Among Religious Groups," *The Journal of Intergroup Relations* (1960), 81–93, for a brief comparison of the Jewish, Protestant and Catholic views.

26 The peculiarly Jansenist qualities of American Catholicism are ascribed by most informed observers less to the influence of American Protestantism and more to the overbearing impact

of the Irish. See Moynihan, *op. cit.;* Rev. James Shannon, "The Irish Catholic Immigration," in McAvoy, *op. ci .,* pp. 204–210.

[27] See the essays by a group of English Catholics in Michael de la Bedoyère (ed.), *Objections to Roman Catholicism* (Philadelphia: J. B. Lippincott, 1965).

[28] See A. Leland Jamison, "Religions on the Christian Perimeter," in Smith and Jamison, *op. cit.,* pp. 182 ff., for a discussion of the historical background of the liberal-orthodox controversy. Also Winthrop S. Hudson, *American Protestantism* (Chicago: University of Chicago Press, 1961), pp. 143 ff.

[29] Browne observes, "It is probably not so well known what a large percentage of Catholics —and Southern Protestants—the Federal Bureau of Investigation is glad to have as employees in work that requires a certain high moral stability." Browne, *op. cit.,* p. 117.

[30] Quoted from Walter Goldschmidt, "Class Denominationalism in Rural California Churches," *American Journal of Sociology,* IX (1944), 354. See also René de Visme Williamson, "Conservatism and Liberalism in American Protestantism," *The Annals of the American Academy of Political and Social Science,* 344 (Nov., 1962), 76–84.

[31] *Cf.* Charles C. Cole, Jr., *The Social Ideas of the Northern Evangelists* (New York: Columbia University Press, 1954); also Liston Pope, *Millhands and Preachers* (New Haven: Yale University Press, 1942).

[32] See Benton Johnson, "Do Holiness Sects Socialize in Dominant Values?" *Social Forces,* XXXIX (1961), 309–316.

[33] Pope, *op. cit.,* Cole, *op. cit.;* Williamson, *op. cit.;* David Danzig, "The Radical Right and the Rise of the Fundamentalist Minority," *Commentary,* XXXIII (April, 1962), 291–298; and Danzig's "Conservatism after Goldwater," *Commentary,* XXX (March, 1965), 31–37. Several of the essays in Bell, *op. cit.,* also draw the link between fundamentalism and ultra-conservatism. Also, Richard Dudman, *Men of the Radical Right* (New York: Pyramid Books, 1962).

[34] *Cf.* John Dillenberger and Claude Welch, *Protestant Christianity* (New York: Charles Scribner's Sons, 1954), pp. 217–223. Also Jamison, *op. cit.;* Hudson, *op. cit.;* and Williamson, *op. cit.*

[35] *Cf.* Walter Rauschenbush, *Christianizing the Social Order* (New York: Macmillan, 1912).

[36] *Cf.* Murray S. Stedman, Jr., *Religion and Politics in America* (New York: Harcourt, Brace & World, 1964), *passim;* Benton Johnson, "Ascetic Protestantism and Political Preference," *Public Opinion Quarterly,* XXVI (1962), 39–40; also Pope, *op. cit.,* p. 164; James Otis Smith and Gideon Sjoberg, "Origins and Career Patterns of Leading Protestant Clergymen," *Social Forces,* XXXIX (1961), 290–296, find that the reasons given for choosing the ministry as an occupation reflect significant denominational orientations. Thus, Episcopalian clergy tend to cite and desire to perform "service," while the fundamentalist Baptists more often speak of "God's calling."

[37] Johnson, "Ascetic Protestantism and Political Preference," *op. cit.* Republicanism is treated as an indicator of conservatism.

PART IX

RACIAL AND ETHNIC GROUPS

The sociology of race and ethnicity encompasses a number of interrelated areas. The terms "minority group," "intergroup relations," and "prejudice" refer to conceptually distinct and empirically associated phenomena. Race, per se, poses unique problems to students of human behavior. Familiarity with genetics and physical anthropology helps us understand race formation and change as well as racial differences. History indicates the effect of previous events and patterns on the present racial situation. In the sociology of race, however, we are concerned with behavior that takes place within and between the social categories known as races. Since these categories, unlike others (except sex), contain an explicit genetic element we are confronted with the issue of the genetic and social determinants of behavior. While many behavioral scientists now see these factors as interactive, serious attempts are still being made to distinguish their effects; studies in the area of intellectual differences are as yet inconclusive. Even when we look at race differences as purely socially determined, however, we must consider such possible "confounding" variables as culture or subculture (within American society), class, and family conditions.

Ethnic groups, by definition, have, at least, elements of their own subculture. To the extent that an individual shares his group's meanings and values, his perspective will be ethnically influenced. In this context Black Americans constitute an ethnic group as well as a racial category.

Tally's Corner: A Study of Black, Lower-Class Streetcorner Men

ELLIOT LIEBOW

The following selection is the concluding chapter of *Tally's Corner* by Liebow. This study describes and analyzes the world of the lower-class, urban, black man in the United States—the "streetcorner man." Liebow rejects the concept of lower-class culture as the basic explanatory idea in studying the black streetcorner man's world. This world is, rather, a product and a response to the culture and the structure of the larger society, not a positive affirmation of a separate and distinct culture.

Failure, particularly in the economic system, and, as a result, in family life, underlies the streetcorner man's perspective. This world view is partially constituted by the beliefs, attitudes, and values of the larger white society. His failure, however, both expected and actual, to perform in terms of this culture leads him to adopt as another part of his perspective a "shadow system of values constructed out of public fictions." This secondary system, which justifies his failures and attempts to make them attributes, is anchored in and perpetuated by the relationships which the lower-class, urban black man has with his peers.

Although he sees failure all around him, and employs the shadow system of values to deal with these failures, it is basically the streetcorner man's own experiences which lead him to his perspective. Liebow rejects the notion of inculcation with streetcorner values simply because of exposure. Rather, "the son goes out and independently experiences the same failures, in the same areas, and for much the same reasons as his father." It is these failures which lead him to embrace the streetcorner men's attitudes as part of his perspective.

THIS study has been primarily concerned with the inside world of the streetcorner Negro man, the world of daily, face-to-face relationships with wives, children, friends, lovers, kinsmen and neighbors. An attempt was made to see the man as he sees himself, to compare what he says with what he does, and to explain his behavior as a direct response to the conditions of lower-class Negro life rather than as mute compliance with historical or cultural imperatives.[1]

This inside world does not appear as a self-contained, self-generating, self-sustaining system or even subsystem with clear boundaries marking it off from the larger world around it. It is in continuous, intimate contact with the larger society—indeed, is an integral part of it- -and is no more impervious to the values, sentiments and beliefs of the larger society than it is to the blue welfare checks or to the agents of the larger society, such as the policeman, the police informer, the case worker, the landlord, the dope pusher, the Tupperware demonstrator, the numbers backer or the anthropologist.

One of the major points of articulation between the inside world and the larger society surrounding it is in the area of employment. The way in which the man makes a living and the kind of living he makes have important consequences for how the man sees himself and is seen by others; and these, in turn, importantly shape his relationships with family members, lovers, friends and neighbors.

Making a living takes on an overriding importance at marriage. The young, lower-class Negro gets married in his early twenties, at approximately the same time and in part for the same reason as his white or Negro working- or middle-class counterpart. He has no special motive for getting married; sex is there for the taking, with or without marriage, and he can also live with a woman or have children—if he has not done this already—without getting married. He wants to be publicly, legally married, to support a family and be the head of it, because this is what it is to be a man in our society, whether one lives in a room near the Carry-out or in an elegant house in the suburbs.

Although he wants to get married, he hedges on his commitment from the very beginning because he is afraid, not of marriage itself, but of his own ability to carry out his responsibilities as husband and father. His own father failed and had to "cut out," and the men he knows who have been or are married have also failed or are in the process of doing so. He has no evidence that he will fare better than they and much evidence that he will not. However far he has gone in school he is illiterate or almost so; however many jobs he has had or hard he has worked, he is essentially unskilled.[2] Armed with models who have failed, convinced of his own worthlessness, illiterate and unskilled, he enters marriage and the job market with the smell of failure all around him. Jobs are only intermittently available. They are almost always menial, sometimes hard, and never pay enough to support a family.

In general, the menial job lies outside the job hierarchy and promises to offer no more tomorrow than it does today. The Negro menial worker remains a menial worker so that, after one or two or three years of marriage and as many children, the man who could not support his family from the very beginning is even less able to support it as time goes on. The longer he works, the longer he is unable to live on what he makes. He has little vested interest in such a job and learns to treat it with the same contempt held for it by the employer and society at large. From his point of view, the job is expendable; from the employer's point of view, he is. For reasons real or imagined, perhaps so slight as to go unnoticed by others, he frequently quits or is fired. Other times, he is jobless simply because he cannot find a job.

He carries this failure home where his family life is undergoing a parallel deterioration. His wife's adult male models also failed as husbands and fathers and she expects no less from him. She hopes but does not expect him to be a good provider, to make of them a family and be head of it, to be "the man of the house." But his failure to do these things does not make him easier to live with because it was expected. She keys her demands to her wants, to her hopes, not to her expectations. Her demands mirror the man both as society says he should be and as he really is, enlarging his failure in both their eyes.

Sometimes he sits down and cries at the humiliation of it all. Sometimes he strikes out at her or the children with his fists, perhaps to lay hollow claim to being man of the house in the one way left open to him, or perhaps simply to inflict pain on this woman who bears witness to his failure as a husband and father and therefore as a man. Increasingly he turns to the streetcorner where a shadow system of values constructed out of public fictions serves to accommodate just such men as he, permitting them to be men once again provided they do not look too closely at one another's credentials.[3]

At the moment his streetcorner relationships take precedence over his wife and children he comes into his full inheritance bequeathed him by his parents, teachers, employers and society at large. This is the step into failure from which few if any return, and it is at this point that the rest of society can wring its hands or rejoice in the certain knowledge that he has ended up precisely as they had predicted he would.

The streetcorner is, among other things, a sanctuary for those who can no longer endure the experience or prospect of failure. There, on the streetcorner, public fictions support a system of values which, together with the value system of society at large, make for a world of ambivalence, contradiction and paradox, where failures are rationalized into phantom successes and weaknesses magically transformed into strengths. On the streetcorner, the man chooses to forget he got married because he wanted to get married and assume the duties, responsibilities and status of manhood; instead, he sees himself as the "put-upon" male who got married because his girl was pregnant or because he was tricked, cajoled or otherwise persuaded into doing so. He explains the failure of his marriage by the "theory of manly flaws." Conceding that to be head of a family and to support it is a principal measure of a man, he claims he was too much of a man to be a man. He says his marriage did not fail because he failed as breadwinner and head of the family but because his wife refused to put up with his manly appetite for whiskey and other women, appetites which rank high in the scale of shadow values on the streetcorner.[4]

Outside of marriage, he sees himself as a ruthless Exploiter of Women. Where women are concerned, he says, a man should take what he can get when he can get it. He claims not to understand men who do otherwise. Establishing his claim in word or deed to being an Exploiter of Women frees him to enter into a love relationship with one or more women, to declare publicly his love for them and to attempt to deal with them on the nonexploitative basis of mutual respect.

In practice, however, he cannot keep separate the exploitative and non-exploitative relationships. As exploiter, his actions sometimes fit his words but just as often he turns away women who offer him their bodies or their money, or he treats them with a solicitousness for their welfare which un-masks the uncompromising Exploiter of Women as a pretentious fraud. Similarly, his sincere profession of undying love for a woman and his offer to put himself and his goods at her everlasting disposal do not long hold up under the weight of his need for money, his desire to consume his own goods, or his desire to confirm his manliness by other conquests. Thus, despite the man's inability or unwillingness to conduct himself as a wholly exploitative animal, the exploitative impulse—supported by the man's poverty of material and inner resources and by the public fiction of man as Exploiter of Women—remains sufficiently strong to compromise the quality and fore-shorten the life of man-woman relationships. The result is that man-woman relationships tend to be relatively brief, one-sided affairs which come to an abrupt and frequently violent end.

Conflicts of interest and a general dearth of material and inner resources eat away at the whole structure of personal relationships. Friendships are precious relationships and of special importance to one's sense of physical and emotional security. Ideally, friendship is seen as a system of mutual aid in which the movement of money, goods, services and emotional support flows freely out of loyalty and generosity and according to need rather than as a mutual exchange resting securely on a quid pro quo basis. But money, goods and the stuff of comfort are normally in short supply, obliging each man to keep careful if secret account of what he gives out and takes in. Moreover, each man knows that his own and his friends' resources are meager and that, unconditional pledges of mutual aid notwithstanding, each will ultimately have to look to himself whenever he requires more than token assistance or aid of the kind that would materially deplete the resources of the giver. And he knows, too, that all friendships are vulnerable to the sudden clash of self-interest, especially where sex and money are concerned.

As if in anticipation of the frailty of personal relationships—to get as much as he can from them while they last and perhaps hopefully to pro-long them—the man hurries each relationship toward a maximum intensity, quickly up-grading casual acquaintances to friends, and friends to best friends and lovers. This rush to up-grade personal relationships, to hurry them on to increasingly intense levels of association, may itself contribute to a foreshortening of their life span, prematurely loading the incumbents with expectations and obligations which their hastily constructed relationships simply cannot support.[5]

The fluidity of personal relationships appears, at another level, as a fluidity in neighbor and kin groups and in families and households which are built up out of these personal relationships. Indeed, transience is perhaps the most striking and pervasive characteristic of this streetcorner world. It characterizes not only the subtler social relationships but the more obvious spatial relationships as well. It characterizes not only the relationships of those within the network of interlocking and overlapping personal communities at any given time but also the movement into and out of these networks. Some men come into this particular area to escape police who have chased them out from another. Some men leave for the same reason. Some men, like Tally, leave the area because they have used up their friendships and alliances and have to start anew elsewhere. But at the same time, another Tally has moved out of his old area and into this one for the same reasons. Here a family is evicted and the sidewalk becomes a staging area for the allocation of the individual family members to households in the same area or in a distant state. The next day or the same day, the same room or apartment is taken over by members of a family evicted from another part of the city. Here a man loses a job and moves out; another finds one and moves in. Here is a man released from prison after seven years and there goes a man who wants to try his luck in New York. Traffic is heavy in all directions.

Thus, this streetcorner world does not at all fit the traditional characterization of the lower-class neighborhood as a tightly knit community whose members share the feeling that "we are all in this together." Nor does it seem profitable—especially for those who would see it changed—to look at it as a self-supporting, on-going social system with its own distinctive "design for living," principles of organization, and system of values.

Whether the world of the lower-class Negro should be seen as a distinctive subculture or as an integral part of the larger society (at the bottom of it, perhaps, but as much a part of it as those in the middle or on top) is much more than an academic question and has important consequences for "intervention." Marriage among lower-class Negroes, for example, has been described as "serial monogamy," a pattern in which the woman of childbearing age has a succession of mates during her procreative years. The label "serial monogamy" clearly has a cultural referent, deriving as it does from the traditional nomenclature used to designate culturally distinctive patterns of marriage, such as polygyny, polyandry, monogamy, and so on. "Serial monogamy," then, as against the unqualified monogamous ideal of American society at large, refer to and *is used as evidence for* the cultural separateness and distinctiveness of the urban, lower-class Negro.

When these same phenomena are examined directly in the larger context of American life, both "serial monogamy" and cultural distinctiveness tend to disappear. In their place is the same pattern of monogamous marriage found elsewhere in our society but one that is characterized by failure. The woman does not have a simple "succession of mates during her procreative years." She has a husband and he a wife, and their hopes and their intentions—if not their expectations—are that this will be a durable, permanent union. More often, however, it is their fears rather than their hopes which materialize. The marriage fails and they part, he to become one of a "succession of mates" taken by another woman whose husband has left her, and she to accept one or more men. While these secondary and subsequent liaisons are, for the most part, somewhat pale reflections of the formal marriage relationship, each is modeled after it and fails for much the same reasons as does marriage itself. From this perspective, then, the succession of mates which characterizes marriage among lower-class Negroes does not constitute a distinctive cultural pattern "with an integrity of its own." It is rather the cultural model of the larger society as seen through the prism of repeated failure. Indeed, it might be more profitable—again, especially for those concerned with changing it—to look on marriage here as a succession of failures rather than as a succession of mates.[6]

In summary, what is challenged here is not that the marriage pattern among urban low-income Negroes does not involve a "succession of mates" but the implication that this succession of mates constitutes prima facie evidence for the cultural distinctiveness of those to whom it is attributed.

Much of what has been dealt with in the foregoing . . . can be looked at from this safe point of view. From this perspective, the streetcorner man does not appear as a carrier of an independent cultural tradition. His behavior appears not so much as a way of realizing the distinctive goals and values of his own subculture, or of conforming to its models, but rather as his way of trying to achieve many of the goals and values of the larger society, of failing to do this, and of concealing his failure from others and from himself as best he can.[7]

If, in the course of concealing his failure, or of concealing his fear of even trying, he pretends—through the device of public fictions—that he did not want these things in the first place and claims that he has all along been responding to a different set of rules and prizes, we do not do him or ourselves any good by accepting this claim at face value.

Such a frame of reference, I believe, can bring into clearer focus the practical points of leverage for social change in this area. We do not have to see the problem in terms of breaking into a puncture proof circle, of trying to change values, of disrupting the lines of communication between parent and child so that parents cannot make children in their own image, thereby transmitting their culture inexorably, ad infinitum. No doubt, each generation does provide role models for each succeeding one. Of much greater importance for the possibilities of change, however, is the fact that many similarities between the lower-class Negro father and son (or mother and daughter) do not result from "cultural transmission" but from the fact that the son goes out and independently experiences the same failures, in the same areas, and for much the same reasons as his father. What appears as a dynamic, self-sustaining cultural process is, in part at least, a relatively simple piece of social machinery which turns out, in rather mechanical fashion, independently produced look-alikes. The problem is how to change the conditions which, by guaranteeing failure, cause the son to be made in the image of the father.

Taking this viewpoint does not reduce the magnitude of the problem but does serve to place it in the more tractable context of economics, politics and social welfare. It suggests that poverty is, indeed, a proper target in the attempt to bring lower-class Negroes "into the mainstream of American life," and it supports the long line of social scientists, from E. Franklin Frazier and Gunnar Myrdal down through Kenneth Clark and Richard Cloward, in seeing the inability of the Negro man to earn a living and support his family as the central fact of lower-class Negro life. If there is to be a change in this way of life, this central fact must be changed; the Negro man, along with everyone else, must be given the skills to earn a living and an opportunity to put these skills to work.

No one pretends that this is an easy matter, to be accomplished at one fell stroke. For many Negro men, jobs alone are no longer enough. Before he can earn a living, he must believe that he can do so, and his women and children must learn to believe this along with him. But he finds it difficult to begin without their support, and they find it difficult to give their support until he begins. The beginning, then, will doubtless be a slow one, but, once started, success will feed on itself just as failure has done.[8] A beginning must be made, however, and it must be made simultaneously at all points in the life cycle. Children and young people must have good schools and good teachers who can give them the skills and the training to compete for jobs and careers, and they must have teachers who believe in them and help them believe in themselves. Jobs that pay enough to support a family must be opened up to the adult generation so that they can support their families, so that the young people can see the changed reality, so that young and old can experience it and gain a vested interest in the world they live in.[9]

Despite the many differences of opinion about how these things are to be achieved, the real problem lies elsewhere. Hundreds of research and demonstration projects have established that we have the know-how to effect these changes. Under the aegis of the Office of Economic Opportunity, a multitude of programs designed to achieve these ends are already under way and some have begun to have a discernible beneficial effect on selected groups and individuals.

What is lacking is not know-how and programs but a clarity of purpose, of motive, and of intention. What do we want to do, why do we want to do it, and how much are we willing to pay for it (not so much in money but in terms of basic changes in the class and racist structure of our society) remain largely unanswered questions.

Notes

[1] There is, fortunately, a growing suspicion that "culture" and "historical continuity" may not be the most useful constructs for dealing with lower-class behavior. Hylan Lewis, for example, suggests that "It is probably more fruitful to think of lower class families reacting in various ways to the facts of their position and to relative isolation rather than to the imperatives of a lower class culture" ("Culture, Class, and the Behavior of Low Income Families," p. 43). Richard Cloward and Lloyd Ohlin argue that "The historical-continuity theory of lower-class values . . . ignores the extent to which lower-class and delinquent cultures today are *predictable responses to conditions in our society rather than persisting patterns . . .*" (*Delinquency and Opportunity: A Theory of Delinquent Gangs*, p. 75; emphasis added.) Thomas Gladwin has similar misgivings: "Defining the multiproblem population as a subculture is only one of several ways of looking at the problem . . . the formulation is useful only if it can bring us closer to a solution" ("The Anthropologist's View of Poverty," p. 75). Elizabeth Bott challenges outright the use of the culture concept as an explanatory device: "I do not believe it is sufficient to explain variations . . . as cultural or sub-cultural differences. To say that people behave differently or have different expectations because they belong to different cultures amounts to no more than saying that they behave differently—or that cultures are different because they are different" (*Family and Social Network*, p. 218).

[2] And he is black. Together, these make a deadly combination and relegate him to the very bottom of our society.

[3] This "shadow system" of values is very close to Hyman Rodman's "value stretch." Members of the lower class, he says, "share the general values of the society with members of other classes, but in addition they have stretched these values, or developed alternative values, which help them adjust to their deprived circumstances" ("The Lower-Class Value Stretch," p. 209).

I would add at least two qualifications to Rodman's and other formulations that posit an alternate system of lower-class values. The first is that the stretched or alternative value systems are not the same order of values, either phenomenologically or operationally, as the parent or general system of values: they are derivative, subsidiary in nature, thinner and less weighty, less completely internalized, and seem to be value images reflected by forced or adaptive behavior rather than real values with a positive determining influence on behavior of choice. The second qualification is that the alternative value system is not a distinct value system which can be separately invoked by its users. It appears only in association with the parent system and is separable from it only analytically. Derivative, insubstantial, and co-occurring with the parent system, it is as if the alternative value system is a shadow cast by the common value system in the distorting lower-class setting. Together, the two systems lie behind much that seems paradoxical and inconsistent, familiar and alien, to the middle-class observer from his one-system perspective.

[4] "The behaviors of lower class persons which are considered deviant, either by the members of their own groups or by the larger society, can be regarded as efforts to attain some sense of valid identity, as efforts to gratify the prompting of needs from inside and to elicit a response of recognition as valid persons from those around them." Lee Rainwater, "Work and Identity in the Lower Class (forthcoming)."

[5] From this point of view, the primary function of pseudo-kinship is to anticipate the frailty of personal relationships by attempting to invest them with the durables of kinship.

[6] "It is important that we not confuse basic life chances and actual behavior with basic cultural values and preferences. . . . The focus of efforts to change should be on background conditions and on precipitants of the deviant behaviors rather than on presumably different class or cultural values." Hylan Lewis, "Culture, Class and the Behavior of Low Income Families," p. 43.

[7] ". . . concealment and ego-protection are of the essence of social intercourse." Everett C. Hughes, *Men and Their Work*, p. 43.

[8] "Feed upon one another" suggests the model of "the vicious circle"—the model which served as Gunnar Myrdal's main explanatory scheme for analyzing the Negro problem in the U.S. In *An American Dilemma*, pp. 1065 ff, the model of the vicious circle—refined as the Principle of Accumulation—is treated in detail. "The theory of the vicious circle is a cause

rather for optimism than pessimism. The cumulative principle *works both ways.*" (P. 1069n, emphasis added.)

[9] For some adults, perhaps many, it will be too late, but we will not know for which ones until it is tried for all. Those for whom it is too late should be bought off, with cash or sinecures, in much the same way and for much the same reasons as the Germans pay reparations to survivors of the Nazi persecutions or as we pay reparations to Japanese Americans disenfranchised, unpropertied, and interned during the war, or as our society sometimes indemnifies men wrongly imprisoned. It is a very small price to pay for their cooperation or neutrality, and there is comfort to be gained from the fact that, in this way, we may not have to buy off generation after generation as we do under our present welfare programs.

The World Views of the Jewish and Italian Subcultures

FRED L. STRODTBECK

Strodtbeck analyzes ethnic influence on perspective to account for differences in occupational achievement. The Southern Italian and East European Jewish cultures had certain contrasting values which account for differences in the perspectives of Americans with these backgrounds. Jewish *shtetl* culture placed a high value on education and scholarship; the Italian peasant saw these values as anathema to his social situation. The community was the inclusive social unit for East European Jews; *La famiglia* was the Italian counterpart. Jewish culture had an orientation toward the future. Such an orientation was meaningless to the Italian in the face of *Destino*.

Strodtbeck contrasts Italians and Jews on five values which relate to differences in occupational achievement, and which are fundamental to the individual's perspective. They concern his relations with the supernatural, with the world at large, with family and community members, and with those he meets on the job. Such fundamental value differences obviously indicate important differences in perspective. As the author states, however, "Differences . . . are greatly attenuated when class level is constant." One of the primary goals of sociological research is to separate the many influences which act upon the phenomenon under investigation.

Italian Jewish Cultural Values

IT is to be assumed that successive generations of Italians and Jews in this country have progressively become more acculturated and thus more like one another. For guidance in the formulation of hypotheses about the way in which value differences between these cultures may have influenced their differential achievement, one needs to turn first to the original cultures from which they emigrated. For the Southern Italian background we found

Originally published as "Family Interaction, Values, and Achievement," in *Talent and Society*, D. C. McClelland *et al.*, eds., D. Van Nostrand Co., Inc., 1958. Reprinted by permission of the author.

some nine substantive sources (*4, 7, 21, 22, 23, 28, 29, 34, 35*), all fairly consistent. For the Jews, the relevant literature was much larger. The present account was based primarily on Zborowski and Herzog's *Life Is With People* (*46*). Their treatment of *shtetl* culture—perhaps idealized—is sympathetic but sharply focused on attitudes of great relevance to contrasts between Italians and Jews.

To begin with one of the most striking differences, Jews have traditionally placed a very high value upon *education and intellectual attainment.* The Jewish parent was expected to provide as much education as the sons showed themselves capable of absorbing, but not in a ritualistic manner. Learning in the *shtetl* society gave the individual prestige, respect, authority— and the chance for a better marriage. The Jews have a folk saying that "parents will blend the sky to educate their sons." Every first-generation Jewish parent can tell heroic stories of the sacrifices made by fellow parents, both in Eastern Europe and in this country, to educate their children.

The essential nature of education is further attested by the prestige associated with "brainwork," and the corresponding lack of prestige associated with physical accomplishments. This pattern of evaluation starts early in the child's career. Traditionally, a 3- or 4-year-old starting *kheyder* (elementary religious school) was regarded as a serious student; brilliant students, though youngsters, were treated with a deference ordinarily reserved for important adults. The weight of the opinion of the young scholar is reflected by the fact that a bearded man would not be ashamed to bring a difficult Talmudic question to a boy of thirteen.

Religious learning and the satisfactions of family life were not in this culture separated, as they were in monastic systems. It was the custom, indeed, to arrange the young scholar's marriage while he was still in his middle teens. In order that such scholars might give more attention to their studies, many of the economic responsibilities of the family were assumed by the wife.

In Southern Italian culture, on the other hand, the traditional attitude toward education was (and is) very different. School and book-learning were alien pursuits, remote from everyday experience. Priests were taken from their families and even their villages in order to be educated. To the typical Southern Italian peasant, school was an upper-class institution and potentially a threat to his desire to retain his family about him. Although education might well serve for some as a means of social advancement, the peasant was disposed to believe that this avenue was not open to his children—in their case, education was not functional. Family life, local political power, and other objectives were stressed as alternative goals to learning.

Even in this country, the attitude of the first-generation Southern Italian was, in part, negative to education. As an Italian educator reports, "Mother believed you would go mad if you read too many books, and Father was of the opinion that too much school makes children lazy and opens the mind for unhealthy dreams." Intellectualism, in itself, was not valued in Southern Italian communities. Learned men were of another class, or, alternatively, they were men of the church. Status in the community changed slowly; property was in all cases more important than learning. Property could be accumulated faster by a trickster-trader than by a scholar (*3*). Scholars were like monks: good men, but not of the real world.

La famiglia in the Southern Italian culture was an inclusive social world. The basic mores of this society were primarily family mores; everyone outside the family was viewed with suspicion. Where the basic code was family solidarity, there was a strong feeling that the family should stay together —physically close together. The essence of the ethos has been most forcefully captured by Edward C. Banfield, who states the one premise from which the political orientation would seem to flow: "Choose so as to maximize the shortrun advantage of the family and assume others will do likewise." [1]

Though the Jewish family was also traditionally a close-knit one, it was the entire Jewish *shtetl* community rather than the family which was considered the inclusive social unit and world. Relatives might be more important than friends, but all Jews were considered to be bound to each other. The primary unit, to be sure, was the family of procreation, but physical proximity was not so heavily stressed. Mandelbaum (*20*, pp. 28, 31) and Joffe (*13*) have both pointed out that the dynamics of benefice for the Jews was not in the nature of reciprocal exchange. Parents' gifts to their children were to be paralleled in the next generation. In the home, as in the community, giving must move in a descending spiral. Giving served not only to enrich the donor and succor the recipient, but also to maintain the constituency of fundamentally equal persons, and in this way, to enrich the community. The charitable contributions of American Jewish communities today owe much to this tradition.

For the Jewish parents, whose theme was so definitely *"Alles für die Kinder,"* there was an emphasis upon a bettered condition in the *future* which made them willing to let children leave the community for opportunities elsewhere. For the Italians, there was less of this emphasis upon the future. The external world for all the Jews was hostile, to be sure, but it was by nature solvable. For all goods there is a proper price, they say; for all labor there is a best way of doing something. For the Italian the equivalent phrasing is perhaps, "There is work which must be done." Perhaps he might go so far as to say that there are ways of doing the work which are more expeditious than others—but no matter how it is done, there is always the chance that fate will intervene. The unpredictable intervention of fate may be for good or evil, but *Destino* is omnipresent. If a man works all his life for something which *Destino* may deny him, well then, why should men look so far ahead? There is always the present, and the chance of a lucky break.

Zborowski, in his study in this country of the reactions of hospitalized

Jews and Italians to pain, employs Florence Kluckhohn's well-known *time* orientation to differentiate the cultural responses (*45*). He finds that both Jews and Italians complain more about pain than do "old Americans." But, more important, sedation alone is enough to relieve the Italian; for the Jew, sedation is not enough. He continues pessimistic, concerned about the implication of the sedation for his eventual recovery. For the Italian there is a *present-oriented* apprehension of the sensation of pain; for the Jew there is a *future-oriented* anxiety concerning the symptomatic meaning of the pain. Neither group wishes to suffer alone; neither group believes it necessarily masculine to deny the existence of pain; neither group believes in suffering as an end in itself.

In the use of folk medicines and in such things as a dread of the "evil eye," Jewish and Italian cultures shared many common elements of irrationality. Religious ritual was strong in both cultures. The behavior involved in an individual's participation in his own salvation, however, deserves separate attention.

In Italian folk theology, Catholic doctrine was popularly understood as requiring sheer obedience to arbitrary prescriptions for the sake of an arbitrary reward. Where the formula did not apply, the matter was of no real significance. Faith in the mystery of the Trinity and the timely interventions of the priest were all that was required. For the Jews, religious improvement was always possible and perfection always denied. The scholar proceeded at his own rate after becoming a Rabbi. There were none to grant a learned and respected man a more advanced degree; his job was ever undone. During the middle years he might have to give more attention to business, but as he grew older he could spend his full time in discussion, study, and prayers.

In the East European *shtetl,* no man could occupy a position so humble that it could not in part be redeemed by his religious scholarship. Without that religious scholarship, a man of means alone could be *prost*—simple, common, vulgar. A diploma of any type which signified learning—even in nonreligious fields—came to be accorded respect like that accorded religious scholarship. It is important to stress that if Talmudic scholarship taught precision, juridic care, and dedication, it taught also attitudes toward learning which might, with a growth of heterodoxy, be transferred to other learning. As long as the ghetto confined the Jew's area of attainment, goals of religious scholarship were highly coveted. Upon release from the ghetto, the status and financial rewards available in such disciplines as law and medicine were also attainable by work of an intellectual character similar to Talmudic scholarship. Jewish mobility has in all probability been facilitated by the transformation of a complex of behavior which had not existed for the Italians.

A peasant's mistrust of books in contrast with veneration of learning does not exist in isolation from other attitudes. Zborowski and Herzog tell us that in the *shtetl* the hair line of babies would in some instances be shaved back so that the child would have a high forehead—hence, appear intelligent. Short, thick hands were thought to be inappropriate and ugly—*prost*. The Jewish attitude toward the body was not ascetic; the body was neither ugly nor inherently evil. Rather, it was looked upon as a vessel for containing the spirit. Rest, food, and procreation on the Sabbath were sanctioned, and keeping one's body at full efficiency was fully approved; but a specialized interest in physical development *per se* was improper. For the Jews the mind was the great tool—but ever under discipline and purposeful direction. In the early morning prayers, the mind is turned to sacred matters; on the Sabbath to non-business matters, etc. There is never a question of whether the mind can win over impulse.[2]

It is perhaps true that the Italian emphasis on good food and proper relaxation is superficially similar to Jewish practice—and, for that matter, to the practice in many cultures. The essential difference as we perceive it is that the Italian manual worker was never ashamed of his strength; to keep his body fit was a desirable end in itself, for it was never perceived to be in competition with other necessarily more important activities.

The contrast in child training in the old Italian and Jewish cultures may be further illustrated by data from one comparative American study which has come to our attention. Field workers from the Harvard University Laboratory of Human Development interviewed an area sample of families in greater Boston concerning methods of child-rearing. For second-generation Italians and Jews, the division of the families by social class was as follows:

	Italian	Jewish
Middle	7	64
Lower	36	15

As is consistent with the predicted differential status mobility, Jews are concentrated in the middle classes, Italians in the lower. Unfortunately, for purposes of comparison, this distribution does not provide many middle-class Italian or lower-class Jewish families, although the class distribution appears to be roughly "modal" for second-generation members of these two groups (see p. 159 *infra*). In an unpublished report of this work, the following points are made: [3]

(a) In the amount of time spent in taking care of the child and in affectionate interaction with it, in the warmth of the mother-child relationship, and in the amount of enjoyment derived from child-care, there is no difference between the two groups. Both are relatively high in infant nurturance, save only for the greater severity of the Italian mothers in toilet training. With regard to sexual play with other children, masturbation, or nudity in the home, Italians are markedly less permissive than Jews.

(b) Italians are less permissive also of aggression toward parents, and impose more restrictions on such things as table manners, conversations with adults, being a "nice" boy or girl, being careful of the furniture, and free-dom to leave home. Jewish children admit deviant behavior more fre-quently than Italian children and, in addition, tend to require more atten-tion from adults.

(c) At the five-year level, both groups of children are about equally depend-ent, but the Jewish mother is significantly more accepting of dependent behavior. In general, the emotional atmosphere of parent-child relations is somewhat warmer in Jewish than in Italian families, although at the same time Jewish families think more highly of the benefits to be gained by spanking.

(d) Jews expect much longer school attendance, but there is less insistence on the child's doing well in school. Perhaps there is implied a disposition to permit the child to set his own level of performance.

There were some marked differences between the 64 middle-class Jewish families and the 15 lower-class Jewish families. While this latter number is small, the lower-class families were significantly more severe in weaning and toilet training, took less pleasure in caring for their babies, and were less warm and nurturant when the child was an infant. Differences between Italians and Jews are greatly attenuated when class level is constant. Since class level was not controlled in the comparisons quoted above, the exact contribution of "class" in contrast with "culture" cannot be ascertained. So, too, the marked difference in "mastery expectations," reported previously from McClelland's work, is not confirmed by the Harvard study, but this may arise simply from differences in the categories of behavior considered.

From all this material, only briefly summarized here, we had now to choose those values which appeared most likely to have accounted for the differences in occupational achievement after these two groups came to the United States. This task entailed likewise a comparison of Italian-Jewish values, with the values we used earlier to describe the Protestant ethic of achievement. Finally the problem narrowed to a comparison at five points, as follows:

(1) *Man's sense of personal responsibility in relation to the external world.* The Calvinist's world was the work of God, its mysteries profound and not to be understood by the slacker. To work to understand and transform this world was the true Christian's personal responsibility. In such a scheme, misfortunes had a definite place; they were the tests which God sets before men. Although hard work was thus understood to be a prerequisite for all worldly accomplishment, there was still no guarantee that even a lifetime of hard work would necessarily be rewarded.

For the present-day achiever in the United States, rational mastery of the situation has taken the place of the "hard work" of the Calvinists, and the threat of almost continuous review of his record has been equated with anxiety over eventual salvation. There is no necessary personal depri-vation which must be endured; indeed, one's accomplishment can be facilitated by "breaks." But the breaks are now of the individual's own making; it is a matter of being available with what is needed at the right place and at the right time. Just as the breaks are not doled out by a beneficent power, neither are failures. Whatever failure an individual has suffered could always have been foreseen and circumvented if the individual had been sufficiently alert. For the modern achiever there is no legitimate excuse for failure. His sense of personal responsibility for controlling his destiny is enormous.

Old-culture Jewish beliefs appear to be congruent in many, if not all, respects with such a belief in a rational mastery of the world. For the Jew, there was always the expectation that everything could be understood, if perhaps not controlled. Emphasis on learning as a means of control was strong. Neither religious nor secular learning, once attained (unlike the Protestant's salvation and the achiever's status), was in continual jeopardy. For men who were learned in trades but not religious scholars, the expectations of charity to others of the community who were less fortunate was a continuing goad to keep working; but if misfortune befell a former benefactor, the community understood. The sense of personal responsibility existed along with a responsibility of the community for the individual which eased somewhat the precariousness associated with "all or none" expectations of the individual.

For the Italian, there was no real logic in striving; the best-laid plans of man might twist awry. Misfortune originated "out there," out beyond the individual. *Destino* decreed whether a particular event would or would not come to pass. A sort of passive alertness was thus inculcated. Although no one knew when he might be slated for a lucky break, at the same time there was no motivation for any rational undertaking of heroic proportions; such an undertaking might be *destined* to fail.

(2) *Familism versus loyalty to a larger collectivity.* The essence of familism is an emphasis on filial obedience and parental authority. Familistic social organization tends to involve a particular locus of activity and a hierarchy of responsibility based upon age and kinship rather than upon impersonal technical requirements. Calvinism was almost anti-familistic in its emphasis upon a first obedience to one's own soul and to God. The achiever in the United States tends, like the Calvinist, to be anti-familistic. Otherwise, the desire to keep two or more generations together would compete with the job and with educational opportunities which require residential moves. On the basis of his technical qualifications alone, the present-day achiever is ready to move with his wife and children to whatever spot offers him maximum opportunities. At the early stages of his career he may even avoid a line of work in which his father could help him, so as to win for himself the privilege of being judged for his own competence.

The old Jewish pattern sanctioned separation from the family for purposes of business and education, and there was a distinct consciousness that a man's first responsibility was toward his children. That is, obligations were primarily from those who have more to those who have less—from which, practically speaking, it followed that children need not always stay to nurture parents who might be better off than they were. Although the Jews did not go so far as the present American achiever in weakening the ties to parents, the pattern contrasts sharply with that of the Southern Italians who put loyalty upward to the extended family first.

(3) *Perfectibility of man.* An aspect of Calvinism perhaps best captured for popular consumption in *Poor Richard's Almanack* by Benjamin Franklin is the insistence that at every moment of every day a man must work to improve himself. The old Jewish culture also, with its emphasis on religious scholarship and study, represented a similar belief in the responsibility for self-improvement. For the achiever in the United States, this perfectibility has, in one sense, been relaxed; but insofar as it remains, it has become even more stringent. Now, we are told, the improvement should be acquired in a relaxed manner, with no apparent effort; self-improvement is something to be "enjoyed" not "endured" as earlier. But in any case, an interest in education should be (and has been) high because it is so obviously one of the ways in which man perfects himself.

For the Southern Italian there has always been considerable doubt as to whether man could perfect himself or, indeed, whether he need try. According to his interpretation of Catholicism, he must conscientiously fulfill his duties, but his "good works" do not form a rationalized system of life. Good works may be used to atone for particular sins, or, as Weber points out, stored up as a sort of insurance toward the end of one's life; but there is no need to live in every detail the ideal life, for there is always the sacrament of absolution. Furthermore, the Southern Italian sees man as living in an uneasy peace with his passions, which from time to time must be expected to break through. Man is really not perfectable—he is all too human. So he would do well not to drive himself or his mind too relentlessly in trying to reach that impossible goal, perfection.

(4) *Consciousness of the larger community.* The Calvinist's dictum that "each man is his brother's keeper" has given way in the United States to a less moralistic rationale based upon a recognition of the interdependencies in modern society. Just as the whole Jewish community could vicariously participate in the charities of its wealthiest members, there is a sense in which the strengthening of various aspects of American society is recognized as contributing to the common good.

The Jew from the older culture, enabled by his success to assume a responsibility for the community, had little choice in the matter. The social pressures were great, and they were ordinarily responded to with pride and rewarded by prominence in the community forum. The identification went beyond the extended family. The giver was not to be rewarded in kind; his reward came from community recognition. Such community identification—as contrasted with family identification—has not been highly developed among

Southern Italians. Reduced sensitivity to community goals is believed to inhibit the near altruistic orientations which in adolescence and early maturity lead individuals to make prolonged personal sacrifices to enter such professions as medicine or the law.

(5) *Power relations.* Insofar as differences in status are perceived to be legitimate—because indeed the person involved *is* technically more competent—then the person in the subordinate position can still give his full commitment to organizational goals without feeling or acting as if he were being dominated by his superior. Early Calvinism laid the groundwork for such limited and specific relationships by insisting that each man had a post assigned him by God and that no one should feel inferior or superior. Today's bureaucracies create for modern achievers a greatly increased number of positions in our society where a person has a specific role to perform in a large impersonal system.

The old-culture Jew, on the other hand, did not see power in the context of some external system of pre-established impersonal relationships. He tended, like the Calvinist, to translate power questions into other terms—to the equity of a particular bargain, for example; but unlike the Calvinist, he saw these relationships always as specific, both as to persons and content, and not part of a larger system. His primary concern was to make his relationships good with others with whom he was in close contact over a particular issue. The specificity of his relations with others, including his separation of business and family matters, is also like the functional specificity of modern bureaucratic society, but again unlike it in overlooking the *system* of such functional relationships.

The old-culture Italian tended to see power entirely in immediate interpersonal terms. Power was the direct expression of who can *control* the behavior of another rather than who knows more for a job in an impersonal system. "Who's boss?" was his constant inquiry. Every relationship he turned into a "for me-against me" or "over me-under me" polarity.

Notes

[1] An address to the Society for Social Research, June, 1956.
[2] See Charles R. Snyder's exhaustive analysis of factors that account for the low rates of inebriety among Jews (*37*).
[3] Summarized from B. Tregoe, "An Analysis of Ethnic and Social Class Differences," unpublished manuscript.

References

1. Alexander, F. *Our Age of Unreason.* Philadelphia: Lippincott, 1942.
2. Bales, R. F. *Interaction Process Analysis.* Cambridge: Addison-Wesley Press, 1950.

3. Brown, N. O. *Hermes the Thief.* Madison: Univ. of Wisconsin Press, 1947.
4. D'Alesandre, J. J. Occupational trends of Italians in New York City. *Italy American Monthly*, 1935, *2*, 11–12.
5. Dynes, R. R., Clarke, A. C., and Dinitz, S. Levels of occupational aspiration: some aspects of family experience as a variable. *Amer. sociol. Rev.*, 1956, *21*, 212–215.
6. Eisenstadt, S. N. *From Generation to Generation.* Glencoe, Illinois: Free Press, 1956.
7. Guilds' Committee for Federal Writers Publications. *The Italians of New York.* New York: Random House, 1938.
8. Henry, W. E. The business executive: the psychodynamics of a social role. *Amer. J. Sociol.*, 1949, *54*, 286–291.
9. Hinkle, Gisela J. Review of Irvin G. Wyllie's *The Self-Made Man in America: The Myth of Rags to Riches. Social Forces*, 1956, *34*, 297.
10. Homans, G. C. *The Human Group.* New York: Harcourt, Brace, 1950.
11. Horwitz, M. Psychological needs as a function of social environments. In L. D. White (ed.) *The State of Social Sciences*, Chicago: Univ. of Chicago Press, 1956, 162–183.
12. Inkeles, A., and Levinson, D. J. National Character: the study of model personality and sociocultural systems. In G. Lindzey (ed.) *Handbook of Social Psychology.* Cambridge: Addison-Wesley Press, 1954, 977–1020.
13. Joffe, N. F., The dynamics of benefice among East European Jews, *Social Forces*, 1949, *27*, 239–247.
14. Kardiner, A. *The Individual and His Society.* New York: Columbia Univ. Press, 1939.
15. Kardiner, A. and others. *The Psychological Frontiers of Society.* New York: Columbia Univ. Press, 1945.
16. King, S. H., and Henry, A. F. Aggression and cardiovascular reactions related to parental control over behavior. *J. abnorm. soc. Psychol.*, 1955, *50*, 206–210.
17. Kohn, M. L., and Clausen, J. A. Parental authority behavior and schizophrenia. *Amer. J. Orthopsychiatry*, 1956.
18. Kluckhohn, C. Culture and Behavior. In G. Lindzey (ed.) *Handbook of Social Psychology.* Cambridge: Addison-Wesley Press, 1954, 921–976.
19. Kluckhohn, F., Strodtbeck, F. L., and Roberts, J. *Variations in Value Orientations.* New York: Harper, 1961.
20. Mandelbaum, D. G. *Change and Continuity in Jewish Life.* Glencoe, Illinois: Oscar Hillel Plotkin Library, 1955.
21. Mangione, J. *Mount Allegro.* Boston: Houghton Mifflin, 1942.
22. Mangione, J. *Reunion in Sicily.* Boston: Houghton Mifflin, 1950.
23. Mariano, J. H. *The Second Generation of Italians in New York City.* New York: Christopher, 1921.
24. McClelland, D. C., Atkinson, J. W., Clark, R. A., and Lowell, E. L. *The Achievement Motive.* New York: Appleton-Century-Crofts, 1953.
25. McClelland, D. C., Rindlisbacher, A., and deCharms, R. Religious and other sources of parental attitudes toward independence training. In D. C. McClelland (ed.), *Studies in Motivation.* New York: Appleton-Century-Crofts, 1955, 389–397.
26. Parsons, T. *The Structure of Social Action.* Glencoe, Illinois: Free Press, 1949.

27. Parsons, T., and Bales, R. F. *Family, Socialization and Interaction Process.* Glencoe, Illinois: Free Press, 1955.

28. Pellegrini, A. *Immigrant's Return.* New York: Macmillan, 1951.

29. Radin, P. *The Italians of San Francisco: Their Adjustment and Acculturation.* Monographs 1 and 2, S.E.R.A. Project, Cultural Anthropology. San Francisco: 1935.

30. Reissman, L. Levels of aspiration and social class. *Amer. sociol. Rev.,* 1953, *18,* 233–242.

31. Ricciuti, H. N., and Sadacca, R. The prediction of academic grades with a projective test of achievement motivation: II. Cross-Validation at the High School Level. Princeton, N.J.: Educational Testing Service, 1955.

32. Robinowitz, R. Attributes of pupils achieving beyond their level of expectancy. *J. Personality,* 1956, *24,* 308–317.

33. Sangree, M. Lucinda. Expectations and interactions in Nisei families, unpublished Master's Thesis, University of Chicago, 1956.

34. Sangree, W., and Hybleum, M. A study of the people of Middletown of Sicilian extraction with special emphasis on the changes in their values resulting from assimilation into the Middletown community, unpublished Master's Thesis, Wesleyan Univ., 1952.

35. Sartorio, E. C. *Social and Religious Life of Italians in America.* New York: Christopher, 1918.

36. Shannon, J. Early detachment and independence in a study of creativity, unpublished manuscript, Univ. of Chicago, 1957.

37. Snyder, C. R. Culture and sobriety, *Quart. J. Studies on Alcohol,* 1955, *16,* 101–177, 263–289, 504–532; 1956, *17,* 124–143.

38. Stein, M. On the role of the industrial research chemist and its relationship to the problem of creativity, unpublished manuscript, Univ. of Chicago, 1956.

39. Strodtbeck, F. L. Husband-wife interaction over revealed differences. *Amer. social. Rev.* 1951, *16,* 468–473.

40. Strodtbeck, F. L. The family as a three-person group. *Amer. sociol. Rev.,* 1954, *11,* 23–29.

41. Strodtbeck, F. L., McDonald, M. R., and Rosen, B. C. Evaluation of occupations: a step toward explaining Jewish-Italian mobility differences. *Amer. sociol. Rev.,* to be published.

42. Vidich, A. J. Methodological problems in the observations of husband-wife interaction. Unpublished manuscript, Cornell Univ., 1957.

43. Warner, W. L., and Abegglen, J. C. *Big Business Leaders in America.* New York: Harper, 1953.

44. Weber, M. *The Protestant Ethic and the Spirit of Capitalism* (translated by Talcott Parsons). New York: Scribner, 1948.

45. Zborowski, M. Cultural components in responses to pain. *J. social Issues,* 1952, *8,* 16–30.

46. Zborowski, M., and Herzog, E. *Life Is With People.* New York: International Univ. Press, 1952.

The Mexican American Subculture

JOHN H. BURMA

Burma's paper is an example of subcultural analysis as an approach to the sociological study of perspective. He defines subculture as "a group adaptation system to a situation." The meanings and attitudes that constitute such a system form a fundamental part of the group member's perspective. With this approach the author compares aspects of the "subculture of poverty," as described by Oscar Lewis, with the Mexican–American subculture and aspects of both subcultures with the parent Mexican and American cultures. He recognizes the view that lower-class life is more usefully analyzed as failure in terms of the larger society (see Liebow's selection), rather than as subcultural behavior. For purposes of comparison, however, he chooses to utilize the concept of subculture of poverty.

Burma focuses on the family as a key area of experience within any subculture. This experience varies in structure and authority from one subculture to another. The Negro subculture is matrifocal and matriarchal; the subculture of poverty in Puerto Rico is matrifocal but not matriarchal, while the Mexican–American family is matrifocal with authority, however, being more equalitarian. The Mexican–American family also differs from the subculture of poverty family because of the greater likelihood of the children being taught the value of respect and obedience. Marriage in the Mexican–American subculture is viewed as "a deep romantic attachment," and ideally it is expected to be permanent. The mother role is based on the values of love and nurturing; the father role on the values of support, defense, and authority. The orientations which underlie marriage and parental roles, then, are quite different in the Mexican–American subculture and the subculture of poverty.

Both subcultures differ from the parent American culture in their orientations toward time, work, and education. In the parent culture, time is a valuable commodity which must be used efficiently. In the subcultures examined here this value "does not make sense." The orientation toward the present and fatalism which are manifested are contrary to the parent culture. Although work is viewed in terms of the

Originally published as "A Comparison of the Mexican American Subculture with the Oscar Lewis Culture of Poverty Model" in *Mexican Americans in the United States*, pp. 17–28, edited by John H. Burma, Schenkman Publishing Company, Inc., Cambridge, Mass., copyright © 1970.

Protestant ethic by the parent culture, it is considered a necessary evil by most Mexican–Americans. Finally, both subcultures believe education ought to be but is not pragmatic. It is therefore little valued. Burma also compares the subcultures on the self-conceptions which they foster. People in the subculture of poverty have feelings of inferiority and a lack of pride, whereas pride and *dignidad* are very important personal qualities in the Mexican–American subculture. The author concludes by assessing the future of the two subcultures.

THE concept of subculture is an increasingly used and useful one in modern sociology and anthropology. Borrowing from the anthropologists, sociologists now study such disparate subcultures as those of prisoners, adolescents, Mexican Americans, Amish, homosexuals, Chinese Americans, hippies, juvenile delinquents, Negro Americans, and persons living in poverty. The concept of a subculture must be defended or condemned on the same grounds as any proper concept; i.e., it is a theoretical tool which produces greater clarity and hence aids theoretical understanding.

Milton Gordon, in his *Assimilation in American Life,*[1] points out that culture as a concept is used to refer to the social heritage or way of life of a particular society at a particular time. Thus one speaks of culture, and subculture, in terms of time, and location, and group. Gordon also points out that in any large, complex, multi-group nation, cultural uniformity is impossible and should not be expected. When any sizable segment of a multi-group society has developed a rather unique way of life, from which members receive status and recognition, norms, sources of support and identification, and meaningful reference groups, it is proper to call that way of life a subculture. Members of a subculture are at least partially aware of the parent, conventional culture and its norms, and they can and usually do behave, on occasion, in terms of the larger culture.

At the present stage of theory building or concept construction relating to subcultures there is no sharp, consensual definition, no "right" or unique definition or usage. James Coleman speaks of adolescent youth culture, and Earl Bell uses the concept of college subculture; Schrag, Sykes, Clemmer, and others make free use of the term prison subculture, and Cohen, Cloward, Ohlin, Miller, Bloch, and others write about delinquent subcultures. Liebow describes the subculture of Negro street-corner men. Schnur uses the concept of the subculture of the dope addict, and so in a somewhat different way does Finestone. Killmorgan's study of the Amish subculture handles the concept differently than Cohen does in his description of homosexual subculture, and my own attempts to describe as a subculture the way of life of the permanent migratory agricultural laborer differ from both.

It is somewhat of a theoretical oversimplification, but a useful one, to think of a subculture as a group adaptation system to a situation, which situation and which adaptation are largely shared by members of a sizeable group. This adaptation system, this subculture, is transmitted by socialization, either generationally or by peers.

One properly may study many aspects of a subculture; its sources, its pervasiveness and limits, its traits, its relation to the parent culture or cultures, or its relation to other subcultures; or one may bend one's efforts toward an exact description of the structure, functions and traits of a subculture. This paper chooses to consider two somewhat related subcultures, and to attempt synoptically to analyze how these cultures compare with each other and with the parent cultures. Thus it deals with the concept "subculture of poverty," especially as described by Oscar Lewis, and also with that more well-known amalgam of the Mexican and American cultures which is properly called the Mexican American subculture.

That the concept "subculture" is a useful and proper one does not prove that every set of traits or behaviors one discovers can properly be called a subculture. It is well agreed that it is proper to apply this concept to the subculture of Mexican Americans; there is less agreement, but considerable evidence, that the subculture of poverty also is a reality.

There is one point of view which holds that no subculture of poverty exists. The "subcultural" uniformities observed among the poor are seen as resulting from strictly limited choices, not subcultural imperatives. Thus the repetitive behavior among delinquent groups is seen as logical and predictable responses to certain conditions, rather than as subcultural patterns. Liebow, in *Tally's Corner,* illustrates this point of view excellently in regard to the observed "serial monogamy" of the lower class urban Negro.[2] His interpretation is that one may look at the succession of mates as being a cultural referent, and by so doing use it as an illustration of subcultural behavior. Liebow believes a more correct appraisal, however, is that this is not a subcultural difference, but rather is to be seen as a series of marriages, each of which it was hoped would follow the pattern of the larger culture, but each of which failed, and was then followed by another which failed, and so on. The succession of mates pattern, using this approach, is seen as seeking the cultural model of the larger society, but being a series of failures to achieve it. Purported subcultural generation similarities in behavior need not result from cultural transmission, but may result instead from failure in both generations to achieve the behavioral patterns of the larger society.

This paper recognizes but does not address itself to the above conflict of opinion. The underlying assumptions presented here are only that a Mexican American subculture does exist, and that a hypothetical model of a subculture of poverty has been presented by Oscar Lewis. Regardless of what is found about the eventual validity of the Lewis model, it can be compared to the Mexican American actuality. Conversely, one legitimately could compare either with Liebow's "failure model" if he wished.

Oscar Lewis, in his *Five Families* says, "Poverty in modern nations . .

becomes a dynamic factor which . . . creates a subculture of its own. One can speak of the culture of the poor, for it has its own modalities and distinctive social and psychological consequences for its members . . . The culture of poverty cuts across regional, rural-urban and even national boundaries. I am impressed . . . by the remarkable similarities in family structure, the nature of kinship ties, the quality of husband-wife and parent-child relations, time orientation, spending patterns, value systems, and the sense of community found in lower class settlements in London, in Puerto Rico, in Mexico City slums, in Mexican villages, and among lower class Negroes in the United States." [3]

Michael Harrington seems correct in *The Other America* [4] when he suggests that what he calls the "old poor" were part of the parent culture, albeit a disadvantaged part; but that many persons in those groups he calls the "new poor" are so alienated from the parent culture that they now possess a separate culture of their own, the subculture of poverty. One of Oscar Lewis' contributions in his book *La Vida* is that a distinction must always be made between poverty, which is financial, and the subculture of poverty, which is a way of life shared by some poverty-stricken people. [5] He repeats this in an article in the *Scientific American*, [6] and hypothesizes that in some societies, especially either primitive or socialistic ones, there is no subculture of poverty; on the other hand, in rapidly developing but not as yet fully developed countries, the great majority of the urban poor participate in the subculture of poverty. He estimates that possibly 20% of poverty-stricken people in the United States participate in the subculture of poverty. The highlander from Appalachia, for example, may be very poor, but he has his own subculture, which in many ways differs from the subculture of poverty. A considerably higher proportion of the Spanish speaking people in the United States partake of the Mexican American subculture. With this as a background, let us first partially describe and analyze the Mexican American subculture.

The parent Mexican culture, which is itself something of an amalgam, has been introduced into the United States by immigrants each year for many decades. Those persons entering our borders from Mexico tend to find themselves in a different situation requiring new adaptations for success. In actual practice the immigrant and his children retain, or retain in modified character, some of the old Mexican culture traits. Also they accept and use, either directly or in modified character, some of the new Anglo culture traits. The result is a mixture, a reasonably fluid one, of the parent cultures, a mixture which quite properly may be considered a Mexican American subculture, with traits and characteristics which stem from both cultures, but whose configuration is unique, and whose amalgamation certainly is different from either of the parent cultures. Because of its dynamic nature, this hybrid culture is shifting, changing in time and place, and Mexican Americans do not all partake of it to the same degree. A number of studies show that there is a significant correlation between generation and culture.

There are marked exceptions, but as a broad generalization the first generation is the most Mexican in culture patterns and the third and fourth generations are nearest the Anglo culture. Celia Heller, in her *Mexican American Youth* [7] says, "Both in the rate and the degree of acculturation and assimilation Mexican Americans are among the least 'Americanized' of all the ethnic groups in the United States." It is only a mild digression to report regarding intermarriage that Burma's studies in southern California and those made by Gary Cretser at California Polytechnic and those by Dr. Joan Moore at U.C.L.A. show that intermarriage of Anglos and Mexican Americans definitely increases by generation and by assimilation out of the Mexican American subculture.

Now, a direct application of this theoretical construct to actual life: in any subculture the family is a major aspect, and it is an excellent example for the comparative analysis we are making. In the subculture of poverty anywhere, the family tends to be matrifocal. In the Negro subculture the tendency is toward a matrifocal, matriarchal family. Frazier, Johnson, Price, and Moynihan have amply described this matriarchy. In the Puerto Rican subculture of poverty described by Lewis, the tendency is toward a matrifocal but patriarchal family; however, in the Mexican American subculture there is a tendency toward a matrifocal family with a mixture of patriarchal and equalitarian authority; considerably more equalitarian than in the case of the parent Mexican culture, for example.

In both the subculture of poverty and the Mexican American subculture the family is not a very stable unit. In each, sexual experimentation begins soon and early pregnancies are common, both in and out of either legal or consensual marriage. The legitimacy of children is likely to be in terms of whether they are recognized or supported by the father. If the family separates, the children in most cases will remain with the mother or her family, which contributes to the aforementioned matrifocal character of the family in the subculture of poverty. In each subculture there is the phenomenon Oscar Lewis [8] calls "the syndrome of the absent father," in which children may grow up either physically or psychically without a real paternal model. Each characteristic above is less true in the Mexican American subculture than in the subculture of poverty, but the differences are of degree, not of kind.

A major difference does exist, however, because in the stable Mexican American home there is a likelihood that the children will receive some training in respectful conduct, and obedience. This carries over into adulthood, and Mexican American men commonly are more polite to each other than an Anglo man is to an Anglo woman. Good manners stand high in the list of desirable attributes. A Mexican American who tried the lower class Negro subcultural behavior called "playing the dozens" would find himself involved in immediate physical violence.

Unlike the subculture of poverty pattern, Mexican American marriage is at least supposed to arise from a deep romantic attachment, and ideally is expected to be permanent. The father and mother are both expected to love the children. The mother ideally will be affectionate, pampering, self-sacrificing; she will minister both to the creature comforts and the psyches of the children and father; she plays a "love" role and is a love symbol. The father, according to the Mexican American subculture, provides for his family, defends them, and wields authority by virtue of his position as husband and father. A man who does not fulfill these expectations loses status in his own eyes as well as those of his community. While these ideal patterns are never fully followed in practice, the existence of the ideal provides a major family difference in the Mexican American subculture and the general subculture of poverty.[9]

A culture trait which illustrates well the overlapping which sometimes occurs between subcultures is that of time and tempo. In the parent American culture one rushes about; wasting time is evil; we say, "time is money." This does not make sense either from the standpoint of the Mexican American subculture or the subculture of poverty. The organization of one's day into short, sharply defined, significant units fits the affluent American parent culture where time is a valuable commodity, but it is not part of either of the subcultures. "Busyness" is a virtue in the American culture; it is an affliction in both subcultures.

Common to both subcultures is an orientation toward the present, with little practical concern for the future or the "deferred gratification pattern." In each subculture this is closely related to what the parent Anglo culture calls fatalism, the feeling that one's destiny is not in one's own hands, so that ambition is not particularly useful because it is so rarely fulfilled.[10] This attitude, which is evaluated negatively by the parent culture, nevertheless has a real subcultural value in helping persons whose upward mobility is blocked, to accept their inability to rise without ego damage to themselves.

Still another trait shared, but differentially shared, is what Weber called the Protestant Ethic. Oversimplified this is the idea that God wants you to work hard, to be thrifty, to be honest, to get ahead financially; and the proof of God's blessing was that one did prosper financially by ambition, hard work, thrift, etc. A typical proverb was "The devil finds work for idle hands to do." All this has been reasonably well incorporated into the parent Anglo culture; in fact, for many Anglos it is a pivotal element of their culture, but it is not a pivotal element of either Mexican or Mexican American cultures. To most Mexican Americans work is a necessary evil; they work because they have to; they may work very hard, but not because they want to; they work to get the things they need and want; and when these needs are satisfied, they are usually willing to stop work. Moreover, the Mexican American is not as materialistic in his values and goals as the Anglo; the Mexican American values, class for class, cover a broader spectrum, and hence material elements are a smaller proportion of the total than is true for the parent Anglo culture.

The same general situation exists for each subculture vis-à-vis education.

Both believe that education ought to be pragmatic, that it usually is not, and that anything beyond grade school is of little use except as it helps get a better job. Although there is a considerable verbalized favoring of education by parents in both subcultures, children are allowed to do poorly, to attend irregularly, and to drop out early.[11] The whole problem is exacerbated by the Mexican American's language difficulty, which usually results in his being lingual, but one to three years retarded in achievement. This problem is doubly accentuated for the children of migratory agricultural workers.

In studies of the subculture of poverty one of the commonly remarked upon traits is the feeling of inferiority, of helplessness, of dependence and of a lack of individual pride and dignity. Social workers and community organizers often give considerable priority to attempts to instill feelings of pride and self-worth in their clients. To the extent this is true, we have a major difference in the two subcultures being compared. In the Mexican American subculture pride, *dignidad,* is very important. It results in an unwillingness to push oneself where one is not wanted, and a desire always to appear at one's best. Sometimes the personal pride which a semi-literate, poverty stricken Mexican American demonstrates seems quite unreasonable by the standards of middle class culture. Many a Mexican American teenage male has dropped out of school, or been kicked out, because of an attitude which he considered necessary pride, but Anglo teachers interpreted incorrectly as insubordination or insolence.

In both subcultures there is the pride of the male in his maleness. In the Mexican American culture, where it is particularly strong, it is called *machismo.* The term does not translate well; it connotes virility, pride, and a self-concept of personal worth in one's own eyes as well as those of his peers. *Machismo* may be demonstrated differently by different persons—for some it means physical violence, the necessity to defend all slights to one's "honor" by fists or knife; for other men it may mean the sexual conquest of many women, and especially being "irresistible" to women. For others it may mean what to an Anglo is reckless disregard for money, through gambling, by buying unneeded articles, or using up one's paycheck setting up drinks for one's friends. Because real or claimed male sexual prowess is always a part of *machismo,* sexual promiscuity is likely to be considered a sort of necessary evil for males, and to some degree for females as well, although there is no question but that there is a very real double standard both in theory and in practice. When an outsider counts the large number of women whom it is claimed have submitted to the overwhelming sexuality of a group of Mexican American males, and then counts the virtuous wives and the virginal sisters and daughters, the total may be about 200% of the actual female population of a Mexican American community!

It is of practical significance that an acceptance by the Mexican American community of *machismo* leads to a differential attitude toward male juvenile delinquency. Mixed with what both Mexican Americans and Anglos consider delinquent acts is other behavior which the Mexican American community sees primarily as a young male proving his manhood, reaching for adulthood, sowing his wild oats, or "getting it out of his system." Whatever you wish to call it, to the Mexican American community this boy is not doing anything which will interfere seriously with his later becoming a good husband and father and provider. The middle class Anglo community, which makes the laws and enforces them, may see the same behavior as clear delinquency, leading, unless punished and stopped, to a life of crime, degradation, and worthlessness. This also illustrates the frequent difficulty of communication and understanding between a subculture and a parent culture.

Walter Miller has suggested that lower class young people live in a world where "trouble" of some sort is an ever present probability.[12] This expectation of "trouble" plays four roles: (1) a self-fulfilling prophecy which helps bring about trouble or at least prevents significant efforts to avoid it; (2) a pre-acceptance of failure, and a consequent bolstering of the ego by other (subcultural) means in order to avoid ego damage; (3) a behavior syndrome (not staying in school or vocational training, not trying for a better job, not really expecting a stable, happy marriage) based on an expectation of failure; (4) a willingness to engage in acts of deviancy, delinquency, or crime which are known to be likely to lead to trouble, because trouble is likely to come, anyway.

In the important characteristic of social interaction, both subcultures seem to have much in common. In each case there is a tendency for narrow social horizons and relatively few formal, organized social relationships. Interaction is with the family, the gang, the corner clique, and in the case of the Mexican American possibly also with the *palomilla* or with the variant of the god-parent pattern called *compadrazco*. In neither subculture is there likely to be much close interaction with neighbors, fellow workers, or groups like the P.T.A. Comparatively, social relationships are few but deep, and possibly quite emotional. Liebow found that the "friendship webs" among his Negro corner men were likely to be based largely on propinquity, to be supported somewhat by friendship behavior but much more by verbalized protestations, to be more fluid than stable, more shallow than deep (despite vows to the contrary), and "as if friendship is . . . a private agreement between two people to act 'as if,' rather than a real relationship between persons."[13] In the middle class parent culture friendship relations are more numerous, more formal, rarely verbalized, and often organization oriented. Related to this trait is the often-noted tendency of many Mexican Americans to tear down rather than support indigenous leaders who arise. Mexican Americans possess many close-knit, small groups, but they have difficulty in achieving lasting, large scale organizations. In fact, it has been said that one of the proofs of the increasing Anglization of Mexican Americans is that they are beginning to set up Anglo-type organizations, with accepted pragmatic priorities and pragmatic, planned means to achieve perceived goals.

Social interaction in the Mexican American subculture, however, has a qualitative difference as well, with a greater stress on politeness, pleasantness, and mutual agreeability. Conversation should be pleasant, and unless the topic is one on which the person feels emotionally, in the Mexican American subculture far more than in the general subculture of poverty, one is likely to agree to someone else's statement, observation or conversational gambit. In the Mexican American subculture one is more likely to say "yes" when he really means "maybe" or even "no." This degree of pleasant agreement, of keeping one's temper, of not reacting aggressively, is not found to the same degree in the subculture of poverty. This quality is not hypocrisy, but it does make for greater superficiality. There is also at least one psychiatric interpretation that because of this characteristic Mexican Americans are "better able to endure stress passively." [14]

The final trait of both subcultures which will be analyzed is that of language and communication; that is, language *differences* between the subcultures and the parent culture. The difference is threefold: first, there are different connotations for the same concepts or mind symbols. If X speaks certain concepts to Y and thereby evokes the same symbols in Y's mind which are in X's mind, then successful and accurate communication has taken place. However, if using the same word or concept evokes different mind symbols, or no mind symbol, then only confusion can result. This is crucial because it is exactly this level at which communication often breaks down between a social worker and a client, between members of an O.E.O. committee from different sides of the tracks, or between an interviewer and a subcultural interviewee. There are important subcultural differences in words and symbols as compared to the parent culture. Secondly, the subculture of poverty furnishes its members with a paucity of word symbols compared to the number in the parent culture. Again and again there are reports from Headstart and similar programs that children from the subculture of poverty cannot converse on many subjects because they simply do not know the words. When they do learn the words, they communicate adequately. Third, the language of the subculture of poverty tends to be stark, realistic, simple, crude, coarse, concrete and is likely to be limited in expressiveness in that it lacks richness of adjectives, adverbs, nouns and verbs, and does not readily express nuances, subtleties, or shades of meaning. Subcultural language is one of the most definitive criteria for drawing boundaries between subcultures and their parent cultures. Even the more transitory types of subcultures such as the adolescent subculture, the homosexual subculture, or the prison subculture have markedly different languages or argots which have been collected and analyzed. One of the best illustrations that there is a true Mexican American subculture is the very real mixture of Spanish and English words in the same sentence, or even the mixture of Spanish and English within the same word: *Que pasa con el* pick-up? *No se. Parece el* timing *o el* carburetor, *o los esparke ploges; y tiene un* flat.

To conclude, one might pause and try to answer the question, "What are the futures of these two subcultures in the United States?" First, it appears that both subcultures do exist. It is true that when a phenomenon first comes under special study, the fact of learning more about it may give the false impression that the phenomenon is increasing when it is really knowledge and identification of the phenomenon which are increasing. Both subcultures seem realities, rather than abstract figments of sociological theory.

Like any pattern of generational socialization, or like any vicious circle, subcultures tend to perpetuate themselves until some outside force breaks in upon them. For analytical purposes one can view social work and community organization as normative attempts to assimilate persons into the middle-class-oriented culture. This analysis views social work as essentially a matter of norms, attitudes, values, and behavior. Then, from this assimilation point of view, it is accurate to say there has been only limited success in such assimilation. In the case of the subculture of poverty, for example, there seems to be an increasing proportion of welfare recipients who are the children of welfare recipients. We have no presently successful way of keeping a flow of people moving out of the inner city ghettos which are the strongholds of the subculture of poverty. This is an index, possibly, of the strength of socialization into the subculture of poverty, and the difficulty of assimilating people out of that subculture into the parent culture. As an oversimplification, and still viewing social work primarily as a normative process, it would seem that we are successful in preventing from entering the subculture of poverty a sizable proportion of what the social workers call "single problem" families, but that we are very unsuccessful in assimilating out of the subculture of poverty any appreciable number of those "multiple problem" families who are the hard core of the subculture of poverty. Certainly the findings of the National Advisory Commission on Civil Disorders, the so-called Kerner Report, point toward an increase rather than a decrease of the significance of subcultural differences and divergences.

In the case of the Mexican American subculture, the future seems somewhat different. First, the number of bearers of the Mexican parent culture entering the United States in the future is likely to be somewhat lessened as the new immigration legislation is enforced. This is important because for many persons the Mexican American culture has been a temporary adjustment on the way to a relatively full assimilation into the Anglo parent culture. Contrariwise, numerous aspects of the Mexican American culture are in areas of indifference to or mesh well with the middle class Anglo culture and hence are subject to no normative stress. Fourth, what limited commitment America has to the concept of cultural pluralism and culture diversity applies much better to the Mexican American subculture than to the subculture of poverty, with the result that there is less concern about securing conformity from the members of the Mexican American subculture. Finally, in it much more than in the subculture of poverty, participants reject assimilation on grounds of self-identity, self-realization, and the "equal value" of the subculture. When to this is added the strong belief of many Mexican Americans that one can and even should choose for himself the best elements from the subculture and both parent cultures, no viable conclusion seems to exist except that the Mexican American subculture will continue into the foreseeable future.

Notes

[1] Milton Gordon, *Assimilation in American Life,* New York, Oxford University Press, 1964, pp. 33–34.

[2] Elliot Liebow, *Tally's Corner,* Boston, Little, Brown, and Co., 1967, pp. 219–223.

[3] Oscar Lewis, *Five Families,* New York, New American Library, 1959, p. 16.

[4] Michael Harrington, *The Other America,* New York, The Macmillan Co., 1963.

[5] Oscar Lewis, *La Vida,* New York, Random House, 1965, p. xlviii.

[6] Oscar Lewis, "The Culture of Poverty," *Scientific American,* Oct. 1966, pp. 19–25.

[7] Celia Heller, *Mexican American Youth,* New York, Random House, 1966, p. 4.

[8] Oscar Lewis, *La Vida, op. cit.,* p. 18.

[9] Liebow, on the basis of his study of Negro street corner men, might deny the validity of this statement on the grounds that the poverty stricken Negro male is aware of this role and ideally would prefer to play it. In practice, he is so sure he will fail, however, that his efforts are so weak as to set in motion a self-fulfilling prophecy. G. D. Suttles, although he does not address himself directly to the subculture of poverty concept in *The Social Order of the Slum,* does propose that the dimensions of the life style of the poor are determined primarily by the struggle for social and economic security as a bulwark against the ravages of economic insecurity, rather than being determined by ethnic subcultural patterns per se.

[10] Liebow interprets present time orientation not as being part of any subculture, but rather as a situation-specific phenomenon present when persons are in distress. Whatever its origin, this present time orientation is very common among persons participating in the subculture of poverty or the lower class Negro subculture.

[11] In all fairness, when children in fact are falling more seriously behind each year, or are not equipped to do the work expected, e.g., a boy who still reads at the third grade level although he has been "passed" to the tenth grade, dropping out may not be irrational.

[12] Walter B. Miller, "Lower Class Culture as a Generating Milieu of Gang Delinquency," *Journal of Social Issues,* XIV, No. 3 (1958), pp. 5–19.

[13] Liebow, *op. cit.,* p. 207.

[14] Unpublished document from the Filfillon Clinic, Los Angeles, 1967.

PART X

SETTLEMENT: RURAL AND URBAN

Rural life in the United States has been associated with basic American values, supposedly fostering individualism, communion with nature, high valuation of work, and an emphasis on family and religion. City life has been considered inimical to the development of these characteristics. As American society becomes increasingly urbanized, however, both by urban expansion and by population movement to the cities, such simple distinctions become less and less useful. We need, rather, information on the influence of sheer numbers. What is the effect of being in a high school class of fifteen hundred as opposed to fifty? The department store clerk may have more human contact in a day than does the farmer in a month. On the other hand, the number of children in one's family or the number of old friends may be greater in rural areas. Furthermore, there are many types of areas in which people live and work. In urban sociology a number of area typologies such as the concentric zone, multiple nuclei, and vector models exist. Land use in more rural areas varies as well. Differences in behavior among the residents of these various areas is an important subject of sociological inquiry. The differences between large apartment complex living, single homes, and the residences between these extremes also merit attention. The rural-urban dichotomy is not as simple as it once was. The emergence of suburban communities on the fringes of urban areas has had considerable impact on the development of a perspective which attempts to encompass the best of both worlds. The recent advent of rural communes is perhaps an indication that the shift in population from rural to urban America is not exclusively a one-way movement.

Springdale's Image of Itself

ARTHUR J. VIDICH AND JOSEPH BENSMAN

In this selection Vidich and Bensman describe some of the views which small-town residents have of their community and of rural and city life in general. A community study of "Springdale," the fictitious name of a rural community of about 2500 inhabitants in upstate New York, provided the data for this description. Springdalers perceive rural life as equalitarian and characterized by "honesty, fair play, trustworthiness, good-neighborliness, helpfulness, sobriety, and clean-living." They believe that their community in particular is the best place to live. Their images of cities are decidedly negative and often stereotypical. The central feeling, however, is that these things do not affect life in Springdale. Neighborliness is considered to be a prime virtue. According to Vidich and Bensman, this view ". . . reinforces itself, serves as a model for achievement, and adds to the essential appearance of community warmth."

There exists a public ideology of equality in Springdale. Public discussions of economic differences are considered improper. Work, rather than wealth, merits respect. To these researchers "social equality based on the humanness of rural life" characterizes the appearance of this community. "Springdale" offers an idyllic and one-sided picture of rural life. Keep in mind, however, that only the part of the Springdalers' perspective that applies to views about their community is being emphasized.

"Just Plain Folks"

WHEN one becomes more intimately acquainted with the people of Springdale, and especially with the more verbal and more prominent inhabitants, one finds that they like to think of themselves as "just plain folks." The editor of the paper, in urging people to attend public meetings or in reporting a social event, says, "all folks with an interest" should attend or "the folks who came certainly had a good time." Almost any chairman of a

---

Pp. 30–42 from "Springdale's Image of Itself," in *Small Town in Mass Society: Class, Power and Religion in a Rural Community,* by Arthur J. Vidich and Joseph Bensman (Princeton University Press, rev. edn., 1968; Princeton Paperback, 1968). Reprinted by permission of Princeton University Press.

public gathering addresses his audience as folks—"all right folks, the meeting will get underway"—and the interviewer in his work frequently encounters the same expression—"the folks in this community," "the townfolk," "the country folk," "good folks," and "bad folks." Depending on context, the term carries with it a number of quite different connotations.

First and foremost, the term serves to distinguish Springdalers from urban dwellers, who are called "city people," an expression which by the tone in which it is used implies the less fortunate, those who are denied the wholesome virtues of rural life. City people are separated from nature and soil, from field and stream, and are caught up in the inexorable web of impersonality and loneliness, of which the public statement in Springdale is: "How can people stand to live in cities?" In an understandable and ultimate extension of this valuation one may occasionally hear references to the rural or country folk, in contrast to the villagers, the former being regarded by Springdalers as the "true folk."

The self-designation as "folk" includes everyone in the community; by its generality of reference it excludes neither the rich nor the poor, for everyone can share equally in the genuine qualities ascribed by the term. This is not to say that the community does not recognize scoundrels and wastrels in its own environment; quite the contrary, the scoundrel and allied types become all the more noticeable in the light of the dominant genuineness of rural life. It is rather to say that the standard of judgment by which character is assessed in Springdale includes no false or artificial values. To be one of the folks requires neither money, status, family background, learning, nor refined manners. It is, in short, a way of referring to the equalitarianism of rural life.

The term also includes a whole set of moral values: honesty, fair play, trustworthiness, good-neighborliness, helpfulness, sobriety, and clean-living. To the Springdaler it suggests a wholesome family life, a man whose spoken word is as good as a written contract, a community of religious-minded people, and a place where "everybody knows everybody" and "where you can say hello to anybody." The background image of urban society and city people gives force and meaning to the preferred rural way of life.

Rural Virtues and City Life

The sense of community-mindedness and identification has its roots in a belief in the inherent difference between Springdale and all other places, particularly the nearby towns and big cities. For the Springdaler surrounding towns all carry stigmata which are not found in Springdale: the county seat is the locus of vice and corruption, the Finnish settlement is "red," University Town is snobbish and aloof, and Industrial Town is inhuman, slummy and foreign. In the big city the individual is anonymously lost in a hostile and dog-eat-dog environment. Being in the community gives one a distinct feeling of living in a protected and better place, so that in spite of occasional internal quarrels and the presence of some unwholesome characters one frequently hears it said that "there's no place I'd rather live . . . there isn't a better place to raise a family . . . this is the best little town in the whole country." In the face of the outer world, Springdalers "stick up for their town."

The best example of community identification occurs when newspapers of neighboring towns choose to publicize negative aspects of Springdale life: making banner headlines over the dismissal of a school principal, publishing the names of youthful criminal offenders who come from good families. In such instances, irrespective of issue or factional position, anyone with an interest in the community comes to its defense: "We may have our troubles, but it's nothing we can't handle by ourselves—and quicker and better if they'd leave us alone." A challenge to the image of Springdale as a preferred place cuts deep and helps to re-create the sense of community when it is temporarily lost.

It is interesting that the belief in the superiority of local ways of living actually conditions the way of life. Springdalers *"make an effort* to be friendly" and *"go out of their way* to help newcomers." The newspaper always emphasizes the positive side of life; it never reports local arrests, shotgun weddings, mortgage foreclosures, lawsuits, bitter exchanges in public meetings, suicides or any other unpleasant happening. By this constant focus on warm and human qualities in all public situations, the public character of the community takes on those qualities and, hence, it has a tone which is distinctly different from city life.

Relationships with nearby towns, in spite of the occasional voicing of hostility, also have a sympathetic and friendly competitive aspect. No one in Springdale would gloat over another town's misfortunes, such as a serious fire or the loss of an industry. Athletic rivalries have long histories and although there is a vocabulary of names and yells for "enemies," these simply stimulate competitiveness and arouse emotions for the night of the contest. No one takes victory or defeat seriously for more than a day or two and only in a very rare instance is there a public incident when outsiders visit the town. "Nobody really wants trouble with other towns."

When one goes beyond neighboring communities, the Springdaler leaps from concrete images of people and places to a more generalized image of metropolitan life. His everyday experiences give him a feeling of remoteness from the major centers of industry, commerce and politics. His images are apt to be as stereotyped as those that city people hold concerning the country. Any composite of these images would certainly include the following:

1. Cities breed corruption and have grown so big and impersonal that they are not able to solve the problems they create.

2. Cities are an unwholesome environment for children and families, and have had an unhealthy effect on family morals.
3. Urban politicians and labor leaders are corrupt and represent anti-democratic forces in American life.
4. Washington is a place overridden with bureaucrats and the sharp deal, fast-buck operator, both of whom live like parasites off hard-working country folk.
5. Industrial workers are highly paid for doing little work. Their leaders foment trouble and work against the good of the country.
6. Cities are hotbeds of un-American sentiment, harbor the reds and are incapable of educating their youth to Christian values.
7. Big universities and city churches are centers of atheism and secularism and in spite of occasional exceptions have lost touch with the spiritual lesson taught by rural life.
8. Most of the problems of country life have their origin in the effects which urban life has on rural ways.

What is central, however, is the feeling of the Springdaler that these things do not basically affect him. While he realizes that machinery and factory products are essential to his standard of life and that taxation and agricultural policy are important, he feels that he is independent of other features of industrial and urban life, or, better, that he can choose and select only the best parts. The simple physical separation from the city and the open rural atmosphere make it possible to avoid the problems inherent in city life. Personal relations are face-to-face and social gatherings are intimate, churchgoing retains the quality of a family affair, the merchant is known as a person, and you can experience the "thrill of watching nature and the growth of your garden." Springdalers firmly believe in the virtues of rural living, strive to maintain them and defend them against anyone who would criticize them.

"Neighbors Are Friends"

Almost all of rural life receives its justification on the basis of the direct and personal and human feelings that guide people's relations with each other. No one, not even a stranger, is a stranger to the circumambience of the community. It is as if the people in a deeply felt communion bring themselves together for the purposes of mutual self-help and protection. To this end the community is organized for friendliness and neighborliness, so much so that the terms "friends" and "neighbors" almost stand as synonyms for "folk."

In its most typical form neighborliness occurs in time of personal and family crises—birth, death, illness, fire, catastrophe. On such occasions friends and neighbors mobilize to support those in distress: collections of money are taken, meals are prepared by others, cards of condolence are sent. A man whose house or barn has burned may unexpectedly find an organized "bee" aiding in reconstruction. Practically all organizations have "sunshine" committees whose sole purpose is to send greeting cards. These practices are so widespread and ultimately may include so many people that an individual, unable to acknowledge all this friendliness personally, will utilize the newspaper's "card of thanks" column to express his public appreciation.

Borrowing and "lending back and forth" is perhaps the most widespread act of neighborliness. Farmers say they like to feel that "in a pinch" there is always someone whom they can count upon for help—to borrow tools, get advice, ask for labor. In spite of the advent of mechanized and self-sufficient farming and consequently the reduction of the need for mutual aid, the high public value placed on mutual help is not diminished. Though a farmer may want to be independent and wish to avoid getting involved in other people's problems and, in fact, may privately resent lending his machinery, it is quite difficult for him to refuse to assist his neighbor if asked. Even where technological advance has made inroads on the need for the practice, to support the public creed remains a necessity.

For housewives in a community where "stores don't carry everything" domestic trading and borrowing is still a reality; they exchange children's clothing and *do* borrow salt and sugar. In Springdale they say "you never have to be without . . . if you need something bad enough you can always get it: of course, sometimes people overdo it and that makes it bad for everybody, but after a while you find out who they are." The process of selectively eliminating the bad practitioners makes it possible to keep the operation of the practice on a high plane.

Neighborliness has its institutional supports and so is given a firm foundation. Ministers and church groups make it a practice to visit the sick in hospitals and homes and to remember them with cards and letters, and all other organizations—the Legion, Masons, Community Club, book clubs—designate special committees to insure that remembrance is extended to the bereaved and ill. The Legion and Community Club "help our own" with baskets of food and clothing at Christmas time and organize fund drives to assist those who are "burned out." The ideology of neighborliness is reflected in and reinforced by the organized life of the community.

To a great extent these arrangements between friends and neighbors have a reciprocal character: a man who helps others may himself expect to be helped later on. In a way the whole system takes on the character of insurance. Of course some people are more conscious of their premium payments than others and keep a kind of mental bookkeeping on "what they owe and who owes them what," which is a perfectly permissible practice so long as one does not openly confront others with unbalanced accounts. In fact, the man who knows "exactly where he stands" with his friends and neighbors is better advised than the one who "forgets and can't keep track." The person who is unconsciously oblivious of what others do for him and distributes his own kindness and favor without thinking is apt to alienate both those whom he owes and doesn't owe. The etiquette for getting and giving in Springdale is an art that requires sensitive adjustments to the moods, needs and expectations of others. This ability to respond appropriately in given situations is the sign of the good neighbor. That this sensitivity is possessed by large numbers of people is attested to by the fact that friendliness and neighborliness contribute substantially to the community's dominant tone of personalness and warmth.

Of course, everyone does not participate equally or at the same level in being a good friend and neighbor. Deviations and exceptions are numerous. Neighborliness is often confined to geographical areas and to socially compatible groups. The wife of the lawyer is on neighborly terms with others like herself rather than with the wife of a carpenter. Farmers necessarily have less to do with people in the village and teachers are more apt to carry on friendly relations with each other. Those who are not willing to both give and take find themselves courteously eliminated from this aspect of local life. "People who are better off" simply by possessing sufficient resources do not find it necessary to call on friends and neighbors for help, though "everyone knows that if you went and asked them for something, they'd give it to you right away." Others have a more "independent turn of mind" and "will get by with what they have, no matter what, just to be free of mind"; the ideology of neighborliness is broad enough to include them "so long as they don't do anyone harm." The foreign elements, particularly the Poles, limit their everyday neighboring to their own group, but still by community definitions they are good neighbors because "you can always trust a Pole to deal square . . . if they owe you anything, they will always pay you back on time." Some folks are known as "just good people" who by choice "keep to themselves." By isolating themselves within the community they neither add nor detract from the neighborly quality of community life and so do not have an effect on the public character of the town.

The only group which does not fall within the purview of the conception of friend and neighbor is the 10 percent of the population that live "in shacks in the hills." The people who live in shacks "can't be trusted"; "they steal you blind"; "if you're friendly to them, they'll take advantage of you"; "if you lend them something you'll never see it again"; "they're bad . . . no good people . . . live like animals." Hence by appropriately extending the social definition to give it a broader base than mutual aid, all groups in the community, except the shack people, fulfill the image of good friend and neighbor. The self-conception then reinforces itself, serves as a model for achievement and adds to the essential appearance of community warmth.

Good Folks and Bad Folks

"Of course, there are some people who just naturally have a dirty mouth. You'll find them anywhere you go and I'd be lying if I said we didn't have a few here." The "dirty mouth" is a person who not only fabricates malicious

gossip about his enemies but also wantonly and carelessly spreads his fabri-
cations. He commits the double *faux pas* of being deliberately malicious and
of not observing the etiquette of interpersonal relations, and he is perhaps
the most despised person in the community.

There are a whole range of personal qualities which are almost unani-
mously disapproved in Springdale. These are identified in the person

"who holds a grudge . . . who won't ever forget a wrong done to him."

"who can't get along with other people . . . who won't ever try to be
friendly and sociable."

"who gives the town a bad name . . . always raising up a ruckus . . .
always trying to stir up trouble."

"who trys to be something he isn't . . . the show-off . . . the braggart."

"who thinks he's better than everybody else . . . who thinks he's too
good for the town . . . who thinks he's a cut above ordinary folks."

"who is bossy . . . thinks his ideas are always the best . . . tries to
run everything . . . wants to be the center of attention all the time
without working for it."

"who makes money by cheating people . . . who hasn't made his money
honestly . . . you can't figure out where he got all that money."

"whom you can't trust . . . whose word is no good . . . who doesn't
do what he says he was going to do . . . who doesn't carry through
on anything."

In almost the exact reverse, the qualities of a good member of the community are found in the person who

"forgives and forgets . . . lets bygones be bygones . . . never dredges
up the past . . . lets you know that he isn't going to hold it against you."

"is always doing something for the good of the town . . . gives willingly
of his time and money . . . supports community projects . . . never
shirks when there's work to be done."

"gets along with everybody . . . always has a good word . . . goes out
of his way to do a good turn . . . never tries to hurt anybody . . . always has a smile for everybody."

"is just a natural person . . . even if you know he's better than you, he
never lets you know it . . . never tries to impress anybody just because
he has a little more money . . . acts like an ordinary person."

"always waits his turn . . . is modest . . . will work along with everybody else . . . isn't out for his own glory . . . takes a job and does it well without making a lot of noise."

"worked hard for what he's got . . . deserves every penny he has . . . doesn't come around to collect the first day of the month . . . you know he could be a lot richer."

"stands on his word . . . never has to have it in writing . . . does what he says . . . if he can't do it he says so and if he can he does it . . . always does it on time."

Springdalers affirm that on the whole most people in the community have these qualities. They are the qualities of "average folk" and "we like to think of ourselves as just a little above the average." "Average people can get things done because nobody has any high-blown ideas and they can all work together to make the community a better place to live."

What is interesting about the usual definitions of good and bad people are the types that are excluded entirely. At this level those who go unrecognized, even in the negative statements, are the intellectuals, the bookish and the introverts. In a community that places a high premium on being demonstrably average, friendly and open, the person who appears in public and "doesn't say much" is a difficult character to understand: "he's a good fellow, but you never know what he's thinking." "Book reading and studying all the time," while they have a place, "shouldn't be carried too far . . . you have to keep your feet on the ground, be practical." The intellectual is respected for his education, is admired for his verbal facility and sometimes can provide the right idea, but nevertheless he is suspect and "shouldn't be allowed to get into positions of responsibility." It is apparent that where stereotyped public definitions do not easily fit, non-conformity is still tolerated so long as it does not seriously interfere with the workings of the town.

In the community setting the test case of the toleration and sympathy for non-conformity lies in attitudes toward cranks, psychotics and "odd" personalities: the ex-minister who writes poetry, the hermit who lives in the woods, the woman obsessed with the legal correctness of her husband's will, the spinster who screams at callers, the town moron and the clinical catatonic. Needless to say these represent only a small percentage of the population. The point is that Springdale is able to absorb, protect and care for them; when in the infrequent instance they intrude on the public scene, they are treated with the same sympathy and kindness accorded a child. So long as non-conformity does not interfere with the normal functioning of the town, no price is exacted from the non-conformist. At the worst, the non-conforming types are surrounded by humor. They become local "characters" who add color and interest to the everyday life of the community; because they are odd and different, they are always available as a standard conversational piece. In this way the community demonstrates its kindness and "lives and lets live."

"We're All Equal"

With the exception of a few "old cranks" and "no goods," it is unthinkable for anyone to pass a person on the street without exchanging greetings. Customarily one stops for a moment of conversation to discuss the weather and make inquiries about health; even the newcomer finds others stopping to greet him. The pattern of everyone talking to everyone is especially characteristic when people congregate in groups. Meetings and social gatherings do not begin until greetings have been exchanged all around. The person who feels he is above associating with everyone, as is the case with some newcomers from the city, runs the risk of being regarded a snob, for the taint of snobbishness is most easily acquired by failing to be friendly to everyone.

It is the policy of the Community Club to be open to "everyone, whether dues are paid or not" and hardly a meeting passes without a repetition of this statement. Those who are the leaders of the community take pride in this organization specifically because it excludes no one, and this fact is emphasized time and again in public situations. Wherever they can, community leaders encourage broad participation in all spheres of public life: everyone is urged and invited to attend public meetings and everyone is urged to "vote not as a duty, but as a privilege." The equality at the ballot box of all men, each according to his own conscience, in a community where you know all the candidates personally, where votes can't be bought and where you know the poll-keepers, is the hallmark of equality that underpins all other equality. "Here no man counts more than any other"; this is stated in every affirmation of rural political equality—"if you don't like the rascals, use your vote to kick them out."

The social force of the idea finds its most positive expression in a negative way. The ladies of the book clubs, the most exclusive and limited membership groups in Springdale, find themselves in the ambiguous position of having to be apologetic for their exclusiveness. Because they are select in a community which devalues standoffishness, they are the only groups that are defensive in meeting the rest of the public. To the observer, they explain, "It's not that we want to be exclusive. It's just that sixteen is all you can manage in a book club. If anybody wants to be in a book club, she can start her own, like the Wednesday Group." By the same token they receive a large share of resentment; any number of vulgar expressions refer to this feminine section of the community.

The public ideology of equality has its economic correlates. One must not suppose that inequalities in income and wealth go unnoticed; rather, they are quite closely watched and known in Springdale. However, such differences, as in the image of the frontier community, are not publicly weighed and evaluated as the measure of the man.

In everyday social intercourse it is a social *faux pas* to act as if economic inequalities make a difference. The wealthiest people in town, though they have big homes, live quite simply without servants. The serviceman, the delivery boy and the door-to-door canvasser knock at the front door and, though they may feel somewhat awkward on carpeted floors, are asked to enter even before starting their business. A man who flaunts his wealth, or demands deference because of it, is out of tune with a community whose "upper class" devalues conspicuous consumption and works at honest pursuits. "What makes the difference is not the wealth but the character behind it."

It is not a distortion to say that the good man is the working man and in the public estimation the fact of working transcends, indeed explains, economic differentials; work has its own social day of judgment and the judgment conferred is self-respect and respectability. Work, in the first instance, is the great social equalizer, and the purest form of work which serves as a yardstick for all other work is farm work. By this mechanism the "hard-working poor man" is superior to the "lazy rich man." The quotation marks are advised and indicate the hypotheticalness of the case because in common usage the two, work and wealth, go together. Where they don't it is because of misfortune, catastrophe, bad luck or simply because the man is young and work has not yet had a chance to pay its dividends. But even wealth is the wrong word. Work is rather juxtaposed beside such terms as rich, solvent, well-off; wealth implies more economic differentiation than Springdalers like to think exists in their community. Thus, the measure of a man, for all public social purposes, is the diligence and perseverance with which he pursues his economic ends; the "steady worker," the "good worker," the "hard worker" in contrast to the "fly-by-night schemer," the "band-wagon jumper," and the "johnny-come-lately." For the Springdaler the test case is the vulgar social climber, the person who tries to "get in with the better people" by aping them in dress and possessions which only money can buy. In spite of the social and economic differences visible to the outside observer, the pervading appearance of the community is that of a social equality based on the humanness of rural life.

Social Conditions for Rationality:

How Urban and Rural Courts

Deal with the Mentally Ill

THOMAS J. SCHEFF

Is urban life related to a more rational perspective than rural life? Scheff deals with this issue through a study of the judicial decision-making process concerning the commitment and hospitalization of the allegedly mentally ill. He finds that the proceedings of urban courts are less rational than those of rural courts. In three of the four metropolitan courts observed there was no serious investigatory purpose in the procedures for institutionalizing the mentally ill. Rather, the procedure was ceremonial since appearance in court virtually assured commitment. Scheff lists the arguments which were offered by metropolitan court officials in defense of these procedures, and he rebuts a blank acceptance of any of these arguments.

The author's description of the handling of mental patient cases in the urban courts indicates a low level of rational decision making. In one court the only contact between judge and patient was in the preliminary hearing which always consisted of the same three questions and averaged 1.6 minutes in length. Although three of the rural courts conducted no proceedings at all, there did appear to be a degree of rationality in the proceedings of most nonmetropolitan courts. Scheff offers four reasons for this difference: (1) metropolitan courts lack time—a resource needed for rational decision making; (2) there is more political pressure on the metropolitan judge to lock up a person defined as potentially dangerous than there is on the rural judge; (3) to the metropolitan judge every patient is a stranger, while the rural judge is often familiar with the case—making him more careful in his decision; (4) the greater psychiatric sophistication of the metropolitan judge leads him to predefine the alleged mentally ill person as "sick" and in "need of help." Furthermore, since the judge feels that the psychiatrist's decision is paramount, and vice versa,

Reprinted from the *American Behavioral Scientist,* Volume VII, No. 7 (March, 1964), pp. 21–24, by permission of the publisher, Sage Publications, Inc.

neither assumes the responsibility for the patient's incarceration. Scheff concludes by suggesting other areas in which rational decision making is problematic.

FORMAL legal procedure is a highly developed instrument for arriving at rational decisions concerning complex and uncertain situations. Legal procedures are institutionalized means for substantial rationality, i.e., for obtaining "intelligent insight into the inter-relations of events in a given situation." [1] Like scientific method, trial procedures and due process serve to control and reduce, though not to eliminate, bias in situations of uncertainty.

One of the central concerns in the sociology of knowledge has been the attempt to determine the social conditions under which substantial rationality occurs. This paper pursues the question by discussing some of the variation in the procedures for hospitalizing and committing persons alleged to be mentally ill, in metropolitan and non-metropolitan jurisdictions in a Midwestern state. My sources of information were interviews with judges, psychiatrists, and other officials in 20 of its counties and observations of judicial hearings, psychiatric interviews, and other procedures in four of the jurisdictions, those courts with the largest number of mental hearings. [2]

Non-rational Procedures and Urban Courts

The major result of our study was the conclusion that in three of the four metropolitan courts, the civil procedures for hospitalizing and committing the mentally ill had no serious investigatory purpose, but were ceremonial in character. Although all four of the courts carried through various procedures required by statute, the psychiatric examination, the judicial hearing, and other steps, hospitalization and treatment appeared to be virtually automatic after the patient had been brought to the attention of the courts. [3]

In nine of the 16 other counties, however, these civil procedures appeared to serve at least some investigatory purpose. At one or more points in the screening process (the application for judicial inquiry, the psychiatric examination, the judicial hearing) detailed investigation was conducted and patients were released or their release was seriously considered.

These observations suggest that for civil procedures concerning mental illness, rationality is associated with a non-metropolitan setting, and bias and the presumption of illness with metropolitan jurisdictions. Before exploring some of the reasons for this relationship, it is necessary to justify the contention that the procedures used in the metropolitan jurisdictions are not rational.

Most of the officials whom we interviewed did not disagree with our description of the typical events in these procedures, but argued that the procedures were justified by larger considerations of a medical and humanitarian character. Their arguments can be summarized in the following five statements:

(1) The condition of mentally ill persons deteriorates rapidly without psychiatric assistance.
(2) Effective psychiatric treatments exist for most mental illnesses.
(3) Unlike surgery, there are no risks involved in involuntary psychiatric treatment: it either helps or is neutral, it can't hurt.
(4) Exposing a prospective mental patient to questioning, cross-examination, and other screening procedures exposes him to the unnecessary stigma of trial-like procedures, and may do further damage to his mental condition.
(5) There is an element of danger to self or others in mental illness. It is better to risk unnecessary hospitalization than the harm the patient might do himself or others.

Although these statements appear to be plausible, statements rebutting each of them are equally plausible.

(1) The assumption that psychiatric disorders usually get worse without treatment rests on very little other than evidence of an anecdotal character. There is just as much evidence that most acute psychological and emotional upsets are self-terminating.[4]
(2) It is still not clear, according to systematic studies evaluating psychotherapy, drugs, etc., that most psychiatric interventions are any more effective, on the average, than no treatment at all.[5]
(3) There is very good evidence that involuntary hospitalization may affect the patient's life—his job, his family affairs, etc. There is some evidence that too hasty exposure to psychiatric treatment may convince the patient that he is "sick," prolonging what might have been an otherwise transitory episode.[6]
(4) This assumption is correct, as far as it goes. But it is misleading because it fails to consider what occurs when the patient who does not wish to be hospitalized is forcibly treated. Such patients often become extremely indignant and angry, particularly in the event, which is common, that they are deceived into coming to the hospital on a pretext.
(5) The element of danger is usually exaggerated both in amount and degree. In the psychiatric survey of new patients in state mental hospitals, conducted as part of the present study, danger to self or others was mentioned in less than a fourth of the cases. Furthermore, in those cases where danger is mentioned, it is not always clear that the risks involved are greater than those encountered in ordinary social life. This issue has been discussed by Ross, an attorney: A truck driver with a mild neurosis who is "accident prone" is probably a greater danger to society than most psychotics; yet, he will not be committed for treatment, even if he would be benefited. The community expects a certain amount of dangerous activity. I suspect that as a class, drinking drivers are a greater danger than the mentally ill, and yet the drivers are tolerated or punished with small fines rather than indeterminate imprisonment.[7]

These latter five statements indicate that arriving at a rational decision concerning hospitalization is not usually a simple and expedient matter. In marginal cases, which frequently arise, a rational disposition would require careful investigation and assessment. Yet in many of the marginal cases we observed, investigation and assessment were quite limited or absent entirely. Some examples of the attitudes and actions of the officials illustrate this point.

Examination and Hearing

The examination by the psychiatrists in the urban courts virtually never led to extensive knowledge of the facts. These examinations appeared to be short (about 10 minutes on the average), hurried, and largely routine. Yet the psychiatrists we interviewed uniformly stated that such a short interview was almost worthless with all but the most extreme cases.

One of the examiners, after stating in an interview (before we observed his examinations) that he usually took about thirty minutes, stated: "It's not remunerative. I'm taking a hell of a cut. I can't spend 45 minutes with a patient. I don't have the time, it doesn't pay." In the examinations that we observed, this physician actually spent 8, 10, 5, 8, 8, 7, 17, and 11 minutes with the patients, or an average of 9.2 minutes.

The key step in the entire sequence is the judicial hearing. Yet these hearings were usually limited to the minimum act required by statute. In one urban court (the court with the largest number of cases) the only contact between the judge and the patient was in a preliminary hearing. This hearing was held with such lightning rapidity (1.6 minutes average) and followed such a standard and unvarying format that it was obvious that the judge made no attempt to use the hearing results in arriving at a decision. He asked three questions uniformly: "How are you feeling?" "How are you being treated?", and "If the doctors recommend that you stay here a while, would you cooperate?" No matter how the patient responded, the judge immediately signified that the hearing was over, cutting off some of the patients in the middle of a sentence.

Even in those courts where some attempt was made to ascertain the circumstances surrounding the case, the judge did not appear to assess the meaning of the circumstances in order to make a rational disposition. For example, in another urban court, the judge seemed to use the hearing to gather information. He attempted to relax the patient, reassure him, get his point of view, and test his orientation. (Of the four courts, the hearings in this court lasted longest: 12 minutes average, as against 1.6, 6, and 9 minutes in the other three courts.) Yet in all the hearings we observed (43), including those in which the judge himself demonstrated that the patient's behavior and orientation were unexceptionable, the judge went on to commit to or continue hospitalization.

The way in which this same judge reacted to a difficult case can be used to illustrate another facet of the concept of substantial rationality. The examining psychiatrists had recommended commitment for the patient, a policeman, whom they had diagnosed as severely depressed. Another psychiatrist (not one of the examiners) had once told the judge that there was always the risk of suicide in severe depression. This patient, however, had no history of suicide attempts, and strenuously denied any suicidal intention. The patient had retained his own attorney (which is unusual) who pleaded at the hearing that the patient be released to the care of a private physician, because if he were committed he would almost certainly lose his job. The judge refused to consider the plea stating that if there were *any* risk of suicide, he did not want to be responsible for having released the patient.

Reaching a decision in this case could never be a simple matter, since it requires the evaluation and comparison of a number of disparate considerations: what is the likelihood that the patient would commit suicide if released? Is this likelihood greater than those which are or should be tolerated in the community? What is the likelihood that the patient would lose his job if committed? How should this likelihood be weighed relative to the likelihood of suicide? This latter question particularly is a complex question, involving joint consideration of likelihoods and "costs" of seemingly incommensurate events. Decisions which meet the criteria of substantial rationality thus require consideration of diverse kinds of information, and equally important, the judicious comparison and weighing of the information.

The Attempt at Rationality in Rural Courts

In some of the non-metropolitan counties we investigated, these kinds of questions were addressed to some degree. In the application for judicial inquiry or in the judicial hearing, or, in two jurisdictions, in the psychiatric screening, serious investigation and assessment were undertaken. In three of the less populated counties, the judge himself heard the testimony before the application for judicial inquiry, and in some cases had the county sheriff or other officer investigate the situation even before issuing an application. In the hearing, several of the judges required that the relatives and the examining psychiatrists be present, allowing for the possibility of confrontation and cross-examination.

It is also true, however, that the procedures in three of the non-metropolitan counties were even more preemptory than in the metropolitan courts. In these three courts, the person alleged to be mentally ill was simply conveyed to the distant state mental hospital, after the application for judicial inquiry had been accepted, without examination or hearing. This occurred even though the Attorney General had issued the opinion that this procedure was illegal.

Allowing for a number of such exceptions, the findings discussed above point to the absence of substantial rationality in the metropolita. courts, and the presence of a degree of rationality in the non-metropolitan courts. On the basis of this relationship, we can now consider some of the conditions which facilitate and impede substantial rationality.

Conditions Favoring Substantial Rationality

Although we ordinarily think of the metropolitan court as being richer in resources than the rural court, there is one commodity which is very rare in the city, *time*. The metropolitan courts are faced with an enormous volume of cases: court B, the extreme example, handled some 14,000 cases (mostly misdemeanors) in 1962. In these circumstances, and with limited numbers of court officers, individual attention to a single case is usually not feasible.

The second condition concerns political pressure. In both rural and metropolitan courts there is considerable public sentiment about cases in which the judge or other official errs by releasing a person whom subsequent events prove should have been retained. There is considerably less sentiment against the opposite error, of retaining a person who should have been released. Officials therefore appear much more careful about erroneously releasing than they are about erroneously retaining. Our impression, however, was that this is less of an issue in rural areas. The absence of sensational treatment of mistakes in the newspapers, and the generally greater personal familiarity with facts of the case, makes for less political pressure on the rural judge.

Court officials in rural areas also usually have greater personal familiarity with the situation than do urban judges. In the typical rural case the judge will personally know the person alleged to be mentally ill, or at least a member of his family. This greater familiarity may lead to delay and investigation that would be absent in the urban court, where virtually every person who comes before the court is a stranger.

Personal familiarity with the patient affects not only the official's knowledge about the patient, but also his attitude. From our interviews, we gained the impression that it was much easier for the officials to consider cases using the impersonal framework of mental illness if they did not know the patient personally. This consideration operated in conjunction with the fact that the rural judges tended to be less psychiatrically sophisticated than the judges in the metropolitan courts, and to use a commonsense framework in most cases.

A fourth condition is also related to the ideological framework within which the officials considered the case. The greater psychiatric sophistication of the metropolitan judges reduces the rationality of their decision procedures in two ways. By establishing the assumption that the person alleged to be mentally ill is "sick" and in "need of help," extra-legal humanitarian considerations are introduced, and tend to break down the investigatory and adjudicatory nature of the court procedures. Introduction of the idea of disease also diffuses the responsibility for a final decision between the judge, who has the legal authority for the decision, and the psychiatrist, whom the judge assumes to have authority by virtue of his technical knowledge. We received the impression that the consequence of this diffusion of authority is that neither the judge nor the psychiatrist assumes the responsibility for decision to continue hospitalization, but each believes that his own decision is unimportant, since the real authority rests with the other.

A final condition is related to the resources of the patient. We formed the impression that an articulate patient, who knew his rights and who had the ability to retain his own lawyer, had a much better chance to obtain summary release from the hospital than the patient who was inarticulate, was unaware of his legal rights, and did not have the money or knowledge to retain a lawyer to represent him.

The Incidence of Mental Illness

To summarize these five conditions, we found that in jurisdictions characterized by a small volume of cases, only moderate public pressures against releasing patients erroneously, personal acquaintance with the patient or his family, little psychiatric sophistication, and where the patient has resources for defending himself against the allegations about him, substantial rationality is a characteristic of civil commitment procedures. In jurisdictions with large numbers of cases, strong public pressures against erroneous releases, lack of personal acquaintance with the persons alleged to be mentally ill, and few resources for patients to defend themselves against the allegations, hospitalization and treatment are virtually automatic once the complaint has been made to the court.

To the extent that all five of the latter conditions are present, hospitalization, far from being a rational decision, becomes an irreversible process. Since the procedures used in the metropolitan areas account for the majority of patients coming to the mental hospitals, the irreversibility of hospitalization has implications which deserve more attention than can be given them here. First, this discussion suggests that the well-established relationship between urban areas and high rates of mental illness may be a product less of greater incidence of mental illness than of the absence of official screening in urban areas.

Secondly, and more generally, since the entire legal and medical decision-making process in metropolitan areas appears to be largely ceremonial, the important decision in hospitalization is that which is made before the complaint comes to the court, i.e., in the community, and particularly in the family. The crucial decision of diagnosis, hospitalization, and treatment is thus made usually not by an expert, but by a layman: the relatives or others who bring the case before the court. This suggests that understanding of the incidence of mental illness requires study of the operation of social control in the community.

Conditions for Rationality in Other Settings

Turning from the topic of decision-making in mental illness to broader concerns, it might be worthwhile to consider some of the conditions discussed here in connection with rationality in other areas. The recent New York bail studies suggest that much the same situation applies to the handling of criminal deviants in the New York legal system as was discussed here.[8] Decisions concerning scientific matters may also be usefully considered within this framework. The decisions of an advisory board evaluating research findings, or, more frequently, research proposals, might be analyzed in this way, to ascertain the effect of volume of cases, political pressure because of erroneous decisions, the ideological framework of the members of the board, the diffusion of responsibility, the effect of personal acquaintance with the applicants, and the power and resources available to the applicants.

A pair of examples will illustrate one of the many parallels between judicial and scientific decision-making which bear on the issue of the conditions for rationality. The diffusion of responsibility between the judge and the psychiatrist, discussed above, puts the judge in the position of having the legal, but not the technical, authority to make final dispositions in hospitalization and commitment. Apparently, however, this conflict is consciously used by some judges who privately have doubts about the seriousness of the psychiatric examination. These judges justify their decisions by referring to the recommendations of the psychiatrists, and thus use the psychiatrists as "fronts" for their own purposes.

Apparently, like psychiatry, the name of science is regularly invoked as a bureaucratic mechanism of defense. The following testimony is by a missile expert, Werner von Braun, before a congressional investigating committee: [9]

> . . . a physics professor may know a lot about the upper atmosphere, but when it comes to making a sound appraisal of what missile schedule is sound and how you can phase a research and development program into industrial production, he is pretty much at a loss. . . . When confronted with a difficult decision involving several hundred million dollars, and of vital importance to the national defense many Pentagon executives like to protect themselves. It helps if a man can say, "I have on my advisory committee some Nobel prize winners, or some very famous people that everybody knows." And if these famous people then sign a final recommendation, the executive feels, "Now, if

something goes wrong, nobody can blame me for not having asked the smartest men in the country what they think about this."

The parallel suggested by these two examples points to regularized organizational techniques for manipulating avowedly rational means to serve non-rational ends, and suggests the need for studies explicitly formulated to determine the social conditions for substantial rationality. Although rationality is a difficult and elusive concept, such studies could help to clarify it and bring empirical materials to bear on an important problem.

Notes

[1] Karl Mannheim, *Man and Society in an Age of Reconstruction* (London: Routledge, 1935), 52–54.

[2] The larger study on which this paper is based is described in "Legal and Medical Decision-making in the Hospitalization of the Mentally Ill: A Field Study" (in press). For a detailed description of the psychiatric screening procedures, see the author's "The Societal Reaction to Deviance: Ascriptive Elements in the Psychiatric Screening of Mental Patients," *Social Problems* (in press).

[3] Similar findings are reported in Herbert J. Jaffe, "Civil Commitment of the Mentally Ill," *Pennsylvania Law Review*, 107 (March 1959), 668–85; John H. Hess and Herbert E. Thomas, "Incompetency to Stand Trial; Procedures, Results and Problems," paper presented at the 1962 convention of the American Psychiatric Association; Luis Kutner, "The Illusion of Due Process in Commitment Proceedings," *Northwestern University Law Review*, 57 (September–October 1962), 383–99; David Mechanic, "Some Factors in Identifying and Defining Mental Illness," *Mental Hygiene*, and Paul D. Rheingold, "Mental Incapacity 46 (January 1962), 66–74; Robert Ross Mezer and Incompetency: A Psycho-Legal Problem," *American Journal of Psychiatry*, 118 (1962), 827–31 (note particularly the comment on p. 829 regarding the presumption of incapacity).

[4] For a review of epidemiological studies of mental disorder see Richard J. Plunkett and John E. Gordon, *Epidemiology and Mental Illness*. Most of these studies suggest that at any given point in time, psychiatrists find a substantial proportion of persons in normal populations to be "mentally ill." One interpretation of this finding is that much of the deviance detected in these studies is of short duration. For a further discussion of this question, see Thomas J. Scheff, "The Role of the Mentally Ill and the Dynamics of Mental Disorder: A Research Framework," *Sociometry* 26 (December 1963), 436–53.

[5] For an assessment of the evidence regarding the effectiveness of electroshock, drugs, psychotherapy, and other psychiatric treatments, see H. J. Eysenck, *Handbook of Abnormal Psychology*, Basic Books, New York, 1961, Part III.

[6] For examples from military psychiatry, see Albert J. Glass, "Psychotherapy in the Combat Zone," in *Symposium on Stress* (Washington, D.C.: Army Medical Service Graduate School, 1953), and B. L. Bushard, "The U.S. Army's Mental Hygiene Consultation Service," in *Symposium on Preventive and Social Psychiatry*, 15–17 (April 1957) Walter Reed Army Institute of Research, Washington, D.C., pp. 431–43. For a discussion of essentially the same problem in the context of a civilian mental hospital, cf. Kai T. Erikson, "Patient Role and Social Uncertainty—A Dilemma of the Mentally Ill," *Psychiatry*, 20 (1957), pp. 263–75.

[7] Hugh Allen Ross, "Commitment of the Mentally Ill: Problems of Law and Policy," *Michigan Law Review*, 57 (1959), 145–1018, p. 962.

[8] Charles E. Ares, Ann Rankin, and Herbert Sturz, "The Manhattan Bail Project: An Interim Report on the Use of Pre-Trial Parole," *New York University Law Review*, 38 (January 1963), 67–95.

[9] U.S. Senate Hearings, *Inquiry into Satellite and Missile Programs*, 1958, quoted in Merton J. Peck and Frederick M. Scherer, *The Weapons Acquisition Process: An Economic Analysis* (Boston: Harvard U. Press, 1962), p. 245.

The Metropolis and Mental Life

GEORG SIMMEL

In this lecture, originally published in 1903, Georg Simmel analyzes some important aspects of the relationship between city life and human perspective. The metropolis demands a larger amount of consciousness than does rural life. It creates a "heightened awareness" in its inhabitants. The intellectual nature of man becomes highly developed as a defense against metropolitan life. In particular, the city individual's perspective is related to his inextricable participation in a money economy and in social relations of great number and diversity. Simmel sees an intrinsic connection between a money economy and the dominance of intellect. Their intimate interrelationship, however, precludes our knowing which first determined which. Metropolitan existence also demands punctuality, calculability, exactness, and a blasé attitude, defined by the author as "incapacity to react to new situations with the appropriate energy." As a protection from both indifference and indiscriminate suggestibility, the city dweller has a perspective characterized by antipathy.

Simmel also considers the metropolis as the locale for personal freedom. He focuses on primary groups, economic specialization, and deviance in this analysis. The city is the arena where the individual's role in society is being worked out since it brings forth, on the one hand, what is universal in man and, on the other, what is unique and irreplaceable in any individual. Much of Simmel's discussion, based on his observations of European society at the turn of the century, appears applicable to most of contemporary industrial society. Fortunately, he indicated those aspects of city life which determine the metropolitan perspective. His analysis, therefore, merits consideration wherever such factors are found.

THE deepest problems of modern life derive from the claim of the individual to preserve the autonomy and individuality of his existence in the face of overwhelming social forces, of historical heritage, of external culture, and of the technique of life. The fight with nature which primitive man has to wage for his *bodily* existence attains in this modern form its latest trans-

Reprinted with permission of The Macmillan Company from *The Sociology of Georg Simmel* translated by Kurt Wolff. Copyright 1950 by The Free Press.

formation. The eighteenth century called upon man to free himself of all the historical bonds in the state and in religion, in morals and in economics. Man's nature, originally good and common to all, should develop unhampered. In addition to more liberty, the nineteenth century demanded the functional specialization of man and his work; this specialization makes one individual incomparable to another, and each of them indispensable to the highest possible extent. However, this specialization makes each man the more directly dependent upon the supplementary activities of all others. Nietzsche sees the full development of the individual conditioned by the most ruthless struggle of individuals; socialism believes in the suppression of all competition for the same reason. Be that as it may, in all these positions the same basic motive is at work: the person resists to being leveled down and worn out by a social-technological mechanism. An inquiry into the inner meaning of specifically modern life and its products, into the soul of the cultural body, so to speak, must seek to solve the equation which structures like the metropolis set up between the individual and the super-individual contents of life. Such an inquiry must answer the question of how the personality accommodates itself in the adjustments to external forces. This will be my task today.

The psychological basis of the metropolitan type of individuality consists in the *intensification of nervous stimulation* which results from the swift and uninterrupted change of outer and inner stimuli. Man is a differentiating creature. His mind is stimulated by the difference between a momentary impression and the one which preceded it. Lasting impressions, impressions which differ only slightly from one another, impressions which take a regular and habitual course and show regular and habitual contrasts—all these use up, so to speak, less consciousness than does the rapid crowding of changing images, the sharp discontinuity in the grasp of a single glance, and the unexpectedness of onrushing impressions. These are the psychological conditions which the metropolis creates. With each crossing of the street, with the tempo and multiplicity of economic, occupational and social life, the city sets up a deep contrast with small town and rural life with reference to the sensory foundations of psychic life. The metropolis exacts from man as a discriminating creature a different amount of consciousness than does rural life. Here the rhythm of life and sensory mental imagery flows more slowly, more habitually, and more evenly. Precisely in this connection the sophisticated character of metropolitan psychic life becomes understandable —as over against small town life which rests more upon deeply felt and emotional relationships. These latter are rooted in the more unconscious layers of the psyche and grow most readily in the steady rhythm of uninterrupted habituations. The intellect, however, has its locus in the transparent, conscious, higher layers of the psyche; it is the most adaptable of our inner forces. In order to accommodate to change and to the contrast of phenomena, the intellect does not require any shocks and inner upheavals; it is only through such upheavals that the more conservative mind could accommodate to the metropolitan rhythm of events. Thus the metropolitan type of man—which, of course, exists in a thousand individual variants—develops an organ protecting him against the threatening currents and discrepancies of his external environment which would uproot him. He reacts with his head instead of his heart. In this an increased awareness assumes the psychic prerogative. Metropolitan life, thus, underlies a heightened awareness and a predominance of intelligence in metropolitan man. The reaction to metropolitan phenomena is shifted to that organ which is least sensitive and quite remote from the depth of the personality. Intellectuality is thus seen to preserve subjective life against the overwhelming power of metropolitan life, and intellectuality branches out in many directions and is integrated with numerous discrete phenomena.

The metropolis has always been the seat of the money economy. Here the multiplicity and concentration of economic exchange gives an importance to the means of exchange which the scantiness of rural commerce would not have allowed. Money economy and the dominance of the intellect are intrinsically connected. They share a matter-of-fact attitude in dealing with men and with things; and, in this attitude, a formal justice is often coupled with an inconsiderate hardness. The intellectually sophisticated person is indifferent to all genuine individuality, because relationships and reactions result from it which cannot be exhausted with logical operations. In the same manner, the individuality of phenomena is not commensurate with the pecuniary principle. Money is concerned only with what is common to all: it asks for the exchange value, it reduces all quality and individuality to the question: How much? All intimate emotional relations between persons are founded in their individuality, whereas in rational relations man is reckoned with like a number, like an element which is in itself indifferent. Only the objective measurable achievement is of interest. Thus metropolitan man reckons with his merchants and customers, his domestic servants and often even with persons with whom he is obliged to have social intercourse. These features of intellectuality contrast with the nature of the small circle in which the inevitable knowledge of individuality as inevitably produces a warmer tone of behavior, a behavior which is beyond a mere objective balancing of service and return. In the sphere of the economic psychology of the small group it is of importance that under primitive conditions production serves the customer who orders the good, so that the producer and the consumer are acquainted. The modern metropolis, however, is supplied almost entirely by production for the market, that is, for entirely unknown purchasers who never personally enter the producer's actual field of vision. Through this anonymity the interests of each party acquire an unmerciful matter-of-factness; and the intellectually calculating economic egoisms of both parties need not fear any deflection because of the imponderables of personal relationships. The money economy dominates the metropolis; it has displaced the last survivals of domestic production and the direct barter of goods; it minimizes, from day to day, the amount of work ordered by customers. The matter-of-fact attitude is obviously so intimately interrelated with the money economy, which is dominant in the metropolis, that nobody can say whether the intellectualistic mentality first promoted the money economy or whether the latter determined the former. The metropolitan way of life is certainly the most fertile soil for this reciprocity, a point which I shall document merely by citing the dictum of the most eminent English constitutional historian: throughout the whole course of English history, London has never acted as England's heart but often as England's intellect and always as her moneybag!

In certain seemingly insignificant traits, which lie upon the surface of life, the same psychic currents characteristically unite. Modern mind has become more and more calculating. The calculative exactness of practical life which the money economy has brought about corresponds to the ideal of natural science: to transform the world into an arithmetic problem, to fix every part of the world by mathematical formulas. Only money economy has filled the days of so many people with weighing, calculating, with numerical determinations, with a reduction of qualitative values to quantitative ones. Through the calculative nature of money a new precision, a certainty in the definition of identities and differences, an unambiguousness in agreements and arrangements has been brought about in the relations of life-elements—just as externally this precision has been effected by the universal diffusion of pocket watches. However, the conditions of metropolitan life are at once cause and effect of this trait. The relationships and affairs of the typical metropolitan usually are so varied and complex that without the strictest punctuality in promises and services the whole structure would break down into an inextricable chaos. Above all, this necessity is brought about by the aggregation of so many people with such differentiated interests, who must integrate their relations and activities into a highly complex organism. If all clocks and watches in Berlin would suddenly go wrong in different ways, even if only by one hour, all economic life and communication of the city would be disrupted for a long time. In addition an apparently mere external factor: long distances, would make all waiting and broken appointments result in an ill-afforded waste of time. Thus, the technique of metropolitan life is unimaginable without the most punctual integration of all activities and mutual relations into a stable and impersonal time schedule. Here again the general conclusions of this entire task of reflection become obvious, namely, that from each point on the surface of existence—however closely attached to the surface alone—one may drop a sounding into the depth of the psyche so that all the most banal externalities of life finally are connected with the ultimate decisions concerning the meaning and style of life. Punctuality, calculability, exactness are forced upon life by the complexity and extension of metropolitan existence and are not only most intimately connected with its money economy and intellectualistic character. These traits must also color the contents of life and favor the exclusion of those irrational, instinctive, sovereign traits and impulses which aim at determining the mode of life from within, instead of receiving the general and precisely schematized form of life from without. Even though sovereign types of personality, characterized by irrational impulses, are by no means impossible in the city, they are, nevertheless, opposed to typical city life. The passionate hatred of men like Ruskin and Nietzsche for the metropolis is understandable in these terms. Their natures discovered the value of life alone in the unschematized existence which cannot be defined with precision for all alike. From the same source of this hatred of the metropolis surged their hatred of money economy and of the intellectualism of modern existence.

The same factors which have thus coalesced into the exactness and minute precision of the form of life have coalesced into a structure of the highest impersonality; on the other hand, they have promoted a highly personal subjectivity. There is perhaps no psychic phenomenon which has been so unconditionally reserved to the metropolis as has the blasé attitude. The blasé attitude results first from the rapidly changing and closely compressed contrasting stimulations of the nerves. From this, the enhancement of metropolitan intellectuality, also, seems originally to stem. Therefore, stupid people who are not intellectually alive in the first place usually are not exactly blasé. A life in boundless pursuit of pleasure makes one blasé because it agitates the nerves to their strongest reactivity for such a long time that they finally cease to react at all. In the same way, through the rapidity and contradictoriness of their changes, more harmless impressions force such violent responses, tearing the nerves so brutally hither and thither that their last reserves of strength are spent; and if one remains in the same milieu they have no time to gather new strength. An incapacity thus emerges to react to new sensations with the appropriate energy. This constitutes that blasé attitude which, in fact, every metropolitan child shows when compared with children of quieter and less changeable milieus.

This physiological source of the metropolitan blasé attitude is joined by another source which flows from the money economy. The essence of the blasé attitude consists in the blunting of discrimination. This does not mean that the objects are not perceived, as in the case with the half-wit, but rather that the meaning and differing values of things, and thereby the things themselves, are experienced as insubstantial. They appear to the blasé person in an evenly flat and gray tone; no one object deserves preference over any other. This mood is the faithful subjective reflection of the completely internalized money economy. By being the equivalent to all the manifold things in one and the same way, money becomes the most frightful leveler. For money expresses all qualitative differences of things in terms of "how much?" Money, with all its colorlessness and indifference, becomes the common denominator of all values; irreparably it hollows out the core of things, their individuality, their specific value, and their incomparability. All things float with equal specific gravity in the constantly moving stream of money. All things lie on the same level and differ from one another only in the size of the area which they cover. In the individual case this coloration, or rather discoloration, of things through their money equivalence may be unnoticeably minute. However, through the relations of the rich to the objects to be had for money, perhaps even through the total character which the mentality of the contemporary public everywhere imparts to these objects, the exclusively pecuniary evaluation of objects has become quite considerable. The large cities, the main seats of the money exchange, bring the purchasability of things to the fore much more impressively than do smaller localities. That is why cities are also the genuine locale of the blasé attitude. In the blasé attitude the concentration of men and things stimulate the nervous system of the individual to its highest achievement so that it attains its peak. Through the mere quantitative intensification of the same conditioning factors this achievement is transformed into its opposite and appears in the peculiar adjustment of the blasé attitude. In this phenomenon the nerves find in the refusal to react to their stimulation the last possibility of accommodating to the contents and forms of metropolitan life. The self-preservation of certain personalities is bought at the price of devaluating the whole objective world, a devaluation which in the end unavoidably drags one's own personality down into a feeling of the same worthlessness.

Whereas the subject of this form of existence has to come to terms with it entirely for himself, his self-preservation in the face of the large city demands from him a no less negative behavior of a social nature. This mental attitude of metropolitans toward one another we may designate, from a formal point of view, as reserve. If so many inner reactions were responses to the continuous external contacts with innumerable people as are those in the small town, where one knows almost everybody one meets and where one has a positive relation to almost everyone, one would be completely atomized internally and come to an unimaginable psychic state. Partly this psychological fact, partly the right to distrust which men have in the face of the touch-and-go elements of metropolitan life, necessitates our reserve. As a result of this reserve we frequently do not even know by sight those who have been our neighbors for years. And it is this reserve which in the eyes of the small-town people makes us appear to be cold and heartless. Indeed, if I do not deceive myself, the inner aspect of this outer reserve is not only indifference but, more often than we are aware, it is a slight aversion, a mutual strangeness and repulsion, which will break into hatred and fight at the moment of a closer contact, however caused. The whole inner organization of such an extensive communicative life rests upon an extremely varied hierarchy of sympathies, indifferences, and aversions of the briefest as well as of the most permanent nature. The sphere of indifference in this hierarchy is not as large as might appear on the surface. Our psychic activity still responds to almost every impression of somebody else with a somewhat distinct feeling. The unconscious, fluid and changing character of this impression seems to result in a state of indifference. Actually this indifference would be just as unnatural as the diffusion of indiscriminate mutual suggestion would be unbearable. From both these typical dangers of the metropolis, indifference and indiscriminate suggestibility, antipathy protects us. A latent antipathy and the preparatory stage of practical antagonism effect the distances and aversions without which this mode of life could not at all be led. The extent and the mixture of this style of life, the rhythm of its emergence and disappearance, the forms in which it is satisfied—all these, with the unifying motives in the narrower sense, form the inseparable whole of the metropolitan style of life. What appears in the metropolitan style of life directly as dissociation is in reality only one of its elemental forms of socialization.

This reserve with its overtone of hidden aversion appears in turn as the form or the cloak of a more general mental phenomenon of the metropolis: it grants to the individual a kind and an amount of personal freedom which has no analogy whatsoever under other conditions. The metropolis goes back to one of the large developmental tendencies of social life as such, to one of the few tendencies for which an approximately universal formula can be discovered. The earliest phase of social formations found in historical as well as in contemporary social structures is this: a relatively small circle firmly closed against neighboring, strange, or in some way antagonistic circles. However, this circle is closely coherent and allows its individual members only a narrow field for the development of unique qualities and free, self-responsible movements. Political and kinship groups, parties and religious associations begin in this way. The self-preservation of very young associations requires the establishment of strict boundaries and a centripetal unity. Therefore they cannot allow the individual freedom and unique inner and outer development. From this stage social development proceeds at once in two different, yet corresponding, directions. To the extent to which the group grows—numerically, spatially, in significance and in content of life—to the same degree the group's direct, inner unity loosens, and the rigidity of the original demarcation against others is softened through mutual relations and connections. At the same time, the individual gains freedom of movement, far beyond the first jealous delimitation. The individual also gains a specific individuality to which the division of labor in the enlarged group gives both occasion and necessity. The state and Christianity, guilds and political parties, and innumerable other groups have developed according to this formula, however much, of course, the special conditions and forces of the respective groups have modified the general scheme. This scheme seems to me distinctly recognizable also in the evolution of individuality within urban life. The small-town life in Antiquity and in the Middle Ages set barriers against movement and relations of the individual toward the outside, and it set up barriers against individual independence and differentiation within the individual self. These barriers were such that under them modern man could not have breathed. Even today a metropolitan man who is placed in a small town feels a restriction similar, at least, in kind. The smaller the circle which forms our milieu is, and the more restricted those relations to others are which dissolve the boundaries of the individual, the more anxiously the circle guards the achievements, the conduct of life, and the outlook of the individual, and the more readily a quantitative and qualitative speciali- zation would break up the framework of the whole little circle.

The ancient *polis* in this respect seems to have had the very character of a small town. The constant threat to its existence at the hands of enemies from near and afar effected strict coherence in political and military respects, a supervision of the citizen by the citizen, a jealousy of the whole against the individual whose particular life was suppressed to such a degree that he could compensate only by acting as a despot in his own household. The tremendous agitation and excitement, the unique colorfulness of Athenian life, can perhaps be understood in terms of the fact that a people of in- comparably individualized personalities struggled against the constant inner and outer pressure of a de-individualizing small town. This produced a tense atmosphere in which the weaker individuals were suppressed and those of stronger natures were incited to prove themselves in the most passionate manner. This is precisely why it was that there blossomed in Athens what must be called, without defining it exactly, "the general human character" in the intellectual development of our species. For we maintain factual as well as historical validity for the following connection: the most extensive and the most general contents and forms of life are most intimately con- nected with the most individual ones. They have a preparatory stage in com- mon, that is, they find their enemy in narrow formations and groupings the maintenance of which places both of them into a state of defense against expanse and generality lying without and the freely moving individuality within. Just as in the feudal age, the "free" man was the one who stood under the law of the land, that is, under the law of the largest social orbit, and the unfree man was the one who derived his right merely from the narrow circle of a feudal association and was excluded from the larger social orbit—so today metropolitan man is "free" in a spiritualized and refined sense, in contrast to the pettiness and prejudices which hem in the small- town man. For the reciprocal reserve and indifference and the intellectual life conditions of large circles are never felt more strongly by the individual in their impact upon his independence than in the thickest crowd of the big city. This is because the bodily proximity and narrowness of space makes the mental distance only the more visible. It is obviously only the obverse of this freedom if, under certain circumstances, one nowhere feels as lonely and lost as in the metropolitan crowd. For here as elsewhere it is by no means necessary that the freedom of man be reflected in his emotional life as comfort.

It is not only the immediate size of the area and the number of persons

which, because of the universal historical correlation between the enlarge-
ment of the circle and the personal inner and outer freedom, has made the
metropolis the locale of freedom. It is rather in transcending this visible
expanse that any given city becomes the seat of cosmopolitanism. The
horizon of the city expands in a manner comparable to the way in which
wealth develops; a certain amount of property increases in a quasi-automatical
way in ever more rapid progression. As soon as a certain limit has been
passed, the economic, personal, and intellectual relations of the citizenry, the
sphere of intellectual predominance of the city over its hinterland, grow as
in geometrical progression. Every gain in dynamic extension becomes a step,
not for an equal, but for a new and larger extension. From every thread
spinning out of the city, ever new threads grow as if by themselves, just as
within the city unearned increment of ground rent, through the mere increase
in communication, brings the owner automatically increasing profits. At this
point, the quantitative aspect of life is transformed directly into qualitative traits
of character. The sphere of life of the small town is, in the main, self-contained and autarchic. For it is the decisive nature of the metropolis that its
inner life overflows by waves into a far-flung national or international area.
Weimar is not an example to the contrary, since its significance was hinged
upon individual personalities and died with them; whereas the metropolis
is indeed characterized by its essential independence even from the most
eminent individual personalities. This is the counterpart to the independence,
and it is the price the individual pays for the independence, which he enjoys
in the metropolis. The most significant characteristic of the metropolis is this
functional extension beyond its physical boundaries. And this efficacy reacts
in turn and gives weight, importance, and responsibility to metropolitan life.
Man does not end with the limits of his body or the area comprising his
immediate activity. Rather is the range of the person constituted by the
sum of effects emanating from him temporally and spatially. In the same
way, a city consists of its total effects which extend beyond its immediate confines. Only this range is the city's actual extent in which its existence is
expressed. This fact makes it obvious that individual freedom, the logical and
historical complement of such extension, is not to be understood only in the
negative sense of mere freedom of mobility and elimination of prejudices and
petty philistinism. The essential point is that the particularity and incomparability, which ultimately every human being possesses, be somehow
expressed in the working-out of a way of life. That we follow the laws of our
own nature—and this after all is freedom—becomes obvious and convincing to ourselves and to others only if the expressions of this nature differ
from the expressions of others. Only our unmistakability proves that our way
of life has not been superimposed by others.

Cities are, first of all, seats of the highest economic division of labor.
They produce thereby such extreme phenomena as in Paris the remunerative
occupation of the *quatorzième*. They are persons who identify themselves by

signs on their residences and who are ready at the dinner hour in correct attire, so that they can be quickly called upon if a dinner party should consist of thirteen persons. In the measure of its expansion, the city offers more and more the decisive conditions of the division of labor. It offers a circle which through its size can absorb a highly diverse variety of services. At the same time, the concentration of individuals and their struggle for customers compel the individual to specialize in a function from which he cannot be readily displaced by another. It is decisive that city life has transformed the struggle with nature for livelihood into an inter-human struggle for gain, which here is not granted by nature but by other men. For specialization does not flow only from the competition for gain but also from the underlying fact that the seller must always seek to call forth new and differentiated needs of the lured customer. In order to find a source of income which is not yet exhausted, and to find a function which cannot readily be displaced, it is necessary to specialize in one's services. This process promotes differentiation, refinement, and the enrichment of the public's needs, which obviously must lead to growing personal differences within this public.

All this forms the transition to the individualization of mental and psychic traits which the city occasions in proportion to its size. There is a whole series of obvious causes underlying this process. First, one must meet the difficulty of asserting his own personality within the dimensions of metropolitan life. Where the quantitative increase in importance and the expense of energy reach their limits, one seizes upon qualitative differentiation in order somehow to attract the attention of the social circle by playing upon its sensitivity for differences. Finally, man is tempted to adopt the most tendentious peculiarities, that is, the specifically metropolitan extravagances of mannerism, caprice, and preciousness. Now, the meaning of these extravagances does not at all lie in the contents of such behavior, but rather in its form of "being different," of standing out in a striking manner and thereby attracting attention. For many character types, ultimately the only means of saving for themselves some modicum of self-esteem and the sense of filling a position is indirect, through the awareness of others. In the same sense a seemingly insignificant factor is operating, the cumulative effects of which are, however, still noticeable. I refer to the brevity and scarcity of the inter-human contacts granted to the metropolitan man, as compared with social intercourse in the small town. The temptation to appear "to the point," to appear concentrated and strikingly characteristic, lies much closer to the individual in brief metropolitan contacts than in an atmosphere in which frequent and prolonged association assures the personality of an unambiguous image of himself in the eyes of the other.

The most profound reason, however, why the metropolis conduces to the urge for the most individual personal existence—no matter whether justified and successful—appears to me to be the following: the development of modern culture is characterized by the preponderance of what one may call the "objective spirit" over the "subjective spirit." This is to say, in language as well as in law, in the technique of production as well as in art, in science as well as in the objects of the domestic environment, there is embodied a sum of spirit. The individual in his intellectual development follows the growth of this spirit very imperfectly and at an ever increasing distance. If, for instance, we view the immense culture which for the last hundred years has been embodied in things and in knowledge, in institutions and in comforts, and if we compare all this with the cultural progress of the individual during the same period—at least in high status groups—a frightful disproportion in growth between the two becomes evident. Indeed, at some points we notice a retrogression in the culture of the individual with reference to spirituality, delicacy, and idealism. This discrepancy results essentially from the growing division of labor. For the division of labor demands from the individual an ever more one-sided accomplishment, and the greatest advance in a one-sided pursuit only too frequently means death to the personality of the individual. In any case, he can cope less and less with the overgrowth of objective culture. The individual is reduced to a negligible quantity, perhaps less in his consciousness than in his practice and in the totality of his obscure emotional states that are derived from this practice. The individual has become a mere cog in an enormous organization of things and powers which tear from his hands all progress, spirituality, and value in order to transform them from their subjective form into the form of a purely objective life. It needs merely to be pointed out that the metropolis is the genuine arena of this culture which outgrows all personal life. Here in buildings and educational institutions, in the wonders and comforts of space-conquering technology, in the formations of community life, and in the visible institutions of the state, is offered such an overwhelming fullness of crystallized and impersonalized spirit that the personality, so to speak, cannot maintain itself under its impact. On the one hand, life is made infinitely easy for the personality in that stimulations, interests, uses of time and consciousness are offered to it from all sides. They carry the person as if in a stream, and one needs hardly to swim for oneself. On the other hand, however, life is composed more and more of these impersonal contents and offerings which tend to displace the genuine personal colorations and incomparabilities. This results in the individual's summoning the utmost in uniqueness and particularization, in order to preserve his most personal core. He has to exaggerate this personal element in order to remain audible even to himself. The atrophy of individual culture through the hypertrophy of objective culture is one reason for the bitter hatred which the preachers of the most extreme individualism, above all Nietzsche, harbor against the metropolis. But it is, indeed, also a reason why these preachers are so passionately loved in the metropolis and why they appear to the metropolitan man as the prophets and saviors of his most unsatisfied yearnings.

If one asks for the historical position of these two forms of individualism which are nourished by the quantitative relation of the metropolis, namely, individual independence and the elaboration of individuality itself, then the metropolis assumes an entirely new rank order in the world history of the spirit. The eighteenth century found the individual in oppressive bonds which had become meaningless—bonds of a political, agrarian, guild, and religious character. They were restraints which, so to speak, forced upon man an unnatural form and outmoded, unjust inequalities. In this situation the cry for liberty and equality arose, the belief in the individual's full freedom of movement in all social and intellectual relationships. Freedom would at once permit the noble substance common to all to come to the fore, a substance which nature had deposited in every man and which society and history had only deformed. Besides this eighteenth-century ideal of liberalism, in the nineteenth century, through Goethe and Romanticism, on the one hand, and through the economic division of labor, on the other hand, another ideal arose: individuals liberated from historical bonds now wished to distinguish themselves from one another. The carrier of man's values is no longer the "general human being" in every individual, but rather man's qualitative uniqueness and irreplaceability. The external and internal history of our time takes its course within the struggle and in the changing entanglements of these two ways of defining the individual's role in the whole of society. It is the function of the metropolis to provide the arena for this struggle and its reconciliation. For the metropolis presents the peculiar conditions which are revealed to us as the opportunities and the stimuli for the development of both these ways of allocating roles to men. Therewith these conditions gain a unique place, pregnant with inestimable meanings for the development of psychic existence. The metropolis reveals itself as one of those great historical formations in which opposing streams which enclose life unfold, as well as join one another with equal right. However, in this process the currents of life, whether their individual phenomena touch us sympathetically or antipathetically, entirely transcend the sphere for which the judge's attitude is appropriate. Since such forces of life have grown into the roots and into the crown of the whole of the historical life in which we, in our fleeting existence, as a cell, belong only as a part, it is not our task either to accuse or to pardon, but only to understand.[1]

Notes

[1] The content of this lecture by its very nature does not derive from a citable literature. Argument and elaboration of its major cultural-historical ideas are contained in my *Philosophie des Geldes* [The Philosophy of Money; München and Leipzig: Duncker und Humblot, 1900.]

PART XI

GENERATIONS

Society is an ongoing process. Individuals are constantly entering into this process (by being born into it), participating in new (to them) facets of it, and leaving it (through death). Persons of the same age category share many important characteristics in terms of their participation in society and its effect upon them. The sociologist studies these phenomena using the concept of generation. Generation often implies only the broadest categorization such as between youth and adult. However, the terms infant, preschooler, adolescent, and so on, are more specific categories. These distinctions note important stages in the socialization process. In American society we make fewer distinctions and have less knowledge concerning age categories at the other end of the average life span—the period we often refer to simply as old age—than do many other societies. American society, however, is constantly changing; therefore, the experiences of "college kids" in the 1970s will be different, perhaps radically so, from those in this category at the turn of the century. Generational analysis must include not only that which is universal to a particular age category, or at least is characteristic of a particular age category in a certain society, but also the historical experience of the group we are studying.

The Sociology
of Parent–Youth Conflict

KINGSLEY DAVIS

This excerpt, from a classic article by Kingsley Davis, describes a
fundamental difference in generational perspectives—adult realism
versus youthful idealism. By middle age most people have replaced
Utopian ideals with the "working ideals current in the society." They
become less concerned with the consistency or even the truth of such
ideals. The young, on the other hand, do have Utopian ideals and often
tend to take them literally. This is primarily because educational institutions inculcate such ideals and "protect" children from much social
experience. Young people necessarily discover the realities concerning ideals and respond with "serious allegiance" to an ideal moral
system. Another, often later response, is a perspective marked by
cynicism. Davis finds that our culture manifests the conditions for
youthful "reformist zeal and cynical negativism" to an extreme degree.
His analysis appears to have stood the test of thirty years.

Psychosocial Differences: Adult Realism
vs. Youthful Idealism

THE decelerating rate of socialization (an outgrowth both of the
human being's organic development, from infant plasticity to senile rigidity,
and of his cumulative cultural and social development), when taken with rapid
social change and other conditions of our society, tends to produce certain differences of orientation between parent and youth. Though lack of space
makes it impossible to discuss all of these ramifications, we shall attempt to
delineate at least one sector of difference in terms of the conflict between
adult realism (or pragmatism) and youthful idealism.

Though both youth and age claim to see the truth, the old are more con-
servatively realistic than the young, because on the one hand they take
Utopian ideals less seriously and on the other hand take what may be called

Reprinted from *The American Sociological Review*, Vol. 5, No. 4 (August, 1940), pp. 526–
529, by permission of the author and The American Sociological Association.

operating ideals, if not more seriously, at least more for granted. Thus, middle-aged people notoriously forget the poetic ideals of a new social order which they cherished when young. In their place, they put simply the working ideals current in the society. There is, in short, a persistent tendency for the ideology of a person as he grows older to gravitate more and more toward the status quo ideology, unless other facts (such as a social crisis or hypnotic suggestion) intervene.[1] With advancing age, he becomes less and less bothered by inconsistencies in ideals. He tends to judge ideals according to whether they are widespread and hence effective in thinking about practical life, not according to whether they are logically consistent. Furthermore, he gradually ceases to bother about the *untruth* of his ideals, in the sense of their failure to correspond to reality. He assumes through long habit that, though they do not correspond perfectly, the discrepancy is not significant. The reality of an ideal is defined for him in terms of how many people accept it rather than how completely it is mirrored in actual behavior.[2] Thus, we call him, as he approaches middle age, a realist.

The young, however, are idealists, partly because they take working ideals literally and partly because they acquire ideals not fully operative in the social organization. Those in authority over children are obligated as a requirement of their status to inculcate ideals as a part of the official culture given the new generation.[3] The children are receptive because they have little social experience—experience being systematically kept from them (by such means as censorship, for example, a large part of which is to "protect" children). Consequently, young people possess little ballast for their acquired ideals, which therefore soar to the sky, whereas the middle-aged, by contrast, have plenty of ballast.

This relatively unchecked idealism in youth is eventually complicated by the fact that young people possess keen reasoning ability. The mind, simply as a logical machine, works as well at sixteen as at thirty-six.[4] Such logical capacity, combined with high ideals and an initial lack of experience, means that youth soon discovers with increasing age that the ideals it has been taught are true and consistent are not so in fact. Mental conflict thereupon ensues, for the young person has not learned that ideals may be useful without being true and consistent. As a solution, youth is likely to take action designed to remove inconsistencies or force actual conduct into line with ideals, such action assuming one of several typical adolescent forms—from religious withdrawal to the militant support of some Utopian scheme—but in any case consisting essentially in serious allegiance to one or more of the ideal moral systems present in the culture.[5]

A different, usually later reaction to disillusionment is the cynical or sophomoric attitude; for, if the ideals one has imbibed cannot be reconciled and do not fit reality, then why not dismiss them as worthless? Cynicism has the advantage of giving justification for behavior that young organisms crave anyway. It might be mistaken for genuine realism if it were not for two things.

The first is the emotional strain behind the "don't care" attitude. The cynic, in his judgment that the world is bad because of inconsistency and untruth of ideals, clearly implies that he still values the ideals. The true realist sees the inconsistency and untruth, but without emotion; he uses either ideals or reality whenever it suits his purpose. The second is the early disappearance of the cynical attitude. Increased experience usually teaches the adolescent that overt cynicism is unpopular and unworkable, that to deny and deride all beliefs which fail to cohere or to correspond to facts, and to act in opposition to them, is to alienate oneself from any group,[6] because these beliefs, however unreal, are precisely what makes group unity possible. Soon, therefore, the youthful cynic finds himself bound up with some group having a system of working ideals, and becomes merely another conformist, cynical only about the beliefs of other groups.[7]

While the germ of this contrast between youthful idealism and adult realism may spring from the universal logic of personality development, it receives in our culture a peculiar exaggeration. Social change, complexity, and specialization (by compartmentalizing different aspects of life) segregate ideals from fact and throw together incompatible ideologies while at the same time providing the intellectual tools for discerning logical inconsistencies and empirical errors. Our highly elaborated burden of culture, correlated with a variegated system of achieved vertical mobility, necessitates long years of formal education which separate youth from adulthood, theory from practice, school from life. Insofar, then, as youth's reformist zeal or cynical negativism produces conflict with parents, the peculiar conditions of our culture are responsible.

Notes

[1] See Footnote 7 for necessary qualifications.

[2] When discussing a youthful ideal, however, the older person is quick to take a dialectical advantage by pointing out not only that this ideal affronts the aspirations of the multitude, but that it also fails to correspond to human behavior either now or (by the lessons of history) probably in the future.

[3] See amusing but accurate article, "Fathers Are Liars," *Scribner's Magazine*, March, 1934.

[4] Evidence from mental growth data which point to a leveling off of the growth curve at about age 16. For charts and brief explanations, together with references, see F. K. Shuttleworth, *The Adolescent Period*, Monographs of the Society for Research in Child Development, III, Serial No. 16 (Washington, D.C., 1938), Figs. 16, 230, 232, 276, 285, 308.

Maturity of judgment is of course another matter. We are speaking only of logical capacity. Judgment is based on experience as well as capacity; hence, adolescents are apt to lack it.

[5] An illustration of youthful reformism was afforded by the Laval University students who decided to "do something about" prostitution in the city of Quebec. They broke into eight houses in succession one night, "whacked naked inmates upon the buttocks, upset beds and otherwise proved their collegiate virtue. . . ." They ended by "shoving the few remaining girls out of doors into the cold autumn night." *Time*, October 19, 1936.

[6] This holds only for expressed cynicism, but so close is the relation of thought to action that the possibility of an entirely covert cynic seems remote.

[7] This tentative analysis holds only insofar as the logic of personality development in a complex culture is the sole factor. Because of other factors, concrete situations may be quite different. When, for example, a person is specifically trained in certain rigid, other-worldly, or impractical ideals, he may grow increasingly fanatical with the years rather than realistic, while

his offspring, because of association with less fanatical persons, may be more pragmatic than he. The variation in group norms within a society produces persons who, whatever their orientation inside the group, remain more idealistic than the average outsider, while their children may, with outside contacts, become more pragmatic. Even within a group, however, a person's situation may be such as to drive him beyond the everyday realities of that group, while his children remain undisturbed. Such situations largely explain the personal crises that may alter one's orientation. The analysis, overly brief and mainly illustrative, therefore represents a certain degree of abstraction. The reader should realize, moreover, that the terms "realistic" and "idealistic" are chosen merely for convenience in trying to convey the idea, not for any evaluative judgments which they may happen to connote. The terms are not used in any technical epistemological sense, but simply in the way made plain by the context. Above all, it is not implied that ideals are "unreal." The ways in which they are "real" and "unreal" to observer and actor are complex indeed. See T. Parsons, *The Structure of Social Action*, 396, New York, 1937, and V. Pareto, *The Mind and Society*, III: 1300–1304, New York, 1935.

An Invasion of Centaurs:
The Making of a Counter Culture

THEODORE ROSZAK

"The Invasion of Centaurs" is an invasion of the youth counter-culture
bearing not guns and weapons of destruction, but rather flowers and the
seeds of rebirth. This counter-culture represents a fundamental break
with dominant middle-class American culture. In its place, these
youths emphasize personal fulfillment and involvement with each
other, the building of a new social pattern. While acknowledging splits
within the youth counter-culture between hippies and members of SDS
as to tactics and political orientation, Roszak attempts to show that
such a dichotomy is superficial, and that beneath it lies a fundamental
search for a new type of community. The counter-culture appears to be
anti-intellectual, partially as response to the social structure and consciousness it is rebelling against.

WHEN one first casts an eye over the varieties of youthful dissent,
it may seem that there is considerably less coherence to this counter culture
than I have suggested. To one side, there is the mind-blown bohemianism
of the beats and hippies; to the other, the hard-headed political activism of
the student New Left. Are these not in reality two separate and antithetical
developments: the one (tracing back to Ginsberg, Kerouac, & Co.) seeking
to "cop out" of American society, the other (tracing back to C. Wright Mills
and remnants of the old socialist left) seeking to penetrate and revolutionize
our political life?

The tension one senses between these two movements is real enough.
But I think there exists, at a deeper level, a theme that unites these variations
and which accounts for the fact that hippy and student activist continue to
recognize each other as allies. Certainly there is the common enemy against
whom they combine forces; but there is also a positive similarity of sensi-
bility.

The underlying unity of these differing styles of dissent is revealed by the extraordinary personalism that has characterized New Left activism since its beginnings. New Left groups like SDS have always taken strong exception to the fashionable thesis that we have reached the "end of ideology" in the Great Society.[1] But there is a sense in which ideology *is* a thing of the past among politically involved dissenters. By and large, most New Left groups have refused to allow doctrinal logic to obscure or displace an irreducible element of human tenderness in their politicking. What has distinguished SDS, at least in its early years, from old-line radical youth groups (as still represented, say, by the Progressive Labor Movement) is the unwillingness of the former to reify doctrine to the extent of granting it more importance than the flesh and blood. For most of the New Left, there has ultimately been no more worth or cogency in any ideology than a person lends it by virtue of his own action: personal commitments, not abstract ideas, are the stuff of politics. Such is the burden of the observation Staughton Lynd offered to the 1968 New University Conference when he lamented the fact that even radically inclined academics too often fail to "provide models of off-campus radical vocation." They teach Marxism or socialism; but they do not "pay their dues."

> The intellectual's first responsibility is, as Noam Chomsky says, "to insist upon the truth. . . ." But what truth we discover will be affected by the lives we lead. . . . to hope that we can understandingly interpret matters of which we have no first-hand knowledge, things utterly unproved upon the pulses . . . is intellectual hubris. . . . I think the times no longer permit this indulgence, and ask us, at the very least, to venture into the arena where political parties and workingmen, and young people do their things, seeking to clarify that experience which becomes ours as well, speaking truth to power from the vantage-point of that process of struggle.[2]

The remarks return us to R. D. Laing's distinction between "theory" and "experience." For the radical intellectual as much as for anyone else, Lynd contends, truth must have a biographical, not merely an ideological, context.

It is this personalist style that has led the New Left to identify alienation as the central political problem of the day. Not alienation, however, in the sheerly institutional sense, in which capitalism (or for that matter any advanced industrial economy) tends to alienate the worker from the means and fruits of production; but rather, alienation as the deadening of man's sensitivity to man, a deadening that can creep into even those revolutionary efforts that seek with every humanitarian intention to eliminate the external symptoms of alienation. Wherever non-human elements—whether revolutionary doctrine or material goods—assume greater importance than human life and well-being, we have the alienation of man from man, and the way is open to the self-righteous use of others as mere objects. In this respect revolutionary terrorism is only the mirror image of capitalist exploitation. As the French students put it in one of their incisive May 1968 slogans: *"Une révolution qui demande que l'on se sacrifice pour elle est une révolution à la papa."* ("A revolution that expects you to sacrifice yourself for it is one of daddy's revolutions.")

The meaning of New Left personalism is cogently expressed by the SDS Port Huron Statement of 1962:

> We are aware that to avoid platitudes we must analyze the concrete conditions of social order. But to direct such an analysis we must use the guideposts of basic principles. Our own social values involve conceptions of human beings, human relationships, and social systems.
>
> We regard *men* as infinitely precious and possessed of unfulfilled capacities for reason, freedom, and love. . . . We oppose the depersonalization that reduces human beings to the status of things. If anything, the brutalities of the twentieth century teach that means and ends are intimately related, that vague appeals to "posterity" cannot justify the mutilations of the present. . . .
>
> Loneliness, estrangement, isolation describe the vast distance between man and man today. These dominant tendencies cannot be overcome by better personnel management, nor by improved gadgets, but only when a love of man overcomes the idolatrous worship of things by man.[3]

The issue the students are addressing themselves to here, with their sentimental regard for "love," "loneliness," "depersonalization," makes for a vivid contrast to the more doctrinaire style of many of their radical predecessors. A generation ago at the time of the Spanish Civil War, Harry Pollitt, the leader of the British Communist Party, could with a clear conscience tell the poet Stephen Spender that he ought to go to Spain and get himself killed: the party needed more martyred artists to bolster its public image. *That* is ideological politics—the total subordination of the person to party and doctrine. Nor have such perversions been confined to the Stalinist Left. It was an adamant anti-Stalinist, Sidney Hook, who in his famous exchange of letters with Bertrand Russell during the early fifties, logic-chopped his way to the conclusion that thwarting the ambitions of the Harry Pollitts of the world would justify wiping out the entire human species.[4] Such anti-Stalinist militancy required two billion martyrs, willy-nilly: surely a political position that wins the world's record for sheer bloody-minded fanaticism. Had the H-bomb existed in the sixteenth century, we might well have expected to hear Calvin and Loyola carrying on with the same hair-raising bravado . . . and meaning it . . . and then perhaps none of us should be here today.

Now this is precisely the sort of corrupted human relations that has been largely absent from New Left politics. Instead, there has been a precociously wise fear of wielding power over others and of unleashing violence in behalf of any ideal, no matter how rhetorically appealing. In the New Left, you pay your *own* dues; nobody pays them for you; and you, in turn, don't enforce payment on anybody else. As Kenneth Keniston of the Yale Medical School observes in a recent study: ". . . in manner and style, these young radicals are extremely 'personalistic,' focused on face-to-face, direct and open relationships with other people; hostile to formally structured roles and traditional bureaucratic patterns of power and authority"—a characteristic Keniston traces to the child-rearing habits of the contemporary middle-class family. The trait is so well developed that Keniston wonders if "it is possible to retain an open, personalistic, unmanipulative and extremely trusting style, and yet mount an effective program on a national scale." [5] The worry is real enough; organizational slackness is bound to be the price one pays for pursuing the ideal of participative democracy. But then it is perhaps a measure of our corruption as a society that we should believe democracy can ever be anything other than "participative."

As I write this, however, I am bleakly aware that an ideological drift toward righteous violence is on the increase among the young, primarily under the influence of the extremist Black Powerites and a romanticized conception of guerrilla warfare. This is especially true of the European young, who rapidly fall back upon stereotyped ideas about revolution; but "confrontation politics" and cheers for the fiction of the "people's war" are becoming more prominent in the United States, too, as frustration with the brutality and sleazy deception of the establishment grows. The tragic search may be on again among radical dissenters for ways to "make murder legitimate," as Camus phrased it—and with this tendency, the New Left runs the risk of losing its original soulfulness. For the beauty of the New Left has always lain in its eagerness to give political dignity to the tenderer emotions, in its readiness to talk openly of love, and non-violence, and pity. It is, therefore, depressing in the extreme when, in behalf of a self-congratulatory militancy, this humane spirit threatens to give way to the age-old politics of hatred, vindictiveness, and windy indignation. At this point, things do not simply become ugly; they become stupid. Suddenly the measure of conviction is the efficiency with which one can get into a fistfight with the nearest cop at hand.

It would be my own estimate that those who give way to the vice of doctrinaire violence and its manipulative ways are still a strict minority among the dissenting young—through an obstreperous minority which, for obvious reasons, attracts much attention from the press. The very inexclusiveness of the New Left style—the willingness to let every man take his own stand even when this produces a hopeless muddle—makes it impossible to turn away those who come to the demonstrations with icons of "Che" and Chairman Mao, and with all the attendant bloodcurdling slogans. Nevertheless, the prevailing spirit of New Left politics remains that reflected in the SDS motto "One man, one soul." The meaning of the phrase is clear enough: at whatever cost to the cause or the doctrine, one must care for the uniqueness and the dignity of each individual and yield to what his conscience demands in the existential moment.

Colin MacInnes, discussing the difference between the youthful radicals of the thirties and the sixties, observes that the contemporary young "hold themselves more personally responsible than the young used to. Not in the sense of their 'duties' to the state or even society, but to themselves. I think they examine themselves more closely and their motives and their own behavior." [6] Anyone who has put in much time with New Left students knows what MacInnes is talking about. It is that quality of sober introspection which almost amounts to what the Catholic Church calls "scrupulosity." It can become nearly intolerable to sit through the soul-searching sessions of these young people, waiting in attendance upon their lint-picking analyses of motivation, their dogged pursuit of a directness and immediacy free of organizational-hierarchical distinctions. And yet it is, at worst, the exaggeration of a virtue to insist that neither theory nor rhetoric must submerge the living reality of our actions as they affect others and ourselves, to insist that the final appeal must be to the person, never to the doctrine.

But then the question arises: what *is* the person? What, most essentially, *is* this elusive, often erratic human *something* which underlies social systems and ideologies, and which now must serve as the ultimate point of moral reference? No sooner does one raise the question than the politics of the social system yields to what Timothy Leary has called "the politics of the nervous system." Class consciousness gives way as a generative principle to . . . *consciousness* consciousness. And it is at this juncture that New Left and beat-hip bohemianism join hands. For even in its most hostile caricatures, the bohemian fringe of our youth culture makes its distinctive character apparent. It is grounded in an intensive examination of the self, of the buried wealth of personal consciousness. The stereotypic beatnik or hippy, dropped out and self-absorbed, sunk in a narcotic stupor or lost in ecstatic contemplation . . . what lies behind these popular images but the reality of a sometimes zany, sometimes hopelessly inadequate search for the truth of the person?

Beat-hip bohemianism may be too withdrawn from social action to suit New Left radicalism; but the withdrawal is in a direction the activist can readily understand. The "trip" is inward, toward deeper levels of self-examination. The easy transition from the one wing to the other of the counter culture shows up in the pattern that has come to govern many of the free universities. These dissenting academies usually receive their send-off from campus New Leftists and initially emphasize heavy politics. But gradually the curricula tend to get hip both in content and teaching methods: psychedelics, light shows, multi-media, total theatre, people-heaping, McLuhan, exotic religion, touch and tenderness, ecstatic laboratories. . . .[7] The same transition can be traced in the career of Bob Dylan, who commands respect among all segments of the dissenting youth culture. Dylan's early songs were traditional folk-protest, laying forth obvious issues of social justice; anti-boss, anti-war, anti-exploitation. Then, quite suddenly, rather as if Dylan had come to the conclusion that the conventional Woody Guthrie ballad could not reach deep enough, the songs turn surrealistic and psychedelic. All at once Dylan is somewhere beneath the rationalizing cerebrum of social discourse, probing the nightmare deeps, trying to get at the tangled roots of conduct and opinion. At this point, the project which the beats of the early fifties had taken up—the task of remodeling themselves, their way of life, their perceptions and sensitivities—rapidly takes precedence over the public task of changing institutions or policies.

One can discern, then, a continuum of thought and experience among the young which links together the New Left sociology of Mills, the Freudian Marxism of Herbert 'Marcuse, the Gestalt-therapy anarchism of Paul Goodman, the apocalyptic body mysticism of Norman Brown, the Zen-based psychotherapy of Alan Watts, and finally Timothy Leary's impenetrably occult narcissism, wherein the world and its woes may shrink at last to the size of a mote in one's private psychedelic void. As we move along the continuum, we find sociology giving way steadily to psychology, political collectivities yielding to the person, conscious and articulate behavior falling away before the forces of the non-intellective deep.

Unrelated as the extremes of this spectrum may seem at first, one would not be surprised to discover the men we name turning up at the same teach-in. The Congress on the Dialectics of Liberation held in London during summer 1967 was pretty much that kind of affair: an effort to work out the priorities of psychic and social liberation within a group of participants that included New Left revolutionaries and existential psychiatrists, with Allen Ginsberg on hand—not to speak, but to chant the Hare Krishna. As one would expect, the priorities never did get established. Significantly, it proved impossible for the congress to maintain more than a stormy rapport with Black Power spokesmen like Stokely Carmichael, for whom, tragically if understandably, real social power, despite all that history teaches us to the contrary, once more looks like something that flows from the muzzle of a gun. And yet, the common cause was undeniably there: the same insistence on revolutionary change that must at last embrace psyche and society. Even for the Black Powerites, the root justification of the cause derives from existentialist theorists like Frantz Fanon, for whom the prime value of the act of rebellion lies in its psychic liberation of the oppressed.[8]

So it is that when New Left groups organize their demonstrations, the misty-minded hippies are certain to join in, though they may tune out on the heavy political speechifying in favor of launching a yellow submarine or exorcizing the Pentagon. In Berkeley after the 1966 troubles, the New Left and local hippies had no difficulty in cosponsoring a "Human Be-In" to celebrate the students' quasi-victory over the administration. Under hip influence, the celebration rapidly took on the character of a massive "love feast"; but no one seemed to find that inappropriate. Perhaps the most important feature of the event was the fact that, of the forty thousand in attendence, a vast number were teen-agers from local high schools and junior high schools— the so-called "teeny-boppers," who currently seem to provide the bulk of the crowd along Berkeley's Telegraph Avenue. For these youngsters, the next wave of the counter culture, the neat distinctions between dissenting activism and bohemianism are growing progressively less clear. No doubt, as the local city fathers fear, these youngsters learn all sorts of bad habits on the avenue—but they probably take their corruption indiscriminately from SDS handouts and psychedelic newspapers without much awareness of the difference between dropping out and digging in for the political fight. It all boils down to disaffiliation for them—and the distinctions are of secondary importance.

We grasp the underlying unity of the counter cultural variety, then, if we see beat-hip bohemianism as an effort to work out the personality structure and total life style that follow from New Left social criticism. At their best, these young bohemians are the would-be utopian pioneers of the world that lies beyond intellectual rejection of the Great Society. They seek to invent a cultural base for New Left politics, to discover new types of community, new family patterns, new sexual mores, new kinds of livelihood, new esthetic forms, new personal identities on the far side of power politics, the bourgeois home, and the consumer society. When the New Left calls for peace and gives us heavy analysis of what's what in Vietnam, the hippy quickly translates the word into *shantih,* the peace that passes all understanding, and fills in the psychic dimensions of the ideal. If investigating the life of *shantih* has little to do with achieving peace in Vietnam, perhaps it is the best way of preventing the next several Vietnams from happening. Perhaps the experiments we find at the hip fringe of the counter culture are still raw and often abortive. But we must remember that the experimenters have only been with us for a dozen or so years now; and they are picking their way through customs and institutions that have had more than a few centuries to entrench themselves. To criticize the experiments is legitimate and necessary; to despair of what are no more than beginnings is purely premature.

Notes

[1] This thesis is, of course, untrue. Ideology is not absent in the technocracy; it is simply invisible, having blended into the supposedly indisputable truth of the scientific world view. Thus the technocrats deal in "rationality," "efficiency," and "progress," speak the purportedly value-neuter language of statistics, and convince themselves that they have no ideological orientation. The most effective ideologies are always those that are congruent with the limits of consciousness, for then they work subliminally.

[2] Lynd's address appears in *The New University Conference Newsletter,* Chicago, May 24, 1968, pp. 5–6.

[3] From the statement as it appears in Mitchell Cohen and Dennis Hale, eds., *The New Student Left* (Boston: Beacon Press, revised ed. 1967), pp. 12–13.

[4] The Russell-Hook exchange appears in Charles McClelland, ed., *Nuclear Weapons, Missiles, and Future War* (San Francisco: Chandler, 1960), pp. 140–57.

[5] See Kenneth Keniston, *Young Radicals* (New York: Harcourt, Brace & World, 1968). The study is based on the National Steering Committee of the 1967 Vietnam Summer.

[6] Colin MacInnes, "Old Youth and Young," *Encounter,* September 1967. For another discussion of the subject, in the course of which the same point emerges, see the symposium "Confrontation: The Old Left and the New," in *The American Scholar,* Autumn 1967, pp. 567–89.

[7] See Ralph Keyes, "The Free Universities," *The Nation,* October 2, 1967.

[8] Black Power frequently gets drawn into the counter cultural style in other respects. In Eldridge Cleaver's book *Soul on Ice* (New York: McGraw-Hill, 1968) there is an engaging analysis of the hidden sexual foundations of racism. See the essay "The Great Mitosis." Unhappily, however, the analysis suggests that, like some of the New Leftists, Cleaver seems to conceive of the struggle for liberation as the province of manly men who must prove themselves by "laying their balls on the line." Too often this suggests that the female of the species must content herself with keeping the home fires burning for her battle-scarred champion or joining the struggle as a camp follower. In either case, the community is being saved *for* her, not *by* her as well. I think this means that invidious sexual stereotyping lies at a deeper level of consciousness than racial prejudice. For a comment on the problem, see Betty Roszak, "Sex and Caste," in *Liberation,* December 1966, pp. 28–31.

Political Generations
in the Cuban Working Class[1]

MAURICE ZEITLIN

In this study, Zeitlin makes a contribution to our understanding of generations. He uses the concept of political generations to explain differences in political outlook. Age categories of Cuban workers constitute the political generations in question; their attitudes toward the revolution are taken as an index of political outlook. The author's major hypothesis is that "the specific historical period in which succeeding generations of workers first became involved in the labor movement had significant consequences for the formation of their political outlook." Cuba, during the last forty years, has had distinct historical periods.

Workers who were eighteen to twenty-five at the start of a particular period constitute a political generation. This categorization is based on: Cuba's political history; the age at which a man "becomes more responsive to the impact of social change"; and the age at which a worker is likely to be significantly affected by the social pressures of the work situation. Zeitlin distinguishes and describes five critical periods in Cuba's recent political history. The conditions, issues, and events of a period provide the most politically relevant experiences for the members of a new political generation.

In the summer of 1962 a randomly selected sample of 202 industrial workers in twenty-one plants scattered throughout Cuba was interviewed. Zeitlin's hypothesis led him to predict that the "generation of '53" would be more supportive of the revolution than any other political generation. The data confirmed this prediction. Of the data on other generations, a good part is also explainable in terms of the major hypothesis. Zeitlin also presents his findings on the effect of employment on political outlook.

This is an abridged version of an article which first appeared in *The American Journal of Sociology*, Vol. LXXI, March, 1966, and is reprinted by permission of the author and the publisher, The University of Chicago Press. The reader is also referred to a full analysis of the topic in the author's *Revolutionary Politics and the Cuban Working Class*, Princeton, N.J.: Princeton Univ. Press; New York: Harper & Row, 1970 (with a special supplement, "Cuba's Workers, Workers' Cuba").

THE concept of political generation focuses on the intersection of biography, history, and social structure. It thus compels us to pay attention to variables of explanatory value that we might otherwise overlook. However, despite the wide interpretive use to which some variant of the concept of generation has been put (whether, for example, in creative literature, literary criticism, or qualitative political analysis), its use has been infrequent in the sociological analysis of politics, and especially so in the analysis of data gathered through survey research methods.[2] The most significant lack in this area is of studies of the formation of political generations elsewhere than in the advanced industrial societies of the West.[3]

This paper is about the formation of political generations in the Cuban working class and the relevance of these generations for the recent social revolution. Its thesis is that (a) different political generations were formed among the Cuban workers as a result of the impact on them of distinct historical experiences and that (b) the differential response of the generations to the revolution is understandable in terms of these experiences.

My approach to the specific problem of generations in Cuba is based essentially on Karl Mannheim's general formulation of the problem. He suggested that common experiences during their youth might create a common world view or frame of reference from which individuals of the same age group would tend to view their subsequent political experiences. Sharing the same year of birth, they "are endowed, to that extent, with a common location in the historical dimension of the social process." Much like the effect of class on its members, the generation also limits its members "to a specific range of potential experience, predisposing them for a certain characteristic mode of thought and experience, and *a characteristic type of historically relevant action.*" (Italics mine.)[4]

From the standpoint of our analysis, it is particularly significant that the Cubans themselves see their history to a great extent in generational terms, a fact that is not at all surprising given the dramatic and profoundly traumatic nature of the events that formed several Cuban generations. Cuban literature—political, historical, fictional—is replete with references to the "generation of '68" or the "generation of '95" or the "generation of the thirties," generations formed during singularly significant historical epochs in Cuba: respectively, the Ten Years' War against Spain (1868–78), the War of Independence (1895–98), and the abortive revolution of the thirties (1933–35). It is especially significant that the movement led by Fidel Castro, in common with other revolutionary nationalist and anticolonial movements, placed special emphasis on its being a new generation, shorn of the cynicism and the betrayal of revolutionary ideals typical of its elders. The movement's cadre consisted predominantly of young people in their late teens and early twenties and, to this extent, shared with other revolutionary youth movements an identification of the general social movement with their particular generation. . . .[5]

Thus, as a result of having lived through a history of rather abrupt social and political transitions and clearly demarcated political intervals, Cubans apparently have developed a relatively high level of generational self-consciousness. Stated formally, the major hypothesis of this paper is that *the specific historical period in which succeeding generations of workers first became involved in the labor movement had significant consequences for the formation of their political outlooks*. Shaped by the early experiences of their youth in the labor movement—that movement's conflicts, organization, tactics and strategy, ideology, and leadership—working-class political generations emerged in Cuba with measurably different attitudes toward the Castro revolution.

For our purposes, the concept of political generation will be defined, as Rudolf Heberle has put it, as "those individuals of approximately the same age who have shared, at the same age, certain politically relevant experiences." [6] The concept leaves open to empirical investigation the decision as to (*a*) which age groups to isolate for analysis and (*b*) which experiences to delineate as of decisive political relevance for that age group. [7]

Thus, in our analysis of political generations in the Cuban working class and their contemporary relevance in the context of the revolution, two strategic methodological decisions were necessary: (1) which age category or categories to locate in time and (2) in which historical periods, depending on which experiences were hypothesized to be politically relevant.

1. Normative expectations of political involvement in Cuba were established and perpetuated by the political activities of students, whose agitation and action since the foundation of the republic were often decisively bound up with the politics of the working class—whether, for instance, in the anti-Spanish colonial struggle for independence or in the abortive revolution of the thirties. The late teens and early twenties have been viewed in Cuba as a period in life demanding political commitment and involvement—the period of coming to manhood politically. In two of Cuba's most significant political periods, the political cadre that predominated in the movement consisted of young men and women; the short-lived government of Ramón Grau San Martín during the revolution of the thirties rested to a considerable extent on the support of the youth. Raúl Roa, a student leader at that time, and now foreign minister of Cuba, dubbed that regime "the ephebocracy," or teenage government. [8] And in the guerrilla struggle and urban *resistencia* against Batista, men and women in their late teens and early twenties apparently formed the majority of the movement's leaders and cadre, whatever their class of origin. On these grounds, I chose the age category of eighteen to twenty-five to locate the generations temporally.

In addition, I chose this age category on more general sociological grounds. First, the meaning of age varies in accordance with social norms governing specific activities and their relationship to age, and it is precisely at the age at which coming to manhood is normatively defined that the individual becomes more responsive to the impact of social change, since he is relatively less subject to parental influence in his new role. That is, it is likely that the individual who has come of age is more "responsive to the impact of social change" than the child who is still "insulated from it by his home environment." [9] It is, therefore, reasonable to assume that the experiences of workers in the period after they enter the labor force, assume their own support, and are no longer under parental supervision would be particularly significant to them, especially if this occurs in a period of social upheaval.

Second, it is a central assumption here that the social pressures arising out of the work situation are fundamental in determining the worker's political outlook. The work place is probably the most important source of the worker's political socialization, more so than for non-workers. A recent study found, for example, that French workers were more likely than other Frenchmen to discuss politics at work.[10] Much of the most significant political socialization of workers—insofar as that involves assimilation of the political orientations current in their class—occurs after the inception of their work career. This being so, crucial historical events impinging on the working class are more likely to affect a worker's personal politics if he has been working for a few years than if he has just begun. These are additional reasons why I chose to focus on historical events when workers were in their late teens and early twenties rather than when they were younger.

2. From the standpoint of our analysis of political generations, five critical periods in Cuban political history of the past several decades can be distinguished. Their general social conditions, political issues, and "concrete internal political and social struggles" [11] constitute the decisive politically relevant experiences of succeeding Cuban generations—that is, of those who were eighteen to twenty-five years old when each of these critical periods began. In Table 1 I have briefly indicated the decisive events of each political generation analyzed in this paper and the predicted political consequences of those events. These events deserve fuller descriptions, nonetheless, so that the reader can ponder their significance for himself.

Sugar speculation in the aftermath of World War I ended abruptly with Cuba's economic collapse in the early 1930's (partly as a consequence of the Great Depression in the United States), and a period of social upheaval began. Working-class and student political strikes throughout the country resulted not only in the overthrow of the repressive Machado regime but also in increasingly more militant political initiatives. These included the students' taking control of the University of Havana and demanding its "autonomy" from government interference and the workers' occupation of several railroad terminals, public utilities, ports, thirty-six sugar centrals, and a number of adjoining towns, in many of which they established "soviets" of workers, peasants, and soldiers. Students, young intellectuals, and workers, aside from taking independent political action, were in liaison with each other, with the former acting in many instances as workers' delegates to the short-lived

Table 1—Temporal Location and Decisive Political Events of Political Generations, and Predicted Political Consequences

Age Category at Time of Study (1962)	Period That Began when Workers Were 18–25	Decisive Politically Relevant Events	PREDICTED RANK OF GENERATION'S SUPPORT FOR	
			Communists	Revolution
21–27	1959 on	Establishment of the revolutionary government and ensuing revolutionary changes, including nationalization of industry and declaration of "socialist" regime	*	4
28–35	1952/53–58	Batista's coup; guerrilla war and urban resistance led by Castro; agitation and organization in working class; rebirth of working-class economic struggle; abortive national general strike; fall of Batista	3	1
36–43	1944–51	Relative political democracy and economic stability; alliance of government and anti-Communist labor officials; purge of Communists from CTC† leadership	4	5
44–51	1936/37–43	Suppression of insurrection; re-emergence of Communist leadership of labor movement; collaboration with Batista; achievement of tangible socio-economic benefits for organized workers	2	2
52–59	1928–35	Mass working-class and student insurrection; "dual power" of "soviets" under Communist leadership; establishment of radical nationalist regime	1	2

* The youngest generation's response to the Communists before the revolution is excluded here and in the following tables, since the question refers to an attitude held before they were adults.
† Confederación de Trabajadores de Cuba.

radical nationalist Grau regime. The young Communist party was dominant in the leadership of the workers, and, despite the equivocal role of the Communists in the final overthrow of the Machado regime, they maintained and increased their influence among the workers throughout the revolutionary period. Repression of the revolutionary movement by Fulgencio Batista, who had led a revolt of the enlisted men and non-commissioned officers and gained leadership of the army, led to his consolidation of power in late 1936 and early 1937.

The suppression of the revolution, forceful dissolution of working-class organizations, and the advent on the international Communist scene of the Popular Front period resulted in the transformation of the radical and independent workers' movement into a reformist movement under Communist leadership, which inaugurated an era of government-labor collaboration. The relative stability and economic security in Cuba during World War II accentuated even further the reformism of the workers' movement, as well as its growing bureaucratization. Under Communist leadership, the organized workers were able to gain certain tangible economic and social benefits.

Batista relinquished power in 1944, and a period of relative political democracy began—a period, however, that also included an alliance of the government and anti-Communist labor officials which increasingly used extra-legal and violent methods to harass the Communist leadership of the labor movement. The Communists were thus finally ousted in 1947 from official leadership of the Confederación de Trabajadores de Cuba (CTC), the national labor organization the Communists themselves had formed in 1938 under Batista's aegis. The growing bureaucratization of the unions, their loss of contact with the mass of the workers, and their collaboration with the government was heightened during this period of comparative internal economic stability and "prosperity."

CTC officials, under the leadership of Eusebio Mujal (whence comes the derogatory term *mujalista*), did not resist Batista's coup d'état of March, 1952, in which he regained power. In the years following, and throughout the guerrilla war and *resistencia,* the CTC was largely an appendage of the regime and was often used as a weapon against the workers themselves; and the already significant union corruption of prior years became increasingly supplemented by gangsterism and intimidation of the workers. The Communists, having lost the government's tutelage and having been outlawed by Batista, regained a measure of grassroots influence among the workers and led some important victorious strikes, especially in the sugar industry. But the regime fell not as the result of a working-class insurrection, which never materialized on a mass level, but as the result of conflict with the guerrilla forces and urban *resistencia* under the leadership of Castro's 26th of July movement, whose cadre included predominantly young men and women. Until the final demise of the regime in 1959, their age peers, whether active in the anti-Batista movement or not, and whatever their class, were both more suspect to the police and the military and more likely than Cubans of other ages to suffer arbitrarily at the hands of the regime.[12]

The role of the workers in the anti-Batista struggle contrasts strikingly with their decisive insurrectionary role against the Machado regime. Nonetheless, the years of the Batista regime saw a reinvigoration of the Cuban tradition of independent working-class economic struggle—under the leadership of Communists and non-Communists alike. The apparent political quiescence of the workers should not be exaggerated. For instance, in the 1955 strike in the sugar industry there were several militant actions, the sugar workers were joined by other workers in cities such as Santa Clara and some sugar towns of Camaguey and Havana provinces, and their economic demands became coupled with such political slogans as "Down with the criminal government!"

In eastern Cuba and in Santiago, Cuba's second largest city, there were especially significant instances of working-class political support of the anti-Batista movement. A spontaneous political strike set off by the funeral of two young 26th of July leaders on August 1, 1957, spread from Santiago to other cities in Oriente Province and several towns throughout the country. The strike was complete in Santiago, shutting down the Nicaro nickel plant and shops in the city for five days. In subsequent months "strike committees" were organized in many plants by 26th of July organizers and other opposition elements, in preparation for a general strike in 1958. The general strike, called for April 9, 1958, collapsed in several hours in Havana, with little mass support; but it completely paralyzed industry and commerce in Santiago, where the workers stayed out despite the regime's threats of arrest and its offers of immunity from prosecution to anyone killing an advocate of the strike. Despite their failure to overthrow the regime, then, the events mentioned here were certainly significant in the movement against Batista's regime and must have affected the workers' political outlook.[13]

If it is correct that the struggle against Batista and the events flowing from it were of decisive significance in shaping the political outlook of the workers of this generation of '53, then clearly they should be far more likely than the members of other generations to support the revolution. How correct this inference is, and the evidence regarding it, will be seen below. First, however, we must briefly describe our methods.

Methods

The data for this study are drawn from interviews with industrial workers in Cuba in the summer of 1962. By that time the revolutionary government had clearly consolidated its power (the Bay of Pigs invasion being a year in the past); the original relatively undifferentiated popular euphoria had already been replaced by relatively clear lines of social cleavage generated in response to actions taken by the revolutionary government; it was two years since the nationalization of industry and more than a year since Castro had declared the revolution to be "socialist." A study of the differential appeals of the ideology and social content of the revolution to Cuban workers could now be meaningful and valuable.

Interviews were carried out with a randomly selected sample of 202 industrial workers employed in twenty-one plants widely scattered throughout the island's six provinces. Plants were chosen from a list of all those functioning under the direction of the Ministry of Industries.[14]

The plants were selected by means of a self-weighting random sample in which the probability that a plant would be chosen was directly proportional to the number of workers employed in it. This sampling method tended to exclude the smaller industrial establishments ("chinchales") that abound in Cuba. In each plant, ten workers were selected by a method designed to obtain a simple random sample. My wife and I each separately interviewed five workers per plant, in Spanish. All interviewing was done in complete privacy, in a location provided within the work center, such as a storage room, office, or classroom. We told each worker interviewed (as well as anyone else concerned) that I was a correspondent for *The Nation;* that we had permission from the Ministry of Industries, the plant administration, and the union delegate to interview workers in the plant; that the worker was chosen by a scientific method of randomization; that he would not be identified personally in any way; and that his answers would be entirely anonymous; we simply wanted to know his opinions about some things at work and in Cuba in general, so as to be able to write an objective report about the condition of the Cuban working class.[15]

It might be objected, of course, that such survey research could not obtain meaningful results since Cuba was already a police state in the summer of 1962. This obviously pertinent question cannot be discussed at length here. The reader will have to be content with the elliptical assertion that this objection is without foundation and that in our observation Cubans could and did inquire and speak freely about whatever they wished—at that time. There were no formal safeguards of freedom of speech and association, and the potentialities for totalitarian rule were great, but that potential had yet to become a reality. We were able to carry out our interviewing without disturbance or interference of any kind and to obtain, I believe, data quite as valid as those obtained in any competent survey research.[16]

The interview schedule began with questions which were, on the surface, far removed from political issues of any kind. These questions pertained to length of residence in a particular place, length of time working in the work place, and so on. Questions of more or less obvious political content came somewhere in the middle of the interview. Five of these, which I think together adequately indicate how the workers view the revolution, were combined into an "index of attitude toward the revolution." Of these five questions, two were open-ended and three were forced-choice questions.

The open-ended questions were: (1) "Speaking generally, what are the things about this country that you are most proud of as a Cuban?" [17] and (2) "What sort [*clase*] of people govern this country now?"

One hundred and fifteen workers gave answers to the first question that were favorable to the revolution. A response was considered "favorable" only if it clearly indicated, or explicitly stated, support for the revolution. . . . [18]

One hundred and twenty-five workers replied to the second question in terms clearly favorable to the revolution. Given the double meaning in Spanish of the word "clase," which can mean "type," "sort," or "kind," as well as "class," the workers could, of course, choose to interpret the question's meaning in a number of ways. As with the preceding question, we counted as "favorable" replies only those that could be clearly regarded as such. . . . [19]

Table 2—Political Generation and Attitude toward the Revolution (Percent)

Age Category at Time of Study (1962) *	Favorable	Indecisive	Hostile	N
21–27	55	19	25	36
28–35	90	2	8	51
36–43	61	17	21	51
44–51	69	15	15	26
52–59	70	9	22	23

* This and the following tables do not include eight workers who were under twenty-one and seven who were over fifty-nine in 1962.

The workers were also asked the following questions with fixed alternatives: (3) "Do you believe that the country ought to have elections soon?" (4) "Do you think that the workers now have more, the same, or less influence on [*en*] the government than they had before the revolution?" (5) "Do you belong to the militia?" [20]

The index of attitude toward the revolution was constructed by coding favorable responses as +1 and all others as 0: [21]

Findings

Comparison of the generations confirms our expectation that members of the rebel generation of Castro, or the generation of '53 are most likely to support the revolution (Table 2). United by the common political frame

Index

Points	Definition	N
3–5	Favorable	142
2	Indecisive	24
0, 1	Hostile	36
Total		202

of reference they developed during the anti-Batista struggle, the generation of '53 stands out as the decisive generational base of the revolution. Further, the two other generations that stand out are precisely those whose members experienced the revolutionary events of the thirties as young men. It is, of course, possible to argue that, having experienced an abortive rather than a successful revolution, they should be cynical and pessimistic rather than optimistic about the Castro revolution, and this argument does make a good deal of sense. Yet, while the *social* revolution was crushed, the Machado regime *was* overthrown, and thus the political revolution in the narrow sense was a success. Moreover, seen in retrospect the revolution also yielded significant gains for the workers in subsequent years—especially the legitimation of their right to political and economic organization, a right that allowed them to win substantial economic benefits. It is also relevant that the repression of the revolution of the thirties, which in any case had significant "anti-imperialist" overtones, was widely believed in Cuba to have been the result of United States political intervention.[22] The anti-imperialism of the revolutionary government may, therefore, be another source of their support. Thus, it is understandable that these generations may view the present revolution as the renascence and continuation of the struggles of their own youth and may be more disposed to support it than the generation who came to manhood during the republican interregnum of relative stability or the present generation for whom prerevolutionary struggles are mere "history."

The low proportion of the present generation who support the revolution is unexpected. My own prediction (see Table 1) was that this generation would be outranked by those of '53 and the thirties but would itself outrank the republican generation. The explanation may be that the workers of this generation knew little if anything through personal experience about the prerevolutionary situation of the working class. Many of them (55 percent) were not yet workers before the revolution and thus could hardly appreciate the positive changes in the situation of the working class wrought by the revolution.

The impact of the anti-Batista struggle on the workers of the generation of '53 has made it the generational base of the revolution. Moreover, in a significant sense it was their generation that brought the revolutionary government to power. The leaders of the revolution itself, it will be remembered, who led the *resistencia* and were the rebel cadres in the hills and in the cities, are members of the generation of '53. In accordance with the hypothesis of political generations, the fact that the members of this generation acquired their political frame of reference in the course of the anti-Batista struggle should have made them more likely than members of other generations to support the revolution now, *regardless of the generation to which the rebel leaders themselves belonged*. But the fact that the rebels *were* predominantly of their own generation may have been an additional source of their support for and identification with the rebels and their cause. It may be surmised that the rebels became, in a significant sense, collectively the reference group of that entire generation, and the chief rebel leaders its foremost culture heroes or "reference individuals." [23] That the rebel leaders couched so much of their program in generational terms also may have considerably increased the likelihood that the members of the generation of '53 would identify with them. In turn, this act of identification may itself have reinforced the attitudes this generation was developing in response to the set of stimuli created by the historical situation.

If our assumption is correct that identification with the members of their generation who were actively participating in and leading the rebel movement was one more element in the complex of elements comprising the distinct politically relevant experiences of the generation of '53, we should expect a similar identification in the present. Are members of the generation of '53 more likely than others to identify with the leaders of the revolution? Using the question "Aside from personal friends or relatives—of all the people you hear or read about—could you name three individuals whom you admire very much?" as a rough empirical indicator, we found that the generation of '53 is distinct in this regard.[24] Its members were more likely than those of other generations to name a revolutionary leader (Fidel Castro, Raúl Castro, Ernesto "Che" Guevara, Juan Almeida, etc.) as at least one of the three individuals whom they admire greatly. . . .

So far, our analysis of the political generations has treated them in terms of their members' common location in the historical process. The common politically relevant experiences of their members have, taken as a whole, differentiated the political generations from each other. It is clear, however, that the generations are themselves internally differentiated by structural factors and that individuals of the same generation sharing different locations in the social structure will have experienced the politically relevant events of their youth differently. As Bennet Berger has put it: "The temporal location of a [generational] group must first be kept analytically distinct from its structural location; second, when considering them together, we should be aware that the impact of structural (e.g., occupational) factors on the nature of the temporal location may, under some conditions, be such as to fragment the cultural 'unity' of a generation beyond recognition." [25]

One of the most significant structural determinants of the Cuban workers' response to the revolution, as I have shown elsewhere,[26] was their prerevolutionary employment status. The workers who were unemployed and underemployed before the revolution were more likely to be pro-Communist before the revolution and are now more likely to support the revolutionary government than those who were employed regularly.

It is therefore important to consider the impact of their prerevolutionary employment status on the workers of different political generations (Table 3).

Table 3—Political Generation, Prerevolutionary Employment Status, and Political Attitudes *

| Age Category at Time of Study (1962) | Under- and Unemployed † | | | Regularly Employed | | |
| | PERCENTAGE SUPPORTING | | | PERCENTAGE SUPPORTING | | |
	Revolution	Communists	N	Revolution	Communists	N
21–27	75	‡	8	42	‡	12
28–35	100	31	22	85	35	20
36–43	81	41	21	43	17	23
44 plus §	82	64	11	68	39	31

* Those who were not workers before the revolution are excluded from this table.

† "Under- and unemployed" refers to workers who worked, on the average, nine months or less per year before the revolution, while "regularly employed" refers to those who worked ten months or more.

‡ Excluded from this table since the question refers to an attitude held before they were adults.

§ This category combines the generations of the second Machado regime and the first Batista regime and is referred to in this paper henceforth as the "generation of the thirties."

As we might expect, within every political generation the workers who were unemployed and underemployed are more likely to support the revolution than those who were regularly employed before the revolution. Moreover, among both the unemployed and the regularly employed, the generation of '53 exceeds the other generations in the proportion of prorevolution workers; and among the employed workers the generation of the thirties comes second, as we should expect. Among the unemployed workers, however, the generation of the republican interregnum has as great a proportion of prorevolution workers as does the generation of the thirties. Here is a particularly instructive instance of how generational peers, located differently in the social structure, are differently affected by historical events. The relative stability, prosperity, and political democracy of the republican interregnum, having left the problem of unemployment and underemployment untouched, proved from the perspective of the unemployed workers to be irrelevant to their situation and may indeed (as our evidence seems to indicate) have inclined them (even more than their unemployment may otherwise have done) toward radical solutions to their problems. . .

Conclusions

In conclusion, then, not only does comparison of the political generations in the aggregate reveal significant political differences in accord with hypotheses based on the concept of political generation, but comparison of *intra*generation subgroups are also in accord with those hypotheses.

The theoretical significance of our findings lies, first, in their demonstration of the analytic utility of formulating specific hypotheses in terms of the concept of political generations. . . .

Second, these conclusions bear indirectly on the issue of the relevance of "history" to sociological analysis and theory. The very concept of political generation implies the hypothesis that social processes, relationships, norms, and values sometimes may be inexplicable without reference to the events of the past and that analyses which are limited to consideration only of contemporary relationships may be deficient in significant ways.

Third, to the extent to which the concept attempts to link up behavior and character with *non*institutionalized but historically significant forms of social interaction, our findings also impinge on social psychological theory. Such decisively relevant experiences as may be included under the rubric of "historically significant events" (major political issues, concrete internal struggles, general social conditions) may or may not themselves have significant consequences for the social structure and, therefore, for the character, norms, and values of the men formed within it. But these very events may have independent psychological effects on their participants, aside from their institutional consequences. "If you wish to understand persons—their development and their relations with significant others—you must be prepared," as Anselm Strauss has put it, "to view them as embedded in historical context. Psychological theory and psychiatric theory, at least of the American variety, underplay this context; and those sociologists and anthropologists who are interested in personal identity tend to treat historical matters more as stage setting, or backdrops, than as crucial to the study of persons." [27] That the historical context in which they came to manhood played a significant role in the formation of the political identities of succeeding generations of Cuban workers—their political allegiances and norms and their response to the revolution—has, of course, been precisely the point of this paper.

Notes

[1] A brief portion of this article appeared in "Political Attitudes of Cuban Workers," a paper delivered at the meetings of the American Sociological Association, August, 1963. I am indebted to the Center of International Studies, Princeton University, for a grant that made my research for this study possible and to its director, Klaus Knorr, for his encouragement. I should also like to acknowledge the theoretical stimulation provided by Norman Ryder's unpublished paper, "The Cohort as a Concept in the Study of Social Change," delivered at the

neetings of the American Sociological Association, August, 1959, and the helpful suggestions of my colleague, Michael T. Aiken, Jerald Hague, and Gerald Marwell.

[2] Seymour Martin Lipset, for instance, recently noted again that, "unfortunately, there has been no attempt to study systematically the effect of generation experiences with modern survey research techniques" (*Political Man* [Garden City, N.Y.: Doubleday & Co., 1960], p. 265). The statement also appeared much earlier in Lipset, Paul F. Lazarsfeld, Allen Barton, and Juan Linz, "The Psychology of Voting," in G. Lindsey (ed.), *Handbook of Social Psychology* (Cambridge, Mass.: Addison-Wesley Publishing Co., 1954), II, 1124–70.

[3] See, however, S. N. Eisenstadt, *From Generation to Generation* (Glencoe, Ill.: Free Press, 1956), and Alex Inkeles and Raymond Bauer, *The Soviet Citizen* (Cambridge, Mass.: Harvard University Press, 1961).

[4] "The Problem of Generations," in Mannheim's *Essays on the Sociology of Knowledge*, ed. Paul Keckskemeti (New York: Oxford University Press, 1952), p. 286.

[5] See Eisenstadt, *op. cit.*, p. 311.

[6] Rudolf Heberle, *Social Movements* (New York: Appleton-Century-Crofts, 1951), pp. 119–20.

[7] This concept is essentially identical with the concept of "cohort" used in demographic analysis; see Ryder, *op. cit.*

[8] Teresa Casuso, *Cuba and Castro* (New York: Random House, 1961), p. 64. Miss Casuso's work emphasizes especially strongly the generational politics of Cuba (see esp. pp. 77 ff).

[9] Herbert Hyman, *Political Socialization* (Glencoe, Ill.: Free Press, 1959), p. 131.

[10] Richard Hamilton, *Affluence and the French Worker: The Fourth Republic Experience* (Princeton, N.J.: Princeton University Press), chap. iv (forthcoming).

[11] Heberle, *op. cit.*, pp. 122–23.

[12] "The most barbaric methods of torture, not excluding castration, were daily incidents in the police stations, where *the groans of a whole generation of youths* were heard as they were tortured for information, or for having aided the revolutionary movement" (Casuso, *op. cit.*, p. 134; italics mine.) Miss Casuso resigned her position as Cuban ambassador to the United Nations in 1960 and sought asylum in the United States. Similar descriptions of the Batista regime's arbitrary violence against young people during the guerrilla war appear in all the accounts of this period, such as Dubois, *op. cit.*; Taber, *op. cit.*; and Ray Brennan, *Castro, Cuba, and Justice* (New York: Doubleday & Co., 1959).

[13] For a more detailed account of these events, see Maurice Zeitlin, "Working Class Politics in Cuba: A Study in Political Sociology" (Ph.D. dissertation, University of California, Berkeley, 1964), and the references therein.

[14] The Ministry of Industries facilitated the completion of this study by providing me with credentials to the administration of the plants I wanted to visit. There was no interference with the wording or content of any questions, nor was there any prearranged schedule for my arrival at the plants, nor, it was evident, had the administrators or union heads been informed of my impending arrival. On several occasions, administrators or personnel chiefs phoned Havana to check my credentials and my insistence that I had permission (which was apparently unbelievable to administrators trying to raise production levels) to take ten workers from their work for as long as the interviews required.

[15] Eight of the 210 workers selected for the sample refused to be interviewed, were not replaced by others, and are not included in our tables. As a precaution, the 8 were included in parallel runs defined as "hostile" to the revolution, and every significant relationship was either the same or strengthened.

[16] Professor Dudley Seers, the well-known British economist, who was also doing research in Cuba at that time, has referred to some preliminary findings of my study as follows: "[Zeitlin's] findings are not inconsistent with the general impression we all [Seers and his co-authors] formed during our stay in Cuba, where we traveled the length of the island and conversed with hundreds of people. (In general, there was clearly little hesitation on their part about speaking their minds.)" (Seers [ed.], *Cuba: The Economic and Social Revolution* [Chapel Hill: University of North Carolina Press, 1964], p. 394, n. 70, and p. 31).

[17] This question was borrowed from the study then in progress by Gabriel Almond and Sidney Verba, *Civic Culture* (Princeton, N.J.: Princeton University Press, 1963), and my use of it is hereby gratefully acknowledged.

[18] Mention of the revolution itself, of the "socialist government," of specific economic and social reforms of the revolutionary government, of increased work security since the revolution, etc., were counted as "favorable." All other responses, whether more or less "neutral" or "clearly hostile," were classified simply as "not clearly favorable."

[19] E.g., "the people," "the humble," "hardworking," "good," "sincere," "moral," "honest," "defenders of the poor and humble," "the working class." Responses such as "socialists" or "revolutionaries" which did not clearly commit the worker were not counted as favorable; neither were such equivocal replies as "Cubans," "Fidel," "Communists," nor hostile ones such as "Russians," "Soviets," "shameless," or "traitors."

[20] Answers to these questions were distributed as follows: (3) "no," 136; "yes," 44; "no

opinion," 22; (4) "more influence," 170; "the same," 17; "less," 8; "no opinion," 7; (5) "yes," 110; "no," 92.

[21] Item analysis of answers to the five questions indicates that the questions form an acceptable Guttman scale, 88 percent of the workers giving answers exactly (67 percent) or consistently (21 percent) in conformity with a Guttman model. The coefficient of reproducibility equals .95.

[22] See Dana Gardner Munro, *The Latin American Republics: A History* (2d ed.; New York: Appleton-Century-Crofts, 1950), p. 501; Charles A. Thompson, "The Cuban Revolution: Reform and Reaction," *Foreign Policy Reports*, XI (January 1, 1936), 261–71; Casuso, *op. cit.*, pp. 68 ff.; Robert F. Smith, *The United States and Cuba: Business and Diplomacy, 1917–1960* (New York: Bookman Associates, 1959), pp. 148–56; and Zeitlin, *op. cit.*, pp. 30–46, and the references therein.

[23] As Robert Merton conceptualizes it, "Emulation of a peer, a parent, or a public figure may be restricted to limited segments of their behavior and values and this can be usefully described as adoption of a role model. Or, emulation may be extended to a wider array of behavior and values of these persons who can then be described as reference individuals" (*Social Theory and Social Structure* [Glencoe, Ill.: Free Press, 1959], p. 303).

[24] This question was also borrowed from the Almond-Verba study (*op. cit.*) and is acknowledged gratefully.

[25] "How Long is a Generation," *British Journal of Sociology*, XI (March, 1960), 16. Cf. also: "In the comparison of different age groups in the *aggregate*, or the same age groups at different historical periods in the *aggregate*, any differences that appear to be generational may simply be *artifacts* of the different social composition of the groups. . . . In principle, this can be solved by the introduction of certain controls or matchings, but it may often be neglected in practice" (Hyman, *op. cit.*, p. 130).

[26] Maurice Zeitlin, "Economic Insecurity and the Political Attitudes of Cuban Workers," *American Sociological Review*, February, 1966.

[27] *Mirrors and Masks: The Search for Identity* (Glencoe, Ill.: Free Press, 1959), p. 164. See also Hans Gerth and C. Wright Mills, *Character and Social Structure* (New York: Harcourt, Brace & World, 1953), p. xix.

Index